MODULA-2: CONSTRUCTIVE F

COMPUTER SCIENCE TEXTS

Modula-2: Constructive Program Development

P.A. MESSER
BSc, MSc
School of Mathematics, Computing and Statistics
Leicester Polytechnic

and

I. MARSHALL
BA, MSc
School of Mathematics, Computing and Statistics
Leicester Polytechnic

BLACKWELL SCIENTIFIC PUBLICATIONS

OXFORD LONDON EDINBURGH

BOSTON PALO ALTO MELBOURNE

© 1986 by
Blackwell Scientific Publications
Editorial offices:
Osney Mead, Oxford, OX2 0EL
8 John Street, London, WC1N 2ES
23 Ainslie Place, Edinburgh, EH3 6AJ
52 Beacon Street, Boston
   Massachusetts 02108, USA
667 Lytton Avenue, Palo Alto
   California 94301, USA
107 Barry Street, Carlton,
   Victoria 3053, Australia

First published 1986

Phototypeset by
Oxford Computer Typesetting

Printed and bound in
Great Britain by
Billing & Sons Ltd
Worcester

DISTRIBUTORS

USA and Canada
   Blackwell Scientific Publications Inc.
   P O Box 50009, Palo Alto
   California 94303

Australia
   Blackwell Scientific Publications
      (Australia) Pty Ltd.
   107 Barry Street
   Carlton, Victoria 3053

British Library
Cataloguing in Publication Data

Messer, P. A.
   Modula-2: Constructive program
   development — (Computer science text)
   1. Modula-2 (Computer program language)
   I. Title   II. Marshall, I.   III. Series
   005.13'3   QA76.73.M63

   ISBN 0-632-01609-4
   ISBN 0-632-01508-X Pbk

Contents

Bibliography, 518

Appendices

Index, 539

Introduction

This book aims to teach you to program in Modula-2. It is suitable for people with little or no programming experience following a taught course, though it will also be of interest to hardened hackers. Modula-2 is a high-level programming language suited for writing programs for a wide range of computer applications. It was designed by Niklaus Wirth in the late 1970's as a successor to his earlier languages Pascal and Modula. The authors' opinion is that Modula-2 is the best language for teaching programming, offering the advantages of languages such as Ada and C in a reasonable sized, strongly typed language. This book concentrates on teaching the language for writing application programs, however the extensive system programming facilities are introduced in later chapters.

We believe that learning to design and develop programs is difficult, but that the difficulties should not be hidden by restricting an introductory text to toy programs. The book is designed in three basic parts.

1. Chapters 1 to 6 introduce a basic subset of the language and illustrate its use for solving small problems. Chapters 1 to 3 provide an overview of fundamental computing and programming concepts so that the important ideas in Chapters 4 to 6 are learnt at an early stage. Students with no computing background should write a number of the programs suggested in the programming exercises of Chapter 3 before going on to Chapter 4.

2. Chapters 7 to 12 amplify the ideas in Chapters 1 to 6 and introduce the majority of the rest of the language, including the important design and construction discipline involved in the the use of modules.

3. Chapters 13 to 15 concentrate on advanced and low-level features of the language and introduce some important topics in Computer Science. The discussions of the topics in these later chapters are rudimentary but suffice to show how Modula-2 can solve problems in these areas without minimising the difficulties.

We thank the staff and students, past and present, of the Department of Mathematics, Computing and Statistics for their encouragement and the opportunity to observe and participate in the difficulties of teaching and learning a programming language. In particular we thank Dr R.B. Coats for his painstaking efforts and advice. Last but not least, we thank Sousan, Robert and Christine for their tolerance, support and encouragement.

Chapter 1

Introduction to a Modula-2 Program, Computers and Syntax Diagrams

This book aims to make you a competent programmer in the programming language Modula-2. This chapter shows an example Modula-2 program and introduces some technical terms used in computing which are relevant to programming in Modula-2. In addition, syntax diagrams are introduced as a notation for describing the parts of the Modula-2 language.

1.1 A MODULA-2 PROGRAM

An example Modula-2 program is shown in Fig. 1.1. When this program is run the statements between the words BEGIN and END are executed in sequence from top to bottom. It should be noted that this program is not very useful as it stands because it does not print out its answer.

```
MODULE SmallExample;
        (* Program to calculate the area of a rectangle. *)
        VAR
            Length,Width,Area: CARDINAL;
        BEGIN
          Length := 10;
          Width  := 20;
          Area   := Length*Width
        END SmallExample.
```

Fig. 1.1.

Figure 1.2 shows a simplified layout of all Modula-2 program modules.

MODULE Name;

| Declarations
A list of instructions describing the properties
of the data used by the program. |

BEGIN

| Module Body (Statement Sequence)
A list of instructions stating what the computer
should do when the program is executed. |

END Name.

Fig. 1.2.

The following sections discuss various aspects of Modula-2 programs.

Programs and Modules

A Modula-2 program is made up of one or more modules. In this very simple example it consists of only the module SmallExample. It is doubtful if you will ever write a practical program which consists of only one module.

Module Names

All modules have a name, for example SmallExample in Fig. 1.1. The name is given at the start of the module and is repeated just before the full stop which terminates the module. Figure 1.2 indicates that this is generally the case.

Comments

The description of the program enclosed within the symbols (* and *) is known as a comment. Such comments are ignored by the computer and are for the programmer's benefit.

Declarations and Statements

A clear distinction is made in Modula-2 between definitions of objects and the way that the objects are used. Declarations describe the properties of objects. The objects must be used in a way that is consistent with the declarations. For example, SmallExample declares a data item called Length and says that it is a CARDINAL variable. CARDINAL variables can only hold CARDINAL values (non-negative whole numbers), so within statements Length cannot be treated as if it holds a sequence of characters. Similarly if a data item is declared so that it can hold a sequence of characters then statements cannot carry out arithmetic operations on it. If attempts are made within a program to perform such illegal operations then errors are reported and the program cannot be run. SmallExample only contains variable declarations though other kinds of objects can also be declared.

Every variable used in a program must be declared so that checks can be made that it is being used appropriately.

Variable Declarations

Variable declarations are introduced by the word VAR, thereby indicating that the objects declared in the following lines are variables. A variable is a program object which can hold a value. Statements in the program can replace a variable's value with other values. Variables can be pictured as containers for data. Figure 1.3 illustrates the variables declared in SmallExample. The question marks indicate that initially the variables contain values which are unknown.

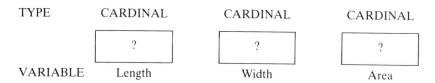

Fig. 1.3.

Variable declarations involve three important ideas,
1. a name is associated with a variable,
2. a variable is associated with a particular type,
3. the value of a variable can be altered to a new value of the appropriate type.

In SmallExample all the variables are of type CARDINAL and therefore can only hold CARDINAL values, which are whole numbers greater than or equal to zero. This is a standard type provided by Modula-2. A careful check is made to see that the operations which are carried out on the data make sense. Thus if a variable has been declared as being of type CARDINAL it does not make sense to try to put a negative value into it.

INTEGER is another standard type whose values are the positive and negative whole numbers and 0. However, no fractional values can be put into such a variable.

In SmallExample three CARDINAL variables are allocated the names Length, Width and Area. Each can hold a CARDINAL value. Note that in Modula-2 a small letter is not treated as the same as its capitalised counterpart, so LENGTH is not the same name as Length. Be sure to check the spelling of names because undeclared names are reported as errors.

Literal Constants

Programs usually need to specify specific values which are to be used. In SmallExample the values 10 and 20 are to be used. These are known as literal constants as the value is literally that written in the program text. This value cannot be altered except by substituting a different value in the text of the program.

Module Body

The module body is surrounded by the words BEGIN and END and contains the instructions, known as statements, for manipulating the data. SmallExample's module body contains three statements, each on a separate line. There are several kinds of statement. Those in SmallExample are all examples of assignment statements.

Assignment Statements

Assignment statements are very important as they are the primary method through which values are placed into variables. After the assignment statement

    Length := 10;

is executed, the variables are as shown in Fig. 1.4.

10	?	?
Length	Width	Area

Fig. 1.4.

After all three assignment statements in the module body have been executed the variables are as shown in Fig. 1.5.

10	20	200
Length	Width	Area

Fig. 1.5.

Let us consider in detail the first statement of SmallExample's module body

    Length := 10;

The distinctive feature which makes this an assignment statement is the := symbol which means 'is assigned the value of'. In English the statement can be thought of as saying 'Length is assigned the value of 10'. As 10 is a literal constant this value is placed inside Length. The second assignment statement is similar, but the third

    Area := Length*Width

has some interesting additional features. The meaning of this is 'Area is assigned the value of Length*Width'. This leaves the problem of interpreting the phrase Length∗Width, which is known as an arithmetic expression. To do this certain conventions must be known. Firstly, the character ∗ means multiply, and secondly, to evaluate the arithmetic expression, the variables named should be replaced by their values. On this occasion the expression means '10 multiplied by 20'. Thus after execution of the third assignment statement, Area holds the value 200.

Punctuation

In Modula-2 the programmer can lay out the text of a program neatly by using spaces and new lines. This freedom should be used to make the program easy to read. In general, each statement should be on a separate line, as in SmallExample.

In Modula-2, punctuation is used to separate parts of the program. Punctuation is indicated by punctuating words and punctuating symbols.

The words MODULE, VAR, BEGIN and END are punctuating words. MODULE indicates the start of a module and VAR indicates the start of a collection of variable declarations. In SmallExample BEGIN and END indicate the start and finish of the module body, though these words are also used in other contexts in the language. Such punctuating words are known as **reserved words** as they can only be used in specific positions and cannot be redefined, for example as a variable's name.

The punctuation symbols in SmallExample are

> ; . , :

1.   The semicolon. This plays two distinct roles in Modula-2 programs, both of which are illustrated in SmallExample. One of its uses is as a **terminator**. For example, a semicolon terminates the heading of the module

```
MODULE SmallExample ;
```

and terminates a declaration, as in the declaration of the three variables.

Its second use is to separate statements from each other. This means that it need not be present when one statement is not immediately followed by another. As it is a **separator** between statements, there is no semi-colon after the third assignment statement in SmallExample because the word END is not a statement.

2.   The full stop. This terminates a program module. The last symbol in a module is always a full stop.

3.   The comma. This is used to separate items in a list, such as the names of variables which are of the same type. The comma is used as a separator in many similar lists which occur in Modula-2 programs.

4.   The colon. The colon is used as part of the assignment operator which is considered to be a composite symbol (:=). Another case is as a separator between variable names and the type name of the variables.

When writing a program you are likely to encounter errors. These fall roughly into three categories,

1.   syntax errors caused by incorrectly punctuating a program, or misspelling names, or omitting declarations,

2.   semantic errors caused by misunderstanding how constructions of the language behave when they are executed, and

3.   logic errors caused by misunderstanding the problem to be solved.

Syntactic errors prevent an executable program from being produced and have to be corrected before the program can be run. Semantic and logic errors do not usually prevent an executable program from being produced but it does not behave as intended. Do not be surprised that the programs you write contain errors. Most programmers' initial attempts contain errors. However you must remove errors when they have been detected.

1.2   COMPUTERS

This section briefly introduces the components of a computer system which are particularly relevant to programming in Modula-2. Further background can be found in the books listed in the bibliography under the heading **Elementary Computing**.

Hardware

A typical microcomputer system comprises a central processor with main memory, disk storage, a visual display unit, a keyboard and printer (see Fig. 1.6). These physical parts of a computer are known as the **hardware**. Modula-2 can be used for programming on larger more sophisticated computers. Thoughout this book, however, we assume such a microcomputer system.

Disk storage is used for storing information on a permanent basis. Floppy disks are one such example of disk storage. Information can be read from and written to a floppy disk via a floppy disk unit. Disk storage has two important characteristics.

1.   Different disks can be put into the disk units to access the information on the disks. The amount of information which can be stored on disks is limited only by the number of disks available.

2.   Information stored on disk is permanent in the sense that it is retained

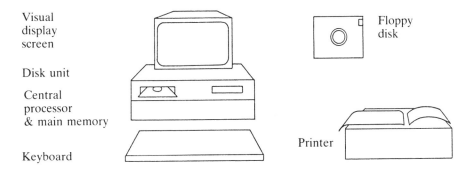

Visual display screen

Disk unit

Central processor & main memory

Keyboard

Floppy disk

Printer

Fig. 1.6.

when the computer is switched off. This information can be used again at a later time. Information can be erased from disks by specific instructions.

Some microcomputers have a hard disk unit built into the machine which works faster than a floppy disk drive unit. Such hard disks cannot be removed, but they can hold large amounts of information. Computers which have hard disks often have a floppy disk drive unit as well so that information can be copied from the hard disk onto floppy disks.

Programs and the information used by them can be stored on disk. This allows programs to be executed a number of times, and modifications to be made to programs written previously.

Information on disks is usually organised into separate **files**. Individual programs are stored in different files, and information required by programs can be stored in other files. Some computer systems use different terminology and support further ways in which information can be held on disks, such as an idea of a **library** which can group together several files.

Main memory is also used to hold information and can be accessed more quickly than disk storage. However main memory is more expensive than disk storage and therefore the amount of main memory is limited. In addition, the information held in it is lost when the machine is switched off. It consists of a sequence of memory locations, often called words, each of which can hold a small amount of information. When the computer executes a program, the program is copied from disk into main memory where it is available to be executed. The information a program processes has to be held in main memory at various stages, but if results are required for later reference then these have to be copied to disk storage before the program finishes.

The central processor executes a program by accessing individual program instructions held in main memory and performing the necessary action for each instruction in turn. These instructions involve primitive operations

which the computer can execute. Some examples are
1. fetch the contents of a memory location
2. write to a memory location
3. process the data read from main memory (e.g. add two pieces of data)
4. modify the normal order of executing instructions.

These instructions are usually called the machine code of the computer, and typically differ from one kind of computer to another.

One of the advantages of a language like Modula-2 is that it hides many of the details of the physical machine and the primitive instructions which it can execute, so that for most programming purposes only a rudimentary understanding of the physical computer is needed. This is useful even for a programmer who knows a computer in detail; a television engineer does not think about the detailed workings of the television when he is watching a television programme.

Operating System

This term is used to describe a collection of programs which provide overall control functions for the computer. Many functions are required by all users and these are normally provided by the operating system. An example of this is the set of control programs required to operate the disk units and keep track of where program files and data files are kept on the disk. Such functions are required by all users and are best provided within the operating system. In larger computers, with powerful processors, the operating system usually provides facilities allowing many users to share the same resources, such as printers. Such programs are very complicated and are normally supplied with the computer. Modula-2 is a very good language in which to write these sophisticated programs.

Software

This is a general term for the computer programs which are used for solving business or scientific problems or to control computers. Some examples of software are a Modula-2 compiler, a Modula-2 program compiled by a Modula-2 compiler, a package used to calculate a company's accounts and a word processor package to aid the production of documents.

It is unfortunate that programs rarely work according to their specification when first developed. This usually means that the program has to be modified many times before a working program is produced. This can be a time consuming process. One aid to speeding up the development is to use a word processor package to enter programs into the computer. In addition, once the source of an error is discovered and the correction deduced, a word processor speeds up the correction process. This can be very useful when using the methods of program development recommended in this book. Whenever possible, you are advised to use a word processor in the development of Modula-2 programs.

Computer Languages

Computer languages are the programmer's medium for communicating with computers. At present such languages are a pale shadow of human languages such as English. Instead computer languages are little more than sets of commands written in very formal and precise phrases. A lot of work is being done to make computer languages more like human languages and therefore more flexible, but progress is slow due to the complexity of human languages and because, in the main, precise commands are necessary.

Most computers only understand a small collection of primitive instructions known as the computer's machine code. These instructions are made up of sequences of numbers and consequently machine code is not suitable for people to use when writing programs. The nearest most people come to programming in machine code is when they use languages called assemblers. These languages are almost equivalent to machine code, but are rather easier to use since the instructions are written to convey a sense of their function to a human programmer. A high level language like Modula-2 is still just a set of instructions, but works at a much higher level of communication than machine codes. One instruction of Modula-2 might be equivalent to twenty instructions in machine code. Programs written in assembler and high level languages must be converted into an equivalent machine code program, and it is this program which is executed by the computer.

Compiler

A **compiler** is a program which translates from one computer language to another. To write Modula-2 programs on a computer, you must have a compiler which translates the Modula-2 program into the equivalent machine code program for that particular computer. It is only after this has been done that the instructions in the machine code program can be executed by the computer. In the compilation process, the code to be translated is known as the **source code** and the translated code is known as the **object code**.

Linker

This term is used for a program which takes separately compiled sections of code and combines them into a single machine code program. If a linker is available then parts of a program can be developed and **compiled separately** from each other. They are combined into a complete machine code program after being compiled. Amongst other things, this allows sections of code to be developed which can be used in many different programs. When a linker is used the compiler produces code, which is acceptable to the linker, rather than direct machine code. This allows the linker to decide where in main memory the machine instructions are to be placed.

Figure 1.7 illustrates the ideas of compilation and linking. Modula-2 is a language able to make maximum use of the facility for separate compilation of parts of a program. It allows many of the traditional linking steps to be carried out at the compilation stage. The linking may be carried out just before execution (during the loading of the program) or in a separate earlier stage.

The machine code program is produced after the linking step. Normally the source code, object code and machine code programs are all stored in files on disk. The machine code program can then be executed many times, or one of the source code files may be altered and recompiled and the object code relinked to produce a new version of the program.

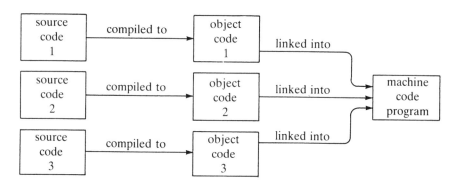

Fig. 1.7.

Program Execution

When a program is executed, it is copied from a file on disk into main memory. The central processor executes it by accessing the program instructions in main memory. The execution of the program often involves the input and output of data (information). Data is input as the program is executed so that it may vary from one execution of the program to the next. The data may be input in several ways; for example the source of the data may be

1.   the user of a program typing data at the keyboard,
2.   a file on disk,
3.   a device connected to the computer (such as a thermostat monitoring the temperature of water in a washing machine).

Data output can be of many kinds, for example
1.   messages in English for the user on the visual display screen,
2.   data written to a file on disk for later analysis,
3.   control codes to some device being controlled by the computer.

1.3   WHY USE MODULA-2?

Modula-2 belongs to the mainstream of computer languages which include such well known languages as FORTRAN, COBOL, ALGOL and Pascal. Modula-2 is a direct descendent of ALGOL and Pascal. In addition Modula-2 embodies significant ideas embodied in lesser known languages such as Simula-67.

FORTRAN was the first language to try to make programming relatively independent of any particular machine. The other languages have continued this drive for machine independence. Inevitably some flexibility is lost in moving from the machine code to a method more natural for people, and this applies to the facilities available within the language, and the efficiency of the code executed by the computer.

Modula-2 has many outstanding points, the more important are listed here.
1.   *Large programs.* It is designed to facilitate the writing of large programs. Though it is an excellent language for writing programs of any size, its distinctive features are most evident when it is used in large projects.
2.   *Error detection.* Modula-2 compilers detect many errors at the compilation stage which in other languages are not detected until the program is run. Since errors at execution time are much harder to correct than compilation errors, this is a powerful facility.
3.   *Low level facilities.* It provides facilities which have been traditionally associated with assembler languages, without losing the advantages of clarity and conciseness normally associated with a high level language.

The above ideas are provided in Modula-2 so that as little as possible of a Modula-2 source program is specific to a particular machine. Those parts of a program which require knowledge of the precise characteristics of a particular computer can be **hidden** from other parts of the program. This maximises
1.   portability — the ability to move the source program from one computer to another type of computer, and then compile it to produce an executable

machine code program for this other computer,

2.   reusability — the ability to use a program to help in solving more than one problem.

All of this is achieved in a language which is relatively small in comparison with other computer languages providing similar facilities.

1.4   SYNTAX DIAGRAMS

An important stage in understanding a programming language is the ability to recognise when a program contains syntax errors. The compiler is of great help in this respect, since it reports any syntax errors and often gives considerable assistance in pinpointing the precise nature of the error. From the viewpoint of the programmer another help is to have precise statements of what is syntactically legal in the language. This is done in this book by the use of syntax diagrams — with extra restrictions expressed in accompanying English. The diagrams in this and subsequent chapters only tell part of the truth, since typically they are concentrating on some aspect under discussion. They should not be used as a definitive statement of the language's syntax. A definitive collection of syntax diagrams is given in Appendix 1. As you progress these should become a major source of reference.

An example of a syntax diagram is given in Fig. 1.8. The arrows indicate the direction of travel along a given path. A legal syntactic item is built up by tracing a path starting at the left hand entry point, exiting at the right hand exit point, and noting the required items on a chosen path through the diagram. It is illegal syntax if the path is truncated before the exit point.

In Fig. 1.8 there is more than one possible path, and each path leads to a legal digit. By following the possible paths through the diagram from left to right it can be seen that a digit is a whole number between 0 and 9 inclusive. Starting at elementary items like a digit the diagrams build up to give a definition of what constitutes a legal module in Modula-2.

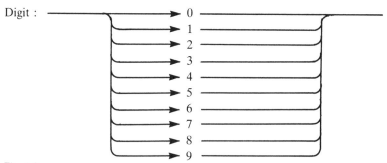

Fig. 1.8.

A more interesting syntax diagram is given in Fig. 1.9. This diagram refers to the syntax diagram for Digit and assumes that a further syntax diagram Letter has been defined as being a small letter (a..z) or a capital letter (A..Z). Paths through a syntax diagram can refer to both symbols which have specific meaning in Modula-2 (such as ;,:= ,END) and to other syntax diagrams. When a syntax diagram refers to another diagram then this latter diagram has to be followed to its exit point before continuing with the former diagram. In addition the diagram for Identifier involves two loops. The leftward pointing arrows rejoin the rightward pointing arrow at an earlier point than they leave it. This indicates that these parts of the diagram can be repeated as many times as is required.

Identifier :

Fig. 1.9.

Figure 1.9 states that a sequence of letters and digits which begin with a letter constitute a valid identifier, which can be used as names in the program, for example as the name of a module or a variable. For example

Length	Width	Area	SmallExample			
L	Len123	WiDTh	w123tHr	ssssssssssssssss	Fig18	R

are all valid identifiers, but the following are all invalid for the reasons given

2length	:– an Identifier must start with a Letter
Fig1.8	:– full stop is not included in either
	of the diagrams for Letter or Digit
John Smith	:– space is not included in either of
	the diagrams for Letter or Digit.

Figure 1.10 illustrates how syntax diagrams can be used to check whether something is syntactically valid. It shows that Fig19 is an identifier by finding a path through the syntax diagram shown in Fig. 1.9. Once an initial letter has been found the syntax chart always terminates successfully because the moment it meets a character that is not a letter or a digit it terminates, having found an identifier. Thus, in the three examples of invalid identifiers, the first is invalid because it does not start with a letter, the second generates the unintended identifier Fig1 and the third generates the unintended identifier John.

To be an Identifier,
    the first character must be a Letter
        F is a Letter
    the Identifier ends or the next character is a Letter or a Digit
        i is a Letter
    the Identifier ends or the next character is a Letter or a Digit
        g is a Letter
    the Identifier ends or the next character is a Letter or a Digit
        1 is a Digit (see Fig. 1.8)
    the Identifier ends or the next character is a Letter or a Digit
        9 is a Digit (see Fig. 1.8)
    the Identifier ends or the next character is a Letter or a Digit
        the Identifier has ended.

Fig. 1.10. Is Fig19 a valid Identifier?

Certain identifiers cannot be used by the programmer because Modula-2 has reserved them for specific uses in the language. These are the punctuating words and are always in capital letters. The ones met in SmallExample are MODULE, VAR, BEGIN and END.

Other identifiers, such as CARDINAL and INTEGER, are said to be predefined. The distinction between reserved identifiers and predefined identifiers is subtle. The former must never be used except as specified in the syntax of Modula-2, but the latter can be redefined under special circumstances. You are advised not to redefine identifiers until you are expert in the use of Modula-2. Lists of reserved and predefined identifiers are available in Appendices 2 and 3.

Figures 1.11 to 1.14 show the syntax diagrams for a simplified version of the assignment statement. Figure 1.14 is the diagram for a simplified form of numeric literal constants such as 10.

Assignment :

Fig. 1.11.

Simple Expression :

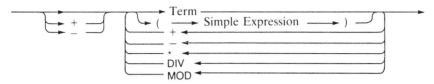

DIV is an INTEGER or CARDINAL divide, e.g. 5 DIV 2 is 2.
MOD is the remainder after an INTEGER or CARDINAL divide, e.g. 5 MOD 2 is 1. In general,

$$p = q*(p \text{ DIV } q) + (p \text{ MOD } q).$$

Fig. 1.12.

Term :

Fig. 1.13.

Number :

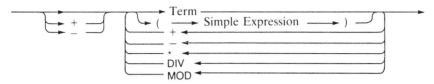

Fig. 1.14.

The following is a valid assignment

    Height := 23*Weight + 32

since it can be analysed as follows

    From Fig. 1.11
            Height has to be an identifier (true from Fig. 1.9).
            23*Weight + 32 has to be a simple expression.
                From Fig. 1.12 this is true if 23,Weight and 32 are all terms.
                    This is true from Figs 1.13 and 1.9 for Weight.
                    This is true from Figs 1.13 and 1.14 for 23 and 32.

Figure 1.15 is a simplified diagram for Statement. It permits two types of statement, the assignment statement and the null statement. A statement sequence is an ordered set of statements separated by semi-colons. This is shown in Fig. 1.16.

Statement :

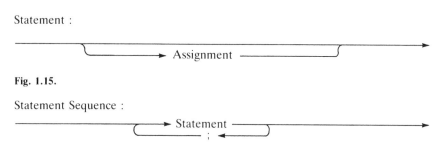

Fig. 1.15.

Statement Sequence :

Fig. 1.16.

Figure 1.15 states that a statement can be empty. This is often called a null statement. Both

```
BEGIN                    BEGIN
   Area := 100              Area := 100;
END                      END
```

are valid. The former is analysed as "BEGIN Statement END" and the latter as "BEGIN Statement;Statement END", the second statement being a null statement. This can be useful as it allows the programmer to treat the semicolon as though it is a terminator of a statement by allowing a semicolon to immediately precede the END symbol.

It is important that you become familiar with the syntax of the language in order that you can express yourself in Modula-2. Syntax diagrams are used throughout this book to indicate the legal form of various parts of the language.

TECHNICAL EXERCISES

1   In the program

```
MODULE OtherExample;
   VAR
      name : INTEGER;
   BEGIN
      name := 20 − 10 * 3
   END OtherExample.
```

state what are the (a) reserved words, (b) predefined words, (c) name of the program, (d) assignment statements, (e) simple expressions.

2   Make the following program valid by inserting punctuation symbols

```
MODULE SillyExample
  VAR
    First Second Sum CARDINAL
BEGIN
  First := 10
  Second := 20
  Sum := First + Second
END SillyExample
```

3 Using the syntax diagrams for Identifier and Number state what the following character sequences represent

a. vAlue   b. Cardinal   c. 123   d. 12fred   e. L56wid

4 Draw a syntax diagram which defines the declaration of variables of type CARDINAL (as, for example, in Fig. 1.1). Extend the definition to include the possibility of the type INTEGER (a positive or negative whole number).

5 Using the syntax diagrams in the text, decide whether or not the following are statement sequences. Assume that all the variables used are of type CARDINAL.

a. joe := 10;   b. num1 := 40;
   fred := 20;   num2 := num1 * 3
   alf := 3 * joe + fred   num3 := num2 − (num1 DIV 7)

c. num4 := 30 + 3(5 + 7)   d. ;;;;;;;;;;

e. joe := 10;   f. joe := 10;
   fred := 20;   fred := 20;
   joe + fred := alf   alf = fred − joe

If a sequence is invalid, say where it is incorrect.

6 Evaluate the following simple expressions:

a. joe := 21 DIV 5   b. fred := 21 MOD 5
c. joe := 5 DIV 6   d. fred := 5 MOD 6

ANSWERS

1 a. MODULE,VAR,BEGIN and END are reserved words.
   b. INTEGER is a predefined word.
   c. OtherExample is the name of the program.
   d. name := 20 − 10 * 3 is the only assignment statement.
   e. 20 − 10 * 3 is a simple expression.

2 One possible answer is

```
MODULE SillyExample;
  VAR
      First,Second, Sum : CARDINAL;
BEGIN
  First := 10;
  Second := 20;
  Sum := First + Second
END SillyExample.
```

The semi-colon before BEGIN is necessary to terminate the declaration section. A semi-colon is not required after the last statement and before END as the semi-colon acts as a separator between statements in the module body. It is not wrong, however, to have a semicolon after the third statement, as the compiler then assumes that there is a fourth statement which is a null statement.

3 a. Identifier.
   b. Identifier, note that it is not the same Identifier as the predefined Identifier CARDINAL.
   c. Number, the literal value 123.
   d. Number 12 followed by Identifier fred
   e. Identifier.

4 A possible diagram is

Variable declaration:

5 a. Valid.
   b. Invalid, due to the missing semi-colon in line 2.
   c. Invalid since implied multiplication is not allowed. A valid simple expression with the most likely equivalent meaning is

   num4 := 30 + 3 * (5 + 7)

   d. Valid, just a sequence of null statements!
   e. Invalid, since line 3 does not have a single identifier on the left hand side of the :=. A probable correction is

   alf := joe + fred

   f. Invalid, since a colon is missing in line 3. The correct expression is

   alf := fred − joe

An interesting point arises if the expression is written as

    alf := joe − fred

The statement sequence is correct, but it is obvious that the answer is incorrect in the sense that it results in a negative number being assigned to alf which is declared as a variable which can only hold non-negative numbers. This is usually considered to be part of the semantics of the language rather than the syntax and compilers do not report an error. Instead an error is indicated when the program is executed. (Some Modula-2 systems fail in this respect, and do not report an error when the program is executed.)

6 It does not matter in this question whether the variables are assumed to be CARDINAL or INTEGER.

a. 4   b. 1   c. 0   d. 5

Chapter 2

Program Modules, Standard Modules
and Procedure Calls

Throughout the book we outline different but complementary approaches to solving problems and writing programs. One approach involves identifying relatively self-contained sub-problems within the original problem, and working on these almost in isolation. The second approach involves identifying recurring sub-problems and writing sections of program code which can be used in several programs.

This chapter describes a program which allows a user to specify the length and width of a rectangle and which then calculates the area of the rectangle. Though this program is elementary it illustrates how larger problems can be tackled using the first approach.

In Chapter 1 a small program module was shown. However, if this was typed into a computer, compiled and executed we would not see anything happen. This is because the program does not ask for any information to be input nor does it write out any results. Typically a program needs to do at least one of these. In theory, we could write a sequence of statements to perform these input and output operations within the program module itself. However, it is apparent that these operations are required by many programs, so Modula-2 provides a facility which effectively allows programmers to extend the language. The way that input and output operations are made available in Modula-2 is an example of the second approach; the language has been extended to allow these operations to be performed easily.

It is important when writing programs that they can be understood by the programmer and by anyone else who may have cause to look at them. The example program of this chapter illustrates how comments and variable names can make a program more intelligible.

2.1 COMMENTS

A Modula-2 program can contain **comments**, which are notes in the program for the benefit of anyone reading the program. Additionally, comments can be used during development to note what work still has to be done. The problem of calculating the area of the rectangle can be broken into three sub-problems

1. read values for the rectangle's length and width,
2. calculate the area,
3. write out the area.

Figure 2.1 shows this information incorporated into a Modula-2 program. The program heading and ending are specified and the three sub-problems are each stated within comments. These are included in a further comment stating that these problems are still to be completed. All characters between the start comment symbol (* and the end comment symbol *) are the comment. They can be placed almost anywhere but they cannot appear in the middle of an identifier name or reserved word. Notice also that comments can be put inside other comments, but for every open-comment symbol (* there must be a matching close-comment symbol *).

Throughout the book we use a sequence of dots at the start and end of a comment to indicate that the comment describes some part of the program which has still to be developed.

The program in Fig. 2.1 can be compiled, though it does not do anything when it is run.

```
MODULE SmallExample ;
BEGIN
  (* The following are 3 comments one for each of the sub-problems
    (*... read the values for length and width ...*)
    (*... calculate the area from length and width ...*)
    (*... print the area ...*)
  *)
END SmallExample .
```

Fig. 2.1.

2.2　VARIABLES AND VARIABLE NAMES

The program needs variables to store the values for the length, width and area of the rectangle. Declarations of variables to hold these values should use identifier names which describe their purpose so that an identifier's role can be understood by looking at the name. Including the lines

```
VAR
        Length,
        Width ,
        Area  : CARDINAL
```

after the module heading allows these variables to be used in the program (see Fig. 2.2).

```
MODULE SmallExample ;
    VAR                       (*module variable declarations*)
        Length,
        Width,
        Area            : CARDINAL ;

BEGIN               (* Module Body *)
    (*... read the values for length and width ...*) ;
    (*... calculate the area from length and width ...*) ;
    (*... print the area ...*) ;
END SmallExample .
```

Fig. 2.2.

If the variables Length and Width are assumed to hold appropriate values for the length and width of the rectangle already, then the sub-problem of calculating the area and storing the result in the variable Area is a simple arithmetic calculation

Area := Length * Width

This leaves the sub-problems of

1. reading the values of the length and width of the rectangle from the keyboard and storing them in Length and Width respectively,
2. writing out the result stored in Area.

These sub-problems can be achieved by using procedures for reading information from the keyboard and writing information to the visual display screen. These are provided in a module which contains procedures to perform input and output operations.

2.3 PROCEDURES FOR INPUT AND OUTPUT, AND PROCEDURE CALLS

High level programming languages generally provide a collection of instructions within the language for performing useful operations which are required in many programs. These are usually known as **procedures** and they can be used or **called** simply by naming the procedure and supplying to it the appropriate information.

Modula-2 provides several procedures for performing such operations. In most programming languages procedures for reading information from the keyboard and writing information to the screen are included within the language. Modula-2 does not provide procedures for performing input and output operations in this way. These procedures are available in a **standard module** supplied with Modula-2, usually called InOut.

Modules in general can be thought of as containers which provide particular facilities. SmallExample is a container for the facility which our program provides. The module InOut contains input and output operations which are commonly required in many programs. Each operation is provided in a separate procedure and other modules can request the use of individual procedures from InOut and then call them when particular operations are required.

InOut contains the procedures ReadCard and WriteCard and several others.

So what do ReadCard and WriteCard do? Briefly

1.   ReadCard reads a CARDINAL number from the keyboard. A CARDINAL number is any sequence of the digits 0 to 9 terminated by any non-numeric character.

2.   WriteCard writes a CARDINAL number to the screen such that it occupies a specific number of character positions when written.

A procedure is called by naming the procedure and supplying it with appropriate information in what are termed the **parameters** of the procedure call. For example, the procedure ReadCard has to be supplied with a parameter, which is a CARDINAL variable, into which it will store the value read from the keyboard. A call to ReadCard looks like

    ReadCard (Length)

where Length has been declared as a CARDINAL variable.

When a CARDINAL value is read from the keyboard by ReadCard, the person using the program types a sequence of numeric characters which are displayed on the visual display screen so that he can see what he has typed. A non-numeric character, for example the space character, has to be typed at the end of the sequence to indicate the end of the number. On this occasion the number is stored in the variable Length as this is the parameter in the procedure call.

WriteCard has to be given two parameters when it is called, which must be CARDINAL values or variables containing CARDINAL values. The first parameter is the value which is written on the screen and the second parameter specifies the minimum number of character positions the number should occupy. For example

    WriteCard (Area,3)

writes the value contained in Area so that it occupies at least three character positions. If Area holds the value 123, then

    |123|

is written on the screen. The lines I are not written out but are used here to indicate the character positions on the screen which are used for writing out the value. If the number needs fewer character positions than indicated in the second parameter then sufficient spaces are written out before the number to make it fill the number of character positions specified. If Area holds the value 12 then a space followed by the number is output so that the number fills the specified number of character positions

I 12I

The value is said to be right justified in that the number always occupies the right most character positions and any unused positions are written as spaces preceding the value. A call of WriteCard

WriteCard (X∗Y,10)

writes the result of multiplying the values in the CARDINAL variables together in an area of the screen ten characters wide. If the values of X and Y are 4 and 6 respectively then the result needs only 2 character positions and WriteCard writes eight spaces and then the number 24 to fill the ten character positions on the screen.

I   24I

WriteCard can be used to format numerical information neatly on the screen.

SmallExample gains access to procedures from standard modules only if it includes instructions stating which procedures are required from which modules. For example the instruction

FROM InOut IMPORT ReadCard,WriteCard ;

should be interpreted as 'from the module InOut import the objects ReadCard and WriteCard'. ReadCard and WriteCard can then be called in SmallExample to read and write information. This instruction is called an **import list** and appears at the top of the module. Several such import lists can appear at the top of a module. In this case the objects are procedures. Other kinds of objects can also be imported. Subsequent chapters discuss where information about imported objects can be found. For the present, all examples of imported objects are restricted to procedures.

SmallExample can now be expanded to include procedure calls for reading values into Length and Width, and for writing the result of the calculation to the screen. The expanded module is shown in Fig. 2.3. Note that the dots have been removed from the comments because statements have been written to achieve the sub-problems. The comments can remain as descriptions of what the different sections of the code achieve. However, in large programs too many comments can obscure the program code. In this chapter such comments are left in programs, however in subsequent chapters only comments essential to understanding the code are retained.

```
MODULE SmallExample ;
 FROM InOut IMPORT ReadCard,WriteCard ;
 VAR                              (*module variable declarations*)
        Length,
        Width,
        Area      : CARDINAL ;

BEGIN
        (* read the values for length and width *)
     ReadCard (Length) ;
     ReadCard (Width) ;

        (* calculate the area from length and width *)
     Area := Length * Width ;

        (* print the area *)
     WriteCard (Area,5) ;
     END SmallExample .
```

Fig. 2.3.

SmallExample is typical of Modula-2 programs. It consists of a main **program module** which uses procedures provided in other modules. These other modules are said to be subservient to the program module in that they do not constitute complete programs in their own right. Instead they provide useful facilities which program modules can use.

SmallExample can now be compiled and run. When two numbers are typed on the keyboard for the length and width (e.g. 6 and 7) the program prints out the area (42). For example

    6 7   42

It is not obvious during the running of this program when information should be typed into the program nor what the information printed by the program means. Programs should also print suitable messages informing the user what to do and what the results written out by the program mean. This implies that the program should format the information in such a way that it is obvious to the person using the program what the information means. It would be preferable for SmallExample to ask the user to input numbers for the length and width of the rectangle and to inform him that the result which has been calculated is the area.

Two other procedures in InOut called WriteString and WriteLn are useful for formatting the input and output of a program.

WriteString writes a sequence of characters to the screen.

WriteLn causes the next input or output operation to be started on the next line of the screen.

The sequence of characters to be written by WriteString is passed to it as a parameter. This can be any sequence of characters enclosed within quotation marks

WriteString ('A sequence of characters to be written on the screen')

WriteString ("Another character sequence to be written")

Sequences of characters enclosed in quotes are literal string constants. They denote a value which is the sequence of characters enclosed within the quotation marks. Either single quotation marks or double quotation marks can be used, but there must be a matching pair at the start and end of the character sequence. This allows quotation marks themselves to be part of a literal string constant. For example

WriteString ("His Master's Voice")

writes out

His Master's Voice

and

WriteString (' " " ')

writes out

" "

Notice that the quotation marks enclosing the entire character sequence are not part of the literal string constant and therefore are not written. A sequence of WriteString calls can be used to write a long character sequence as each statement starts writing where the previous one finished. For example

WriteString ('Customer Name   Credit Card No.   Amount Due') ;

WriteString (' Amount Paid Balance') ;

would write

Customer Name   Credit Card No.   Amount Due Amount Paid   Balance

which could form a heading for columns of information on a report or account statement.

WriteLn causes a new line on the screen to be started, and in combination
with other procedures this permits the design of well presented information.
For example, the sequence of statements

```
WriteLn ;
WriteString ('Gross Pay                    ') ;
WriteCard (5000,5) ;
WriteLn ;
WriteString ('Tax Payable                  ') ;
WriteCard (1000,5) ;
WriteLn ;
WriteString ('Net Pay                      ') ;
WriteCard (5000–1000,5) ;
WriteLn ;
```

causes the information to appear as

Gross Pay	5000
Tax Payable	1000
Net Pay	4000

The completed version of SmallExample with suitable messages and reasonably
formatted input and output is shown in Fig. 2.4.

```
MODULE SmallExample ;
FROM InOut IMPORT ReadCard,WriteCard,WriteLn,WriteString ;
VAR                             (*module variable declarations*)
      Length,
      Width,
      Area       : CARDINAL ;

BEGIN
      (* read the values for length and width *)
      WriteString ('Type the length of the rectangle – ') ;
      ReadCard (Length) ;
      WriteLn ;
      WriteString ('Type the width of the rectangle – ') ;
      ReadCard (Width) ;
      WriteLn ;

      (* calculate the area from length and width *)
      Area := Length * Width ;

      (* print the area *)
      WriteString ('The area of the rectangle is – ') ;
      WriteCard (Area,5) ;
      WriteLn
END SmallExample .
```

Fig. 2.4.

When this program is compiled and run and two numbers are typed at the keyboard the following appears on the screen

Type the length of the rectangle - 10
Type the width of the rectangle - 5
The area of the rectangle is - 50

The procedures in InOut allow the sub-problems of accepting input from the keyboard and writing information to the screen to be solved relatively easily. However, these are complicated operations and are dependent upon the particular type of computer being used. Notice that in writing SmallExample it is not necessary to know how ReadCard, WriteCard, WriteString and WriteLn perform the input and output operations. It is sufficient to know that when they are called correctly they achieve particular operations.

2.4 EXAMPLE. TAX CALCULATION

Suppose the problem to be solved is to calculate a person's annual net pay from his annual gross pay and the amount to be paid in tax, assuming that he pays tax at a rate of 30% on all earnings. Figures 2.5–2.7 show similar stages of program development for a module Pay to solve this problem. In Fig. 2.5 the major sub-problems are identified.

```
MODULE Pay ;
BEGIN
        (*... Read in the person's gross pay ...*)
        (*... Calculate his tax payable and net pay ...*)
        (*... Write out the tax payable and net pay ...*)
END Pay .
```

Fig. 2.5.

The possibly more complex sub-problem of calculating the taxable and net pay is developed first. Any necessary declarations for achieving this sub-problem are also included in the developing module (see Fig. 2.6).

Notice how the taxable pay is calculated. The statement

TaxPayable := GrossPay DIV 100 * 30

produces a less accurate result in TaxPayable because CARDINAL division performed by DIV disregards the remainder. Hence

7299 DIV 100 * 30   equals   72 * 30   equals   2160

because the initial division disregards the remainder of 99 thereby rendering this non-taxable. If the multiplication is performed before the division then all GrossPay is taxable

7299 * 3 DIV 10   equals   21897 DIV 10   equals   2189

```
MODULE Pay ;
 VAR
      GrossPay,
      NetPay,
      TaxPayable : CARDINAL ;
 BEGIN
      (*... Read in the person's gross pay ...*)

      (* Calculate his tax payable and net pay *)
   TaxPayable := GrossPay * 3 DIV 10 ;
   NetPay := GrossPay − TaxPayable ;

      (*... Write out the tax payable and net pay ...*)
   END Pay .
```

Fig. 2.6.

A further possibility is to write the calculation as

TaxPayable := GrossPay * 30 DIV 100

but this also has a drawback. As there is a maximum CARDINAL value, multiplication by a large number is more likely to produce a result which is larger than this maximum than multiplication by a smaller number. When the multiplication is performed before the division, multiplication by 30 produces an intermediate result which is larger than that produced by multiplication by 3. Multiplication by 3 increases the range of values for GrossPay for which the program produces sensible results.

Finally the sub-problems of reading information from the keyboard and writing information to the screen are tackled in a similar way to that used in SmallExample (see Fig. 2.7).

The problems discussed in this chapter are very straightforward, but nevertheless the approach of breaking a problem down into smaller sub-problems helps us to focus on one aspect of the problem at a time. With more complex, larger problems this approach is indispensable. Modula-2 encourages this way of thinking.

```
MODULE Pay ;
 FROM InOut IMPORT ReadCard,WriteCard,WriteString,WriteLn ;
 VAR
        GrossPay    ,
        NetPay      ,
        TaxPayable : CARDINAL ;
BEGIN
        (* Read in the person's gross pay *)
        WriteLn ;
        WriteString ( 'Gross Pay                    ') ;
        ReadCard (GrossPay) ;

        (* Calculate his tax payable and net pay *)
        TaxPayable := GrossPay * 3 DIV 10 ;
        NetPay := GrossPay − TaxPayable ;

        (* Write out the tax payable and net pay *)
        WriteLn ;
        WriteString ('Tax Payable                  ') ;
        WriteCard (TaxPayable,5) ;
        WriteLn ;
        WriteString ('Net Pay                      ') ;
        WriteCard (NetPay,5) ;
        WriteLn ;
END Pay .
```

Fig. 2.7.

2.5 SUMMARY

1 There are several kinds of module in Modula-2, two of which are

a program modules, which begin with the word MODULE,

b standard modules which are supplied with Modula-2. These contain procedures which may be useful in many programs. The standard module we have seen is usually called InOut and contains procedures for performing input and output operations.

2 The import list of a program module states that procedures from other modules will be used in this module. In order to use procedures contained in the module InOut the programmer has to specify which procedures are to be imported in the module's import list.

3 InOut contains procedures for performing input from the keyboard and output to the screen. These procedures include

a ReadCard which when used has to be supplied with a CARDINAL variable as a parameter in the procedure call

```
ReadCard (X)
```

where X has been declared as a CARDINAL variable. This causes the program to wait for a value to be typed by the user at the keyboard and then stores this value in X.

b WriteCard which has to be called with two CARDINAL values (or variables holding CARDINAL values) as parameters

    WriteCard (X,Y)

the first is the value to be written and the second determines the number of character positions the value is to occupy on the screen,

c WriteLn which does not take any parameters and causes subsequent input and output to begin on the next line of the screen, and

d WriteString which takes a sequence of characters enclosed within quotes as its parameter

    WriteString ('A string of characters')

and writes this string on the screen.

A complete list of the procedures available in InOut is given in Appendix 4, though at this stage you do not know what all of these do.

TECHNICAL EXERCISES

1 Given the following declarations

    VAR X,Z : CARDINAL ;

state which of the following calls of procedures in InOut are valid.

a READCARD (X)

b ReadCard (Z)

c ReadCard (X,Z)

d WriteCard (X)

e WriteCard (X,6)

f WriteCard (X,Z)

g WriteString (A sequence of characters)

h WriteString ('A sequence of characters')

j WriteLn (X)

k WriteLn

l WriteString ("Another sequence of characters.")

m WriteString ("Different quotation marks at each end.')

2. State the errors apparent in the following program module. How could the program be improved to help others understand it? How could the program be improved to help someone using the program? Try to write a corrected and better version of the program.

```
PROGRAM Mistakes ;
VAR
       FRED,George : CARDINAL ;
BEGIN
 ReadCard (Fred) ;
 George := Fred * Fred ;
 WriteCard (George,6)
END .
```

3 Show what the output from the following program module will be.

```
MODULE OutputExample ;
 FROM InOut IMPORT WriteCard,WriteString,WriteLn ;
BEGIN
 WriteString ('————————————————————') ;
 WriteLn ;
 WriteLn ;
 WriteLn ;
 WriteString (' ————————————————') ;
 WriteLn ;
 WriteString ('|          ') ;
 WriteCard (50,2) ;
 WriteString ('          |') ;
 WriteLn ;
 WriteString (' ————————————————') ;
 WriteLn ;
 WriteLn ;
 WriteString ('————————————————————————') ;
 WriteLn ;
END OutputExample .
```

4 Write a statement sequence which asks a user of a program to type the time as three numbers separated by spaces and reads the numbers into three CARDINAL variables Hours, Minutes and Seconds.

PROGRAMMING EXERCISES

1 Type the example programs into a computer and get them running. Do not worry about typing them correctly the first time, as it is instructive to see the kinds of error messages you receive when there are errors in a module. If errors are reported by the compiler then compare your versions carefully with those in the figures and correct them. The error messages are dependent upon the compiler you are using, some will be more helpful in identifying what the error is than others.

2 Write a program module which asks the user for the price of an item, and the number of items purchased and writes out the total cost of the purchase.

Assume that the price is an exact number of pence. Modify the module so that it writes out the total price in pounds and pence by using MOD and DIV.

ANSWERS TO TECHNICAL EXERCISES

1   **a** invalid as the name of the procedure is ReadCard.
   b valid.
   c invalid as ReadCard requires precisely one parameter.
   d invalid as WriteCard requires two parameters.
   e valid.
   f valid — the width of the area on the screen for displaying X will be determined by the current value in Z.
   g invalid as the quotation marks are missing around the sequence of characters. As it stands a compiler could well report that there are commas missing between four parameters to the procedure and that WriteString does not accept four parameters.
   h valid
   j invalid as WriteLn does not take a parameter
   k valid
   l valid
   m invalid as the quotation marks must match.

2   A module begins with the word MODULE not PROGRAM. The module uses procedures which are available in the standard module InOut but does not import these. Fred has not been declared, Fred and FRED are not the same name. The module name Mistakes must appear before the fullstop ending the module.

The variable names Fred and George do not contribute towards the understanding of the program. In this particular case names such as Number and Square would be more suitable.

When the program is run the person using it will not be told what is happening. He will be expected to input a number but there will be no indication of this appearing on the screen. Additionally the result of the calculation will be written but no indication of what calculaton has been performed or what the result means will be given. Only someone who knew exactly what the program does could use it.

The following is one possible corrected and improved version.

```
MODULE SquareANumber ;
 FROM InOut IMPORT Readcard,WriteCard,WriteString,WriteLn ;
 VAR
        Number,Square : CARDINAL ;
BEGIN
        (* Read the number. *)
  WriteString ('Type a number – ') ;
  ReadCard (Number) ;
  WriteLn ;

        (* Calculate the square. *)
  Square := Number * Number ;

        (* Write the result. *)
  WriteString ('The square of the number is – ') ;
  WriteCard (Square,6)
END SquareANumber .
```

3

```
|          50              |
```

4
```
WriteString ('Type the time (in the format HH MM SS) – ') ;
ReadCard (Hours) ;
ReadCard (Minutes) ;
ReadCard (Seconds) ;
WriteLn ;
```

Chapter 3

Variable and Constant Declarations, Expressions and Control Structures

This chapter gives a preliminary explanation of several ideas central to writing Modula-2 programs. These ideas are

1. variable and constant declarations,
2. expressions,
3. control structures.

The discussion in this chapter uses simplified forms of these ideas. Later they are expanded to incorporate all constructs in Modula-2. Nevertheless after studying these ideas we will be in a position to write programs to solve reasonably sophisticated and interesting problems.

3.1 VARIABLE AND CONSTANT DECLARATIONS

Declarations allow the programmer to introduce names to identify program objects, hence these names are known as identifiers. In addition, declarations associate identifiers with certain attributes which determine how the objects can be used.

This section concentrates on two kinds of declaration: variable declarations and constant declarations. Examples of the former have appeared in programs already and are discussed in further detail. Constant declarations are closely related to variable declarations and it is important to appreciate the similarities and differences between them.

Program Module :

Block :

Declaration :

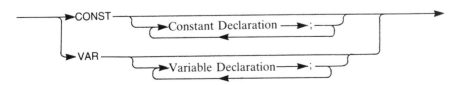

Fig. 3.1.

Simplified syntax diagrams for program module, block and declaration are shown in Fig. 3.1. It should be noted that collections of constant and variable declarations can occur in any order. Constant declarations can precede or follow variable declarations, or they can be interleaved with one another.

Variable Declarations

All but the most trivial of programs require that information is held in the computer's main memory when it is executed. In the program module in the previous chapter the following declaration occurred

```
VAR
      Length,Width,Area : CARDINAL ;
```

This declaration introduces three variables with the names Length, Width and Area. When a program containing this declaration is executed, memory locations are allocated for each of the variables. In general, variable declarations are instructions to reserve memory locations for holding information. Once a variable has been declared its identifier can be used subsequently to refer to the variable. When the program is executed, references to the variable access the memory location allocated for the variable.

In a variable declaration it is necessary to specify the **type** of each of the variables. The type of a variable determines the range of values which it can hold and the permissible operations applicable to it. Variable declarations have the general form shown in Fig. 3.2 where an identifier list is defined as a sequence of identifiers separated by commas.

Variable Declaration :

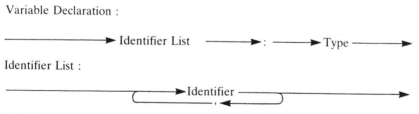

Identifier List :

Fig. 3.2.

Variables of the same type can be listed in an identifier list in the same variable declaration so that the type need only be stated once. The syntax diagram for declarations (see Fig. 3.1) permits sequences of variable declarations, so variables of the same types can be given in the same declaration or in separate declarations. The following consists of two variable declarations in which the first declares two CARDINAL variables and the second declares a further CARDINAL variable.

```
VAR
        Length,Width : CARDINAL ;
        Area        : CARDINAL ;
```

Alternatively Length, Width and Area could have been declared in the same declaration

```
VAR
        Length,Width,Area : CARDINAL ;
```

or in separate collections of variable declarations

```
VAR Length      : CARDINAL ;
VAR Width       : CARDINAL ;
VAR Area        : CARDINAL ;
```

Variables of differing types must be declared in separate variable declarations. The following declaration introduces two CARDINAL variables A and B, and a variable CH whose type is CHAR.

```
VAR
        A,B : CARDINAL ;
        CH : CHAR ;
```

Assignment operations are allowed on variables and therefore variable identifiers can occur on the left hand side of the assignment symbol in assignment statements. For example

```
Length := 2*3
```

is permitted. When this statement is executed the value 6 is stored in the memory location for Length. The previous value held in Length is overwritten and lost. Hence the contents of a variable can vary during the execution of the program.

The Type CARDINAL

A declaration that a variable's type is CARDINAL restricts the variable to hold only CARDINAL values (non-negative whole numbers). It is then permitted to place CARDINAL values in the variable. For example

```
Length := 5
ReadCard (Length)
```

are legal statements. However it is illegal to try to put a non-CARDINAL value into the variable. For example the following assignment statements are all invalid

Length := −2	(negative value)
Length := 'String'	(a sequence of characters)
Length := 'A'	(one character)
Length := '9'	(one character)

Notice that the last example is invalid because of the quotation marks around the number which indicate that it is a character rather than a CARDINAL value. This distinction is made clear in the section on the type CHAR later in this chapter.

The following operations are allowed on a CARDINAL variable

1. a CARDINAL value can be stored in the variable by an assignment statement,

2. the operations +, −, ∗, DIV (CARDINAL divide) and MOD (CARDINAL modulus) can be used,

3. a CARDINAL value can be read into the variable using ReadCard,

4. the value in the variable can be written using WriteCard,

5. the value in the variable can be compared with another CARDINAL value to see if they are equal or not, or whether one is greater than the other.

So far, examples and discussion have centred on the predefined type CARDINAL, but Modula-2 also provides several other predefined types. One of these is INTEGER, which is a type that has many similarities with the type CARDINAL but differs in that negative whole numbers are permissible INTEGER values. The type CHAR contrasts with CARDINAL more markedly.

The Type CHAR

CHAR variables hold a single character as their value. Characters include all the alphabetic and numeric characters that appear on a keyboard, punctuation marks and several special characters such as [, +, @ etc. In Modula-2 characters are denoted by enclosing them in quotation marks. Either single or double quotation marks may be used but the closing quotation mark must match the opening quotation mark.

Modula-2 uses the ISO standard set of 128 characters, a common variant of which is the ASCII character set shown in Table 3.1.

Each character is associated with a unique number, which is known as the character code of the character. The alphabetic characters are ordered so that the character code of **A** is associated with a lower number than the code of **B** and this is lower than that of **C** etc. The lower case characters are ordered in a similar manner from **a** to **z** and additionally there is a fixed difference of 32 between the character code of a capital letter and its lower case equivalent.

			LOW					
	0	1	2	3	4	5	6	7
0	null	soh	stx	etx	eot	enq	ack	bel
1	bs	ht	lf	vt	ff	cr	so	si
2	dle	dc1	dc2	dc3	dc4	nak	syn	etb
3	can	em	sub	esc	fs	gs	rs	us
4	sp	!	"	#	$	%	&	'
H 5	(	)	*	+	,	–	.	/
I 6	0	1	2	3	4	5	6	7
G 7	8	9	:	;	<	=	>	?
H 8	@	A	B	C	D	E	F	G
9	H	I	J	K	L	M	N	O
10	P	Q	R	S	T	U	V	W
11	X	Y	Z	[	/	]	^	←
12	`	a	b	c	d	e	f	g
13	h	i	j	k	l	m	n	o
14	p	q	r	s	t	u	v	w
15	x	y	z	{			}	~	del

Character Code = (HIGH * 8 + LOW)

Table 3.1. The ASCII character set.

The numeric characters **0** to **9** are ordered in the same way, however the code of a numeric character is not identical to the number. The code of **9** is 57 in ASCII. The difference between the character **9** and the number 9 is indicated by the use of quotation marks when the character is intended. '9' is the character nine and 9 is the number nine.

The low numbers in the character set are associated with special characters and for the most part we will not be concerned with these. However the space (sp) character and the null character are frequently used. The space character is typed at the keyboard by pressing the space bar and generates a character which we will depict as △ where it would not otherwise be obvious, though when it is displayed on the screen or on printout it appears as a blank character. The null character is a special character in that it cannot be written out and whose significance is illustrated later.

There are other character sets beside the ASCII character set. If your version of Modula-2 and computer use a different character set you will have to refer to the system documentation for precise details. In many situations the ordering of the characters is irrelevant, however in discussion and examples where the ordering of the characters is important, the ASCII character set will be assumed.

Declarations of character variables look very similar to declarations of CARDINAL variables, except that the word CHAR is used instead to indicate the type of the variable(s)

```
VAR
     ch,CH : CHAR ;
```

Some of the operations which are then permitted on the variable are
1.   assignment of a character to the variable, e.g.

```
CH := 'A'
```

which puts the character **A** into the variable CH.
2.   read a character into the variable using a procedure Read which is one of
the other procedures provided in the module InOut, e.g.

```
Read(ch)
```

which reads a character from the keyboard and assigns it to ch.
3.   write out the character held in a variable using Write, a further procedure
supplied in InOut, e.g.

```
Write(ch)
```

4.   compare the value of a character variable with another character value.

One important use of CHAR variables is to accept a one character reply
from a user. For example the program fragment in Fig. 3.3a will accept one
character from the keyboard which may then be used to determine how the
program continues. The decision of what the program should do next can
then be made on the basis of whether Reply holds **y** after the Read statement.
This makes the program a easier to understand than trying to do the same
thing using a CARDINAL variable as in Fig. 3.3b. With this version the person
using the program has to remember that 1 means continue and 0 means stop,
as does the programmer when reading the program. In addition, the end of a
CARDINAL number has to be signalled by a character after the number, so the
user has to type two characters (e.g. **1△**).

```
VAR
     Reply : CHAR ;
     (*...    ...*)
BEGIN
 (*...    ...*)
 WriteString ('Do you wish to continue? (y/n)') ;
 Read (Reply) ;
 (*...    ...*)
END
```

(a) using Read.

```
VAR
      Reply : CARDINAL ;
      (*...   ...*)
BEGIN
(*...   ...*)
WriteString ('Type 1 to continue or 0 to stop.') ;
ReadCard (Reply) ;
(*...   ...*)
END
```

(b) using ReadCard.

Fig. 3.3.

Constants

Constants are values and therefore cannot be changed during program execution. There are two kinds of constant, one of which has already appeared in example programs. In the statements

```
X   := 3
CH  := 'A'
ch  := '3'
```

the right hand side of the assignment symbol is a reference to a constant value. Characters in quotation marks and numbers used in this way are referred to as **literal constants** and do not have to be declared.

The second kind of constant is introduced in a **constant declaration** which allows identifiers to be associated with specific values. For example the following constant declaration

```
CONST
      SpeedOfSound = 5 ; (* miles per second *)
```

associates the value 5 with the identifier SpeedOfSound.

Choosing names for constant identifiers which are suggestive of the purposes for which they are used can greatly aid someone trying to understand a program. It can also reduce the number of modifications which may have to be made to a program if the requirements of the program are changed.

Consider the following situation. A program is to read some information and a particular character signals the end of the information. The character chosen to signal the end of the data is [. It is therefore reasonable to include the declaration

```
CONST
      Terminator = '[' ;
```

in the program. The name Terminator can be used in place of '[', so anyone reading the program does not have to remember that [is being used to mark the end of the data.

In addition, if it is subsequently found that the data can include the character [, it will not be possible to use this as the marker signalling the end of the data. A different character has to be used. The only modification required to the program is to alter this constant declaration and replace [by the new character which marks the end of the data. If the character [had been used throughout the program then modifying the program requires that on each occasion that [is used to mean 'the character signalling the end of data' this must be changed by the programmer. This can be a time consuming and error prone exercise.

Constant declarations can refer to identifiers declared in previous declarations. For example if the space character is used as a terminator of a list of input items and it is used in other places in a module then it is permissible to make the declarations

```
CONST
      Space       = ' '  ;
      Terminator = Space ;
```

Altering the terminating character would then only involve changing the declaration of Terminator but other references to the constant Space would not be affected. The above declarations have to be made in the order illustrated, because a constant declaration cannot refer to identifiers whose declarations follow it. For example

```
CONST
      Terminator = Space ;
      Space       = ' '  ;
```

is illegal because the declaration of Terminator requires the declaration of Space to precede it.

In some situations constants suggest themselves naturally. These tend to be values which have some natural or conventional meaning as illustrated by the examples in Fig. 3.4.

```
CONST
      MiddleC              =     264 ;
      RadiusOfEarth        =    3960 ;
      WeeksInYear          =      52 ;
      HeightOfEverest      =   29028 ;
      Comma                =     ',' ;
      Fullstop             =     '.' ;
```

Fig. 3.4.

More usually constant declarations involve values which are unique to the problem being tackled. In writing a program which is to deal with the customer accounts of a shop it may be agreed that the program need only cater for a maximum of a thousand customers. It is appropriate to declare a constant

```
CONST
       MaxNoCustomers        = 1000 ;
```

If, at a future date, business is so good that the program has to cater for more customers some modifications will be required, but modifying the number of customers only requires replacing 1000 by the new maximum and recompiling the program. Alternatively it might be the case that another shop is interested in the program but has fewer customers and a smaller computer. Again altering the value of this constant creates a new version of the program which copes with fewer customers and presumably requires less computer facilities.

Even if neither of these situations is likely, it is still good programming practice to use constant declarations for the sake of clarity.

Notice that in a constant declaration the type of the constant is not specified. This is because its type is implicit in the value which is associated with the identifier. Hence the type of Comma and Fullstop is CHAR as the identifiers are each associated with a CHAR value, whilst MiddleC and WeeksIn-Year are CARDINAL constants because they are associated with CARDINAL values. It is therefore permissible to assign Comma or Fullstop to character variables but not to CARDINAL variables, and assignment of WeeksInYear or MiddleC to CARDIN-AL variables is allowed but not to CHAR variables. Assuming the variable declarations

```
VAR
       CH : CHAR        ;
       Days,
       X  : CARDINAL    ;
```

then

```
       CH := Comma
       Days := WeeksInYear * 7 + 1
       X   := MiddleC * 2
```

are valid assignment statements, but

```
       CH := WeeksInYear
       X   := Comma
```

are not.

The Structured type ARRAY

The types CARDINAL, INTEGER and CHAR are predefined basic types. There are other predefined basic types which will be discussed later. In addition Modula-2 provides **structured types** which are types built up from other types. Basic types are types whose values cannot be broken into any component parts. Structured types are collections of information packaged together in some way.

One such structured type is known as an array. For example, the declaration

```
VAR
    ArrayOfNumbers : ARRAY [1..10] OF CARDINAL ;
```

declares a variable ArrayOfNumbers which can hold 10 CARDINAL values. ArrayOfNumbers is therefore a collection of components or elements each of which can hold a CARDINAL value. We can picture this as in Fig. 3.5.

ArrayOfNumbers

23	5	46	0	6	23	7	123	9	0
1	2	3	4	5	6	7	8	9	10

ARRAY [1..10] OF CARDINAL

Fig. 3.5.

In order to place a value into ArrayOfNumbers there has to be some way of referring to one of the elements of the array individually. This is done by using the subscript (also known as the index) of that element. For example if we wish to change the third element of ArrayOfNumbers from 46 to 57 then the following assignment statement achieves this

```
ArrayOfNumbers[3] := 57
```

The value in the square brackets is the subscript or index of the array which selects the third element of the array.

Similarly if a value is to be read from the keyboard and stored in the fourth component of ArrayOfNumbers then this can be done by the statement sequence

```
ReadCard (NewValue) ;
ArrayOfNumbers[4] := NewValue ;
```

assuming that NewValue is a CARDINAL variable, or by the single statement

```
ReadCard (ArrayOfNumbers[4])
```

In this example the array elements are numbered from 1 to some upper limit, but this does not have to be the case. The only restriction when specifying the limits of the array is that the upper limit is not smaller than the lower limit.

There is usually some logical reason for wanting to treat a collection of information as a bundle in this way. For example consider a situation where a company's annual profit over a period of ten years is of interest. We could declare ten variables, one for each year and store the profit for each year in a separate variable

```
VAR
        Profit80, Profit81, Profit82, Profit83, Profit84,
        Profit85, Profit86, Profit87, Profit88, Profit89: CARDINAL ;
```

however this is longwinded and gets much worse if we are interested in the annual profit over a period of fifty years. Alternatively we can group the information together in a variable which can hold the profits for all years of interest

```
VAR
        AnnualProfit    : ARRAY [80..89] OF CARDINAL ;
        GrossProfit,
        TaxPayable,
        ProfitThisYear : CARDINAL ;
```

which declares AnnualProfit to be an array of ten CARDINAL values. The components of the array are indexed from 80 to 89 so that the index corresponds to the year in question. The following are then valid statements

```
AnnualProfit[80] := GrossProfit − TaxPayable
ProfitThisYear := AnnualProfit[85]
```

but the following are not

```
AnnualProfit[6] := 5
ProfitThisYear := AnnualProfit[7]
```

The statement

```
ProfitThisYear := AnnualProfit[ThisYear]
```

is meaningful only if ThisYear is a variable or constant whose value is currently between 80 and 89 inclusive.

Constants can be used to make the declarations and statements even more meaningful and to help if subsequent modifications are required. AnnualProfit could have been declared by the following collection of declarations

```
CONST
      FirstYear = 80 ;
      LastYear  = 89 ;
VAR
      AnnualProfit : ARRAY [FirstYear .. LastYear] OF CARDINAL ;
```

Access to individual components is then expressed as previously

```
AnnualProfit[82] := 45
```

or by using the starting index as an offset

```
AnnualProfit[FirstYear+2] := 45
```

It was stated earlier that the syntax diagrams relating to declarations allow collections of constant and variable declarations to occur in any order. However, just as a constant decaration must precede any other constant declarations which refer to it, so the declaration of a constant must precede any variable declarations which use the constant. In the above example the declarations of FirstYear and LastYear must precede the declaration of Annual-Profit.

Just as arrays of CARDINAL values are permitted so are arrays of other types. The declaration

```
VAR
      Name : ARRAY [1..15] OF CHAR ;
```

declares a variable which can hold fifteen characters. Characters can be assigned to its elements so that it holds a person's name (see Fig. 3.6a). The resulting array is illustrated in Fig. 3.6b.

Characters are assigned to elements of a CHAR array in a similar manner to the way values are assigned to the elements of a CARDINAL array. For example,

```
Name[5] := 'r'
```

replaces the character in the fifth element of Name by **r**. If subsequently the value stored in the fifth element of the array is assigned to a character variable then this variable also holds **r**, as in

```
ch := Name[5]
```

Values can be assigned directly from one element of an array to another, as in

```
Name[12] := Name[10]
```

which copies the character in the tenth element into the twelfth element. As was the case with the CARDINAL array, we can read characters directly into the array and write out the characters in the array by using the procedures Read

```
Name[1]   := 'P' ;
Name[2]   := 'E' ;
Name[3]   := 'T' ;
Name[4]   := 'E' ;
Name[5]   := 'R' ;
Name[6]   := ' ' ;
Name[7]   := 'M' ;
Name[8]   := 'E' ;
Name[9]   := 'S' ;
Name[10] := 'S' ;
Name[11] := 'E' ;
Name[12] := 'R' ;
Name[13] := ' ' ;
Name[14] := ' ' ;
Name[15] := ' ' ;
```

(a)

Name

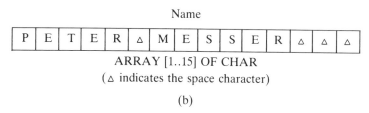

ARRAY [1..15] OF CHAR
(△ indicates the space character)

(b)

Fig. 3.6.

and Write from InOut rather than ReadCard and WriteCard

```
Read (Name[13])
Write (Name[Index])
```

In the latter case this is only valid if Index is a CARDINAL variable which currently has a value between 1 and 15.

InOut has two procedures which allow sequences of characters to be read from the keyboard and written to the visual display screen. These are Read-String and WriteString.

1. ReadString reads into a character array a sequence of characters from the keyboard until a character is read whose code is 32 or less. Normally the character terminating a character sequence is either the space character or the return (cr) character. For example

```
ReadString (Name)
```

reads a sequence of characters and stores them in Name. ReadString ignores any spaces preceding the character sequence before it begins reading characters into the array. If the number of characters typed at the keyboard is less than the number the array can hold then ReadString assigns the null character to all the remaining components. If the number of characters typed is greater than the size of the array then the excess characters are ignored. The backspace key can be used to delete characters.

2. WriteString writes the sequence of characters in a variable or a constant out to the visual display screen. For example

>   WriteString (Name)

writes out the sequence of characters in Name up to the first null character or all the characters in the array if there is no null character in the array.

Modula-2 has a special array of characters known as a **string**. This is simply an array of characters whose lower index is 0. For example

>   VAR
>   AnotherName : ARRAY [0..14] OF CHAR ;

declares a string variable called AnotherName which can hold 15 characters. The index of the first element is 0 and the index of the fifteenth element is 14.

Strings variables are special because literal string constants can be assigned to them directly. The statement

>   AnotherName := 'IAN MARSHALL'

is equivalent to the sequence of assignment statements shown in Fig. 3.7a. Notice the last three of these assignment statements. The literal string constant 'IAN MARSHALL' only contains 12 characters but AnotherName has fifteen elements so the remainder of the string variable is padded out with null characters (indicated by ∇). The resulting array is shown in Fig. 3.7b.

A string cannot be assigned to another string if the latter is not long enough to hold the character sequence of the former. Consider the declarations

>   VAR
>   LongString : ARRAY [0..40] OF CHAR ;
>   ShortString: ARRAY [0..10] OF CHAR ;

A literal string with more than 10 characters cannot be assigned to Short-String, so the statement

>   ShortString := 'Too long a character sequence'

is reported as an error.

Assignment of one string variable to another string variable

>   s1 := s2

```
AnotherName[0]   := 'I' ;
AnotherName[1]   := 'A' ;
AnotherName[2]   := 'N' ;
AnotherName[3]   := ' ' ;
AnotherName[4]   := 'M' ;
AnotherName[5]   := 'A' ;
AnotherName[6]   := 'R' ;
AnotherName[7]   := 'S' ;
AnotherName[8]   := 'H' ;
AnotherName[9]   := 'A' ;
AnotherName[10] := 'L' ;
AnotherName[11] := 'L' ;
AnotherName[12] := '▽' ;
AnotherName[13] := '▽' ;
AnotherName[14] := '▽' ;      (a)
```

AnotherName

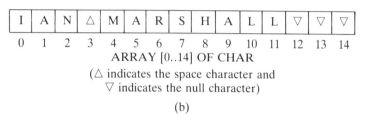

I	A	N	△	M	A	R	S	H	A	L	L	▽	▽	▽
0	1	2	3	4	5	6	7	8	9	10	11	12	13	14

ARRAY [0..14] OF CHAR
(△ indicates the space character and
▽ indicates the null character)

(b)

Fig. 3.7.

is permissible so long as the number of characters up to the first null character in s2 will fit in s1. Assuming the declarations of LongString and ShortString above, the following statement sequence is permitted

```
LongString   := 'A sequence of 27 characters' ;
ShortString  := '10     chars' ;
LongString   := ShortString ;
ShortString  := LongString ;
```

but the following statement sequence is not permitted

```
LongString := 'A sequence of 27 characters' ;
ShortString := '10     chars' ;
ShortString := LongString ;
```

In the former there are only 10 characters in LongString before the first null character so it can be assigned to ShortString without causing an error. In the latter case there are too many characters in LongString before the first null character so an error will be reported when the statements are executed.

The ideas of constants and variables have been introduced, as have three types and three different ways of reading and writing information. Figure 3.8

	CARDINAL	CHAR	ARRAY[M..N] OF CHAR (string)
Literal Constant	634 23	"z" 'A'	"James O'Neill" "A" 'A message' 'H'
Constant Decl'tion	CONST Length = 16	CONST Comma = ','	CONST Title = 'Macbeth'
Variable Decl'tion	VAR X : CARDINAL	VAR CH : CHAR	VAR Message : ARRAY[0..9] OF CHAR Name : ARRAY[1..9] OF CHAR
Assign- ment	X := 3 X := Length	CH := '4' CH := Comma CH := Message[3]	Message := 'Hello' Message := Title Message[5] := 'b' (Name := 'Fred' *****) (Name := Title *****) Name[2] := 'r'
Reading	ReadCard (X)	Read (CH)	ReadString (Message) ReadString (Name) Read (Name[4])
Writing	WriteCard(X:5) WriteCard(6:X) WriteCard(Length:3)	Write (CH) Write (Comma) Write ('x')	WriteString (Message) WriteString (Title) WriteString ('Hello') WriteString (Name) Write (Message[3])

***** not permitted — an array of characters whose lower index is not 0 cannot be assigned the values of string constants directly.

Fig. 3.8.

	ARRAY[M..N] OF CARDINAL
Variable Declaration	VAR Nums : ARRAY[1..8] OF CARDINAL
Assignment	Nums[3] := 7 Nums[4] := Nums[8] X := Nums[5]
Reading	ReadCard (Nums[2]) ReadCard (Nums[X])
Writing	WriteCard (Nums[3],6)

Fig. 3.9.

summarises these ideas. Arrays of CARDINAL and CHAR values have also been discussed. The ways in which these can be used are summarised in Fig. 3.8 and Fig. 3.9. Notice that constants of structured types such as arrays (excluding strings) are not permitted, and that there are no procedures supplied for reading and writing such structured types (again with the exception of strings). Nevertheless we will find structured types to be very useful for solving more complicated problems.

3.2   EXPRESSIONS

An expression is a construct which produces a result when it is evaluated. It is most readily apparent in assignment statements. The syntax diagram for the assignment statement is shown in Fig. 3.10.

Assignment Statement :

————————▶Identifier ————————▶ := ————————▶ Expression ————————▶

Fig. 3.10.

In the assignment statement

    Area := 2*3

Area is assigned the result of evaluating 2 multiplied by 3. In general an expression consists of operands separated by operators. The operands provide values and the operators determine the operation to be performed on these values in order to produce the result. In this example the multiplication operation is to be performed on the operands 2 and 3.

The values used in the evaluation of an expression can be provided by variables. In the assignment statement

    Area := Length * Width

the expression is

    Length * Width

The multiplication operation is to be performed on the values held in the variables Length and Width.

Notice that there is a distinct difference in the way that the name of the variable is used depending upon whether it occurs on the left hand side or right hand side of the assignment symbol. When a variable name occurs on the right hand side of the assignment symbol it is part of an expression and therefore the value held by the variable is to be used. When the variable name occurs on the left hand side this is simply stating that the result of the expression on the right hand side is to be put in this variable. This is apparent in an assignment statement

```
X := X * 3
```

which multiplies the value held in X by 3 and then assigns the result to X. If X originally held the value 6 then after the statement is executed it holds the value 18.

When an expression is evaluated it produces a result which has a particular type. The type of the result is determined by the types of the values of the operands used in the expression and the operations performed on the values. Assuming the declarations

```
CONST
        LetterA       = 'A'        ;
        VAR
                ch,CH : CHAR        ;
                X,Y     : CARDINAL  ;
```

then the assignment statements

```
CH := 'Z'
CH := LetterA
X   := 3
```

are valid statements involving the most trivial kind of expression. These are all valid assignment statements as all the values on the right hand side of the assignment statement are constants and no operations are involved, and the types of the constants are identical to the types of the variables to which they are assigned. In these cases the result of the expression is the same as the value of the constant.

Another straightforward form of an expression is the case where the expression consists only of a variable name, for example

```
Y  := X
ch := CH
```

In these cases the result of the expression is the value held by the variable (or you can think of it as the present value represented by the variable name).

The situation is only slightly more complicated with arrays, if the following declarations are made

```
VAR
        Name            : ARRAY [1..15] OF CHAR ;
        AnnualProfit    : ARRAY [80..89] OF CARDINAL ;
        CH              : CHAR ;
        ProfitThisYear  : CARDINAL ;
```

then the assignments

```
CH := Name[3]
ProfitThisYear := AnnualProfit[83]
```

are valid. In the first case the result of the expression is the value in the third element of Name, and in the second case the result is the value in the fourth element of AnnualProfit (whose index is 83).

Arithmetic expressions can be more complex than those involving CHAR values as they permit a wide range of arithmetic operators. For the present we will concentrate on expressions which evaluate to a result whose type is CARDINAL. These will be called CARDINAL arithmetic expressions. The points discussed are also applicable to the type INTEGER.

CARDINAL Arithmetic Expressions

CARDINAL arithmetic expressions are expressions which produce a result whose type is CARDINAL. Such expressions can involve the arithmetic operations of addition, subtraction, multiplication, CARDINAL division and CARDINAL modulus. However programming languages require a notation different from that used in mathematical formulae. For example the mathematical forms

$$\frac{a \times b}{c} \qquad \text{or} \qquad \frac{ab}{c}$$

are written in Modula-2 as

```
a * b DIV c
```

The symbol for multiplication is * because x is a possible identifier, and CARDINAL division is indicated by the word DIV.

Multiplication, addition and subtraction are the normal arithmetic operations. However, CARDINAL division and modulus produce CARDINAL results. The result of CARDINAL division does not include any fractional part. For example

```
5 DIV 2
```

evaluates to 2 (not 2.5). CARDINAL modulus gives the remainder left by a CARDINAL division. For example

```
5 MOD 2
```

evaluates to 1.

Figure 3.11a shows examples of valid assignment statements, assuming that X and Y are declared as CARDINAL variables. Notice that though the spaces before and after the addition, subtraction and multiplication symbols are optional, spaces must be left before and after MOD and DIV. In Fig. 3.11b YMOD11 satisfies the syntax of identifiers and hence the compiler would report that YMOD11 had not been declared. In the second case the same problem occurs with MOD11 which most compilers analyse as an identifier.

```
X := 23 + 46
Y := 12+6
X := 345−56
Y := 34∗22
X := Y ∗ 2
X := 2334 MOD 11
X := X ∗ Y
X := X∗Y
Y := 2334 DIV 11
```

(a)

```
X := YMOD11
X := 123MOD11
```

(b)

Fig. 3.11.

The usual mathematical interpretation of arithmetic expressions which involve combinations of arithmetic operations is that multiplication and division have precedence over addition and subtraction. Hence

12 + 4 ∗ 2	is interpreted as	12 + (4 ∗ 2)
3 + 2 ∗ 5 + 2 DIV 6	is interpreted as	3 + (2 ∗ 5) + (2 DIV 6)
X + Y ∗ Z	is interpreted as	X + (Y ∗ Z)

where the brackets indicate that the operation inside the brackets are to have precedence over those outside. This is the case with expressions where the operators ∗, MOD and DIV have precedence over the + and − operators. Hence the assignment statement

X := 12 + 4 ∗ 2

assigns 20 to X, and

Y := 3 + 2 ∗ 5 + 2 DIV 6

assigns 13 to Y (as 2 DIV 6 evaluates to 0).

It is permissible to use brackets in expressions to indicate that the bracketed part of the expression is to have precedence over other parts which would otherwise have higher precedence. If in the above examples the intention is that the addition operations are to be carried out before the division or multiplication then brackets can be used to indicate this

```
X := (12 + 4) * 2
Y := (3 + 2) * (5 + 2) DIV 6
```

X will then be assigned the value 32, and Y the value 5. Brackets can also be used to emphasise the normal ordering of evaluation. The following assignment statements are equivalent

```
Y := 3 + 2 * 5 + 2 DIV 6
Y := 3 + (2 * 5) + (2 DIV 6)
```

but note again the need for spaces before and after DIV (and MOD).

The Standard Procedures INC **and** DEC

The previous chapter illustrated how programs can use procedures which are contained in the module InOut. Modula-2 also provides several standard procedures which are part of the language and do not have to be imported from another module. INC and DEC are two such procedures.

Certain arithmetic expressions are so common that Modula-2 provides an abbreviated way of writing them. For example the statement

```
Count := Count + 1
```

can be written using INC as

```
INC(Count)
```

to increment Count by 1. There is a further version of INC which permits the value of the increment to be specified. A call of INC

```
INC (Count,7)
```

is equivalent to the statement

```
Count := Count + 7
```

and a call of INC

```
INC (Count,X*Y)
```

where X and Y are CARDINAL variables is equivalent to

```
Count := Count + X * Y
```

A further procedure called DEC is provided for decrementing the values of variables. It also has two forms analogous to those of INC,

```
      DEC (Count) is equivalent to Count := Count - 1
and   DEC (Count,5) is equivalent to Count := Count - 5
```

Standard Function Procedures

Some of the standard procedures are **function procedures**. These **return** a value which can be used in an expression.

For example, there is a standard function procedure CAP which, when given a character, returns the capitalised version of the character. If CH has been declared as a character variable then

    CH := CAP('a')

assigns the character **A** to CH. If the character given as the parameter is not a noncapitalised letter then CAP simply returns the character as its result, hence a statement

    CH := CAP('A')

leaves CH unaltered. It is usual to talk of noncapitalised letters as 'lower case characters' and capitalised letters as 'upper case characters'. A statement

    CH := CAP(CH)

converts the value of CH to its upper case counterpart if it holds a lower case character, otherwise it leaves CH unaffected.

There are other useful standard function procedures which are concerned with converting a value from one type into a corresponding value of another type. The functional procedure ORD can be used to convert a character to its corresponding CARDINAL character code, whilst CHR converts a CARDINAL value between 0 and 127 to the corresponding character value. For example

    CH := CHR(65)

assigns to CH the character whose character code is 65 (**A** in the ASCII character set), and the assignment statement

    X := ORD('0')

assigns to X the code of character **0**.

As an example of the use of ORD and CHR consider the problem of radix conversion. Suppose that an array of characters called NumSeq holds a sequence of numeric characters between **0** and **7** representing an octal number (a number in base 8). Assume that NumSeq is declared as

    VAR
        NumSeq : ARRAY [1..3] OF CHAR ;

and that currently it contains 3 numeric characters, one in each element as shown in Fig. 3.12.

NumSeq

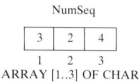

ARRAY [1..3] OF CHAR

Fig. 3.12.

The character in the first element indicates that there are 3 sixty-fours, the second element that there are 2 eights, and the third element that there are 4 ones in the number. Note that the character code for **3** in ASCII is 51, therefore we cannot simply multiply the character code by 64, it is necessary first to subtract an offset of 48 from the code and then multiply by 64. In fact 48 is the code of the character **0**, so a numeric character can be converted to its corresponding numeric value by

    ORD (CH) − ORD ('0')

The contribution of the first element of NumSeq to the octal number can be calculated by the expression

    (ORD(NumSeq[1]) − ORD ('0')) ∗ 64

which evaluates to the CARDINAL value 192.

The entire character sequence can be converted to the corresponding CARDINAL value by the assignment statement

    X := (ORD(NumSeq[1]) − ORD('0')) ∗ 64 +
         (ORD(NumSeq[2]) − ORD('0')) ∗ 8 +
         (ORD(NumSeq[3]) − ORD('0'))

which assigns the CARDINAL value 212 to X.

There are better ways of expressing this conversion which are discussed later. For the present it is important to note how ORD is being used. As the numeric characters are ordered from **0** to **9** in the character set, subtracting the character code of **0** from the character code stored in the element of the array gives a CARDINAL value between 0 and 9 which is then multiplied by 64 or 8 depending upon the position in the array. Notice that arithmetic operations are not performed on characters, but are performed on the character codes provided by ORD. These are CARDINAL values which can be used like other values in arithmetic expressions.

We have seen that CARDINAL variables can be assigned the result of complex arithmetic operations if the result is itself a CARDINAL value. In addition we have seen that some of the function procedures which are provided in Modula-2 allow a value of one type to be converted into a value of another type. In particular CHR and ORD have been discussed for converting CHAR values into CARDINAL values and vice versa. The idea that values of different types cannot be mixed within an expression is central to Modula-2. If for some reason you need to divide 163 by the character **B**, or some similar operation, then a suitable type conversion has to be performed. The insistence on compatibilities of types is called **strong typing**, and its restrictions prevent the programmer from writing code which involve absurd operations. If such type conversions are needed the programmer has to explicitly ask for them, which usually means that the programmer has thought about and intends the conversions.

Note that INC and DEC are procedures which calculate a new value but do not **return** a value in the technical sense of the word. They are not function procedures.

3.3   STATEMENTS AND CONTROL STRUCTURES

The sequence of statements that constitute a module body determine the way the module behaves. It is usual to talk of control being passed from one statement to another to express the idea that when the execution of one statement is completed execution of another commences. The purpose of some kinds of statements is partly or solely concerned with which statement to execute next.

The statements we have met to date provide two different ways in which control is passed from one statement to another. The assignment statement and the null statement have no effect on control in the program and therefore control is automatically passed onto the following statement if there is one. For example, the statements of the following statement sequence are executed in order.

```
X := 1 ;        (∗ executed first ∗)
Y := 2 ;
       ;        (∗ a null statement ∗)
Z := X + Y ;    (∗ executed fourth ∗)
```

The situation with procedure calls is slightly more complicated. When a procedure is called the computer remembers the point reached in the current statement sequence, goes away and executes the procedure and then continues with the statement following the procedure call. Again control is essentially sequential in that the statement following the call is executed as soon as the procedure has been executed.

Often we need greater flexibility than this. Sometimes it is necessary to execute certain statements only in specific situations, whilst on other occasions the program needs to execute a sequence of statements repeatedly. These two kinds of situation are permitted through two kinds of constructs which are normally referred to as **conditional statements** and **repetitive statements**. Modula-2 provides several different ways of achieving each. Here we introduce only one example of each.

Conditional Statements: The IF Statement

Conditional statements are used to allow certain statements to be executed in a precisely stated set of circumstances. For example a program may ask a user to type two numbers and then calculate the value of the first number divided by the second number. However division by 0 is not permitted and the result is either in error or unpredicatable, therefore it makes sense to calculate the result only if the second number is not 0. The program fragment in Fig. 3.13 assumes that X and Y are CARDINAL variables which have been declared previously and that the appropriate procedures from InOut have been imported.

```
ReadCard (X) ;
ReadCard (Y) ;
IF Y <> 0 THEN
    WriteString ('The result is – ') ;
    WriteCard (X DIV Y,6) ;
    WriteLn ;
ELSE
    WriteString ('Division by 0 is not permitted.') ;
END (* IF *) ;
```

Fig. 3.13.

The condition to be tested appears between the words IF and THEN. In Fig. 3.13 the condition is that Y is not equal to 0 (<> is the Modula-2 way of writing 'not equal to'). The sequence of statements between the words THEN and ELSE is executed if the condition is true, otherwise the statement sequence between the words ELSE and END is executed.

As a further example suppose that a program allows a user to try to guess a number known to the program. The program can use an IF statement to tell the user whether or not he has guessed correctly. Assuming that Guess is a CARDINAL variable then the sequence of statements in Fig. 3.14 will do this.

```
ReadCard (Guess) ;
WriteLn ;
IF Guess = 42 THEN
    WriteString ('Correct')
ELSE
    WriteString ('Wrong')
END (* IF *) ;
```

Fig. 3.14.

The general form of the version of the IF statement we have been considering is illustrated in Fig. 3.15. The condition is tested and if it is true then control is passed to the statement sequence immediately following the word THEN. If it is false control is passed to the statement sequence following the word ELSE. In both cases after the appropriate statement sequence has been executed the program continues at the statement following the END of the IF statement.

IF   condition   THEN

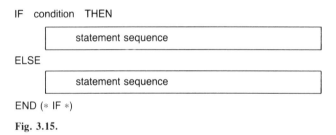

END (* IF *)

Fig. 3.15.

Situations also arise where no specific action is required when the condition is false. This can be written with an empty statement sequence for the ELSE alternative as in Fig. 3.16a. However a further form is provided for this situation which allows the alternative to be left out entirely as illustrated by Fig. 3.16b. The general form of this version is shown in Fig. 3.17.

The syntax diagram in Fig. 3.18 incorporates both versions. There are further versions of the IF statement but these two forms suffice at present. The condition can become complex. For the present it should be noted that typical conditions involve testing whether two things are the same or whether they are different, and testing whether one thing is less than or greater than something else. Figure 3.19 lists the operators for performing these tests with examples of conditions which could be included in an IF statement as the condition. Note carefully that these conditions are not statements in their own right, they can only occur within other statements at particular points.

```
ReadString (Name) ;
IF Name[1] = CHR(0) THEN
     WriteString ('Please type your name.') ;
     WriteLn ;
     ReadString (Name) ;
ELSE      (* do nothing *)
END (* IF *) ;
```

(a) an empty ELSE part of an IF statement.

```
ReadString (Name) ;
IF Name[1] = CHR(0) THEN
     WriteString ('Please type your name.') ;
     WriteLn ;
     ReadString (Name) ;
END (* IF *) ;
```

(b) an alternative form for the IF statement.

Fig. 3.16.

```
IF   condition   THEN

          ┌─────────────────────────────────────┐
          │   statement sequence                 │
          └─────────────────────────────────────┘

END   (* IF *)
```

Fig. 3.17.

If Statement :

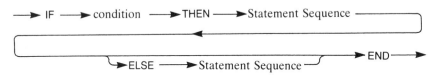

Fig. 3.18.

	Examples	
Test	CARDINAL	CHAR
= (equal to)	Num = 12	Ch = 'A'
<> (not equal to)	Num <> X	Ch <> CHR (0)
> (greater than)	Num > 45	Ch > ' '
< (less than)	Num1 < Num2	Ch < '7'
>= (greater than or equals)	Num >= 0	Ch >= '0'
<= (less than or equals)	Num <= ORD ('7')	Ch <= Space

Fig. 3.19.

Repetitive Statements: The WHILE Statement

Repetitive statements permit a sequence of statements to be executed over and over again. The WHILE statement allows a sequence of statements to be executed while some condition is true.

Consider the following problem. A program is to allow a user to type in an indefinitely long list of numbers and is to add these numbers together and print out the total. This cannot be done by a sequence of ReadCard procedure calls as it is not known how many numbers will be input. The repetitive statement allows us to effectively say 'keep reading numbers until there are no more to read'. The program in Fig. 3.20 keeps reading numbers until the user types the number 0.

Figure 3.21 shows an expansion of the earlier program of guessing a number to allow the user to keep guessing until he guesses the number correctly. The program gives the user help by telling him whether he has guessed too high or too low.

```
MODULE TotalUp ;
 FROM InOut IMPORT ReadCard,WriteCard,WriteLn,WriteString ;
 CONST
    Terminator = 0 ;
 VAR
    NextNum          : CARDINAL ;
    Total            : CARDINAL ;
BEGIN
 Total := 0 ;
 WriteString ('Type the first number (') ;
 WriteCard (Terminator,4) ;
 WriteString (' to indicate you have finished) − ') ;

 ReadCard (NextNum) ;
 WriteLn ;
 WHILE NextNum <> Terminator DO
    INC (Total,NextNum) ;
    WriteString('Type the next number − ') ;
    ReadCard (NextNum) ;
    WriteLn ;
 END (∗ WHILE ∗) ;

 WriteString ('Total is ') ;
 WriteCard (Total,6) ;
 WriteLn ;
 END TotalUp .
```

Fig. 3.20.

```
MODULE GuessingGame ;
  FROM InOut IMPORT ReadCard, WriteLn, WriteString ;
  CONST
     Answer = 42 ;
  VAR
     Guess : CARDINAL ;
BEGIN
  WriteString ('Guess the number I am thinking of – ') ;

  ReadCard (Guess) ;
  WriteLn ;
  WHILE Guess <> Answer DO
     IF Guess > Answer THEN
        WriteString ('You are too high.')
     ELSE
        WriteString ('You guessed too low.')
     END (* IF *) ;
     WriteString (' Try again – ') ;
     ReadCard (Guess) ;
     WriteLn ;
  END (* WHILE *) ;

  WriteString ('Correct.') ;
END GuessingGame .
```

Fig. 3.21.

The general form of the WHILE statement is shown in Fig. 3.22. The condition is tested and if it is true then control is passed to the statement sequence inside the WHILE statement. When these statements have been executed control returns to the top of the WHILE statement and the test is performed again. If the test is again true then the statement sequence inside the WHILE statement is executed and control cycles back to the condition at the top of the WHILE loop. This continues until the test is false, when control is passed to the statement after the END of the WHILE statement. Any of the tests in Fig. 3.19 can be used to form the condition of the WHILE statement.

```
WHILE   condition   DO
       ┌─────────────────────────────────────────┐
       │    statement sequence                    │
       └─────────────────────────────────────────┘
END   (* WHILE *)
```

Fig. 3.22.

Note that the comments (* IF *) and (* WHILE *) are present to aid clarity. They are not obligatory.

As the sequence of statements is executed repeatedly until the condition becomes false it follows that something should happen within these statements to cause the condition to become false. In the number guessing module this was achieved by reading a new value for Guess inside the WHILE statement's statement sequence. In the program fragment in Fig. 3.23 the condition is not affected by the statements in the statement sequence of the WHILE statement so the program will never come out of the WHILE loop. When this problem arises the program is said to have gone into a non-terminating loop. There are other reasons why a program may go into a non-terminating loop, so it is advisable to check that the condition governing a WHILE loop becomes false at some stage and therefore that the loop terminates.

```
X := 0 ;
Z := 0 ;
WHILE X = 0 DO
        ReadCard(Y) ;
        Z := Z + Y ;
END ; (* WHILE *)
WriteCard(Z,6) ;
```

Fig. 3.23.

3.4   EXAMPLE. Reading a Number in a Specified Base

Let us assume that it is necessary to write statements to read a sequence of characters representing a number followed by further number indicating the base of the first number. The first number of the pair is then to be converted into its equivalent CARDINAL value which by the definition of Modula-2 is a decimal value. The number which indicates the base is always a decimal number in the range 2 to 36. The pair of numbers are separated by a space character. For bases larger than 10, upper case letters denote digits, A denoting 10, B denoting 11 etc.

A solution to this problem is to use ReadString to read the sequence of numeric characters representing the number into an array of characters, and to use ReadCard to read the number indicating the base. Once these have been read the program can calculate the CARDINAL value of the number which the array represents in the specified base.

Let us assume that the maximum CARDINAL value is 65535 ($2^{16}-1$). As binary numbers require the longest sequence of characters to represent a number, an array of 16 characters is sufficient to hold all possible character sequences representing CARDINAL values in any base.

The program module in Fig. 3.24 outlines the code to read the pairs of numbers and perform the conversion.

```
MODULE NumberConversion ;
 FROM InOut IMPORT ReadString, ReadCard ;
 VAR
        CharSeq              : ARRAY [0..15] OF CHAR ;
        Base                 ,
        Result               : CARDINAL ;
BEGIN
 ReadString (CharSeq) ;
 ReadCard (Base) ;
 (*... convert the sequence of characters in CharSeq into
       the equivalent CARDINAL value and store this in Result. ...*) ;
END NumberConversion .
```

Fig. 3.24.

The sub-problem of converting the sequence of characters involves two further sub-problems; converting the characters in the array denoting digits to their appropriate CARDINAL equivalent and of amalgamating the values for each digit into the required result.

Ignoring the problem of converting each character to its numeric equivalent, the value of the resulting number for a sequence of 4 characters can be calculated by the formula

$$((CharSeq[1] * Base + CharSeq[2]) * Base + CharSeq[3]) * Base + CharSeq[4]$$

For example, the conversion of the hexadecimal number 1A2B as illustrated in Fig. 3.25 to its decimal equivalent is

$$((1 * 16 + A) * 16 + 2) * 16 + B$$

Base   CharSeq

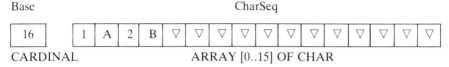

CARDINAL   ARRAY [0..15] OF CHAR

Fig. 3.25.

This can be written as a WHILE loop which maintains the result so far. Each time the loop is executed, the result so far is multiplied by the base and the character's numeric equivalent added, thereby producing the new value for the result so far. This is incorporated in the developing module shown in Fig. 3.26. Note that a CARDINAL variable Count has been introduced to index CharSeq at successive positions in the array.

```
MODULE NumberConversion ;
 VAR
    Base ,
    Count ,
    Units ,
    Result: CARDINAL ;
BEGIN
  ReadString (CharSeq) ;
  ReadCard (Base) ;
  Result := 0 ;
  Count := 0 ;
  WHILE (*... not finished ...*) DO
        (*... convert the character and treat as units digit
            and store in Units ...*) ;
            (* multiply the result-so-far by the number base
               and add the new units digit *)
        Result := Result*Base + Units ;
        INC (Count) ;
  END (*WHILE*) ;
END NumberConversion .
```

Fig. 3.26.

Characters in the array denoting digits of the number must be converted into the appropriate CARDINAL value. This involves a complication for bases larger than base 10 which involve digits denoted by alphabetic characters. Alphabetic characters are not in strict sequence with the numeric characters in ASCII. An IF statement can differentiate between the two cases.

```
IF CharSeq[Count] > '9' THEN
    Units := ORD(CharSeq[Count]) − ORD('A') + 10 ;
ELSE
    Units := ORD(CharSeq[Count]) − ORD('0') ;
END (* IF *)
```

The completed program module in Fig. 3.27 incorporates this character conversion.

It only remains to determine under what circumstances the WHILE statement should terminate. The longest sequence of numeric characters which the program needs to handle is sixteen characters, so if we declare CharSeq to be an array which can hold seventeen characters, there will always be at least one unused element at the end of the array. Remember that when ReadString reads a sequence of characters it also fills unused elements at the end of the array with null characters. By providing an extra component in CharSeq a test can be made to find the end of the sequence of numeric characters by testing for the null character. This provides the terminating condition for the WHILE statement. The completed program module is shown in Fig. 3.27.

```
MODULE NumberConversion ;
 FROM InOut IMPORT ReadString, ReadCard, WriteCard, WriteLn ;
 VAR
    CharSeq              : ARRAY [0..16] OF CHAR ;
    Count,
    Base,
    Units,
    Result               : CARDINAL ;
 BEGIN
  ReadString (CharSeq) ;
    (* CharSeq contains at most 16 numeric characters terminated by
       a null character *)
  ReadCard (Base) ;
    (* initialise the variables used in the loop *)
  Result := 0 ;
  Count := 0 ;
  WHILE CharSeq[Count] <> CHR(0) DO
                    (* convert the character and treat as units digit *)
       IF CharSeq[Count] > '9' THEN
                    Units := ORD(CharSeq[Count]) – ORD('A') + 10 ;
       ELSE
                    Units := ORD(CharSeq[Count]) – ORD('0') ;
       END (* IF *) ;
                    (* multiply the result-so-far by the number base
                       and add the new units digit *)
       Result := Result*Base + Units ;
                    (* move to the next character position *)
       INC (Count) ;
  END (* WHILE *) ;
  WriteCard (Result,10) ;
  WriteLn ;
 END NumberConversion .
```

Fig. 3.27.

Notice that the condition of the WHILE loop is affected by the incrementing of Count inside the statement sequence of the WHILE loop, and the necessity for CharSeq to hold a null character so that the loop will terminate. If the number completely filled the array then the computer would try to test for a null character over the end of the array and this would give an error. Note that ReadString will not guarantee that this is the case. In addition, note that there is no check that only characters in the ranges 0 to 9 and A to Z are in the array.

See technical exercises 7 and 8 for hints on essential improvements to this program module.

3.5 SUMMARY

In this chapter several ideas and constructs have been introduced. These are summarised as

1 Modules have to declare program objects. Two kinds of declarations have been discussed. These are variable declarations and constant declarations.

2 Variable declarations associate an identifier with a memory location which can hold a value of a particular type. Different values can be stored in the variable.

3 Constant declarations introduce an identifier and associate the name with a particular value.

4 Both variable and constant identifiers are associated with a particular type. In the case of variable identifiers the type has to be stated in the variable declaration and only values of that type can then be stored in the variable. In the case of constant declarations the type of the constant is implicit because its type is the same as the type of the value which is associated with the identifier in the declaration.

5 The types of variables and constants determine operations which can be performed involving the constant or variable. The types introduced are CARDINAL (which allows CARDINAL arithmetic), CHAR, and arrays of these types. The type INTEGER has been discussed briefly. A special type ARRAY [0..N] OF CHAR known as a string is slightly more flexible than other forms of character arrays.

6 In situations where values need to be converted from one type to a corresponding value of another type, special type conversion function procedures are provided, for example ORD and CHR.

7 Two important control structures are the conditional statement and repetitive statement.

8 Conditional statements allow certain actions to be performed only if a particular condition is true. The IF statement is one such conditional statement.

9 Repetitive statements allow a sequence of actions to be performed repeatedly. The WHILE statement is one such repetitive statement.

TECHNICAL EXERCISES

Assuming the declarations

CONST	Max	= 300 ;
	Message1	= 'Press any key to continue' ;
	Yes	= 'Y' ;
VAR	X,Y	: CARDINAL ;
	CH	: CHAR ;
	String	: ARRAY [0..49] OF CHAR ;
	ShortString	: ARRAY [0..9] OF CHAR ;
	NotAString	: ARRAY [1..50] OF CHAR ;

State which of the following assignment statements are illegal and why.

1 a CH := Yes   b CH := 'A'
   c Yes := 'Y'   d Yes := CH
   e CH := Max   f Yes := Max
   g String := Message1   h String := Max
   j String := 'A'   k String := Yes
   l Message1 := Hello   m ShortString := Yes
   n ShortString := 'Hello'   p ShortString := Message1
   q X := 10   r Y := Max
   s Max := 10   t String := ShortString
   u ShortString := String   v NotAString := Message1
   w NotAString := String

2 a X := X + 1   b X := 2−3
   c X := Y*5 + 2   d X := (Y * 5) + 2
   e X := (Max * 2) + 3   f X := Max * (2 + 3)
   g X := Max (*2 + 3)   h X := Max + Yes
   j X := (3*2) DIV 4   k X := (24 DIV 3) * (3+2)

3 a CH := String[1]   b CH := String[Max-280]
   c CH := String[Max]   d CH := ShortString[10]
   e CH := NotAString[0]   f X := Yes
   g X := CHR(Yes)   h X := ORD(Yes)
   j X := ORD(String[4])   k CH := CHR(71)
   l CH := CAPS(Yes)

4 Assume that X and Y are CARDINAL variables with initial values of 8 and 54
   respectively. State the values of each variable after each of the statements
   in the following statement sequence.

       INC (X) ;
       INC (X) ;
       INC (Y) ;

```
INC (Y,5) ;
INC (X,10) ;
INC (X,Y) ;
INC (Y,X) ;
DEC (X) ;
DEC (X) ;
DEC (X,23) ;
DEC (Y,X) ;
```

5 Describe the contents of ShortString after each of the following assignment statements.

  a ShortString := 'Hello'

  b ShortString := Message1

  c ShortString := ' '

6 During execution of the following statement sequence describe the contents of the array NumSequence at each of the points indicated by a letter on the right hand side, assuming that initially it holds the values depicted by

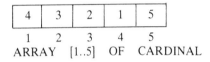

NumSequence

4	3	2	1	5
1	2	3	4	5

ARRAY   [1..5]   OF   CARDINAL

(Assume that j and k are CARDINAL variables, and note that the effects of the statements are cumulative)

```
NumSequence[5] := 0 ;                                              (* a. *)
NumSequence[3] := 4 ;                                              (* b. *)
NumSequence[2] := NumSequence[3] ;                                (* c. *)
NumSequence[1] := NumSequence[4] ;                                (* d. *)
NumSequence[4] := NumSequence[3] + NumSequence[2] ;               (* e. *)
NumSequence[3] := NumSequence[2] +NumSequence[1] ;                (* f. *)
j := 1 ;
WHILE j <> 5 DO
        INC (NumSequence[j],NumSequence[j+1]) ;
        INC (j) ;
END (* WHILE *) ;                                                  (* g. *)
k := 0 ;
j := 1 ;
WHILE j <= 5 DO
        INC (k,NumSequence[j]) ;
        INC (j) ;
END (* WHILE *) ;
NumSequence[1] := k ;                                              (* h. *)
IF NumSequence[1] > 50 THEN
        DEC (NumSequence[1],50) ;
```

```
END (* IF *) ;                                          (* j. *)
j := 1 ;
WHILE j <= 5 DO
        INC (NumSequence[j],k) ;
        INC (j) ;
END (* WHILE *) ;                                       (* k. *)
IF NumSequence[1] > 50 THEN
        DEC (NumSequence[1],50) ;
ELSE
        INC (NumSequence[1],50) ;
END (* IF *) ;                                          (* l. *)
```

7 a State what the following program fragment does.

```
ReadCard (GrossPay) ;
IF GrossPay > 2000 THEN
        Tax    := (GrossPay − 2000) * 3 DIV 10 ;
        NetPay := GrossPay − Tax ;
        WriteCard (NetPay,8) ;
        WriteCard (Tax,8) ;
ELSE
        WriteString ('      No Tax Payable.') ;
END (* IF *) ;
WriteLn ;
```

b Write the rest of the code necessary to make this program fragment into a compilable module, and make any modifications which would make it easier to understand and modify.

c Include statements in the module to request input from the user and inform the user of the meaning of any results where appropriate.

8 In the following program fragment, assuming that Number is a CARDINAL variable, what messages would you output to the user to let him know what he should do and what the program does?

```
ReadCard (Number) ;
Count := 0 ;
Total := 0 ;
WHILE Count <> Number DO
        INC (Count) ;
        INC (Total,Count) ;
END (* WHILE *) ;
WriteCard (Total,6) ;
```

9 The following program fragment is supposed to calculate the sum of all whole numbers between two positive whole numbers inclusive.

```
ReadCard (LowerNumber) ;
ReadCard (HigherNumber) ;
WHILE LowerNumber <> HigherNumber+1 DO
     INC (Total,LowerNumber) ;
     HigherNumber := HigherNumber + 1
END (* WHILE *) ;
WriteCard (Total,6) ;
```

State what is wrong with this program fragment and how you would correct it.

PROGRAMMING EXERCISES

1 Write a program module to read in a CARDINAL value and to print out the next higher odd number.

2 Write a program module to read in two CARDINAL values and then write out the smaller followed by the larger on separate lines.

3 **a** Write a program module to read in 10 CARDINAL values and then write them out in the opposite order to which they were read in.

b Write a further program module to read a list of CARDINAL values. Write them out in reverse order, using the value 0 to indicate the end of the list. The number 0 is not to be included in the list.

4 Write a program module to read in a sequence of characters terminated by the character * (up to a maximum of twenty characters) and write out the sequence with all alphabetic characters capitalised. The * is not to be included in the character sequence and an error should be reported if * is not read in the first 20 characters.

5 Write a program module to read up to twenty characters terminated by the character * , add the ordinal values of the characters together and write out the sequence of characters and the ordinal total. It should be obvious throughout to anyone using the program what to do and what the information on the screen means.

6 Write a program module to read in a list of CARDINAL values representing credits and debits to and from a bank account. The information is input as

     236 C
     34 D

for credits and debits respectively. Decide how the list will be terminated. Write out the information in two columns with totals and a balance such as

	CREDIT	DEBIT		
	340	23		
	49	94		
	211	145		
	34	67		
		50		
Total	634	379	Balance	255

Note that there is a problem if the total debits is greater than the total credits as the balance will be negative and therefore cannot be held in a CARDINAL variable. One solution is to maintain separate totals for credits and debits and test for the total debits being greater than the total credits before working out the balance. (Alternatively the balance could be held in a variable of type INTEGER which allows negative values.)

7 Write a program module which uses an array of 10 components, each component representing the number of Too-Aludoms which a retail outlet currently holds in stock.

Initialise the array to some sensible values.

Allow the user to enter a value for each outlet indicating the number of Too-Aludoms sold at an outlet in the past week. As each value is entered perform the following checks and, where appropriate, the associated actions.

a If the number is greater than a reorder level of 20, inform the user that the outlet should be supplied with more,

b If the number sold is greater than the number indicated in stock, inform the user that the there has been an error,

c If the number left in stock is 0, inform the user that the outlet is out of stock.

At the end of collecting data allow the user to see the resulting stock levels of all outlets if he wishes.

8 Write a program module to read a sequence of characters terminated by the character * and for each letter of the alphabet count how many times it occurs in the sequence. Write out the totals in a suitable format, for example

A	3	B	4	C	5	D	12
E	34	F	7	G	8	H	45

etc.

ANSWERS TO TECHNICAL EXERCISES

1 **a** legal
   b legal
   c and **d** illegal as Yes is a constant and so cannot have values assigned to it

e illegal as CH is a CHAR variable and Max is a CARDINAL constant

f illegal as Yes is a constant (also Yes and Max are different types so it would not be legal even if Yes was a variable)

g legal

h illegal as String is an array of characters and Max is a CARDINAL constant so they are different types

j and **k** legal

l illegal as Message1 is a constant and cannot have values assigned to it, (also the identifier Hello has not been declared)

m and **n** legal

p illegal as ShortString does not have enough components in the array to hold the constant Message1

q and **r** legal

s illegal as Max is a constant and so cannot have values assigned to it

t legal

u legal if String only has 10 or fewer characters before the first null character in the string, otherwise an error will be generated when the program is executed

v and **w** illegal as NotAString does not have a lower bound of 0 and therefore is not a **string** so string constants cannot be assigned directly to it, nor can other arrays of characters which are not identical in type to it

2 **a**
> legal (equivalent to INC (X))

b illegal as the result of the expression is not a CARDINAL value but is a negative number

c, d, e, and **f** are all legal

g illegal as Max (∗2+3) is not a well-formed expression
> Max ∗ (2+3) would be legal

h illegal as Yes is not a CARDINAL value and so cannot be part of an expression producing a CARDINAL result in this way

j illegal as the operators DIV and MOD must be followed by a space

k legal

3 **a** and **b** are both legal

c, d and **e** are all illegal as in each case the index of the array lies outside the range for the array

f illegal as Yes is a CHAR constant and X a CARDINAL variable so their types are different

g illegal as CHR does not take a character as a parameter but a CARDINAL value

h legal and X will be assigned the character code of the character Y

j legal

k legal

l legal

4

	X	Y
initially	8	54
INC (X) ;	9	54
INC (X) ;	10	54
INC (Y) ;	10	55
INC (Y,5) ;	10	60
INC (X,10) ;	20	60
INC (X,Y) ;	80	60
INC (Y,X) ;	80	140
DEC (X) ;	79	140
DEC (X) ;	78	140
DEC (X,23) ;	55	140
DEC (Y,X) ;	55	85

5 a ShortString := 'Hello'

H	e	l	l	o	▽	▽	▽	▽	▽

b ShortString := Message1 is an error as ShortString cannot hold all the characters in Message1

c ShortString := ' '

▽	▽	▽	▽	▽	▽	▽	▽	▽	▽

6

Element Number	1	2	3	4	5
Initially	4	3	2	1	5
a.	4	3	2	1	0
b.	4	3	4	1	0
c.	4	4	4	1	0
d.	1	4	4	1	0
e.	1	4	4	8	0
f.	1	4	5	8	0
g.	5	9	13	8	0
h.	35	9	13	8	0
j.	35	9	13	8	0
k.	70	44	48	43	35
l.	20	44	48	43	35

```
7    MODULE TaxCalculation ;
     FROM InOut IMPORT ReadCard, WriteCard, WriteString, WriteLn ;
     CONST
         TaxThreshold = 2000 ;
     VAR
         GrossPay,
         NetPay,
         Tax                 : CARDINAL ;
     BEGIN
      WriteLn ;
      WriteString ('Type your Salary − ') ;
      ReadCard (GrossPay) ;
      IF GrossPay > TaxThreshold THEN
          Tax := (GrossPay − TaxThreshold) * 3 DIV 10 ;
          NetPay := GrossPay − Tax ;
          WriteString ('Net Pay is − ') ;
          WriteCard (NetPay,8) ;
          WriteLn ;
          WriteString ('Tax to pay is −') ;
          WriteCard (Tax,8) ;
          WriteLn
      ELSE
          WriteString ('     No Tax Payable.') ;
      END (* IF *) ;
      WriteLn ;
     END TaxCalculation .

8    WriteLn ;
     WriteString ('This program will calculate the Summation of ') ;
     WriteString ('all numbers from 1 to the number.') ;
     WriteLn ;
     WriteString ('Type the number − ') ;

     ReadCard (Number) ;
     Count := 0 ;
     Total := 0 ;
     WHILE Count <> Number DO
         INC (Count) ;
         INC (Total,Count) ;
     END (* WHILE *) ;

     WriteLn ;
     WriteString ('Total of all the whole numbers from 1 to ') ;
     WriteCard (Number,3) ;
     WriteString (' is ') ;
     WriteCard (Total,6) ;
```

9 Inside the WHILE loop HigherNumber is incremented so no progress is made towards the terminating condition and therefore the loop will not terminate. In fact the program will terminate with an execution error when

HigherNumber or, more likely, Total becomes too large a value to be represented as a CARDINAL. There are two possible solutions. Either HigherNumber should be decremented and Total should be incremented by the current value of HigherNumber each time round the loop, or LowerNumber should be incremented_. The following code fragment illustrates the latter solution.

```
ReadCard (LowerNumber) ;
ReadCard (HigherNumber) ;
WHILE LowerNumber <> HigherNumber+1 DO
      INC (Total,LowerNumber) ;
      LowerNumber := LowerNumber + 1
END (* WHILE *) ;
WriteCard (Total,6) ;
```

In addition, messages should be written to the screen requesting input and stating the meaning of the output.

Chapter 4

Procedures and Definition Modules

A program to solve a real-world problem can result in thousands of lines of program code. When programs are this size, they must be constructed in such a way that they can be understood at different levels of detail. Often it will be sufficient to have a general understanding of some parts of the code whilst detailed attention is being given to other parts of the program. Modula-2 provides several ways to present a program so that it is understandable at different levels of detail. These enable a programmer to look at programs written some time ago and quickly understand how the program works at a general level. As it is rarely the case that a program can be written during one session of programming, they are also of assistance during the development of a program.

We have already considered the use of comments and variable names in Chapter 2. This chapter concentrates on how the programmer can declare procedures and how these can be used to organise a program so that it is comprehensible. In addition, definition modules are introduced as a source of information about procedures available in other modules.

4.1 PROCEDURES

Chapter 2 considered the development of a program to calculate the area of a rectangle. In Fig. 2.1 a first attempt at developing the solution to the problem using comments to indicate the organisation of the solution was shown, and is reproduced here as. Fig 4.1. In Chapter 2 each sub-problem was considered separately until the program was completed. In this chapter each of the sub-problems is considered as a separate procedure, and working on each sub-problem then involves completing each procedure.

```
MODULE SmallExample ;
BEGIN
        (*... read the values for length and width ...*)
        (*... calculate the area from length and width ...*)
        (*... print the area ...*)
END SmallExample .
```

Fig. 4.1.

Procedures are a way of grouping together and naming a collection of statements in such a way that they are distinct and separate from other groups of statements. It is useful to consider each of the sub-problems as a separate procedure thereby keeping the groups of statements for sub-problems separate from each other. This is done in a procedure declaration.

Each of the comments of Fig. 4.1 can be treated as a specification of what the procedure for that sub-problem achieves. The choice of appropriate names for procedures greatly increases the readability of a program. Figure 4.2 incorporates this extension to the developing program.

```
MODULE SmallExample ;
   VAR                           (*module variable declarations*)
         Length,
         Width,
         Area        : CARDINAL ;


                                  (*procedure declarations*)
   PROCEDURE ReadLengthAndWidth ;
         (*... read the values for length and width ...*)
   END ReadLengthAndWidth ;

   PROCEDURE CalculateArea ;
         (*... calculate the area from length and width ...*)
   END CalculateArea ;

   PROCEDURE WriteArea ;
         (*... print the area ...*)
   END WriteArea ;

   BEGIN                         (* Module Body *)
   ReadLengthAndWidth ;
   CalculateArea ;
   WriteArea
   END SmallExample .
```

Fig. 4.2.

The procedures have no statements in them so the program does not do anything, but notice that the module body has three statements in it. These are **procedure calls** similar to the statements for calling ReadCard and WriteCard. The three procedure calls in the module body are instructions to execute the statements in ReadLengthAndWidth, CalculateArea and WriteArea in this order.

It is now possible to work on each of the procedures individually. When CalculateArea is called the variables Length and Width hold the values for the length and width of the rectangle, so these values must be given to the procedure. The procedure needs to return the result of the calculation to the rest of the program in the variable Area. This is achieved by passing Length, Width and Area as parameters to CalculateArea. In order to do this, the declaration of the procedure has to specify the number and types of parameters it requires. The declaration of CalculateArea is modified to

```
PROCEDURE CalculateArea (VAR LenTimesWid : CARDINAL ;
                              Len,Wid : CARDINAL) ;
BEGIN
  LenTimesWid := Len * Wid
END CalculateArea ;
```

This states that the procedure should be given values for the length and width of the rectangle. These values are multiplied together and the result is given back to the rest of the program. The procedure should be called by the statement

```
CalculateArea (Area,Length,Width) ;
```

which states that Length and Width supply the appropriate values to the procedure and that Area will hold the result calculated by the procedure. The way in which information is given to a procedure and how it gives information back are considered in greater detail later in this chapter. For the present it is sufficient to note that the programmer has to be concerned with this aspect when developing the program, as it is rarely the case that a procedure is totally independent of the rest of the program.

At this point attention can be given to either of the other procedures. ReadLengthAndWidth has to read values for the length and width of the rectangle from the keyboard and put these in the variables Length and Width. WriteArea has to write out the value held in the variable Area. These are included in the completed program in Fig. 4.3.

When this program is run it will behave in exactly the same way as the program in Fig. 2.4.

SmallExample is a trivial program, but its basic structure is typical of many data processing problems where some information is read into the computer's memory, some calculations are performed, and some new information is written out. The use of procedures in SmallExample emphasises its similarity to other problems and contributes to the ease with which the program can be understood. In more complex problems each of the sub-problems will involve a substantial amount of program code. Separating these programs into a number of procedures aids in the development of the program and subsequently to understanding it when alterations may be required.

SmallExample illustrates the major benefits of procedures which are
1.   to organise a program so that it is more readable and therefore can be understood more readily.

```
MODULE SmallExample ;
 FROM InOut IMPORT ReadCard,WriteCard,WriteLn,WriteString ;
 VAR                          (*module variable declarations*)
         Length,
         Width,
         Area      : CARDINAL ;

                         (*procedure declarations*)
 PROCEDURE ReadLengthAndWidth (VAR Len,Wid: CARDINAL) ;
 BEGIN
  WriteString ('Type the length of the rectangle – ') ;
  ReadCard (Len) ;
  WriteLn ;
  WriteString ('Type the width of the rectangle – ') ;
  ReadCard (Wid) ;
  WriteLn
 END ReadLengthAndWidth ;

 PROCEDURE CalculateArea (VAR LenTimesWid: CARDINAL ;
                               Len,Wid: CARDINAL) ;
 BEGIN
  LenTimesWid    := Len * Wid
 END CalculateArea ;

 PROCEDURE WriteArea (A : CARDINAL) ;
 BEGIN
  WriteString ('The area of the rectangle is – ') ;
  WriteCard (A,5) ;
  WriteLn
 END WriteArea ;

 BEGIN                        (* Module Body *)
  ReadLengthAndWidth (Length,Width) ;
  CalculateArea (Area,Length,Width) ;
  WriteArea (Area)
 END SmallExample .
```

Fig. 4.3.

2. to reduce the length of a program because a procedure can be called in more than one statement in the program. This is illustrated by the calls of the procedures in InOut. Each of these procedures is declared only once but is called several times. A procedure can be called as many times as is needed once it has been declared.

3. to increase the reusability of parts of a program. Procedures which have been written for one program may be useful in other programs and therefore intelligent use of procedures can reduce the time and effort in the development of programs.

Modula-2 is an excellent language in these respects and we encourage you to try to think of problems in terms of a collection of relatively independent sub-problems each of which can be treated as a procedure.

4.2 PROCEDURE DECLARATIONS AND PROCEDURE CALLS

This section discusses more formally how to declare and call procedures.

The first point of note is that SmallExample has several distinct sections. One of these is concerned with the procedure declarations of ReadLengthAndWidth, CalculateArea and WriteArea. Another is the module body which calls each of these in turn. Procedure declarations like other declarations precede the module body, and they can occur in any order with other declarations as indicated by the simpified syntax diagram for Block and Declaration in Fig. 4.4.

Each of the procedure declarations looks very similar to a program module. Figure 4.5 shows the general form of a procedure declaration and the corresponding syntax diagrams. The sequence of statements is executed when the procedure is called. These constitute the procedure body and determine what the procedure does.

The order in which procedures are executed is determined by the order in which they are called and is not affected by the order in which procedures are declared. In the above program the declaration of the procedure CalculateArea could have followed the declaration of WriteArea but this would not have affected how the program is executed. In normal circumstances it is preferable to list the procedure declarations in some organised manner.

Block :

Declaration :

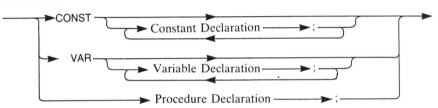

Fig. 4.4.

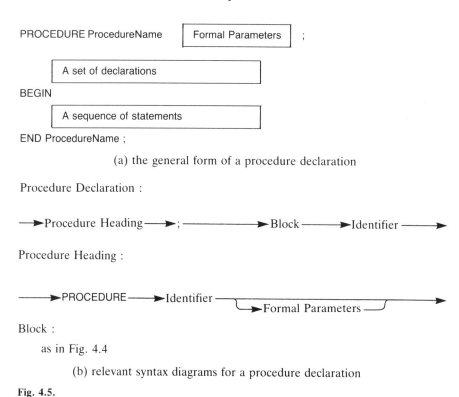

(a) the general form of a procedure declaration

Procedure Declaration :

——►Procedure Heading——►; ————————►Block————►Identifier ————►

Procedure Heading :

————————►PROCEDURE————►Identifier ——————————————————————►
                                      └——►Formal Parameters ——┘

Block :
   as in Fig. 4.4

(b) relevant syntax diagrams for a procedure declaration

Fig. 4.5.

None of the procedures in SmallExample have their own declarations so this section of the procedure is empty. If you follow the possible routes through the syntax diagrams for Block and Procedure Heading you will find that all of the formal parameters, the set of declarations and the sequence of statements are optional. The following, therefore, is a valid procedure

```
PROCEDURE dummy ;
END dummy ;
```

It does not declare anything, nor does it specify any statements to be executed when the procedure is called. However such dummy procedures can be of use to indicate that the procedure has yet to be fully developed as in Fig. 4.2. Comments were used in a similar manner in Chapter 2.

Procedures can consist solely of a statement sequence with no parameters and no declarations of its own. For example a procedure called Introduction could be declared which would simply write on the screen what a program does

```
PROCEDURE Introduction ;
BEGIN
 WriteString ('This program calculates the area of a rectangle.') ;
END Introduction ;
```

This is called by a statement naming the procedure

```
Introduction
```

which causes the message to be printed.

4.3 FORMAL PARAMETERS AND ACTUAL PARAMETERS

It is often necessary for information to be supplied to a procedure, or for it to supply results to the rest of the program. This is achieved by passing values and variables as parameters to the procedure. For example the call of the procedure WriteArea

```
WriteArea (Area)
```

indicates that WriteArea should be executed using information supplied by the variable Area. Similarly the call of ReadLengthAndWidth

```
ReadLengthAndWidth (Length,Width)
```

specifies that the variables Length and Width are to be used when executing ReadLengthAndWidth. The list of parameters in a procedure call are known as the **actual parameters**. These are the values and variables which are actually used when executing the procedure on a particular occasion. The actual parameters are enclosed within brackets and are separated by commas.

The declaration of a procedure determines what information has to be supplied in the list of actual parameters of a corresponding procedure call. This information is known as the procedure's **formal parameters**. The formal parameters constitute a set of restrictions on the actual parameters which appear in the call of the procedure. These restrictions are
1. the number of actual parameters in the call must be the same as the number of formal parameters in the declaration of the procedure,
2. the actual parameters are associated with the formal parameters in order (the first actual parameter with the first formal parameter etc.),
3. if the procedure declaration indicates that a parameter is a variable parameter then the corresponding actual parameter must be a variable of the same type as the formal parameter,
4. if the procedure declaration indicates that a parameter is a value parameter the corresponding actual parameter must be a value which is assignment compatible with the formal parameter.

The restrictions in points 3 and 4 are discussed in the following section. In the case of WriteArea

```
PROCEDURE WriteArea (A: CARDINAL) ;
BEGIN
  WriteString ('The area is ') ;
  WriteCard (A,5) ;
  WriteLn
END WriteArea ;
```

the formal parameter of the procedure declaration states that for WriteArea to be called correctly it must be given one parameter which is a value of type CARDINAL. If these restrictions are not met then an error will be reported stating that the procedure is being called inappropriately.

For example, both of the following calls would be detected as errors

```
WriteArea (Area,6)
```

and

```
WriteArea ('The area is ')
```

The first is wrong because it has been supplied with two actual parameters and the second because the actual parameter is a sequence of characters rather than a CARDINAL value.

The reason that a procedure has to be declared in this way is that the compiler uses the formal parameters of a procedure to check that all actual parameters in the calls of the procedure are consistent with its declaration. The compiler can often be of assistance in detecting errors in our programs thereby protecting us from our own carelessness or foolishness.

Formal Parameters

Information can be passed directly between a procedure and the rest of the program in two ways and this is reflected in two kinds of formal parameters. These are

1.   value parameters. Every time a procedure is called, a variable which can only be used inside the procedure is created for each formal value parameter. The value of the corresponding actual parameter in the procedure call is assigned to this variable. When execution of the procedure is complete these variables are discarded. If the procedure is called again then variables for its formal parameters are recreated and are initialised with the values passed as the actual parameters in this further call.

2.   variable parameters. Instead of creating a new variable the specified variable is passed directly to the procedure.

In the list of formal parameters a variable parameter is indicated by the presence of the word VAR, If a formal parameter is not specified as a variable parameter then it is a value parameter.

Value Parameters

The formal parameter of WriteArea's procedure declaration

```
PROCEDURE WriteArea (A : CARDINAL) ;
```

indicates that its parameter is a value parameter whose type is CARDINAL. If WriteArea is called by a statement

```
WriteArea (34)
```

then the value 34 is passed to the procedure and the new variable A is initialised with the value 34. When WriteArea is called in the statement

```
WriteArea (Area)
```

the **value** inside the variable Area is copied into A as indicated in Fig. 4.6. The formal parameter A is a variable available only within WriteArea. A is initialised with the value of the actual parameter specified within the call. In this case it is initialised with the value held in the variable Area.

Fig. 4.6.

It follows that variables in an actual parameter list whose matching formal parameters are value parameters merely initialise the formal parameters with the values in the variables, but cannot be used for trying to communicate results back to the rest of the module. For example, suppose CalculateArea were to be declared as

```
PROCEDURE CalculateArea (LenTimesWid : CARDINAL ;
                         Len,Wid : CARDINAL) ;
BEGIN
  LenTimesWid       := Len * Wid
END CalculateArea   ;
```

then this procedure would calculate the area and store the value in the formal parameter LenTimesWid, but because this is a value parameter this result is not communicated back to the rest of the module. At the end of the execution of the procedure, the variables for the value parameters are discarded. Therfore, the result of the calculation is thrown away. Procedures can return results through variable parameters.

Variable Parameters

ReadLengthAndWidth, in contrast to WriteArea, has to supply information to the rest of the program. The purpose of the procedure is to use ReadCard to read values for the length and width of the rectangle and to make these values available to the rest of the program. Consequently the formal parameter list of ReadLengthAndWidth specifies that the parameters are variable parameters by preceding them with the word VAR.

    PROCEDURE ReadLengthAndWidth (VAR Len,Wid : CARDINAL) ;

When ReadLengthAndWidth is called, the **variables** specified in the actual parameter list are passed to the procedure rather than the values in the variables. We can think of this as the formal parameter providing a direct reference back to the actual parameter as in Fig. 4.7.

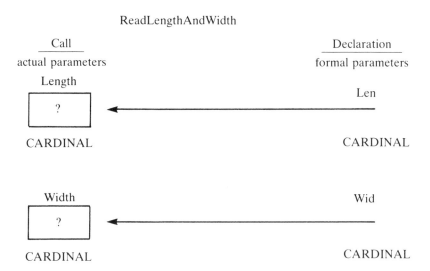

Fig. 4.7.

The consequence of this is that within ReadLengthAndWidth the formal parameter Len is essentially a pseudonym (or an alias) for the variable passed as the actual parameter. Whenever a value is assigned to Len this results in the actual parameter Length acquiring this value. If we accept for the present that ReadCard's parameter is also a variable parameter then when ReadCard is called by the statement

```
ReadCard (Len)
```

this results in the value being read into the module's variable Length.

Note that it is not permitted to pass constants to ReadLengthAndWidth. A call

```
ReadLengthAndWidth (10,6)
```

is an error because the procedure is expecting two variables to be supplied to it. 10 and 6 are not variables. An actual parameter whose corresponding formal parameter is a variable parameter must be a variable.

More about Formal Parameters

The relevant syntax diagrams for the formal parameters of a procedure are shown in Fig. 4.8.

Formal Parameters :

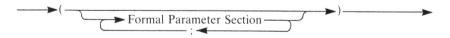

Formal Parameter Section :

Fig. 4.8.

In the declaration of a procedure the list of formal parameters is enclosed within brackets. The list consists of a sequence of Formal Parameter Sections separated by semi-colons in which parameters with the same characteristics are listed. The list can be empty, the earlier declaration of the procedure Introduction could have looked like

```
PROCEDURE Introduction () ;
BEGIN
  WriteString ('This program calculates the area of a rectangle.') ;
END Introduction ;
```

and would be called by a statement

    Introduction () ;

The brackets seem unnecessary, but they are useful as they indicate at a
glance that this is a procedure call.

Each Formal Parameter Section can introduce a sequence of variable
parameters of the same type, or a sequence of value parameters of the same
type. (An identifier list is a sequence of identifiers separated by commas.) For
example a formal parameter list

            (Fred,Joe,June,Harry : CARDINAL ;
                     William : INTEGER ;
            VAR Georgina,Charles : INTEGER)

specifies that the procedure has, in order, four value parameters of type
CARDINAL, one value parameter of type INTEGER, and two variable parameters
of type INTEGER. Notice that though William is specified as being of type
INTEGER it differs from Georgina and Charles in that they are variable parameters
and so must be listed in a separate section.

Both kinds of formal parameter are illustrated in the declaration of
CalculateArea

    PROCEDURE CalculateArea (VAR LenTimesWid : CARDINAL ;
                                    Len,Wid : CARDINAL) ;
    BEGIN
     LenTimesWid := Len * Wid
    END CalculateArea;

CalculateArea's formal parameters state that the procedure takes three parameters. The first parameter is a variable parameter whose type is CARDINAL,
the second and third parameters are value parameters which hold CARDINAL
values. Throughout the rest of the procedure declaration the parameters are
called LenTimesWid, Len and Wid respectively.

Whenever CalculateArea is called it must be supplied with three actual
parameters, the first must be a variable which can hold a CARDINAL value, the
second and third must be CARDINAL values. In SmallExample the call of CalculateArea in the module body is

    CalculateArea (Area,Length,Width)

CalculateArea's second and third formal parameters are value parameters, so
the values of Length and Width are assigned to the variables created for Len and
Wid respectively. Len and Wid are then new variables which can only be used
inside CalculateArea. The formal parameter list indicates that the first parameter is a variable parameter. This means that the variable Area is passed

directly to the procedure. Thus when CalculateArea assigns the result of the calculation to its formal parameter LenTimesWid this has the effect of assigning the result to the module variable Area (see Fig. 4.9).

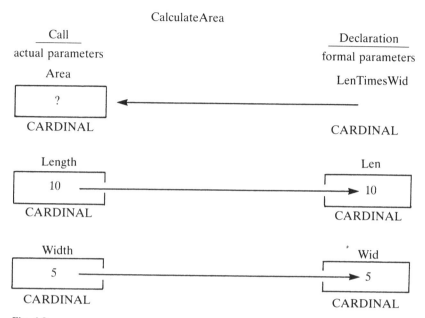

Fig. 4.9.

It is possible for the name of an actual parameter in a procedure call to be the same as the name of the corresponding formal parameter in the procedure declaration. Figure 4.10 shows a module for calculating the squares of numbers. The names of the two variables declared at the top of the module are used again as the names of formal parameters in the declarations of GetNum, Square and WriteSquare. Figure 4.11 illustrates how the parameters are passed to Square to emphasise that the association between an actual parameter and a formal parameter is established by the order of identifiers in the parameter lists and not by coincidental names. Technically there is nothing wrong with this way of naming variables and parameters. However, it can lead to confusion and, in larger modules, uncertainty about where the declaration of an identifier is to be found. Until you feel confident coding in Modula-2, we recommend that you avoid using the same identifiers in different parts of a module.

```
MODULE SquaresOfNumbers ;
 FROM InOut IMPORT ReadCard, WriteCard, WriteString, WriteLn ;
 VAR
      SquareNum          ,
      Num                : CARDINAL ;

      (* this procedure is discussed in the following section *)
 PROCEDURE WriteLnString (Message: ARRAY OF CHAR) ;
 BEGIN
  WriteLn ;
  WriteString (Message) ;
 END WriteLnString ;

 PROCEDURE Introduction () ;
 BEGIN
  WriteLnString ('Squares of Numbers') ;
  WriteLnString ('==================') ;
  WriteLnString ('Type 0 for the number to end the program.') ;
  WriteLn
 END Introduction ;

 PROCEDURE GetNum (VAR Num: CARDINAL) ;
 BEGIN
  WriteLnString ('Type the number – ') ;
  ReadCard (Num) ;
 END GetNum ;

 PROCEDURE Square (Num : CARDINAL;
            VAR SquareNum : CARDINAL) ;
 BEGIN
  SquareNum := Num * Num
 END Square ;

 PROCEDURE WriteSquare (SquareNum : CARDINAL) ;
 BEGIN
  WriteString (' its square is – ') ;
  WriteCard (SquareNum,10)
 END WriteSquare ;

 BEGIN
  Introduction () ;
  GetNum (Num) ;
  WHILE Num <> 0 DO
       Square (Num,SquareNum) ;
       WriteSquare (SquareNum) ;
       GetNum (Num) ;
  END (* WHILE *) ;
  WriteLn ;
 END SquaresOfNumbers .
```

Fig. 4.10.

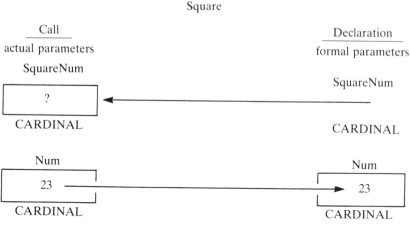

Fig. 4.11.

Notice that it is not possible to tell which parameters are value parameters and which are variable parameters simply by looking at the procedure call. This can only be determined by looking at the procedure declaration and its formal parameters.

A common programming error is to intend that a procedure return some information through a variable parameter but to omit the word VAR in the formal parameter list thereby specifying that the parameter is a value parameter. The procedure may perform the correct calculations but will then fail to communicate the result to the rest of the program. Subsequent calculations will use whatever value the actual parameter held prior to the call of the procedure, resulting in erroneous calculations.

4.4 EXAMPLE. OCTAL ARITHMETIC

Suppose an educational establishment which teaches computing wishes students to understand the principles of octal representation of numbers and requires a small program to test their understanding. This program is required to

a. perform octal addition and multiplication,

b. accept a sequence of octal numbers, each number terminated by a space character and separated from other octal numbers by a character indicating an operator, either +, * or =,

c. accept a student's answer in octal,

d. check an answer and indicate whether or not it is correct,

e. if an answer is incorrect inform the student of the correct answer.

The program can convert the octal numbers typed at the keyboard to CARDIN-
AL values, use the normal processes of addition and multiplication of CARDIN-
AL values within the program, and write out the answer as an octal number.

A first formulation of a solution to this problem is given in Fig. 4.12.

```
MODULE OctalAdditionAndMultiplication ;
  (*... IMPORT lists and declarations ...*)
BEGIN
  (*... read an octal number typed by the user ...*) ;
  (*... read an arithmetic operator typed by the user ...*) ;
  (*... while the operator is not an = sign
    (*... read an octal number typed by the user ...*) ;
    (*... if the operator is + perform addition
      if it is * perform multiplication ...*) ;
    (*... read an arithmetic operator typed by the user ...*) ;
  ...*) ;

  (*... read an octal number typed by the user for the answer ...*) ;
  (*... if the user's answer is correct tell him so
    if it is not correct then tell him the correct answer ...*) ;
END OctalAdditionAndMultiplication .
```

Fig. 4.12.

Certain parts of this problem are reasonably straightforward.
1. Variables are required to hold
    a. the CARDINAL equivalent of the octal number which has been read
    (NewNumber),
    b. to hold the operator typed on the keyboard (Operator),
    c. to keep a total of the correct answer to date (CurrentAnswer),
    d. to accept the answer the user thinks is correct (UserAnswer).
2. The user inputs octal numbers and operators until the operator is an =
sign so we can code the repetition of these operations inside a WHILE statement.
3. Reading an arithmetic operator can be achieved by reading a character by
a call of Read.
4. As an octal number is accepted it can be converted to a CARDINAL value.
The accumulative answer can be updated using INC or CARDINAL multiplication
depending upon the operator.
5. Once the number for the answer has been accepted and converted to a
CARDINAL value it can be compared with CurrentAnswer. If the user's answer is
correct he can be informed that this is the case, otherwise the program can
inform him of the correct answer using another procedure available in InOut
called WriteOct which writes out a CARDINAL value as an octal number.

Figure 4.13 shows these extensions to the module.

```
MODULE OctalAdditionAndMultiplication ;
(*... IMPORT lists ...*)
VAR
        NewNumber                       ,
        CurrentAnswer                   ,
        UserAnswer                      : CARDINAL ;
        Operator                        : CHAR ;
BEGIN
(*... read an octal number typed by the user ...*) ;
(*... read an arithmetic operator typed by the user ...*) ;
WHILE Operator <> '=' DO
        (*... read an octal number typed by the user ...*) ;
        IF Operator = '+' THEN
            INC (CurrentAnswer,NewNumber) ;
        END (* IF *) ;
        IF Operator = '*' THEN
            CurrentAnswer := CurrentAnswer * NewNumber
        END (* IF *) ;
        (*... read an arithmetic operator typed by the user ...*) ;
END (* WHILE *) ;

(*... read an octal number typed by the user for the answer ...*) ;
IF UserAnswer <> CurrentAnswer THEN
    WriteLn ;
    WriteString ('The correct answer is ') ;
    WriteOct (CurrentAnswer,8) ;
ELSE
    WriteLn ;
    WriteString ('Your answer is correct.') ;
END (* IF *) ;
END OctalAdditionAndMultiplication .
```

Fig. 4.13.

Let us assume that a procedure ReadOct is available with a formal CARDINAL variable parameter. ReadOct reads a sequence of numeric characters in the range 0 to 7 and converts these to the equivalent CARDINAL value which is returned to the rest of the program in the variable parameter. Its heading is

```
PROCEDURE ReadOct (VAR OctalNum : CARDINAL) ;
```

Additionally, we can assume that a procedure ReadOperator is available whose procedure heading is

```
PROCEDURE ReadOperator (VAR NewOperator : CHAR) ;
```

and which reads an arithmetic operator.

Calls to these procedures can now be included in the module body where these operations are needed, so the module can be extended to that shown in Fig. 4.14.

```
MODULE OctalAdditionAndMultiplication ;
(*... IMPORT lists ...*)
VAR
      NewNumber                    ,
      CurrentAnswer                ,
      UserAnswer             : CARDINAL ;
      Operator               : CHAR ;

  PROCEDURE ReadOct (VAR OctalNum : CARDINAL) ;
  BEGIN
  END ReadOct ;

  PROCEDURE ReadOperator (VAR NewOperator : CHAR) ;
  BEGIN
  END ReadOperator ;

BEGIN
  ReadOct (CurrentAnswer) ;
  ReadOperator (Operator) ;
  WHILE Operator <> '=' DO
      ReadOct (NewNumber) ;
      IF Operator = '+' THEN
          INC (CurrentAnswer,NewNumber)
      END (* IF *) ;
      IF Operator = '*' THEN
          CurrentAnswer := CurrentAnswer * NewNumber
      END (* IF *) ;
      ReadOperator (Operator) ;
  END (* WHILE *) ;

  ReadOct (UserAnswer) ;
  IF UserAnswer <> CurrentAnswer THEN
      WriteLn ;
      WriteString ('The correct answer is ') ;
      WriteOct (CurrentAnswer,8) ;
  ELSE
      WriteLn ;
      WriteString ('Your answer is correct.') ;
  END (* IF *) ;
END OctalAdditionAndMultiplication .
```

Fig. 4.14.

This module illustrates the major advantage of procedures that they need only be declared once but can be called at different places in a module. In addition, they can be given different actual parameters to operate upon. Thus, in Fig. 4.14, ReadOct is called to pass back a result in NewNumber and UserAnswer on different occasions.

The procedures ReadOct and ReadOperator can now be developed. ReadOct reads a sequence of characters in the range '0' to '7' inclusive

1. ignoring leading space characters
2. using the space character to indicate the end of the sequence
3. ignoring all other characters outside the range.

ReadOperator should check that only characters denoting valid operators are input, however this is omitted for the present. The procedures are shown in the completed module in Fig. 4.15.

```
MODULE OctalAdditionAndMultiplication ;
  FROM InOut IMPORT Read,WriteLn,WriteString,WriteOct ;
  VAR
        NewNumber, CurrentAnswer, UserAnswer       : CARDINAL ;
        Operator                                   : CHAR ;
  CONST
        Space = ' ' ;

  PROCEDURE ReadOct (VAR OctalNum: CARDINAL) ;
  VAR
          Ch            : CHAR ;
  BEGIN
   Read (Ch) ;                        (* read over any leading spaces *)
   WHILE Ch = Space DO
    Read (Ch) ;
   END (* WHILE *) ;

   OctalNum := 0 ;                    (* read the sequence of characters *)
   WHILE (Ch <> Space) DO             (* up to the next space, ignoring *)
     IF (Ch >= '0') THEN              (* characters other than '0' to '7'*)
        IF (Ch <= '7') THEN
             OctalNum := OctalNum * 8 + ORD(Ch) – ORD('0') ;
        END (* IF *)
     END (* IF *) ;
     Read (Ch)
   END (* WHILE *) ;
  END ReadOct ;

  PROCEDURE ReadOperator (VAR NewOperator : CHAR) ;
  (*... This procedure should only allow the characters *, + and =
       as valid operators. For the present no validation is included
       to check that this is so. ...*)
  BEGIN
   Read (NewOperator) ;
   WHILE NewOperator = Space DO
          Read (NewOperator) ;
   END (* WHILE *) ;
  END ReadOperator ;
```

```
BEGIN
  ReadOct (CurrentAnswer) ;
  ReadOperator (Operator) ;
  WHILE Operator <> '=' DO
      ReadOct (NewNumber) ;
      IF Operator = '+' THEN
          INC (CurrentAnswer,NewNumber)
      END (* IF *) ;
      IF Operator = '*' THEN
          CurrentAnswer := CurrentAnswer * NewNumber
      END (* IF *) ;
      ReadOperator (Operator) ;
  END (* WHILE *) ;

  ReadOct (UserAnswer) ;
  IF UserAnswer <> CurrentAnswer THEN
      WriteLn ;
      WriteString ('The correct answer is ') ;
      WriteOct (CurrentAnswer,8) ;
  ELSE
      WriteLn ;
      WriteString ('Your answer is correct.') ;
  END (* IF *) ;
END OctalAdditionAndMultiplication .
```

Fig. 4.15.

4.5   OPEN ARRAY PARAMETERS

The procedure WriteLnString in Fig. 4.10 introduces a further possibility when declaring a procedure and its formal parameters. The syntax diagram for a formal parameter section in Fig. 4.8 indicates that the type of a formal parameter is specified by Formal Type. The syntax diagram for Formal Type is given in Fig. 4.16, and it allows the words ARRAY OF to be optionally placed before the type identifier.

Formal Type :

Fig. 4.16.

In the procedure heading of WriteLnString

```
PROCEDURE WriteLnString (Message : ARRAY OF CHAR) ;
```

the formal parameter Message requires that the actual parameter passed to the procedure is an array of characters. If we assume the following declarations

```
VAR
    Line   : ARRAY [0..80] OF CHAR ;
    Name : ARRAY [0..20] OF CHAR ;
```

then the calls of WriteLnString in the following sequence of statements are all permissible

```
WriteLnString ('A short message.') ;
WriteLnString ('A much longer sequence of characters.') ;
Line := 'This is a line of text to be written out' ;
WriteLnString (Line) ;
Name := 'Fred' ;
WriteLnString (Name) ;
```

WriteLnString accepts arrays with differing numbers of components. The formal parameter of the procedure is said to be an **open array parameter** as the number of components in the array of the actual parameter is left open and does not have to be specified when the procedure is declared. This is not so very new, as you have already seen the procedure heading of WriteString which has such an open array parameter and we have illustrated its use for writing sequences of characters of various lengths on many occasions.

When writing a procedure which uses an open array parameter it is often necessary for the procedure body to know how many components are in the array of the actual parameter. Suppose that while working on a problem, a sub-problem of totalling up the values of the components of an array of CARDINAL values is identified. In addition, suppose that this sub-problem recurs frequently throughout the problem so that it is worthwhile having a procedure which can perform this operation on any array of CARDINAL values. Therefore, a procedure is required which accepts as an actual parameter an array of CARDINAL values, adds up the values in the array and returns the total in a variable parameter. A first attempt at writing such a procedure is shown in Fig. 4.17.

There are problems in writing this procedure which still have to be resolved. The value of the lower bound of the array is needed so that ThisComponent can be initialised to be the first component of the array. Similarly the value of the upper bound of the array is required so that LastComponentPlusOne can be initialised to prevent the WHILE statement trying to access components beyond the end of the array. Both problems centre around the lack of information about the lower and upper bounds of the array passed as

```
PROCEDURE SumComponents (Components : ARRAY OF CARDINAL ;
                                      VAR Total : CARDINAL) ;
    (*... declare ThisComponent and LastComponentPlusOne ...*) ;
BEGIN
  Total := 0 ;
    (*... initialise ThisComponent and LastComponentPlusOne ...*) ;
  WHILE ThisComponent <> LastComponentPlusOne DO
    INC (Total,Components[ThisComponent]) ;
    INC (ThisComponent) ;
  END (* WHILE *) ;
END SumComponents ;
```

Fig. 4.17.

the actual parameter. However this imprecision is necessary as it permits the procedure to be used to process arrays with differing lower and upper bounds. For example, assuming the declarations

```
VAR
    ArrayOne        : ARRAY [10..20] OF CARDINAL ;
    ArrayTwo        : ARRAY [0..100] OF CARDINAL ;
    Total1,Total2   : CARDINAL ;
```

and that the arrays have been suitable initialised, then the following calls of SumComponents are permitted

```
SumComponents (ArrayOne,Total1)
SumComponents (ArrayTwo,Total2)
```

How then can the procedure know the lower and upper bound of the array which has been passed as the actual parameter? The answer is straightforward. The lower bound of an open array parameter is assumed to be 0, regardless of whatever the lower bound of the array of the actual parameter is. A Modula-2 standard function procedure named HIGH can be used to find out the upper bound of the array. When HIGH is passed an array, it returns a CARDINAL value indicating the index of the last component in the array. As an open array parameter has a lower bound of 0 this is equivalent to one less than the number of components in the array of the actual parameter. For example, if SumComponents is called with ArrayOne as the actual parameter then inside the procedure

```
HIGH (Components)
```

evaluates to 10 for the upper bound of the array, and the lower bound is treated as 0.

This information permits SumComponents to be declared fully as in Fig. 4.18 with ThisComponent initialised to 0 and LastComponentPlusOne initialised to one greater than the value returned by HIGH. SumComponents can be used to total the values of any array of CARDINAL values irrespective of the lower and upper bound specified in the declaration of the array.

```
PROCEDURE SumComponents (Components : ARRAY OF CARDINAL :
                                      VAR Total : CARDINAL) ;
VAR
    ThisComponent ,
    LastComponentPlusOne: CARDINAL ;
BEGIN
 Total := 0 ;
 ThisComponent := 0 ;
 LastComponentPlusOne := HIGH (Components) + 1 ;
 WHILE ThisComponent <> LastComponentPlusOne DO
    INC (Total,Components[ThisComponent]) ;
    INC (ThisComponent) ;
 END (* WHILE *) ;
END SumComponents ;
```

Fig. 4.18.

A procedure which has a formal open array parameter can only process the array component by component. Within such a procedure the array cannot be treated as though it is string even though it has a lower bound of 0. This prevents assignment of a string constant or a string variable to an open array parameter. Figure 4.19 shows a procedure which tries to use an open array parameter illegally. However, open array parameters can be passed as parameters to other procedures, which permits a general procedure to be written for copying the contents of an array into another array. This can be used with open array parameters (see technical exercise 7).

```
PROCEDURE NotPermitted (VAR CharArray : ARRAY OF CHAR) ;
 CONST
    StringConstant = 'A literal String' ;
 VAR
    StringVariable : ARRAY [0..79] OF CHAR ;
 BEGIN
 CharArray := StringConstant ;                      (* invalid *)
 CharArray := 'A literal string' ;                  (* invalid *)
 StringVariable := StringConstant ;
 CharArray := StringVariable ;                      (* invalid *)
 END NotPermitted ;
```

Fig. 4.19. Illegal use on an open array parameter.

4.6   FUNCTION PROCEDURES

The previous sections demonstrate how a procedure can communicate the results of its actions to the rest of the program through variable parameters. There is a further way in which a procedure can give a result back to the rest of the program. This is through a **function procedure**.

Function procedures differ from normal procedures in the way that they give a result back to the rest of the program. This affects the form of the declaration and the way in which the function procedure can be called. As an example, consider a function procedure for calculating the volume of a cuboid when it is given the cuboid's length, width and height as parameters

```
PROCEDURE CuboidVolume (Len,Wid,Hgt : CARDINAL) : CARDINAL ;
BEGIN
  RETURN Len * Wid * Hgt ;
END CuboidVolume ;
```

This differs from a declaration of a normal procedure in two ways.

1.   Following the closing bracket, which terminates the list of formal parameter sections, it is necessary to specify the type of the result that the function procedure gives back.

2.   One or more of the statements of the statement sequence of the procedure body is a RETURN statement. This is often the final statement in the sequence and it causes the expression following RETURN to be evaluated and the resulting value to be given back as the result of the function procedure. The RETURN statement also causes execution of the function procedure to terminate so if this is not the last statement in the sequence subsequent statements are not executed.

Function procedures are called in a different way to normal procedures. Remember that a normal procedure call is a statement. The call of a function procedure is not a statement but appears as part of an expression. For example if we wish to call CuboidVolume then this can be done in an expression

```
Volume := CuboidVolume (2,3,4)
```

When this assignment statement is executed it returns the result of 2*3*4 (24) and assigns this value to Volume.

Suppose that the outer dimensions of a hollow cuboid are 10, 11 and 12, and that the walls of the cuboid are 1 unit thick. The dimensions of the hollow inside the cuboid are therefore 8, 9 and 10. From this we can calculate the volume of material in the cuboid as the volume of the outer cuboid minus the volume of the inner cuboid. We can write an assignment statement to calculate this as

```
VolumeOfMaterial := CuboidVolume (10,11,12) − CuboidVolume (8,9,10)
```

In this case the expression is a CARDINAL arithmetic expression which involves two calls of CuboidVolume. When we call a function procedure we can think of it as standing for the result which the function returns. In this case it is a CARDINAL value computed from the values of its parameters.

Results from function procedures can be passed directly to procedures if the corresponding formal parameter is a value parameter. For example, in the statement sequence

```
ReadCard (Length) ;
ReadCard (Width) ;
ReadCard (Height) ;
WriteCard (CuboidVolume(Length,Width,Height),10) ;
```

the result returned by CuboidVolume is passed as an actual parameter to WriteCard.

Figure 4.20a shows a function procedure that asks the user a question and accepts a CARDINAL value as a reply which is returned as the result. Examples of calling this function procedure are

```
Length := NewCardValue ('Type the Length')
```

and

```
Width := NewCardValue ('Type the Width ')
```

```
PROCEDURE NewCardValue (Message : ARRAY OF CHAR) : CARDINAL ;
VAR
    Reply : CARDINAL ;
BEGIN
 WriteLn ;
 WriteString (Message) ;
 ReadCard (Reply) ;
 RETURN Reply
END NewCardValue ;
```

(a) returning a CARDINAL result.

```
PROCEDURE ExtractCharacter (CharSeq : ARRAY OF CHAR ;
                            N : CARDINAL) : CHAR ;
BEGIN
 DEC (N) ;
 IF N <= HIGH (CharSeq) THEN
    RETURN CharSeq[N]
 ELSE
    RETURN CHR (0)
 END (* IF *)
END ExtractCharacter ;
```

(b) returning a CHAR result.

Fig. 4.20.

The type of the result of a function procedure need not always be CARDIN-AL. Figure 4.20b shows a function procedure declaration which either returns the Nth character in an array of characters if N is a valid index of the array, or it returns the null character. For example, a call

```
SecondCharacter := ExtractCharacter ('Any old character array',2)
```

assigns to SecondCharacter the character 'n'.

Note that

1. ExtractCharacter uses the standard function procedure HIGH,

2. function procedures which you declare yourself behave in exactly the same way as standard function procedures, and must appear within expressions.

The inclusion of function procedures requires revision of the syntax diagram of Fig. 4.8 to include the type of the result of a function procedure (see Fig. 4.21).

Formal Parameters :

Fig. 4.21.

The formal parameters part of the declaration is obligatory for a function procedure, so that the type of the result can be specified. If a function procedure does not require any parameters to be declared there must still be an opening and closing bracket. One useful parameterless function procedure is a random number generator. Its declaration could look like

```
PROCEDURE RandomNumber (): CARDINAL ;
VAR
        Rand      : CARDINAL ;
BEGIN
    (* statements to generate random number *)
    RETURN Rand
END RandomNumber ;
```

When RandomNumber is called, an empty list of actual parameters must be specified.

```
NewNumber := RandomNumber()
```

Though this may seem unnecessary there are good reasons for the empty formal and actual parameters lists. For example, it prevents a call of Random-Number as

NewNumber := RandomNumber

which can be confusing as it looks like the assignment of the value in a variable or a constant called RandomNumber to NewNumber. A programmer could waste time looking for the declaration of a variable or constant called Random-Number. The first version is unambiguously a function procedure call.

These function procedures could have been written as normal procedures which return the result through a variable parameter. Why then have function procedures in the language? The answer to this comes down to readability of a program. Remember that it is not possible to tell which parameters are value parameters and which are variable parameters just by looking at a procedure call. If we need to find out how it passes information back to the rest of the program then we might guess from the names of variables but if we want to be certain then we have to look for the declaration of the procedure and look at its formal parameters. If a function procedure is used it is obvious from the call of the function procedure that it returns a result and what is subsequently done with the result.

From a different point of view, it is not unreasonable to ask that if functions are so useful why have the distinction between value and variable parameters. Why not give information needed by a procedure as value parameters and get information back through the result of a function procedure? The answer to this is that function procedures have certain restrictions which are

1.   a function procedure can only return a single value as a result. It is possible to give additional results back in variable parameters, but this is unwise. If a procedure has to give two or more results then it should be written as a normal procedure and all results should be given back through variable parameters.

2.   the result of a function procedure cannot be a structured type. For the present this means that a function procedure cannot return an array as its result. There are other structured types in Modula-2 and these also cannot be returned as the result of a function procedure.

4.7   DEFINITION MODULES

The idea that modules can make procedures available for use by other modules was introduced in Chapter 2. The module InOut is one such module. Its procedures are available for performing input operations from the keyboard and output operations to the screen. This chapter has so far concentrated on the ideas of procedure declaration and procedure call and in particular that the declaration of the procedure determines how the procedure should be called.

Whilst a module's import list can list procedures to be imported from other modules, it says nothing about the parameters required by the procedures. So how do we know how to call procedures imported from other modules correctly? In fact only the procedure heading of a procedure is necessary in order to determine how to call it correctly.

A standard module such as InOut has a **definition module** associated with it. This contains the procedure headings of the procedures which other modules can import from InOut. The full declarations for the procedures occur in another kind of module known as an **implementation module**. This contains the procedure headings and bodies for each of the procedures, and therefore contains the statements which implement the procedure.

A typical definition module for InOut is shown in Fig. 4.22. All definition modules begin with the word DEFINITION and a module name. The rest of the definition module is a list of items which can be exported from the corresponding implementation module and can be imported into other modules. In the case of procedures the definition module specifies the name and formal parameter list of each procedure. Thus WriteCard takes two value parameters which must be CARDINAL values, and WriteString takes one value parameter which must be an ARRAY OF CHAR. This is precisely the information needed by the programmer to call the procedures appropriately within other modules. Note that Read and ReadCard could be written as function procedures, but ReadString has to return its result in a variable parameter as arrays cannot be returned as the results of function procedures. InOut, therefore, uses a convention of returning the result in a variable parameter for all its reading procedures.

The comments describe what the procedures do for the benefit of the programmer. They are an essential part of a definition module as they give a more precise description of what the procedures do than the names of the procedures and parameters.

The definition module of InOut is therefore a summary of the facilities provided by its implementation module. It is a kind of go-between for the implementation module and modules which use its facilities.

For the present, there are three major kinds of module. These are
1. a main program module. This is a module which determines the behaviour of the entire program whose body contains statements which control how the program should be executed, often through a sequence of calls to procedures which may or may not be declared in the module itself.
2. implementation modules. These are modules containing declarations of objects which can be used in other modules and may itself use objects in other implementation modules. An implementation module is supplied with Modula-2 which contains the code for each of the procedures ReadCard, WriteCard,

DEFINITION MODULE InOut ;

PROCEDURE ReadCard (VAR x : CARDINAL) ;
(∗ reads a CARDINAL value into the variable parameter x,
ignoring leading spaces.
A CARDINAL value consists of a sequence of numeric characters
terminated by any non-numeric character. ∗)

PROCEDURE Read (VAR ch : CHAR) ;
(∗ reads a character into the variable parameter ch ∗)

PROCEDURE ReadString (VAR s : ARRAY OF CHAR) ;
(∗ reads a sequence of characters into the variable parameter s,
ignoring leading spaces.
The character sequence is terminated by any character whose
ordinal value is less than or equal to that of the space
character. This terminating character is not stored in the
array.
The backspace character (bs) deletes the last character. ∗)

PROCEDURE WriteCard (x,n : CARDINAL) ;
(∗ writes the value of the CARDINAL parameter x in a fieldwidth
n characters wide. ∗)

PROCEDURE WriteString (s : ARRAY OF CHAR) ;
(∗ writes the sequence of characters in s up to the first null
character or the entire array if there is no null character
in the array. ∗)

PROCEDURE Write (ch : CHAR) ;
(∗ writes out the character held in ch. ∗)

PROCEDURE WriteOct (x,n : CARDINAL) ;
(∗ writes the value of the CARDINAL parameter x as an octal number
in a fieldwidth of n characters. ∗)

PROCEDURE WriteHex (x,n : CARDINAL) ;
(∗ writes the value of the CARDINAL parameter x as a hexadecimal
number in a fieldwidth of n characters. ∗)

PROCEDURE WriteLn ;
(∗ causes subsequent input and output to start on the next line. ∗)

END InOut.

Fig. 4.22.

WriteString and WriteLn. This contains the code which is executed when any of
the procedures are called. This module is usually called InOut.
3.   definition modules. For every implementation module there must exist a

corresponding definition module. This includes within it sufficient information to allow the objects in the implementation module to be used appropriately. It is this kind of module which allows the programmer to know about the facilities available in an implementation module without knowing the detail of exactly how these facilities are provided. It additionally provides the compiler with the exact detail required to check that the objects are used correctly.

4.8 SUMMARY

The effective design and coding of programs is aided considerably by being able to see similarities with, and differences between, the requirements of various problems. The organisation of a program should reflect the perceived structure of a problem. Good program organisation is acquired mainly through experience, however the facilities provided by Modula-2 allow a programmer to organise programs to correspond to the structure that he sees in the problem.

The following ideas are central to a thorough understanding of Modula-2.

1 Modula-2 provides several ways of organising programs. One of these is the provision for the programmer to define his own procedures so that the structure of the program mirrors the structure he sees in the problem he is solving.

2 A procedure declaration consists of a list of parameters, a collection of declarations and a procedure body which is a sequence of statements.

3 A procedure declaration's formal parameters state the number of parameters, the type of each parameter (CARDINAL, ARRAY OF CHAR, etc) and the kind of parameter (variable or value). The compiler checks that a call to the procedure passes actual parameters which are consistent with the declaration of the procedure's formal parameters.

4 There are two kinds of formal parameter, variable parameters and value parameters. Value parameters are used for giving information to a procedure. Variable parameters are used for allowing a procedure to give information back to the procedure or module body from which the procedure was called. Variable parameters have the word VAR in front of them in the procedure's formal parameter list, after the word VAR all parameters listed up to the next semi-colon are variable parameters.

5 A function procedure is a special kind of procedure which returns a result. The type of the result is specified after the closing bracket of the list of formal parameter sections. In the case of the function procedures the formal parameter part of the declaration of the procedure is obligatory. This means that even if the function does not require any parameters to be passed to it, it must have an empty list of formal parameter sections indicated by an opening and closing bracket. A RETURN statement indicates the value to be returned as the result and terminates execution of the function procedure. It is usual for the RETURN statement to be the last statement of the function procedure body. A procedure body may, however, contain more than one RETURN statement. The call of a function procedure always appears as part of an expression rather than a statement in its own right. If the function procedure has no formal parameters then the call must indicate an empty actual parameter list by an open and close bracket. A function can only return one result and this cannot be a structured object such as an array.

6   Programs can be split across several modules. Several standard modules are supplied with Modula-2. These consist of an implementation module which contains the declarations of procedures and therefore the code which performs the operations. In addition, an implementation module has a definition module associated with it which is essentially a summary of the implementation module. For procedures, the definition module contains a copy of the procedure heading of procedures which can be imported into other modules. In later chapters we will see that Modula-2 allows the programmer to write his own implementation modules and thereby organise his program across several modules.

TECHNICAL EXERCISES

1   Given the following declarations

```
VAR A,B : CARDINAL ;
    C   : INTEGER ;
PROCEDURE Cube (VAR Y : CARDINAL ;
                    X : CARDINAL) ;
BEGIN
 Y := X*X*X
END Cube ;
```

State which of the parameters are variable parameters and which are value parameters.

State which parameter can pass back a result to the rest of the program.

State which of the following calls of Cube are valid.

a   Cube (2,B)

b   Cube (B,2)

c   Cube (A,B)

d   Cube (C,B)

e   Cube ('CARDINAL',B)

f Cube (B)

g Cube (A,B,C)

Assume that the valid calls of Cube are executed in sequence, what will be the final values of A and B?

Which of the parameter lists above are formal parameters and which are actual parameters?

2 Given the declarations

```
VAR X,Y,Z : CARDINAL ;
PROCEDURE HighestCommonDenominator (Num1,Num2 : CARDINAL ;
                                    VAR Result : CARDINAL) ;
(* Result is assigned the largest CARDINAL value which both Num1 and Num2
are divisible by without leaving a remainder *)
BEGIN
  (*... ...*)
END HighestCommonDenominator ;
```

Write procedure calls to calculate the highest common denominator of

a 81 and 27

b X and 11

c X and Y

d X and Z

in each case the result is to be held in Z after the procedure call.

3 Correct the following procedure declaration so that it is syntactically correct.

```
Procedure Fred (VAR firstparam ; secondparam : CARDINAL ,
                thirdparam , fourthparam ; CARDINAL)
(* firstparam is assigned the value of thirdparam DIV fourthparam,
   secondparam is assigned the value of thirdparam MOD fourthparam
BEGIN
  firstparam = thirdparam DIV fourthparam ;
  secondparam := ThirdParam MOD fourthparam ;
END ;
```

4 The following procedure is part of a program

```
PROCEDURE AreaOfTriangle (Area : CARDINAL ;
                          BaseLen,Height : CARDINAL) ;
BEGIN
    Area := BaseLen * Height DIV 2
END AreaOfTriangle ;
```

but when the program runs the user types in the values 4 and 6 and an incorrect result for the area is printed. What is wrong with the procedure and how could the problem be rectified?

Rewrite the procedure as a function procedure.

5   What is wrong with the following procedure.

```
PROCEDURE ReadName () : ARRAY OF CHAR ;
VAR
      Name : ARRAY [1..10] OF CHAR ;
BEGIN
      ReadString (Name) ;
      RETURN Name ;
END ReadName ;
```

Rewrite the procedure so that it legally reads a sequence of characters into a character array which is then available to the rest of the program.

6   The following procedure headings are included in a definition module (descriptions of what each procedure does have been omitted, though it is possible to hazard a guess from the procedure names)

```
DEFINITION MODULE PersonalDetails ;
  PROCEDURE WriteName (Name : ARRAY OF CHAR) ;
  PROCEDURE ReadName (VAR Name : ARRAY OF CHAR) ;
  PROCEDURE ChangeName (VAR Name : ARRAY OF CHAR ;
                    NewName : ARRAY OF CHAR) ;
  PROCEDURE ReadDateOfBirth (VAR Day,Month,Year : CARDINAL) ;
  PROCEDURE WriteDateOfBirth (VAR Day,Month,Year : CARDINAL) ;
  PROCEDURE ChangeDateOfBirth (VAR Day,Month,Year,
                    NewDay,NewMonth,NewYear : CARDINAL) ;
  END PersonalDetails .
```

state which of the following are valid procedure calls.

a ReadName (MyName)

b MyName := ReadName ()

c WriteName (MyName)

d ReadName ('Fred')

e WriteName ('Fred')

f ChangeName (MyName,'Fred')

g ChangeName ("Fred",MyName)

h ChangeName (MyName,")

j WriteName ('Fred")

k ReadDateOfBirth (A,B,C)

l WriteDateOfBirth (28,11,56)

m ChangeDateOfBirth (A,B,C,A,B,C)

n ChangeDateOfBirth (A,B,C,25,12,84)

What is wrong with this as a definition module?

What alterations to the procedure headings could be justified in the light of the limitations you may have identified while deciding which of the calls are valid and which are invalid? Rewrite the definition module with these alterations.

7 State what is wrong with the following procedure and rewrite it correctly.

```
PROCEDURE SetToNulls (CharacterArray : ARRAY OF CHAR) ;
(* initialise the actual parameter array with null characters *)
BEGIN
 CharacterArray := '' ;
END SetToNulls ;
```

PROGRAMMING EXERCISES

1 Rewrite the module SmallExample in Fig. 4.3 so that it uses function procedures where appropriate.

2 Write a function procedure PerimeterOfRectangle which returns as its result the perimeter of a rectangle given its length and width.

What modifications would you need to make to the procedures ReadLengthAndWidth and WriteArea to make them appropriate for a program for calculating the perimeter of a rectangle. Make the required modifications and write a module RectanglePerimeter which asks the user to state the length and width of the rectangle and writes out the perimeter.

3 Rewrite OctalAdditionAndMultiplication to use function procedures for ReadOct and ReadOperator.

4 Write procedures to complete the following program module.

```
MODULE SubStringSubstitution ;

BEGIN
 Introduction () ;
 ReadTargetString (TargetString) ;
 ReadSubstituteSubString (SubString) ;
 SubstituteIn (TargetString,SubString) ;
 WriteNewString (TargetString) ;
END SubStringSubstitution .
```

The program must substitute a sub-string for every occurrence of the character '*' in a target string. For example, substituting 'Will' in '* you ask * for the pen?' results in the new target string 'Will you ask Will for the pen?'. The strings are to be read from the keyboard and the result of the substitution is to be written to the screen. Note that depending upon the length of the sub-string and the number of substitutions to be made, the length of the target string may be unable to cope with all substitutions. The program should inform the user of such situations if they occur and perform the substitutions up to the point when the target string becomes full.

5 Write a program module called TitlePage which requests the user for

a the title of a report,

b the author names,

c the length of the page as the number of lines of characters,

d the width of the page as the number of characters on a line,

and writes the report title and author names centred in the middle of the screen. For example the input

> Modula-2: Constructive Program Development
> P.Messer and I.Marshall
> 25
> 80

should write the title and names in the centre of the screen (assuming that the screen is 25 rows of 80 columns).

Many operating systems allow you to send the output from a program to both the screen and to a printer by using some facility before running the program. Find out if this can be done with your computer and if so specify the length and width of the paper so that the output can be sent to a printer to produce a title page.

6 Write a program module called Volumes which allows the user the option of asking for the volume of a sphere, cube or cuboid to be computed. Once the user has selected one of these the program should then request the data it needs from the user. Take care that the user understands what is happening at all times and understands the information which is presented. Allow the user to repeat this as many times as he wishes until he indicates that he wishes the program to stop.

ANSWERS

1 Y is a variable parameter and X is a value parameter. Y can return a result back to the rest of the program.

a invalid as Cube's first formal parameter is a variable parameter so the actual parameter must be a variable

b valid

c valid

d invalid as C is not a CARDINAL variable

e invalid as 'CARDINAL' is a string (ARRAY OF CHAR)

f invalid as Cube takes two parameters

g invalid as Cube takes two parameters

If calls to Cube in **b** and **c** were executed in sequence then we can picture what happens as shown in Fig. 4.23.

The parameters in the declaration are the formal parameters, the parameters in procedure calls are the actual parameters.

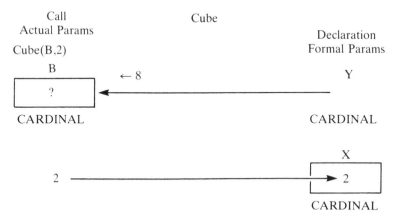

As 2 is a CARDINAL value it is copied into the new variable X and the cube of 2 is put into B in the procedure.

Cube(A,B)

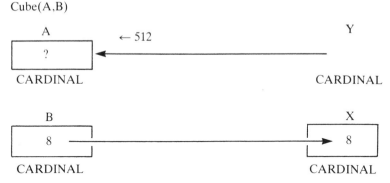

A would have the value 512 and B would hold the value 8.

Fig. 4.23.

2 **a** HighestCommonDenominator(81,27,Z)   or HighestCommonDenominator(27,81,Z)
   b HighestCommonDenominator(X,11,Z)   or HighestCommonDenominator(11,X,Z)
   c HighestCommonDenominator(X,Y,Z)   or HighestCommonDenominator(Y,X,Z)
   d HighestCommonDenominator(X,Z,Z)   or HighestCommonDenominator(Z,X,Z)

3   Procedure(*a*) Fred (VAR firstparam ;(*b*) secondparam : CARDINAL , (*c*)
               thirdparam , fourthparam ; (*d*) CARDINAL) (*e*)
         (* firstparam is assigned the value of thirdparam DIV fourthparam,

secondparam is assigned the value of thirdparam MOD fourthparam (*f*)
BEGIN
    firstparam = (*g*) thirdparam DIV fourthparam ;
    secondparam := ThirdParam (*h*) MOD fourthparam ;
    END (*j*) ;

a PROCEDURE
b the separator between parameters with the same characteristics is a comma
c the separator between parameters with different characteristics is a semi-colon
d the separator between parameters and their type is colon
e a procedure heading is terminated by a semi-colon
f missing end of comment bracket
g assignment is denoted by := not =
h ThirdParam is a different variable from thirdparam because of the different upper and lower case letter
j missing procedure name, the procedure name must be repeated at the end of the procedure

4 The result of the calculation is assigned to the formal parameter but this is a value parameter so the result is never communicated back to the rest of the program. The problem can be rectified by placing VAR before Area in the parameter list thereby making Area a variable parameter, or better still, in this case, by writing it as a function procedure.

```
PROCEDURE AreaOfTriangle (BaseLen,Height : CARDINAL) : CARDINAL ;
BEGIN
 RETURN BaseLen * Height DIV 2
END AreaOfTriangle ;
```

5 Essentially the problem with the procedure is that a function procedure cannot return a result whose type is a structured type such as an array. The only way to pass back arrays to the rest of the program is by a variable parameter. A possible rewriting of this is

```
PROCEDURE ReadName (VAR Name : ARRAY OF CHAR) ;
BEGIN
     ReadString (Name) ;
END ReadName ;
```

though it is now obvious that all this does is give a procedure which does exactly the same as ReadString. A possible reason for such a procedure would be that it may also include a message to the user asking for a name to be typed at the keyboard.

6 a valid

   b invalid as ReadName is not a function procedure

   c valid

   d invalid as 'Fred' is a constant value not a variable

   e valid as WriteName takes a value parameter

   f valid

   g invalid as "Fred" is a constant value not a variable

   h valid as ' ' is the empty string

   j invalid due to mismatch ' "

   k valid

   l invalid as the parameters are constant values, not variables

   m valid though it is only exceptional circumstances which warrant passing the same variables to a procedure in different parameters. As a consequence, inside ChangeDateOfBirth OldDay and NewDay will refer to the same variable, which can cause confusion and programming difficulties.

   n invalid as all parameters are variable parameters and therefore CARDINAL values cannot be passed as parameters

```
DEFINITION MODULE PersonalDetails ;
  PROCEDURE WriteName (Name : ARRAY OF CHAR) ;
  PROCEDURE ReadName (VAR Name : ARRAY OF CHAR) ;
  PROCEDURE ChangeName (VAR OldName : ARRAY OF CHAR ;
                            NewName : ARRAY OF CHAR) ;
  PROCEDURE ReadDateOfBirth (VAR Day,Month,Year : CARDINAL) ;
  PROCEDURE WriteDateOfBirth (Day,Month,Year : CARDINAL) ;
  PROCEDURE ChangeDateOfBirth (VAR Day,Month,Year : CARDINAL ;
                            NewDay,NewMonth,NewYear : CARDINAL) ;
END PersonalDetails.
```

A major criticism of this as a definition module is that the only clue to what each procedure does is the procedure name and parameter names. A precise description of each procedure should also be given in a comment.

The formal parameters of WriteDateOfBirth could be changed to be value parameters as routines for writing information do not usually need to communicate information back to the program. Similarly, the last three parameters of ChangeDateOfBirth could be value parameters. This assumes that these parameters are the new values to be stored in the actual parameters given as the first three parameters. In both cases this would permit the actual parameters to be constant values or results of expressions rather than merely variables.

7 Open array parameters can only be processed element by element so the assignment statement is not permitted. In addition the parameter should be a variable parameter rather than a value parameter. This procedure has to be written

```
PROCEDURE SetToNulls (VAR CharacterArray : ARRAY OF CHAR) ;
(* initialise the actual parameter array with null characters *)
VAR
    EndPlusOne ,
    Pos          : CARDINAL ;
BEGIN
 EndPlusOne := HIGH(CharacterArray) + 1 ;
 Pos := 0 ;
 WHILE Pos <> EndPlusOne DO
    CharacterArray [Pos] := CHR (0) ;
    INC (Pos) ;
 END (* WHILE *) ;
END SetToNulls ;
```

It can then be used to initialise any character array.

Chapter 5

Scope Rules and the Use of Procedures

An important stage in writing Modula-2 programs is to become fluent in the writing of collections of procedures which together form a logical unit. In this chapter a collection of procedures is developed to manipulate a data structure known as a queue which is an idealisation of a real life queue.

To achieve this it is necessary to understand the rules under which program objects, such as variables and procedures, can and cannot be referenced. These rules are called the scope rules of the language and are discussed first.

5.1 SCOPE RULES

The syntax diagrams for modules and procedures, in Figs 3.1 and 4.5 respectively, state that each contains a block and that a block is a collection of declarations and statements. Typically a module involves a collection of procedure declarations, but each of these procedures consists of a block. This means that they can introduce declarations of their own, some of which may be other procedures containing their own declarations. The position of an object's declaration crucially affects where the object can be used within the program. Scope rules allow the programmer to determine where and how identifier names can be used simply by inspecting the program text.

Scope Rule 1

> An object can be referenced throughout the block in which its declaration occurs, including any procedures declared within the block.

The most fundamental idea of the scope rules is that constants, variables and procedures declared in a module's declarations can be referred to throughout the module. Such objects are said to be **global** to the module (see Fig. 5.1). In SmallExample (see Fig. 4.3) the procedures could have been written without any parameters, but with the procedures referring directly to the module's global variables Length, Width and Area. This has the disadvantage that the procedures have no independence from the rest of the module. If the name of one of the global variables is changed then all references to the name inside the procedures must also be changed.

121

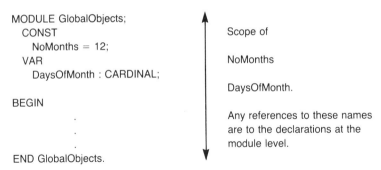

```
MODULE GlobalObjects;
   CONST
      NoMonths = 12;
   VAR
      DaysOfMonth : CARDINAL;

BEGIN
         .
         .
         .
END GlobalObjects.
```

Scope of

NoMonths

DaysOfMonth.

Any references to these names
are to the declarations at the
module level.

Fig. 5.1. Declarations at the outer level of a Module.

We have already seen objects declared in a module's block. In addition, a procedure can declare objects which are local it. In fact such objects have already been met in Chapter 4 in normal declarations of objects and in the guise of value parameters in formal parameter lists. In Fig. 5.2 the variable Count can be referenced anywhere within the module LocalObjects, but Count1 can only be referenced inside the procedure Demo.

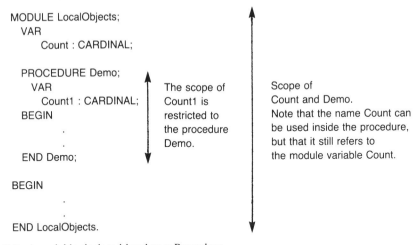

```
MODULE LocalObjects;
   VAR
      Count : CARDINAL;

   PROCEDURE Demo;
      VAR
         Count1 : CARDINAL;
      BEGIN
            .
            .
      END Demo;

   BEGIN
         .
         .
   END LocalObjects.
```

The scope of
Count1 is
restricted to
the procedure
Demo.

Scope of
Count and Demo.
Note that the name Count can
be used inside the procedure,
but that it still refers to
the module variable Count.

Fig. 5.2. A variable declared local to a Procedure.

It is possible to declare procedures within procedures to any number of levels, as procedures themselves consist of blocks. Figure 5.3 shows a procedure declared within another procedure thereby introducing a block within a block within the module's block. The boxes around parts of the code indicate the blocks of the module and procedures. It is usual to talk about such nesting of blocks as different block levels. The module block can be considered to be block level 0, and each nesting of a block within another as increasing the block level by 1. For example, procedure OuterProc establishes a new block level numbered 1, and InnerProc creates block level 2. Scope rule 1 essentially states that a name which is declared at block level N can be used throughout this block and in blocks of procedures which are nested within it and therefore have a block level greater than N.

Notice that the name of a procedure is declared in the block surrounding the block which it establishes, so that it can be called from outside the procedure's block! The name of the procedure is also in scope within its own block so it can call itself, this is discussed at length in Chapter 13. Note also that in Fig. 5.3 the module body cannot call InnerProc as it is not within scope of the main module, it can only be called from within OuterProc. This procedure is local to OuterProc.

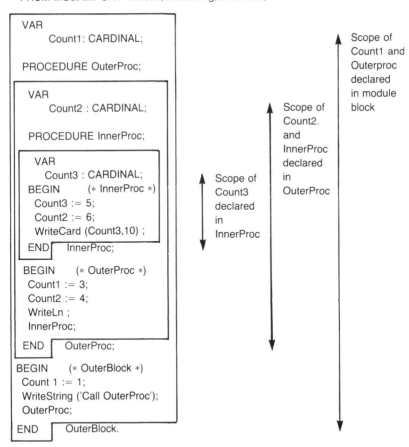

```
MODULE OuterBlock;
   FROM InOut IMPORT WriteLn,WriteString,WriteCard;

VAR
      Count1: CARDINAL;

   PROCEDURE OuterProc;

   VAR
         Count2 : CARDINAL;

      PROCEDURE InnerProc;

      VAR
         Count3 : CARDINAL;
      BEGIN          (* InnerProc *)
      Count3 := 5;
      Count2 := 6;
      WriteCard (Count3,10) ;
      END  InnerProc;

   BEGIN       (* OuterProc *)
   Count1 := 3;
   Count2 := 4;
   WriteLn ;
   InnerProc;
   END  OuterProc;

BEGIN     (* OuterBlock *)
Count 1 := 1;
WriteString ('Call OuterProc');
OuterProc;
END  OuterBlock.
```

Scope of Count1 and Outerproc declared in module block

Scope of Count2. and InnerProc declared in OuterProc

Scope of Count3 declared in InnerProc

Fig. 5.3. A procedure local to a procedure.

Figure 5.3 illustrates a further point about scope rules.

Scope Rule 2

> Objects can be imported into a module through its import lists. The
> scope of the imported objects is the module's block.

In Fig. 5.3 WriteLn, WriteString and WriteCard are imported into the module and
therefore can be used anywhere within the module, just as if they had been
declared in the module's block. A consequence of this is that the module
cannot use these names for objects declared in the outer block of the module.
The standard procedures, such as INC, CAP, etc, and the standard types, such
as CARDINAL, CHAR etc, are implicitly imported into every module and consequently these names cannot be used as names for objects declared at the
module level.

```
MODULE InvalidDuplicateNames;
  CONST
        Separator = 0;
        Count = 4;
  VAR
        Count : CARDINAL;        (* This declaration is invalid as the name    *)
                                 (* Count is already being used in this block. *)
  CONST
        Separator = 20;          (* This is invalid as the name Separator      *)
                                 (* has already been used in this block.       *)

        Count1 = 30;             (* This is valid, Count1 is a new identifier. *)

  PROCEDURE Count ;             (* This is invalid as the name Count is       *)
                                 (* already being used in the module block.    *)
     VAR
        Fred : CARDINAL ;        (* This is valid as it is declared in a new   *)
     CONST                       (* block and therefore is a new variable.     *)
        Fred = 50 ;              (* This is invalid as Fred has already been   *)
  BEGIN                          (* used in a declaration in this block.       *)
        .
        .
        .
  END Count ;

BEGIN
        .
        .
        .
END InvalidDuplicateNames.
```

Fig. 5.4. Incorrect uses of the same name.

Care must be taken if the same name is used more than once.

Scope Rule 3

> Two objects cannot have the same name if they are declared at the same block level within the same block.

Figure 5.4 illustrates invalid declarations of the same identifier in the same block. Note that the attempt to declare the procedure Count is invalid because the identifier is already being used for a different object in the module's block.

A procedure can declare an object with the same name as an object which is declared in a block enclosing the procedure. Inside the procedure, use of the name is restricted to the object declared in the procedure. The object declared in the outer block is not accessible within the procedure, and there is said to be a **hole in its scope**. Figure 5.5 illustrates the phenomenon, the module's variables Zero and Count cannot be accessed inside Demo as it reuses their names.

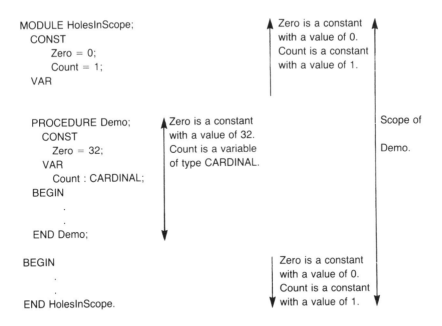

Fig. 5.5. Local declarations of objects with the same name as objects declared in surrounding blocks — holes in scope.

The reuse of the same name is not recommended since it is possible that the local and global variable may be required in the same procedure if some change to the program specification is made. This objection does not apply to uses of the same name in different blocks at the same level, because their names cannot be confused.

It is recommended that in general the names for objects should be chosen to be unique.

An object's scope is determined by the position of its declaration and not by the positions where it is used. This is particularly important when procedures are called from different places in a program. When the module StaticScoping in Fig. 5.6 is executed it writes out the value 20. This is because UseSep writes out the value of the module variable Separator. The fact that UseSep is called from within Static, which has its own declaration involving the same name, is irrelevant. UseSep would have to be declared as a local procedure inside Static for it to write out the value of Static's local variable Separator. Be careful in situations like this, for even if the result seems obvious it is easy to get it wrong when other matters of program development are dominating your thoughts.

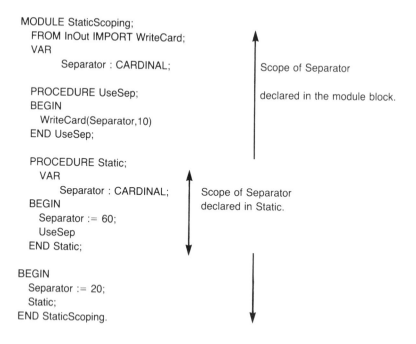

```
MODULE StaticScoping;
    FROM InOut IMPORT WriteCard;
    VAR
            Separator : CARDINAL;                    Scope of Separator

    PROCEDURE UseSep;                                declared in the module block.
    BEGIN
        WriteCard(Separator,10)
    END UseSep;

    PROCEDURE Static;
        VAR
            Separator : CARDINAL;                    Scope of Separator
    BEGIN                                            declared in Static.
        Separator := 60;
        UseSep
    END Static;

BEGIN
    Separator := 20;
    Static;
END StaticScoping.
```

Fig. 5.6. Static Scoping.

The formal parameters of procedures are handled in the same way as other variables. The names of all formal parameters are local to the procedure, just as if they had been declared in the normal part of the procedure declarations. Figure 5.7 illustrates this.

```
MODULE FormalParameterNames;
VAR
        Count1,Count2 : CARDINAL;

PROCEDURE Demo(Count1 :CARDINAL;VAR Count2 :CARDINAL);
(*  Within the procedure, Count1 and Count2 refer to the parameters and not to the
    global variables. *)
BEGIN
   Count1 := 1;
   Count2 := 2
END Demo;

BEGIN
   Count1: = 4;
   Count2: = 5;
   Demo(Count1,Count2);   (* The call Demo(Count2,Count1) is legal, but is very
                              confusing.*)
      (* Count1 has the value 4 at this point.*)
      (* Count2 has the value 2 at this point, because it was passed to Demo as a variable
         parameter.*)
END   FormalParameterNames.
```

Fig. 5.7. Procedure parameters which reuse names.

There is an additional restriction on references to names within declarations.

Scope Rule 4

The names introduced in constants and user-defined type declarations (see Chapter 8) can only be used in other **declarations** which **follow** them. However these and variable and procedure names can be used within **statements** anywhere in their scope, either following or preceding the declaration.

Figure 5.8 shows examples of valid and invalid references to names which are declared after references are made to them. CanUse can refer to LaterDec, DeclaredLater and UsedBeforeDeclared because these references occur in the statements of its procedure body. The declaration of Illegal is invalid because it refers to the constant NotInScope which has yet to be declared. As a general rule, when declaring an object check that other identifiers used in its declaration are in scope and that their declarations precede this one.

```
MODULE ForwardReferences;

   PROCEDURE CanUse;
   BEGIN
     LaterDec    := 20;
     DeclaredLater := UsedBeforeDeclared()
   END CanUse;

   VAR
        DeclaredLater,
        LaterDec      : CARDINAL;

   PROCEDURE UsedBeforeDeclared () : CARDINAL;
   BEGIN
     RETURN 67
   END UsedBeforeDeclared;

   CONST
        Illegal       = NotInScope;      (* This is a syntax error *)
        NotInScope = 5;

BEGIN
   CanUse
END ForwardReferences.
```

Fig. 5.8. Restrictions within declarations.

Lifetime

In addition to the idea of the scope of an object's name, which determines where in the program text a declared object can be used, there is an important related concept of lifetime. Lifetime is concerned with the periods of time that objects exist during a program's execution, when they come into existence and when they cease to exist. The rules covering the lifetime of an object are as follows

1.   An object declared at module level exists as long as the module exists.

2.   An object declared locally to a procedure only exists while the procedure is being executed. The object is created when the procedure is called and ceases to exist when the procedure call is completed. If a procedure is called again, a new object of the same name is created for the lifetime of this procedure call. As a consequence of this, objects local to a procedure do not retain their values between calls to the procedure. Note that the idea of lifetime is concerned with the value associated with an identifier and so is primarily concerned with variables.

The program in Fig. 5.9 is incorrect due to a misunderstanding of the idea of lifetime. The behaviour of this program in detailed in the following steps.

```
MODULE Lifetimes;
  FROM InOut IMPORT WriteCard;
  VAR
      Count : CARDINAL;

  PROCEDURE Demo;
    VAR
        Count1 : CARDINAL;
    BEGIN
    IF Count = 1 THEN
      Count1 := 20
    END (*IF*);
    WriteCard(Count1,5)
    END Demo;

BEGIN
  Count := 1;
  Demo;
  Count := 2;
  Demo
END Lifetimes.
```

Fig. 5.9. The lifetime of variables local to a procedure.

Step1. Count is set to one.

```
┌─────────┐
│    1    │
└─────────┘
   Count
```

Step2. Call Demo. This causes the variable Count1 to be created producing

```
┌─────────┐    ┌─────────┐
│    1    │    │    ?    │
└─────────┘    └─────────┘
   Count          Count1
```

Step3. The IF test in Demo checks to see if Count is one and since it is, sets Count1 to twenty producing

```
┌─────────┐    ┌─────────┐
│    1    │    │   20    │
└─────────┘    └─────────┘
   Count          Count1
```

Step4. The value twenty is written out.

Step5. The call to Demo is complete and so control is returned to the main module which called Demo. This results in Count1 ceasing to exist. The position becomes

```
┌─────────┐
│    1    │
└─────────┘
   Count
```

Step6. The value of Count is set to two producing

Count

Step7. Call Demo. This creates a new local variable called Count1. This does NOT contain the old value of twenty, instead it is undefined so the result is

Count   Count

Step8. Since Count is two, the IF statement has no effect.

Step9. The write statement tries to write out a variable whose value is undefined which is an error. In some systems this might give the result twenty by coincidence (i.e. it uses the same physical memory location each time) but this is very dangerous — you are better off with a system which tells you that an error has occurred since this enables you to correct it.

Step10. The call to Demo is completed and the module terminates execution.

Summary

1.   An object declared at the module level is accessible throughout the module, except for blocks in which there is a hole in its scope. Such objects are said to be global to the module and their lifetime is the entire life of the module.

2.   An object imported into the module has the same status as if it had been declared at the module level. It can be referenced anywhere in the module except for blocks in which there is a hole in its scope.

3.   An object declared within a procedure can be referred to anywhere in the procedure including procedures which are declared locally to it, again with the exception of blocks in which there is a hole in its scope. The lifetime of such objects is the invocation of the procedure. They are created at the beginning and destroyed at the end of each invocation of the procedure.

4.   Two objects cannot be declared to have the same name in the same block at the same block level. However a name can be reused in an inner block. In such situations the object declared in the outer block cannot be referred to directly from within the inner block. There is said to be a hole in the scope of the outer object.

5.   Constants and types can only be used in other declarations from the point of their declaration onwards.

6. Some compilers do not meet the requirements of Modula-2 in regard to scoping, in particular some compilers always require that a name has been declared before it is used and therefore do not permit forward references in statements. Care should be taken in using the scope rules on any particular implementation.

7. When in doubt always declare objects before using them and do not reuse names.

5.2 MISUSE OF GLOBAL VARIABLES

In Modula-2 a procedure can access variables outside the procedure either because the scope of the variable includes the procedure or because the variable has been passed as an actual parameter to the procedure. It is confusing, however, to use both mechanisms to access the same variable. If a variable is accessed in both ways it effectively has two names within the procedure; its declared name and the name of the formal parameter which gives access to it. If the procedure's formal parameter is a value parameter it makes the program more difficult to read. If the procedure's formal parameter is a variable parameter some very curious program behaviour can result. You are advised not do this with value parameters and warned for your own good NEVER to do it with variable parameters.

When the program of Fig. 5.10 is executed the values of both Temp and Num are written onto the screen by WriteCard and the value of both is 4. This is clearly not what the procedure is intended to do. The problem is that the intermediate variable Temp is declared as global to the module and can legitimately be passed as a variable parameter. When Interchange is called with Temp as its first parameter, Interchange refers to the same variable using two different names, Temp and Temp1. The procedure effectively executes the three statements

```
Temp  := Temp;
Temp  := Temp2;
Temp2 := Temp;
```

which do not exchange the contents of Temp1 and Temp2. This is rectified by declaring Temp local to the procedure (see Fig 5.11). The module is even easier to understand if the name of one of the variables called Temp is changed, but the module in Fig 5.11 is correct as it stands.

```
MODULE SameVariableDifferentNames;
  FROM InOut IMPORT WriteCard;
  VAR
      Temp,Num : CARDINAL;

  PROCEDURE Interchange(VAR Temp1,Temp2 : CARDINAL);
  (* This interchanges the contents of the two variables passed as actual parameters. *)
  BEGIN
    Temp  := Temp1;
    Temp1 := Temp2;
    Temp2 := Temp
  END Interchange;

BEGIN
  Temp := 3;
  Num  := 4;
  Interchange(Temp,Num);
  WriteCard(Temp,10);
  WriteCard(Num,10)
END SameVariableDifferentNames.
```

Fig. 5.10. Misused global variables.

```
MODULE LocalSolution;
  FROM InOut IMPORT WriteCard;
  VAR
      Temp,Num : CARDINAL;

  PROCEDURE Interchange(VAR Temp1,Temp2 : CARDINAL);
  (* This interchanges the contents of the two variables passed as actual parameters. *)
    VAR
      Temp : CARDINAL;
  BEGIN
    Temp  := Temp1;
    Temp1 := Temp2;
    Temp2 := Temp
  END Interchange;

BEGIN
  Temp := 3;
  Num  := 4;
  Interchange(Temp,Num);
  WriteCard(Temp,10);
  WriteCard(Num,10)
END LocalSolution.
```

Fig. 5.11.

5.3 THE USE OF LOCAL AND GLOBAL VARIABLES

The full implications of the scope rules are difficult to appreciate initially until experience is gained in using them. A principle to follow is that variables should be declared as local to their place of use as possible. Only those parts of code that need to know about a variable should be within its scope.

1. If a variable is only required within a procedure it should be declared local to the procedure. Efficiency considerations caused by the creation and destruction of local variables on calling procedures may occasionally override this guideline — but seldom.

2. Variables and values should be passed as parameters rather than referred to directly unless there is a good reason for doing otherwise.

The second is very important as often there are good reasons for deciding not to pass variables as parameters. It is important to develop criteria to help in deciding when to contravene the general guideline. Consider the following typical elementary uses of parameter passing.

1. A value parameter allows a value to be passed to the procedure for use within the procedure.

2. A variable parameter passes a variable to the procedure which is assigned a value as a result of the procedure. (The variable may also supply a value to the procedure when the procedure is called.)

In certain kinds of modules there exist data structures whose purpose is central to all the procedures in the module. In such circumstances it is justifiable to allow the procedures to refer directly to the global data structures rather than pass them as parameters to the procedures. The following program illustrates one such situation.

5.4 PROGRAM DEVELOPMENT: THE DEVELOPMENT OF A QUEUE

Writing a program of any size or complexity is a major task requiring careful planning and implementation. Even quite small programs can seem very difficult until a considerable amount of experience is gained. This is not surprising since programming requires a combination of many different skills. In particular, extreme precision in the use of the language is necessary. Until a thorough understanding of Modula-2 syntax is obtained, just writing code which does not contain syntax errors is difficult. Do not be dismayed by this, perseverance will be amply rewarded.

Conversely, an overview of the problem that is being solved is necessary if the program code is not to be turgid and imprecise. The ability to pay extreme attention to the detail of the code while keeping in mind the general purpose of the code requires experience. It is difficult to appreciate the subtleties of Shakespeare if you have to keep an English dictionary on your knee.

A standard method of writing programs is known as **stepwise refinement**, which involves working from an overview and refining the ideas at each stage until each idea is small enough to be directly coded in the programming language. At each stage of refinement, only the most immediately important ideas are refined further and in this way a high degree of flexibility is maintained in the design of the code.

This idealistic method of developing a program requires a large amount of knowledge about what facilities are available in the language so that refinements are chosen which lead to subproblems which are easier to solve. Similarly, it requires experience to choose refinements which are relatively independent of each other. If they are chosen inappropriately subproblems, which on the surface seem to be easier, can actually lead to difficulties. Our objective in this book is to help you to be able to code in this fashion. Modula-2 has a structure which directly reflects these ideas and makes their use much easier than in many other languages. However, it has to be recognised that a mixture of design strategies is required until you have gained experience and this approach will be used to help you overcome the difficulties.

Stepwise refinement is typically referred to as a **top down** method reflecting the idea that it starts from the most general statement of the problem and works down to the intricate detail of the code. The method of starting by writing sections of code and then merging them together to form the program is called a **bottom up** method. In larger programs this latter technique tends to lead to ill designed code because of the lack of a general strategy, but it has the advantage of allowing the programmer to experiment with how to achieve solutions to a problem. Thus it is often the preferred method of inexperienced programmers who are unsure of the techniques of problem solving, and who have found it highly effective in solving the small problems typically presented when learning how to program. The bottom up technique is most useful for studying small parts of code suggested by the top down analysis where the best solutions for a sub-problem are not obvious. One or two different bottom up attempts at the solution are usually sufficient to give enough insight into the problem to continue the top down analysis.

Rather than preach the superiority of the top down method, the following example uses an approach which develops solutions top down, but also studies how to solve parts of the problem in a bottom up manner. As you grow more experienced you will find the requirement to look in a bottom up manner becomes much less of a necessity, but it is doubtful if it will ever become completely unnecessary. If it does it will probably be because you have built up large libraries of modules to carry out general purpose tasks for the types of problems you are required to solve.

Development of a Queue

The development of a module embodying a queue is now discussed. The fundamental idea is to hide the details of how the queue is represented by restricting access to the queue to specific procedures which manipulate the queue. By doing this, it is possible to design and test the module as a unit independent of any particular use of the queue. The queue is not used for a specific purpose here but later it will be used in several programs. The objective at this stage is to construct the facilities which would make the use of a queue in a program easy to achieve. The layout of the module is given in Fig. 5.12.

MODULE QueueModule;

> A set of declarations which define a data structure
> to represent a queue. None of the variables declared will
> be altered in the module body.

> A set of procedures to allow data items to be added to
> or taken from the queue. In addition, certain procedures
> can be made available to enquire about properties of the
> queue. These procedures provide access to the variables
> representing the queue.

BEGIN
   (*... This section can be used to contain a test program for the
      procedures. ...*)
END QueueModule.

Fig. 5.12.

To develop the problem further it is necessary to appreciate precisely what is meant by the term queue. That is, what necessary features of a real life queue, for example a bus queue, are to be represented in the computer? The essential characteristics of a queue are that objects are added to the end of the queue and are removed from the head of the queue.

Head   End

| 10 | 15 | 20 | 9 | 25 | 4 |

If an object is removed from the queue it must be the one at the head, in this case 10, and the new head of the queue is then 15. If an object is added to the queue it must be added onto the end, that is after 4, and this new object becomes the end of the queue. Note that removals or additions from other positions are not allowed. This restriction retains the pure idea of a queue, though this may not always correspond to real life.

Typical operations that can be performed on a queue are
1. add an item to the queue
2. remove an item from the queue
3. check if the queue is full
4. check if the queue is empty
5. give the length of the queue.

It appears from this that five procedures are required to manipulate a queue in a useful way. All information modifying or enquiring about the queue is relayed via parameter passing. The proposed procedures and their headings are shown in Fig. 5.13. Note that the data items to be held in this queue are CARDINAL values. This is an arbitrary decision for the purpose of illustrating the development of the queue. The formal parameter of AddTo-Queue is a value parameter. As RemoveFromQueue requires an item from the queue to be returned, its parameter is a formal variable parameter.

```
PROCEDURE AddToQueue(Data : CARDINAL);
PROCEDURE RemoveFromQueue(VAR Data : CARDINAL);
PROCEDURE FullQueue() : CARDINAL;
(* RETURN 0 if the queue is not full
   RETURN 1 if the queue is full
*)
PROCEDURE EmptyQueue() : CARDINAL;
(* RETURN 0 if the queue is not empty
   RETURN 1 if the queue is empty
*)
PROCEDURE LengthOfQueue() : CARDINAL;
```

Fig. 5.13.

The next stage is to consider how to represent a queue in Modula-2. The previous diagram illustrating a queue could clearly be represented as an array. Consider the following

Array : QueueData

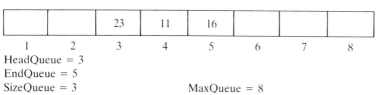

		23	11	16			
1	2	3	4	5	6	7	8

HeadQueue = 3
EndQueue = 5
SizeQueue = 3   MaxQueue = 8

This represents the queue as an array with three supporting CARDINAL variables, HeadQueue which indicates the front of the queue where removal of items occur, EndQueue which indicates the end of the queue where new items are added, and SizeQueue which indicates the number of items currently in the queue. Positions 1,2,6,7,8 are free components. A small problem arises when, as a result of insertions and deletions, the following situation results

Array : QueueData

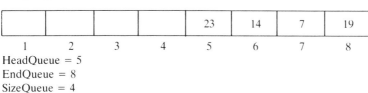

				23	14	7	19
1	2	3	4	5	6	7	8

HeadQueue = 5
EndQueue = 8
SizeQueue = 4

An addition of an item to the queue in this situation causes EndQueue to index a component which is beyond the end of the array. Yet to say that the queue is full is wasteful. This requires some detailed bottom up consideration to find a method by which the queue is considered full only when no components are free. When an item is added to the queue in this situation, it can be inserted in position 1 and EndQueue set to 1. This produces the new situation

Array : QueueData

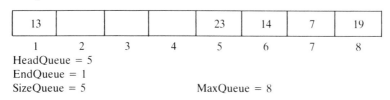

13				23	14	7	19
1	2	3	4	5	6	7	8

HeadQueue = 5
EndQueue = 1
SizeQueue = 5   MaxQueue = 8

This allows the entire array to be used to store items in the queue, even though the front of the queue will not typically correspond to the start of the array. However, it is necessary to study the behaviour of the queue in certain situations to gain insight into how this can be coded. In fact there are very simple techniques available to do this. When an item is added, either of the following pieces of code suffices to update EndQueue to the next available component where the item can be added.

```
1.   IF EndQueue < MaxQueue THEN
         EndQueue := EndQueue + 1
     ELSE
         EndQueue := 1
     END (* IF*)
2.   EndQueue := (EndQueue MOD MaxQueue) + 1
```

Clearly the second statement is more concise and so is used. You may find it necessary to write a short test program to see why it works or at least try some sample values to convince yourself that this does what is required.

The same problem arises with removal of items from the front of the queue. After the removal of an item the new head of the queue can be calculated by the code

```
HeadQueue := (HeadQueue MOD MaxQueue) + 1
```

A further difficulty occurs in the following case

Array : QueueData

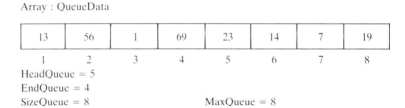

13	56	1	69	23	14	7	19
1	2	3	4	5	6	7	8

HeadQueue = 5
EndQueue = 4
SizeQueue = 8   MaxQueue = 8

If an item is added to the queue in this situation, it would overwrite the front of the queue. Insertions must be prevented in this situation, and the clue to a simple way of detecting this situation is given by the values of SizeQueue and MaxQueue. Thus an insertion into the queue must be prevented whenever SizeQueue equals MaxQueue. Similarly a removal from the queue is not allowed when SizeQueue is 0.

The final consideration is how to initialise HeadQueue and EndQueue to represent an empty queue. This is best decided by seeing what happens when an item is removed from a queue of length 1

Array : QueueData

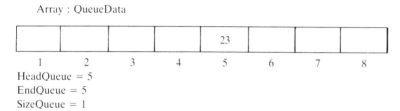

1 2 3 4 5 6 7 8
HeadQueue = 5
EndQueue = 5
SizeQueue = 1

If the above technique is used, on the removal of an item the result is

Array : QueueData

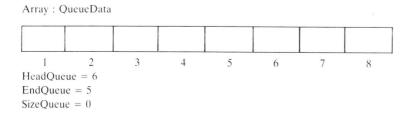

1 2 3 4 5 6 7 8
HeadQueue = 6
EndQueue = 5
SizeQueue = 0

When the length is zero EndQueue is one less than HeadQueue (MOD MaxQueue). Adding an item back in leads to a correct situation for a queue of one item, so this seems to be a valid initialisation. It follows that a natural set of initialisation values is

    HeadQueue = 1
    EndQueue = 8
    SizeQueue = 0

EndQueue could have been initialised to 0, but initialising it to the value of MaxQueue is more natural as it is a valid index of the queue array.

This ends the detailed bottom up analysis of the behaviour of a queue. Note how *ad hoc* it has been and how easy it is to miss something of importance. You may well have not thought of some of the points that have been discussed and perhaps some important ideas have been omitted. The top down analysis should take care of any such omissions.

Having established a method by which a queue can be represented, it is now necessary to investigate the integration of the queue data structure with the procedures to implement the permissable operations on the queue. Note that the queue array is used by each of the procedures and is therefore best declared outside the procedures and not passed as a parameter to the procedures. When an addition or deletion is made to the queue, only the data item is relevant. The array and its attendant variables, HeadQueue, EndQueue and MaxQueue are global variables. Under normal conditions all references to the queue data are restricted to these procedures. The justification of this assumption is given in full in Chapter 6, for the present it is sufficient to note

that by designing the procedures which manipulate the queue to be independent of the rest of the program we are isolating those parts of a program
which are distinct from each other. The module can now be writen as that
shown in Fig. 5.14.

```
MODULE QueueModule;
    (* Data declarations which form an abstract representation of a queue of CARDINAL
       values. *)
    CONST
        MaxQueue = 1000;
    VAR
        QueueData                              : ARRAY[1..MaxQueue] OF CARDINAL;
        HeadQueue,EndQueue,SizeQueue    : CARDINAL;


    PROCEDURE AddToQueue(Data : CARDINAL);
    BEGIN
    END AddToQueue;

    PROCEDURE RemoveFromQueue(VAR Data : CARDINAL);
    BEGIN
    END RemoveFromQueue;

    PROCEDURE FullQueue() : CARDINAL;
    (* RETURN 0 if the queue is not full
       RETURN 1 if the queue is full *)
    BEGIN
    END FullQueue;

    PROCEDURE EmptyQueue() : CARDINAL;
    (* RETURN 0 if the queue is not empty
       RETURN 1 if the queue is empty *)
    BEGIN
    END EmptyQueue;

    PROCEDURE LengthOfQueue() : CARDINAL;
    BEGIN
    END LengthOfQueue;

BEGIN
    (*... This section can be used to contain test programs for the
         procedures. ...*)
END QueueModule.
```

Fig. 5.14.

The next task is to write the code for each of the procedures. Note that the procedures are divided into two classes

1. those which modify the queue, AddToQueue and RemoveFromQueue, and

2. those which reference the queue, but do not modify it, FullQueue, Empty-Queue and LengthOfQueue.

A principle of stepwise refinement is always to tackle the most critical problem first and leave easy decisions to the end. This leads to greater flexibility in the solution. In this case it implies that the procedures of class 1 should be attempted first as they are more likely to cause problems. Both these procedures are of equal difficulty, in fact they are mirror images, so it does not matter which is developed first.

Development of AddToQueue

To write the code, it helps to start with a statement of the situation which is true on entry to the procedure and what should be true on exit from the procedure.

Entry : A correctly formed queue and an object to add to the queue.
Exit　: A correctly formed queue with:
　　　　a. the object added
　　　　or
　　　　b. some message that the queue is full and the object is not added.

As there is a special procedure available to enquire about whether or not the queue is full, no special measures are needed if an attempt is made to insert an item into a full queue. The procedure need only write a message saying that it is full, though later a better technique will be introduced for reporting such errors.

```
PROCEDURE AddToQueue(Data : CARDINAL);
BEGIN
  IF SizeQueue < MaxQueue THEN
    EndQueue                := (EndQueue MOD MaxQueue) + 1;
    QueueData[EndQueue]     := Data;
    SizeQueue               := SizeQueue + 1
  ELSE (* SizeQueue = MaxQueue *)
    WriteLn;
    WriteString('Error : Queue is full,no insertion allowed')
  END (* IF *)
END AddToQueue;
```

Fig. 5.15.

A queue, which is correctly formed before an insertion, is correct after the insertion if

1. EndQueue is correctly updated (see earlier discussion)
2. the object is added in the next free position
3. SizeQueue is incremented by one.

This leads to the procedure shown in Fig. 5.15.

Development of RemoveFromQueue

The entry and exit situations for RemoveFromQueue are

Entry : A correctly formed queue and a variable into which the first object in the queue can be placed.

 Exit : A correctly formed queue with:

   a. the object removed from the queue and placed in the given variable

   or

   b. a message that the queue is empty.

A queue, which is correctly formed before removal, is correctly formed after removal if

1. The head object is placed in the supplied variable
2. HeadQueue is correctly updated
3. SizeQueue is decremented by one.

This leads to the procedure in Fig. 5.16.

```
PROCEDURE RemoveFromQueue(VAR Data : CARDINAL);
BEGIN
  IF SizeQueue > 0 THEN
    Data         := QueueData[HeadQueue];
    HeadQueue  := (HeadQueue MOD MaxQueue) + 1;
    SizeQueue   := SizeQueue − 1
  ELSE (∗ SizeQueue = 0 ∗)
    WriteLn;
    WriteString('Error: queue is empty, cannot remove object')
  END (∗ IF ∗)
END RemoveFromQueue;
```

Fig. 5.16.

The other three procedures are simple functions which test the value held in SizeQueue. They can be found in Fig. 5.17. Note how the procedures have been defined to protect references directly to the queue data structure. The variable SizeQueue is protected by writing a procedure whose only purpose is to return its value. Also of note is the way that the scope rules of the language are exploited. QueueData, HeadQueue, EndQueue and SizeQueue are variables which are global to the module and the procedures refer to these directly. The only local variables are the formal parameters of AddToQueue and RemoveFrom-Queue. In the following section the module body is developed as a test program.

```
MODULE QueueModule;
  FROM InOut        IMPORT WriteString,WriteLn;
  (* Data declarations which form an abstract representation of a queue of CARDINAL
    values. *)
  CONST
    MaxQueue = 1000;
  VAR
    QueueData                        : ARRAY[1..MaxQueue] OF CARDINAL;
    HeadQueue,EndQueue,SizeQueue    : CARDINAL;

  PROCEDURE AddToQueue(Data : CARDINAL);
  BEGIN
    IF SizeQueue < MaxQueue THEN
      EndQueue                := (EndQueue MOD MaxQueue) + 1;
      QueueData[EndQueue]    := Data;
      SizeQueue              := SizeQueue + 1
    ELSE (* SizeQueue = MaxQueue *)
      WriteLn;
      WriteString('Error: Queue is full,no insertion allowed')
    END (* IF *)
  END AddToQueue;

  PROCEDURE RemoveFromQueue(VAR Data : CARDINAL);
  BEGIN
    IF SizeQueue > 0 THEN
      Data          := QueueData[HeadQueue];
      HeadQueue    := (HeadQueue MOD MaxQueue) + 1;
      SizeQueue    := SizeQueue - 1
    ELSE (* SizeQueue = 0 *)
      WriteLn;
      WriteString('Error: queue is empty, cannot remove object')
    END (* IF *)
  END RemoveFromQueue;

  PROCEDURE FullQueue() : CARDINAL;
  (* RETURN 0 if the queue is not full
    RETURN 1 if the queue is full *)
```

```
BEGIN
  IF SizeQueue = MaxQueue THEN
    RETURN 1
  ELSE (* SizeQueue < MaxQueue *)
    RETURN 0
  END (* IF *)
END FullQueue;

PROCEDURE EmptyQueue() : CARDINAL;
(* RETURN 0 if the queue is not empty
   RETURN 1 if the queue is empty *)
BEGIN
  IF SizeQueue = 0 THEN
    RETURN 1
  ELSE (* SizeQueue > 0 *)
    RETURN 0
  END (* IF *)
END EmptyQueue;

PROCEDURE LengthOfQueue() : CARDINAL;
BEGIN
   RETURN SizeQueue
END LengthOfQueue;

(*... Special declarations for the test data are inserted here ...*)

BEGIN
  (*... Queue initialisation statements go here ...*)
  (*...This section can be used to contain test programs for the
      procedures.
   ...*)
END QueueModule.
```

Fig. 5.17.

Testing the Module

An important stage after writing a collection of procedures such as these is to remove errors from the code. The compiler reports obvious syntax errors and picks up some more difficult errors, but errors in what the programmer is trying to achieve are much harder to discover. The following points are aids to error elimination.

1. A precise statement of what is to be achieved by the program must be available. If it is not then it is hard to spot errors.

2. It is extremely difficult to write programs without errors, but it is even more difficult to find errors after they have been introduced.

3. Except for trivial programs, testing can never be exhaustive so tests will only ever discover errors, they will not prove that no more errors exist.

4.   Most errors occur at the boundaries of events, at initialisation or when selections are made or when loops start and finish or accessing data structures which are full or are empty. Boundaries should be carefully checked when writing programs and in the subsequent testing.

5.   Finding that an error exists is not the same as correcting the error. Even if the correction seems obvious, be careful since the original error is likely to be due to a misunderstanding of what the program needed to do. It is important to see clearly both the source and the reason for the error, otherwise one error is likely to be replaced by another.

6.   Since most errors are caused by a misunderstanding of what the program should do or what a piece of code does, it is useful to check carefully for further errors close to where an error has been found. A lack of understanding is quite likely to lead to more than one error.

The queue manipulaton procedures can be tested using the module body as a test program. By applying a planned series of insertions and removals it is possible to search for errors in the performance.

The test program can be very simple, it need only allow insertions and deletions and write out details of the queue after each update. To enable this to work effectively it is necessary to make the array representing the queue very small. In this case a size of four is chosen as suitable. Despite the crudity of the test program it is developed using top down techniques. The method used here is a general one of considerable usefulness, stepwise refinement using pseudo code.

```
BEGIN (* Test program for QueueModule *)
    (*... Initialise the queue ...*);
    (*... Write an insertion/removal/end message ...*);
    (*... Read an insertion/removal/end answer ...*);
    WHILE (*... insertion/removal ...*) DO
        IF (*... insertion ...*) THEN
            (*... insert a newly generated item ...*)
        ELSE
            (*... remove an item ...*)
        END (* IF *);
        (*... Write out the queue abstraction ...*);
        (*... Write out empty, full, length tests ...*);
        (*... Write an insertion/removal/end message ...*);
        (*... Read an insertion/removal/end answer ...*);
    END (* WHILE *)
END QueueModule.
```

Fig. 5.18.

The basic steps of the program are laid out in code involving instructions written in English which are structured by the use of the Modula-2 syntax for sequence, selection and repetition. This is illustrated in Fig. 5.18. Normally the most important code phrase is chosen for refinement as it is most likely to lead to critical structural decisions, but in this case they are all straightforward, the completed module body is shown in Fig. 5.19.

```
MODULE QueueModule;
    (*... Add ReadCard,WriteCard to the IMPORT list from InOut ...*)
    (* Declarations of constants and variables to represent the queue
        as in Fig. 5.17 but with MaxQueue = 4. *)
    (* Procedures for manipulating the queue as in Fig 5.17. *)

    VAR
        Count,Data,Counter,How,RemOrIns: CARDINAL;
BEGIN
    (* initialise the queue *)
    HeadQueue := 1;
    EndQueue  := MaxQueue;
    SizeQueue  := 0;
    Counter := 0;
    WHILE Counter <> MaxQueue DO
        INC(Counter);
        QueueData[Counter] := 0
    END (* WHILE *);

    (* test the queue *)
    Count: = 1;(* Used to generate a unique data value for the queue *)
    WriteString('Type 0 for add, 1 for remove,other end'); WriteLn;
    ReadCard(RemOrIns);
    WHILE RemOrIns < 2 DO
        IF RemOrIns = 0 THEN
            AddToQueue(Count);
            INC(Count)
        ELSE
            RemoveFromQueue(Data)
        END (* IF *);

        Counter := 0;
        WriteString('The queue is'); WriteLn;
        WHILE Counter <> MaxQueue DO
            INC(Counter);
            WriteCard(QueueData[Counter],3)
        END (* WHILE *);
        WriteLn;
        WriteString('Head = ');      WriteCard(HeadQueue,3);      WriteLn;
        WriteString('End  = ');      WriteCard(EndQueue,3);       WriteLn;
        WriteString('Length = ');    WriteCard(SizeQueue,3);      WriteLn;
        How := FullQueue();
```

```
              WriteString('FullQueue ');        WriteCard(How,3);              Writeln;
              How := EmptyQueue();
              WriteString('EmptyQueue ');       WriteCard(How,3);              WriteLn;
              WriteString('Length ');           WriteCard(LengthOfQueue(),3);  WriteLn;

              WriteString('Type 0 for add, 1 for remove,other end');          WriteLn;
              ReadCard(RemOrIns);
         END (* WHILE *);
      END QueueModule.
```

Fig. 5.19.

Figure 5.20 shows a table of suitable test data and the kind of planning that goes into generating test data. The programmer writes this table to predict the values of the variables after particular operations and sequences of operations are performed. Note that no data is entered without a reason and that tests at boundaries dominate. The tests are dependent on the data structure that represents the queue, but are largely independent of the code within the procedures. It is often useful to generate test data before the detailed code is written as this can lead to more carefully written code.

Test Steps	Result				Head	End	Length	Reason for the Test
	Queue							
1 initial	0	0	0	0	1	4	0	
2 remove	0	0	0	0	1	4	0	invalid initial remove
3 four additions	1	2	3	4	1	4	4	fill the queue with valid additions
4 add	1	2	3	4	1	4	4	invalid addition
5 remove	1	2	3	4	2	4	3	valid removal
6 add	5	2	3	4	2	1	4	add: MOD tested
7 add	5	2	3	4	2	1	4	invalid add, after MOD
8 four removals	5	2	3	4	2	1	0	remove: MOD tested. Only Length has changed!
9 remove	5	2	3	4	2	1	0	invalid remove
10 add	5	6	3	4	2	2	1	start queue, non initial
11 remove	5	6	3	4	3	2	0	removal just after start

Fig. 5.20.

The test data presented here is by no means exhaustive, but all of it is chosen for a specific reason. Nevertheless, it is a fundamental precept that testing is a necessary evil and is no substitute for a carefully planned and implemented program. It is almost better that a person other than the programmer tests the program, as most people wish their programs to be correct and so do not test as carefully as they might. This is unprofessional. Instead you should take the view that the tests are designed to raise the confidence level of the correctness of the program. Testing should stop only when no errors have been found recently! The subject of testing will be discussed in the context of other programs, but it is a large topic. If you find it interesting, and you should, consult the references in the bibliography under the heading **Program Development**.

5.5 GUIDELINES FOR PROGRAM DEVELOPMENT

The points made in this section are general and require experience before they can be put into practice as a matter of routine, so do not worry if they seem difficult when you first try to apply them. They are based on top down design, but remember that a liberal amount of bottom up analysis may also be necessary.

General Principles

1 Goal Oriented Development

Program development essentially consists of defining a set of goals and then finding solutions to achieve these goals. This is the case at different levels of the problem solution, from a statement of what the entire program is to achieve to the detail of using constructs in the language. These differing levels can be categorised
1.   the program. This is a specification of what the program should do.
2.   a collection of procedures accessing a data structure. This is a specification of how the data structure should behave and the goal of each procedure.
3.   a procedure in isolation. This requires a specification of the goal of the procedure.
4.   individual statements and groups of statements. These can be considered as contributing to achieving a goal. For example the goal of a WHILE statement is for the loop to terminate with some required property holding.

A further important idea is that of **interfaces** between programs and between parts of a program. For example the entire program interfaces with the outside world through the keyboard and the visual display screen and input and output statements. The interface between a procedure and the rest of a program is its procedure heading and any access it has to variables declared outside of itself. Individual statements interface with each other in the way that they affect variables and set up particular states which allow other statements to be executed.

Throughout the book we will try to encourage you to think in terms of the goals which a module or procedure or Modula-2 construct is trying to achieve, and to then consider what needs to be the case initially in order that the goal can be achieved.

2 Pseudo Code: design of statement sequences

The use of pseudo code, as in the preliminary analysis for Fig. 5.18, is a powerful technique. It is based on the three kinds of statement, sequence, selection and repetition. The syntax of the language is maintained as far as is practical and at each stage refinements are made to the sections of pseudo code which seem most critical. Eventually all the pseudo code is converted to Modula-2 code.

Selection statements are typically of the form

```
IF (*... some cases ...*) THEN
   (*... make the goal true for 'some cases' ...*)
ELSE (* all other cases *)
   (*... achieve the goal for 'all other cases' ...*)
END (* IF *)
(* goal is achieved *)
```

Repetition statements are typically of the form

```
(*... initialise data for the WHILE statement ...*);
WHILE (*... goal is not yet true ...*) DO
   (*... make some progress towards the goal ...*)
END (* WHILE *);
(* goal is achieved *)
```

Whenever possible the pseudo code should be written in this goal-oriented fashion. That is, try to state the goal first and then work towards this goal by choosing pseudo-code constructs and instructions to establish the goal so that eventually the conditions which must pertain prior to the pseudo-code constructs are determined.

3   *Pseudo Code: data structure development*

Refinement of pseudo code is not solely concerned with writing statements, it is also concerned with decisions regarding the introduction of variables and collections of variables representing data structures. A basic principle is that data structures should be designed and introduced when a refinement of a piece of pseudo code cannot be done without knowledge of the data structure. This kind of decision may be implicit in the specification of the problem or it may be quite a late decision during the coding phase. Usually there is no problem with individual variables. Their types should be specified and an expressive name chosen to indicate their purpose with an accompanying comment if the purpose cannot be adequately expressed by a name.

Larger structures of data are more problematic. At the moment the only candidate for large amounts of data storage is the array, but try to avoid a reflex action of introducing an array every time a large data area is needed. Later, other possibilities will become apparent.

However, as the queue example shows clearly, there are many ways in which an array can be used and it may be better to hide the general properties of the array from view by allowing only specific procedures to act on the data structure. It follows that when a requirement is found for a data structure the first reaction should be a very careful consideration of the kind of behaviour required of the data structure and to design the structure and procedures to provide this kind of behaviour. It is a disadvantage if the structure is able to exhibit other kinds of unnecessary behaviour. The important attribute of an array which makes it so important is that any array item can be accessed very efficiently by stipulating its relative position in the array. This powerful property makes it a suitable choice for many data structures. If the full power of the array is not required then it is wise to protect the array from the rest of the program by providing procedures to access the array which restrict the normal operations that can be performed on them.

In passing it is worth noting two properties of arrays which restrict their usefulness and may result in other Modula-2 structures being used.
1.   An array must be declared as a fixed size, so it can waste space if the maximum space required is much larger than the average. In some cases the maximum cannot be sensibly specified.
2.   An array holds items of precisely the same type so it is not useful, in its simple form, for cases where the type of the items may vary.

In general, the problem of choosing a data structure involves implementing the required structure by using an appropriate combination of the variables of types provided in Modula-2. Thus the queue is developed by using an array in combination with three CARDINAL variables specifing the head, end and length of the queue. The subject of implementing complex data structures is an important topic in its own right in Computer Science. Do not be restricted in your thinking by the basic facilities of the language. The basic structures in Modula-2 are a starting point for constructing more complex objects which act like the structures you require.

4 *Refinement Techniques*

On the basis of the ideas of the previous sections it is possible to lay down some criteria for the choice of refinements of a pseudo code program outline.

a *Independence*

Refinements should be chosen to be as independent of one another as possible. Given a choice between two ways of refining a piece of pseudo code look at the interfaces between the proposed refinements. Normally the simpler the interface, the better the refinement. This corresponds with the idea that, whenever possible, code should be written as separate procedures. Relative independence tends to produce pseudo code which contains the potential for construction as a procedure.

Certain parts of pseudo code are by their nature closely interfaced with other parts of the code. An example of this is the initialisation before a WHILE statement. It is almost certain that any initialisation will be refined immediately after refining the WHILE body. Note that the initialisation code is usually written after the more critical code of the WHILE body has been written as decisions made in refining the WHILE body may affect the kind of initialisation required.

b *Critical choice*

The order in which pseudo code should be refined is important and some ground rules are
i. Only pseudo code at a particular level is refined at any one time. Refinements of refinements are not considered until the complete code has been rewritten so that the overall top down structure has been checked.
ii. At a given stage only pseudo code statements of greatest difficulty or importance are refined. In addition only refinements of the same order of difficulty are attempted before the complete code is rewritten.

c *Level of refinement*

It is better to proceed slowly with refinements and break any one section of pseudo code into at most four or five sub-refinements. This reduces the complexity of the detail to be considered at any one time.

5 *Procedure Development*

The decision to make a pseudo code statement into a procedure is dependent on the criteria adopted for using procedures. These can vary from program to program, but include

a.   a section of code that performs an identifiable operation which is used in more than one place in the program.

b.   a section of code which carries out tasks almost completely independent of the rest of the code (e.g. output procedures).

c.   a section of code which carries out a particular operation on a data structure.

Once a decision has been made to write a procedure, it should be treated as a separate sub-problem. The decision as to when it is written depends on how separate its data structures are from the rest of the program, but certainly it should be developed in its entirety and separately from the program which uses it. Thus the decision to make a part of the code a procedure can result in a quite different development order.

Programming is difficult and you must not expect to find it easy just because you know a few guidelines. The act of refining is often pragmatic. An initial hazy version of how to solve the problem frequently turns out to be inadequate and this applies as much to individual subgoals as to the overall goal. Even very experienced and talented programmers find that they have to rewrite many of their refinements. This implies that you should always keep a record of your refinements as a way of documenting the program design to help with subsequent modifications. It is much easier to modify a program which includes design documentation than it is to modify bare code. By modifying the pseudo code first the overall integrated design can be maintained. Changes made to the program code, with no account taken of the overall design, tend to produce a badly constructed program which is hard to understand and modify further. Thus a program which started life as well designed and readable code can end up as a disorganised series of patches which no one understands properly. Many of the programming exercises are designed as maintenance problems and these should be solved on the basis of making refinements.

TECHNICAL EXERCISES

1 Find any violations of scope rules in the following code fragments.

a
```
MODULE Test;
    CONST
        Sample = 42;
        Universe = Sample ;
    VAR
        Guide : CHAR;
    PROCEDURE Galaxy(Hiker:CARDINAL);
        VAR
        Guide : CARDINAL;
    BEGIN
            .
        Guide := 'e';
            .
    END Galaxy;
BEGIN
            .
    Guide := Universe;
            .
END Test.
```

b
```
MODULE WhatScope;
    CONST
        First = 1;
        Second = Third;
    VAR
        Count : CARDINAL;
    CONST
        Third = First;
            .
            .
END WhatScope .
```

c
```
MODULE IsScope;
    PROCEDURE Idea(A:CARDINAL);
        VAR
        A,B : CARDINAL;
        ...

END IsScope .
```

d
```
MODULE NoScope;
    VAR
        A,B : CARDINAL;
    PROCEDURE Idea(A:CARDINAL);
        ...

END NoScope .
```

2 State the output when the following modules are executed.

a

```
MODULE TestValue;
    FROM InOut IMPORT WriteCard,WriteLn;
    VAR
            D,E : CARDINAL;
    PROCEDURE Result (VAR A : CARDINAL;
                               B : CARDINAL);
        VAR
            C : CARDINAL;
    BEGIN
      C := 1;
      WriteCard(A,6);
      WriteCard(B,6);
      WriteCard(C,6);
      WriteLn;
      A := 7;
      B := 8
    END Result;

BEGIN
  D := 20;
  E := 10;
  Result(D,E+20);
END TestValue.
```

b

```
MODULE TestValue;
    FROM InOut IMPORT WriteCard,WriteLn;
    VAR
            A,C : CARDINAL;
    PROCEDURE Result (VAR A : CARDINAL;
                               B : CARDINAL);
        VAR
            C : CARDINAL;
    BEGIN
      C := 1;
      WriteCard(A,6);
      WriteCard(B,6);
      WriteCard(C,6);
      WriteLn;
      A := 7;
      B := 8
    END Result;

BEGIN
  A := 3;
  C := 4;
  Result(A,C);
  WriteCard(A,6);
  WriteCard(C,6)
END TestValue.
```

3 The text suggests that 'boundaries' should be carefully tested. State what the boundaries are in QueueModule.

4 Check whether or not the test data for QueueModule causes every statement of the module to be executed at least once.

5 Is it a matter for concern that the test program in QueueModule's module body is more complicated than the procedures which manipulate the queue?

PROGRAMMING EXERCISES

1 The internal testing for QueueModule is incomplete in a serious way (remember practical testing is always incomplete) because it does not check that Data, the object removed from the queue, is correct. It is a common error that variables like Data have incorrect values (why?), so add this check into the test program and retest the module.

2 Sometimes programs fail in degenerate cases. Try testing QueueModule when MaxQueue has the sizes 2 and 1.

3 Change the internal testing routine to print out a '?' when an array position is not in the queue. This makes the output easier to read. Explain why, even though it makes the output easier to read, it is not an improvement as a test program.

4 An alternative internal representation of the queue is to have EndQueue pointing at the next free location in the queue rather than the last item entered. Reconstruct QueueModule using this representation.

5 Construct a version of QueueModule which does not contain a procedure giving the length of the queue. On this basis implement the queue without an internal variable which holds the length.

6 Add a procedure to QueueModule which makes the queue empty. In effect it should discard any items in the queue.

7 Add a procedure to QueueModule which returns the head item in the queue without removing the item. That is, the queue remains unchanged as a result of a call of the procedure.

8 A stack is a data structure similar to a queue except that the most recently added object is the one first removed. If the numbers 1,2,3 are added to a stack in that order, then they are removed in the order 3,2,1. Write a module called Stack to implement a stack.

Typical procedures are

>   AddToStack (often called Push)
>   RemoveFromStack (often called Pop)
>   LookAtTopOfStack (without removing the item)
>   EmptyStack
>   FullStack

Develop comprehensive test programs and data to test the stack.

ANSWERS

1   a Guide := 'e' is a syntax error as the identifier Guide represents a CARDINAL variable at this point of the module.
Guide := Universe is a syntax error as the identifier Guide represents a CHAR variable at this point of the module.

b The declaration Second = Third is a syntax error because the declaration of Third, used in defining Second, does not textually precede the declaration of Second.

c The declaration A,B: CARDINAL is a syntax error since this tries to declare a second meaning to A within the procedure Idea. This is because the formal value parameter A is a declaration local to the procedure.

d There are no syntax errors in this code fragment.

2   a   20   30   1
      b   3   4   1
                  7   4

3   There are two structures that have boundaries
     a the queue, with boundaries empty, full
     b the array, with boundaries empty, full.

Commentary on the boundaries. The queue is the logical unit and the array is the program structure unit. The boundaries do not normally coincide. The array boundaries are concerned with checking that the references to positions of the array do not go outside those that exist, e.g. QueueData[0] or QueueData[5]. The queue boundaries are concerned with whether there are no items in the queue or whether there are four items in the queue. The test data checks all four boundaries, some of them in combination. A check of a boundary should investigate, the last legal possibility and the first illegal possibility. There is a fundamental difference in the queue and array checks, the queue checks are independent of the implementation, but the array checks can only be written after it is known how the queue is implemented. Thus the queue checks can be written before the code is written (though there is a slight problem about what 'full' means), but the array checks can only be written after certain design decisions have been made about the code.

4   All the procedures of the module are called and the initialisation is checked to begin with, so the only problem arises with the conditional statements (there are no WHILE statements in the procedures).
     a AddToQueue
         test step 3 causes the IF statement's condition to be true and execution of the first statement sequence

test step 4 causes the IF statement's condition to be false and execution of the second statement sequence (the ELSE alternative)

b RemoveFromQueue

test step 5 causes the IF statement's condition to be true and execution of the first statement sequence

test step 2 causes the IF statement's condition to be false and execution of the second statement sequence (the ELSE alternative)

c FullQueue

test step 4 causes the IF statement's condition to be true and execution of the first statement sequence

test step 3 causes the IF statement's condition to be false and execution of the second statement sequence (the ELSE alternative)

d EmptyQueue

test step 2 causes the IF statement's condition to be true and execution of the first statement sequence

test step 3 causes the IF statement's condition to be false and execution of the second statement sequence (the ELSE alternative)

e LengthOfQueue

all tests allow this to be completely executed.

It is easy to design test data which does not satisfy the criterion that every statement in the program should be executed at least once. Yet it is only a necessary condition on the adequacy of the test data. It is not nearly sufficient.

5 There are a number of major points to be made on this question.

a The test program is not very complicated, it is input/output statements that cause most of the apparent complexity.

b The danger of the test program being incorrect and giving answers which make the queue look correct when it is incorrect is small though it does happen occasionally.

c There is considerable danger of a test program giving false confidence because it does not test all aspects of a program, this is true of the test program under discussion! See the programming exercises for details.

The answer to the question is that it is a matter of concern, but that there are other problems with testing which are of higher priority.

Chapter 6

Implementation Modules

In preceding chapters the ideas of

a. declarations of constants and variables,

b. procedure declarations and procedure calls,

c. different kinds of modules,

d. scoping rules

have been introduced. In this chapter modules are discussed further. Implementation modules are discussed in detail and their use is illustrated. The advantages of organising a program such that it is contained in several modules are stressed.

To date, the use of other modules has focused exclusively on their use for importing procedures from other modules, however other kinds of objects can be imported from a module into other modules. In this chapter it is shown that these objects include variables and constants as well as procedures. A full understanding of modules requires revision of the idea of scope rules introduced in Chapter 5.

6.1 DEFINITION MODULES AND IMPLEMENTATION MODULES

Programs in previous chapters have used procedures from the module InOut to perform input from the keyboard and output to the visual display screen. In Chapter 4 a possible definition module of InOut is presented which provides the procedure headings for each of the procedures available in InOut. Chapter 4 also states that there exists a further module which contains the full declarations of these procedures.

A definition module is one part of a pair of modules. For every definition module there is a further module known as an **implementation module** which contains the full declarations of the procedures. The implementation module contains the code which implements the facilities provided by that module pair. The definition module provides sufficient information for that module pair to be used by other modules. It defines how the facilities provided in the implementation module should be used.

Figure 6.1 shows an abbreviated version of the definition module of InOut similar to that shown earlier in Fig. 4.22. A skeleton of the corresponding implementation module is shown in Fig. 6.2.

```
DEFINITION MODULE InOut ;
(* The early definition of Modula-2 required an explicit
   EXPORT QUALIFIED list here to stipulate what can be exported.
       EXPORT QUALIFIED ReadCard,WriteString,WriteCard,WriteLn ;
   This was later removed and anything that is included in the
   definition module can be exported from the implementation module *)

PROCEDURE WriteString (s : ARRAY OF CHAR) ;
    (* writes the sequence of characters in s *)

PROCEDURE WriteCard (x,n: CARDINAL) ;
    (* writes the value of the CARDINAL parameter x in a fieldwidth of n characters wide *)

PROCEDURE WriteLn ;
    (* starts a new line *)

PROCEDURE ReadCard (VAR x : CARDINAL) ;
    (* reads a value into the variable parameter x *)

END InOut .
```

Fig. 6.1.

```
IMPLEMENTATION MODULE InOut ;
    (* Import objects required by the implementation module
       from other modules. *)

PROCEDURE WriteString (s : ARRAY OF CHAR) ;
    (* any local declarations for WriteString *)
BEGIN
    (* statements to write out the sequence of characters in s *)
END WriteString ;

PROCEDURE WriteCard (x,n : CARDINAL) ;
    (* any local declarations for WriteCard *)
BEGIN
    (* statements to perform writing of the CARDINAL value in x *)
END WriteCard ;

PROCEDURE WriteLn ;
    (* any local declarations for WriteLn *)
BEGIN
    (* statements to perform start a new line *)
END WriteLn ;

PROCEDURE ReadCard (VAR x : CARDINAL) ;
    (* any local declarations for ReadCard *)
BEGIN
    (* statements to read a CARDINAL value into x *)
END ReadCard ;
END InOut .
```

Fig. 6.2.

Several points are noteworthy.

1. An implementation module begins with the words IMPLEMENTATION MODULE, the corresponding definition module begins with the words DEFINITION MODULE. Both modules have the same name, InOut in this case, which occurs at the top and at the end of the module.

2. Both implementation and definition modules can import items from other modules, this is often the case with implementation modules but is more rare with definition modules. The implementation module for InOut may actually use procedures provided in further modules, but the programmer using InOut does not need to know this. These are imported into the implementation module of InOut but not into its definition module.

3. The implementation module contains the full definition of the procedures. This means that the procedure heading occurs in full in the implementation module as it does in the definition module and that the procedure bodies contain statements for performing the operation provided by the procedure. Each of the procedures may have local declarations as with any other procedure declaration.

In the early definition of the language it was necessary for a definition module to include an **export list** shown as a comment in Fig. 6.1. This redundantly listed the names of objects which the definition module allowed to be imported into other modules. It was later removed from the language definition. The entire definition module, therefore, can now be understood as a list of items which are exportable from the corresponding implementation module. However, some implementations of Modula-2 may not have been updated yet, in which case the names will have to be listed after the words EXPORT QUALIFIED at the top of the definition module. Throughout this chapter we will include such an export list in a comment at the top of definition modules as a reminder that this might be necessary, but through the rest of the book we will omit such comments.

In Fig. 6.2 the full declarations of the procedures have been replaced by comments. These comments are different in kind from those in the definition module. In the definition module the comments are written by the programmer who wrote the definition module so that other programmers can use the corresponding implementation module appropriately. The comments in the implementation module have been written by us (the authors) to avoid telling you (the reader) the actual statements needed to provide each procedure. If you have been writing Modula-2 programs, as suggested in the programming exercises, you will have already used these procedures without having to know precisely how they work.

Let us consider how input and output to the visual display screen could be easier if we had some further procedures available which performed higher

level operations than those provided in InOut and would allow other modules
to be shorter. For example in Chapter 4 a procedure WriteLnString was declared
as starting a new line and then writing a message. A call to this procedure
shortens other statement sequences and reduces the likelihood of forgetting a
call of WriteLn which would result in poor formatting of the output on the
screen. The complementary statement sequence of writing an array of characters and then starting a new line may also be useful. A further useful
procedure, WriteStringCard starts a new line and writes a sequence of characters
and a CARDINAL value in a specified fieldwidth. Procedure headings for these
procedures will then be included in the definition module.

```
PROCEDURE WriteLnString (Message : ARRAY OF CHAR) ;
PROCEDURE WriteStringLn (Message : ARRAY OF CHAR) ;
PROCEDURE WriteStringCard (Message : ARRAY OF CHAR ;
                           CardVal ,
                           FieldWidth : CARDINAL) ;
```

There are other common sequences of statements for accepting information from the keyboard which have been required in the modules shown so
far. Typically when input is required a message is written out to inform the
user what information is required and this often starts on a new line. The kind
of reply which is required may vary, for example on occasions a CARDINAL
value is to be input and on other occasions a sequence of characters is
required. Two useful procedures would be a procedure which starts a new
line, asks a question and accepts a CARDINAL value as a reply, and a procedure
which again starts a new line, asks a question but accepts a sequence of
characters as a reply. The procedure headings for these might be

```
PROCEDURE NewCardValue (Message : ARRAY OF CHAR) : CARDINAL ;
PROCEDURE OpenEndedQuestion (Question : ARRAY OF CHAR ;
                             VAR Reply: ARRAY OF CHAR) ;
```

which again would be included in the definition module. A further common
sequence of statements is concerned with asking a yes/no question and accepting a valid response of Y or N. The module can contain another function
procedure, similar to NewCardValue, to perform this operation whose procedure heading is

```
PROCEDURE YesNoQuestion (Question : ARRAY OF CHAR) : CHAR ;
```

Question will be written out on a new line and the character Y or N will be
returned as the result of the procedure.

The entire definition module now looks like that shown in Fig. 6.3. This
can then be compiled so that other modules can import procedures from

MoreInOut and be compiled. It is also necessary for this definition module to be compiled before MoreInOut's implementation module can be compiled.

```
DEFINITION MODULE MoreInOut ;

(* EXPORT QUALIFIED WriteLnString,WriteStringLn,NewCardValue,
                    OpenEndedQuestion,YesNoQuestion ; *)

PROCEDURE WriteLnString (Message : ARRAY OF CHAR) ;
  (* starts a new line and then writes out Message. *)

PROCEDURE WriteStringLn (Message : ARRAY OF CHAR) ;
  (* writes out the message and then starts a new line. *)

PROCEDURE WriteStringCard (Message : ARRAY OF CHAR ;
                           CardVal ,
                           FieldWidth : CARDINAL) ;
  (* starts a new line, writes the message and then writes the
     CARDINAL value CardVal in the specified FieldWidth. *)

PROCEDURE NewCardValue (Question : ARRAY OF CHAR) : CARDINAL ;
  (* starts a new line, writes out Question and accepts
     a sequence of numeric characters terminated by any non-numeric
     character, and converts these to the corresponding CARDINAL
     value which is returned as its result. *)

PROCEDURE OpenEndedQuestion (Question : ARRAY OF CHAR ;
                             VAR Reply : ARRAY OF CHAR) ;
  (* starts a new line, writes out Question accepts
     an array of characters terminated by any character
     whose ordinal value is 32 or less, and passes this
     character sequence back in Reply. *)

PROCEDURE YesNoQuestion (Question : ARRAY OF CHAR) : CHAR ;
  (* start a new line, writes out Question and accepts a character
     as a reply to the question. If the character is 'Y' or 'y'
     then the result is the character 'Y', otherwise 'N' is returned
     as its result. *)

END MoreInOut .
```

Fig. 6.3.

Figure 6.4 shows a short module called CubesOfNumbers which uses some of these procedures and WriteLn and WriteString from InOut. CubesOfNumbers can be compiled if the definition module of MoreInOut has been compiled. However, it cannot be linked or executed yet. Linking is a stage where separately compiled modules are combined together to produce an executable program. This is only possible once the implementation module of MoreInOut has been written and compiled.

The definition module can be thought of as a control panel on the front of a definition and implementation module pair. It allows other modules to use it correctly, similar to the control panel on the front of a television set or washing machine which allows people to use them appropriately. The comments in the definition module function as a manual providing additional necessary information. It follows that the implementation module must be consistent with the definition module — a control on a washing machine labelled 'spin speed' is not expected to control the water temperature.

```
MODULE CubesOfNumbers ;
  FROM MoreInOut      IMPORT WriteLnString, YesNoQuestion,
                            NewCardValue, WriteStringCard ;
  CONST
      Again           = 'Do you wish to find the cube of a further number?' ;
  VAR
      Number          : CARDINAL ;
      DoItAgain       : CHAR ;

  PROCEDURE CubeOf (N : CARDINAL) : CARDINAL ;
      (* Assumes N*N*N is not greater than the largest CARDINAL value *)
  BEGIN
    RETURN N * N * N
  END CubeOf ;

BEGIN
  WriteLnString ('Cubes Of Numbers.') ;
  DoItAgain := 'Y' ;
  WHILE DoItAgain = 'Y' DO
      Number := NewCardValue ('Type the number – ') ;
      WriteStringCard ('Its cube is – ',CubeOf(Number),8) ;
      DoItAgain := YesNoQuestion(Again) ;
  END (* WHILE *) ;
END CubesOfNumbers .
```

Fig. 6.4.

In the implementation module of MoreInOut each of the procedures whose headings are listed in the definition module has to be declared in full. Initially we can take the definition module and substitute the word DEFINITION by IMPLEMENTATION. Each of the procedure headings can be changed to a dummy procedure by adding END, the procedure name and a semi-colon as illustrated in Fig. 6.5. Note that the implementation module must not redeclare these identifier names as some other object, such as a variable. Any inconsistency between the implementation and definition modules is reported as an error by the Modula-2 compiler when the implementation module is compiled.

```
IMPLEMENTATION MODULE MoreInOut ;

PROCEDURE WriteLnString (Message : ARRAY OF CHAR) ;
    (* starts a new line and then writes out Message. *)
END WriteLnString ;

PROCEDURE WriteStringLn (Message : ARRAY OF CHAR) ;
    (* writes out the message and then starts a new line. *)
END WriteStringLn ;

PROCEDURE WriteStringCard (Message : ARRAY OF CHAR ;
                           CardVal ,
                           FieldWidth : CARDINAL) ;
    (* starts a new line, writes the message and then writes the
       CARDINAL value CardVal in the specified FieldWidth. *)
END WriteStringCard ;

PROCEDURE NewCardValue (Question : ARRAY OF CHAR) : CARDINAL ;
    (* starts a new line, writes out Question and accepts
       a sequence of numeric characters terminated by any non-numeric
       character, and converts these to the corresponding CARDINAL
       value which is returned as its result. *)
END NewCardValue ;

PROCEDURE OpenEndedQuestion (Question : ARRAY OF CHAR ;
                             VAR Reply : ARRAY OF CHAR) ;
    (* starts a new line, writes out Question accepts
       an array of characters terminated by any character
       whose ordinal value is 32 or less, and passes this
       character sequence back in Reply. *)
END OpenEndedQuestion ;

PROCEDURE YesNoQuestion (Question : ARRAY OF CHAR) : CHAR ;
    (* start a new line, writes out Question and accepts a character
       as a reply to the question. If the character is 'Y' or 'y'
       then the result is the character 'Y', otherwise 'N' is returned
       as its result. *)
END YesNoQuestion ;

END MoreInOut .
```

Fig. 6.5.

Figure 6.6 shows the completed implementation module. The procedure bodies for WriteLnString, WriteStringLn are straightforward. These procedures are global to the module so they are in scope for other procedures to use. WriteStringCard, OpenEndedQuestion, NewCardValue and YesNoQuestion can call them when needed. OpenEndedQuestion and NewCardValue use ReadString and ReadCard respectively to accept input from the keyboard.

YesNoQuestion is slightly more complex as some provision has to be made for the user typing characters other than 'Y' and 'N' and some provision should be made for the user typing these in their lower case equivalents 'y' and 'n'. One possible formulation of YesNoQuestion is shown in MoreInOut. This means that any character other than 'Y' or 'y' is interpreted as 'N', which may not be unreasonable but can cause problems in certain situatons. Suppose that a program editor asked a question

Do you wish to save your editing?

then if the user mistyped 'Y' and pressed another key instead this would be interpreted as 'N' and any editing would be discarded. If characters other than 'Y' and 'y' are to be interpreted as 'N' then this must be clearly documented in the definition module so that programmers using the procedure can phrase their questions to minimise the dangers of mistyping. In this example the question can be phrased as

Do you wish to discard your editing?

so that any mistyping of 'N' would have the consequence of saving the editing.

```
IMPLEMENTATION MODULE MoreInOut ;
  FROM InOut IMPORT WriteLn, WriteString, WriteCard,
                    ReadString, ReadCard, Read ;

  PROCEDURE WriteLnString (Message : ARRAY OF CHAR) ;
      (* starts a new line and then writes out Message. *)
  BEGIN
    WriteLn ;
    WriteString (Message)
  END WriteLnString ;

  PROCEDURE WriteStringLn (Message : ARRAY OF CHAR) ;
      (* writes out the message and then starts a new line. *)
  BEGIN
    WriteString (Message) ;
    WriteLn
  END WriteStringLn ;

  PROCEDURE WriteStringCard (Message : ARRAY OF CHAR ;
                             CardVal ,
                             FieldWidth : CARDINAL) ;
      (* starts a new line, writes the message and then writes the
         CARDINAL value CardVal in the specified FieldWidth. *)
  BEGIN
    WriteLnString (Message) ;
    WriteCard (CardVal,FieldWidth)
  END WriteStringCard ;
```

```
PROCEDURE NewCardValue (Question : ARRAY OF CHAR) : CARDINAL ;
      (* starts a new line, writes out Question and accepts
         a sequence of numeric characters terminated by any non-numeric
         character, and converts these to the corresponding CARDINAL
         value which is returned as its result. *)
   VAR
      Reply : CARDINAL ;
BEGIN
   WriteLnString (Question) ;
   ReadCard (Reply) ;
   RETURN Reply
END NewCardValue ;


PROCEDURE OpenEndedQuestion (Question : ARRAY OF CHAR ;
                                 VAR Reply : ARRAY OF CHAR) ;
      (* starts a new line, writes out Question accepts
         an array of characters terminated by any character
         whose ordinal value is 32 or less, and passes this
         character sequence back in Reply. *)
BEGIN
   WriteLnString (Question) ;
   ReadString (Reply) ;
END OpenEndedQuestion ;


PROCEDURE YesNoQuestion (Question : ARRAY OF CHAR) : CHAR ;
      (* start a new line, writes out Question and accepts a character
         as a reply to the question. If the character is 'Y' or 'y'
         then the result is the character 'Y', otherwise 'N' is returned
         as its result. *)
   VAR
      Reply : CHAR ;
BEGIN
   WriteLnString (Question) ;
   Read (Reply) ;
   Reply := CAP (Reply) ;
   IF Reply <> 'Y' THEN
      Reply := 'N' ;
   END (* IF *) ;
   RETURN Reply
END YesNoQuestion ;


END MoreInOut .
```

Fig. 6.6.

MoreInOut's implementation module can now be compiled and CubesOfNum-bers can then be linked and executed.

In Chapter 5 a module was developed to implement a data structure known as a queue. This was developed as a program module with a test program as its body. However, for other modules to be able to use the queue it is necessary to make this into an implementation module and to make the procedures which operate on the queue available through its definition module. Figure 6.7 shows the definition module consisting of the procedure headings for the operations which are made available from the implementation module to other modules.

QueueModule's implementation module is shown in Fig. 6.8. It is very similar to the program module in Chapter 5 with the code for testing the procedures removed. However, the variable declarations at the top of the module and the statements in the module body have special significance in an implementation module.

The way that AddToQueue and RemoveFromQueue report that an error has occurred, by writing out an error message, is inadequate. There are better ways of reporting errors from inside an implementation module which will be discussed at the end of the chapter.

```
DEFINITION MODULE QueueModule ;
  (* EXPORT QUALIFIED AddToQueue,RemoveFromQueue,FullQueue,EmptyQueue,
            LengthOfQueue ; *)

  PROCEDURE AddToQueue(Data : CARDINAL);
      (* Data is added as a new item at the end of the queue. *)

  PROCEDURE RemoveFromQueue(VAR Data : CARDINAL);
      (* The item at the front of the queue is removed and passed
         back in the variable parameter Data. *)

  PROCEDURE FullQueue () : CARDINAL ;
      (* RETURN 0 if the queue is not full
         RETURN 1 if the queue is full. *)

  PROCEDURE EmptyQueue () : CARDINAL ;
      (* RETURN 0 if the queue is not empty
         RETURN 1 if the queue is empty. *)

  PROCEDURE LengthOfQueue () : CARDINAL ;
      (* returns the current number of items in the queue.*)

  END QueueModule .
```

Fig. 6.7.

```
IMPLEMENTATION MODULE QueueModule ;
FROM MoreInOut IMPORT WriteLnString;


(* Data declarations which form an abstract representation of a queue of CARDINAL values.
*)
CONST
    MaxQueue = 1000;
VAR
    QueueData                              : ARRAY[1..MaxQueue] OF CARDINAL;
    HeadQueue,EndQueue,SizeQueue   : CARDINAL;

(* Procedures available for use by other modules because they are
  named in the definition module *)

PROCEDURE AddToQueue(Data : CARDINAL);
      (* Data is added as a new item at the end of the queue. *)
BEGIN
 IF SizeQueue < MaxQueue THEN
    EndQueue                     := (EndQueue MOD MaxQueue) + 1;
    QueueData[EndQueue]        := Data;
    SizeQueue                    := SizeQueue + 1
 ELSE (* SizeQueue = MaxQueue *)
    WriteLnString('Error : queue is full, no insertion allowed')
 END (*IF*)
END AddToQueue;


PROCEDURE RemoveFromQueue(VAR Data : CARDINAL);
      (* The item at the front of the queue is removed and passed
         back in the variable parameter Data. *)
BEGIN
 IF SizeQueue > 0 THEN
    Data              := QueueData[HeadQueue];
    HeadQueue         := (HeadQueue MOD MaxQueue) + 1;
    SizeQueue         := SizeQueue - 1
 ELSE (* SizeQueue = 0 *)
    WriteLnString('Error : queue is empty, cannot remove object')
 END (*IF*)
END RemoveFromQueue;


PROCEDURE FullQueue () : CARDINAL ;
      (* returns 0 if the queue is not full
                 1 if the queue is full. *)
BEGIN
 IF SizeQueue = MaxQueue THEN
    RETURN 1
 ELSE (* SizeQueue < MaxQueue *)
    RETURN 0
 END (*IF*)
END FullQueue;
```

```
PROCEDURE EmptyQueue () : CARDINAL ;
    (* returns 0 if the queue is not empty
                 1 if the queue is empty. *)
BEGIN
 IF SizeQueue = 0 THEN
    RETURN 1
 ELSE (* SizeQueue *)
    RETURN 0
 END (*IF*)
END EmptyQueue;

PROCEDURE LengthOfQueue () : CARDINAL ;
    (* returns the current number of items in the queue.*)
BEGIN
 RETURN SizeQueue
END LengthOfQueue;

BEGIN               (* Initialisation *)
 HeadQueue := 1 ;
 EndQueue   := MaxQueue ;
 SizeQueue := 0
END QueueModule .
```

Fig. 6.8.

An Implementation Module's Declarations

The declarations at the top of an implementation module can be used any-where within the module just like those in a program module. That is, the scope of these declarations is the entire module and they are said to be **global** to the module. However variables declared in the module's declarations exist throughout the entire time that a program is being executed. It is said that the **lifetime** of these variables is the entire program. This is in contrast to variables which are declared within procedures which are created and destroyed each time the procedure is called.

The implications of this are that the variables QueueData, HeadQueue, End-Queue, and SizeQueue exist throughout the entire time that any program which incorporates QueueModule is being executed. However these variables can only be accessed by the procedures in QueueModule's implementation module. This effectively hides them from the entire program, except for those parts in QueueModule's implementation module.

This ability to hide variables from other parts of a program is a major advantage of Modula-2. If it is found that QueueModule's global variables hold values known to be in error then the possible places from which the error(s) stems are limited to within QueueModule or to calls to the procedures provided by the module. Conversely if an implementation module has been thoroughly tested and shown to be reliable but a program which uses the module is not behaving correctly, then the code within that module can be discounted as being a source of the problem. The implementation module acts rather like a protective skin around its variables and procedures and the only parts of itself which it makes visible are those presented in its definition module. As already suggested it is possible to code the user module and compile it in the absence of QueueModule's implementation module.

Even more importantly, the implementation module could be completely rewritten and as long as the interface given in the definition module has not changed, the code in the user module does not require changing. Naturally this assumes that the semantics of QueueModule have not changed.

It should be noted that an implementation module does not have to make all procedures within it visible to other modules. Both MoreInOut and QueueModule export all the procedures declared in the implementation module. However procedures can be declared in an implementation module, for use by other procedures in the module, which are not exportable to other modules because their procedure headings are not included in the definition module. Examples of modules where this is the case will be seen shortly. For the present it is sufficient to note that the definition module determines which parts of the corresponding implementation module are visible and therefore directly accessible by other modules.

The Body of an Implementation Module — Initialisation

The general form of an implementation module is given in Fig. 6.9, it can optionally include a sequence of statements as the module body. This sequence of statements is executed once before the statement sequence of the body of the program module, thereby performing any initialisation needed within that module before the main program runs.

```
IMPLEMENTATION MODULE ModuleName ;
  FROM OtherModule IMPORT Whatever, Is, Needed ;

        ┌─────────────────────────────────────────┐
        │ Declarations of this modules global     │
        │ constants,variables and procedures      │
        └─────────────────────────────────────────┘

BEGIN
        ┌─────────────────────────────────────────┐
        │ Module Body – a sequence of statements  │
        └─────────────────────────────────────────┘
END ModuleName .
```

Fig. 6.9.

MoreInOut is exceptional in that it does not have any global variables of its own and therefore requires no initialisation. In QueueModule this initialisation is concerned with setting HeadQueue, EndQueue and SizeQueue to represent an empty queue. Most modules require some such initialisation. This applies to all modules including predefined modules.

```
MODULE QueueTest ;    (* A test module for QueueModule. *)
  FROM MoreInOut  IMPORT WriteLnString, NewCardValue, WriteStringCard ;
  FROM QueueModule IMPORT AddToQueue, RemoveFromQueue, FullQueue,
                          EmptyQueue, LengthOfQueue;
  VAR
      Count, RemOrIns, DataValue, IsIt : CARDINAL;
BEGIN
  Count := 0 ;
  RemOrIns := NewCardValue('Type 0 for add, 1 for remove, other end ');
  WHILE RemOrIns < 2 DO
      IF RemOrIns = 1 THEN
          RemoveFromQueue(DataValue);
          WriteStringCard('Data item removed is ',DataValue,6);
          IsIt := EmptyQueue();
          IF IsIt = 0 THEN
              WriteLnString('Queue is not empty');
          ELSE
              WriteLnString('Queue is empty');
          END(*IF*)
      ELSE
          INC (Count) ;
          AddToQueue(Count);
          WriteStringCard('Data item added is ',Count,6);
          IsIt := FullQueue();
          IF IsIt = 0 THEN
              WriteLnString('Queue is not full');
          ELSE
              WriteLnString('Queue is full');
          END(*IF*)
      END(*IF*);
      WriteStringCard('The length of the queue is now ',
                                              LengthOfQueue(),4);
      RemOrIns := NewCardValue('Type 0 for add, 1 for remove, other end ');
  END(*WHILE*)
END QueueTest.
```

Fig. 6.10.

Further Testing Of QueueModule

One of the elegant points about such modular programming is the near certainty that a tested module works properly in any circumstances for which it is designed. The testing carried out on QueueModule in Chapter 5 is effective in isolation, but it is always possible that the interface between the modules is incorrect. The Modula-2 compiler picks up any syntactic incompatibility, but errors across the boundaries can occur due to the fact that the use of global variables in the internal test module may have obscured an error. Figure 6.10 shows a program module which acts as a test of QueueModule's interface. It is well worthwhile implementing QueueModule and QueueTest to get used to the ideas of importing from modules of your own creation. Remember that QueueModule's definition module must be written and compiled before QueueTest is compiled, but QueueModule's implementation module can be written and compiled later.

Module Organisation

QueueTest is a complex program in its own right. It imports procedures from two other modules. In addition QueueModule's implementation module imports procedures from MoreInOut and MoreInOut's implementation module imports procedures from InOut. We can think of the structure between these modules as illustrated in Fig. 6.11.

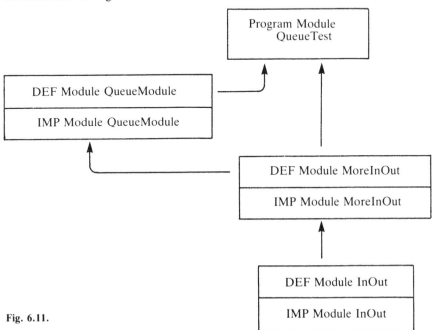

Fig. 6.11.

Program Modules, Definition Modules and Implementation Modules

Main program modules, definition modules and implementation modules are all termed **compilation units** as each can be compiled separately. Figure 6.12a shows simplified syntax diagrams for compilation units and those relevant to implementation modules and main program modules. Figure 6.12b shows those which are relevant to definition modules.

Compilation Unit :

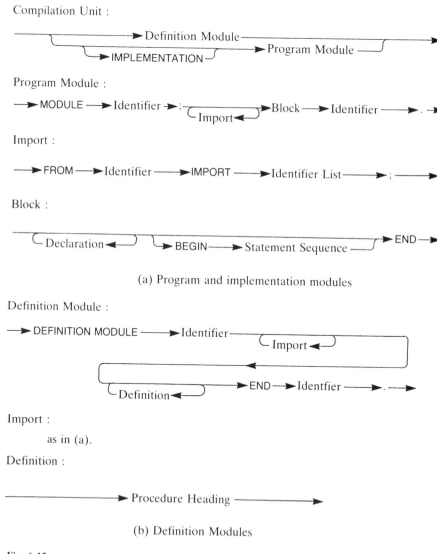

(a) Program and implementation modules

Import :

as in (a).

Definition :

(b) Definition Modules

Fig. 6.12.

Syntactically the only difference between a main program body and an implementation module is that the latter is introduced by the word IMPLE-MENTATION. Both consist of a block so that they can have their own declarations of constants, variables, types and procedures and both can have a module body consisting of a sequence of statements. However the purposes of main program modules and implementation modules are different, a main program module has overall control of a complete program. In contrast implementation modules provide a facility which is used by other modules. Implementation modules and the procedures within them are therefore subservient to a main program module which is controlling the program execution through the order in which procedures in the implementation module are called. The module body of an implementation module is subservient to the main program body, its purpose is to make any necessary initialisation to data structures within the implementation module, and therefore is executed **before** the body of the main program module is executed.

Definition modules are again compilation units, however they are syntactically very different to both main program modules and to implementation modules. Simplified syntax diagrams relevant to definition modules are given in Fig. 6.12b.

In contrast to program and implementation modules, definition modules consist of an optional sequence of import lists and a sequence of definitions. To date the definitions we have considered have only been concerned with the exporting of procedures but later in this chapter the syntax diagram of **Definition** will be expanded to include other Modula-2 constructs which can be exported from modules into other modules. Notice that a definition module does not involve a block and therefore does not contain a module body. This is because the purpose of definition modules is very different from those of main program modules and implementation modules. Whereas the latter two contain statements to be executed, definition modules are never executed and consequently do not contain constructs which allow statements in them. Their purpose is solely for reference so that the programmer (and the compiler) is able to know how to use the corresponding implementation module appropriately.

Usually the compiler will insist on certain orderings in which compilation units can be compiled. A definition module must be compiled
1. before its corresponding implementation module,
2. and before modules which import items from the corresponding module pair.

The first requirement is straightforward and insists that QueueModule's definition module must be compiled before its implementation module.

The second requirement means that the definition module for InOut must have been compiled before either MoreInOut's or QueueTest's implementation modules are compiled. This will normally have been done by the supplier of the compiler or someone responsible for looking after the compiler. In addition MoreInOut's definition module will have to be compiled before QueueModule's implementation module and QueueTest, though the order in which the last two are compiled with respect to each other is arbitrary.

These requirements on the ordering of compilation emphasise the primary role of definition modules as go-betweens for the implementation modules and other modules which use the facilities of the implementation module.

Development of Definition and Implementation Modules

There are several reasons for encapsulating procedures in an implementation module and definition module.

1.   The procedures provide some general operations which are required by numerous programs. For example, the procedures in InOut and MoreInOut.

2.   The procedures manipulate a data structure hidden in the implementation module, as in the case of QueueModule. Once the procedures have been tested and shown to behave correctly these can be largely discounted as a source of any errors in the program and therefore make debugging and maintaining a program easier.

3.   The solutions to many problems result in large programs. Such programs are written by identifying relatively self-contained sub-problems and developing their solutions as separate modules. Some of these modules will be more generally useful than others. The ability to develop and test modules independently allows large programs to be developed and tested in tandem and allows several programmers to work on the same program.

The common feature in all these cases is the way that modules are used to allow the programmer to develop a solution to some manageable part of an entire problem independently of the detail of the rest of the problem.

The definition module of a definition and implementation module pair is usually determined first so that the facilities provided in the module are known. However, the implementation module will often be developed as a program module so that the behaviour of the procedures can be tested in the module body. Later, when the procedures are believed to behave as required, the test program can be removed from the module body leaving only essential initialisation to convert the program module to an implementation module. The definition and implementation modules can then be compiled. A further test module should test that the interface to the implementation module presented by the definition module is adequate and permits the module to be used appropriately.

6.2   EXAMPLE. MODULAR DEVELOPMENT OF FREQUENCY COUNTING PROGRAMS

Consider a situation where a program is to be written which counts the number of occurrences of each of the vowels in a sequence of English sentences and presents a bar chart showing the frequency of each of the vowels. An initial formulation of the solution is shown in Fig. 6.13.

```
MODULE VowelCount ;
  (*... import lists and declarations ...*) ;
BEGIN
  (*... read a character ...*) ;
  (*... while the character does not indicate the end of the input text do
    (*... if the letter is in lower case
          convert it to upper case ...*) ;
    (*... if the letter is an upper case vowel then
          increment the count for that vowel ...*) ;
    (*... read a character ...*)
  end while ...*) ;
  (*... print the bar chart ...*)
END VowelCount .
```

Fig. 6.13.

Concentrating on the control structure of the solution and the reading of the characters this can be refined further using Modula-2 control structures and inclusion of suitable declarations to that shown in Fig. 6.14.

The parts of the problem still to be refined are concerned with incrementing the counts associated with the vowels and printing the bar chart. The sub-problem of printing the bar chart will have to refer to each of the counts associated with each vowel. This suggests that these sub-problems can be suitably developed within an implementation module which hides the detail of how the counts are represented and allows VowelCount to be completed without concern about this detail. Note that in VowelCount there is no mention of any variables which are used for counting the frequency of the vowels.

```
MODULE VowelCount ;
  FROM InOut          IMPORT Read ;
  FROM MoreInOut      IMPORT WriteStringLn ;
  CONST
        Terminator    = '*' ;
  VAR
        Ch            : CHAR ;
BEGIN
  WriteStringLn ('Type the text to be processed, and type *') ;
  WriteStringLn (' to indicate the end of the character sequence.') ;
  Read (Ch) ;
  WHILE Ch <> Terminator DO
      Ch := CAP(Ch) ;
      (*... if Ch is any of 'A','E','I','O','U'
                  increment the count for that vowel ...*) ;
      Read (Ch) ;
  END (* WHILE *) ;
  (*... print the bar chart ...*)
END VowelCount .
```

Fig. 6.14.

We shall call this second module Frequencies, it must provide two operations allowing

1. the count associated with any vowel to be incremented by one, and
2. the bar chart to be printed.

In order to permit these operations two procedures IncrementBy1 and BarChart will be assumed.

In order to increment one of the counts, Frequencies will have to know which one to increment, which suggests either passing the character or some other information determining which count should be incremented. For the present let us assume that the character will be passed as a parameter to IncrementBy1. The procedure headings for IncrementBy1 and BarChart could then be defined as

PROCEDURE IncrementBy1 (Ch : CHAR)

and

PROCEDURE BarChart

As the procedure headings have been determined we are now in a position to state what the definition module of Frequencies will look like. It will conform to the syntax of a definition module and will include these procedure headings (see Fig. 6.15).

```
DEFINITION MODULE Frequencies ;

(* EXPORT QUALIFIED IncrementBy1, BarChart ; *)

PROCEDURE IncrementBy1 (Ch : CHAR) ;
    (* increment the count associated with Ch by 1 *)

PROCEDURE BarChart ;
    (* draws a Bar Chart based upon the current values of the counts
      associated with characters *)

END Frequencies .
```

Fig. 6.15.

Vowelcount must now include an instruction in its import list to say that
these procedures are to be imported from Frequencies and can then call these
procedures in order to achieve the required operations as illustrated in Fig.
6.16.

```
MODULE VowelCount ;
  FROM Frequencies      IMPORT IncrementBy1, BarChart ;
  FROM InOut            IMPORT Read ;
  FROM MoreInOut        IMPORT WriteStringLn ;
  CONST
      Terminator        = '*' ;
  VAR
      Ch                : CHAR ;
BEGIN
  WriteStringLn ('Type the text to be processed, and type *') ;
  WriteStringLn ('to indicate the end of the character sequence.') ;
  Read (Ch) ;
  WHILE Ch <> Terminator DO
      Ch := CAP(Ch) ;
      IF Ch = 'A' THEN IncrementBy1 ('A') END (* IF *) ;
      IF Ch = 'E' THEN IncrementBy1 ('E') END (* IF *) ;
      IF Ch = 'I' THEN IncrementBy1 ('I') END (* IF *) ;
      IF Ch = 'O' THEN IncrementBy1 ('O') END (* IF *) ;
      IF Ch = 'U' THEN IncrementBy1 ('U') END (* IF *) ;
      Read (Ch) ;
  END (* WHILE *) ;
  BarChart ;
END VowelCount .
```

Fig. 6.16.

This only leaves Frequencies' implementation module to be written, which must declare the procedures IncrementBy1 and BarChart fully. Let us assume that the counts of the frequencies of the vowels are held within an array

    FrequencyArray : ARRAY [1..5] OF CARDINAL ;

IncrementBy1 has to determine which component of the array to use each time it is called and then add 1 to the current value of this component. BarChart has to take each of the values in the array and represent it graphically in some way, for example by a sequence of asterisks. These procedures are shown in a possible implementation module for Frequencies in Fig. 6.17.

```
IMPLEMENTATION MODULE Frequencies ;
FROM InOut IMPORT Write,WriteString,WriteLn ;
VAR
     FrequencyArray : ARRAY [1..5] OF CARDINAL ;

PROCEDURE IncrementBy1 (Ch : CHAR) ;
 VAR
     CategoryNo    : CARDINAL ;
 BEGIN
  IF Ch = 'A' THEN CategoryNo := 1 END ;
  IF Ch = 'E' THEN CategoryNo := 2 END ;
  IF Ch = 'I' THEN CategoryNo := 3 END ;
  IF Ch = 'O' THEN CategoryNo := 4 END ;
  IF Ch = 'U' THEN CategoryNo := 5 END ;
  INC(FrequencyArray[CategoryNo]) ;
 END IncrementBy1 ;

PROCEDURE BarChart ;
 VAR      Count, CategoryNo       : CARDINAL ;

 PROCEDURE WriteRowHeading ;
 BEGIN
   IF CategoryNo = 1 THEN WriteString ('A ') END ;
   IF CategoryNo = 2 THEN WriteString ('E ') END ;
   IF CategoryNo = 3 THEN WriteString ('I ') END ;
   IF CategoryNo = 4 THEN WriteString ('O ') END ;
   IF CategoryNo = 5 THEN WriteString ('U ') END ;
 END WriteRowHeading ;

BEGIN (* BarChart body *)
 WriteLn ;
 CategoryNo := 0 ;
 WHILE CategoryNo <> 5 DO
    INC (CategoryNo) ;
    WriteRowHeading ;
    Count := 0 ;
```

```
        WHILE Count <> FrequencyArray[CategoryNo] DO
              INC (Count) ;
              Write ('*') ;
        END (* WHILE *) ;
        WriteLn ;
   END (* WHILE *) ;
   END BarChart ;

VAR
   CatNo : CARDINAL;

BEGIN          (* Module Body − Initialisation *)
   CatNo := 0 ;
   WHILE CatNo <> 5 DO
        INC (CatNo) ;
        FrequencyArray[CatNo] := 0 ;
   END (* WHILE *) ;
END Frequencies.
```

Fig. 6.17.

Notice that Frequencies' implementation module does not make all procedures within it visible to other modules. WriteRowHeading is a procedure local to BarChart and so it can only be called from within BarChart. However, even if WriteRowHeading were not declared locally to BarChart other modules would not be able to call it directly as it is not included in the definition module. In addition the comments of Frequencies are imprecise because IncrementBy1 will not work if the character given to the procedure is not a vowel and the comment should be altered to reflect this.

An Alternative Organisation

VowelCount and Frequencies, when compiled and linked together, allow the frequency of vowels to be determined in a sequence of characters. However the solution illustrated in Figs. 6.15 to 6.17 is not a good example of how to use separate modules for different parts of a program.

The major failing is that both VowelCount and Frequencies are currently tied to the particular problem of counting vowels. VowelCount determines if a character is a vowel and then passes the character to IncrementBy1 in Frequencies. This determines which vowel it is and then increments the count for the vowel. Other situations may arise where the problem is concerned with determining the frequency of things other than vowels, for example all letters, or particular names, or the ranges of people's incomes. Particular subproblems in these problems would have similarities with the procedures provided in Frequencies and it would save a programmer time and effort if the procedures available in Frequencies were more generally useful.

The solution to the problem of counting vowels can be reformulated with a restriction that Frequencies must not make any assumptions about the categories of the things being counted. What implications does this have for Frequencies and for modules which use it?

1. A module using Frequencies must determine which count should be incremented so that IncrementBy1 only increments the appropriate count.

2. BarChart is not able to make any assumptions concerning the row headings for the categories. It is necessary for the programmer using Frequencies to tell the module what the row headings are.

3. Five categories are restrictive. Provision for a greater number of categories is useful. The programmer needs to inform Frequencies how many of the available categories he uses in his program.

Figures 6.18 and 6.19 give an alternative formulation of Frequencies to allow for these modifications. IncrementBy1 and BarChart have the same effects as before, however IncrementBy1 has to be passed a CARDINAL value indicating which count the Frequencies module should increment. A procedure Associate associates a heading, which will be used on the bar chart, with a CARDINAL value. Hence a call

```
Associate ( 1 , 'Red Cars' )
```

associates the heading 'Red Cars' with the first category and calls of

```
IncrementBy1 (1)
```

increment this category by 1. When the bar chart is printed the heading 'Red Cars' will be printed, and the number of asterisks printed against this category heading will be the same as the number of times IncrementBy1 is called with 1 as its actual parameter.

The headings in Frequencies' implementation module are held in a character array. This array holds all the headings with the heading for category 1 is held in the first 20 characters, the heading for category 2 in the second group of 20 characters, etc. When Associate and BarChart have to pick out individual headings, GetStartAndFinishOfCategoryName is called to indicate the starting and finishing positions in the array. There are easier ways of manipulating an array to hold category names in Modula-2 which will be discussed in Chapter 10.

```
DEFINITION MODULE Frequencies ;
(* EXPORT QUALIFIED NumberOfCategories,Associate,IncrementBy1,
                   BarChart ; *)
(* Module to allow an importing module to count the frequency of
   occurrence of items falling in various categories.
```

How to use
NumberOfCategories should be called at the beginning of the
program to determine how many categories will be used.
Associate should be called for each category to associate
a category number with a category heading. This category
number should then be passed to IncrementBy1 when the
category count requires incrementing.
N.B. that no checks are incorporated to prevent repeated
calls of NumberOfCategories and Associate with the same
category number *)

PROCEDURE NumberOfCategories (Number : CARDINAL) ;
(* requests a Number of categories to be used by the importing module *)

PROCEDURE Associate (CategoryNo : CARDINAL ;
                                      Heading : ARRAY OF CHAR) ;
(* associates a Heading with a CategoryNo used internally in
Frequencies, each item which is to be classified under
the Heading is recorded by calling IncrementBy1 with the
corresponding CategoryNo as its parameter. *)

PROCEDURE IncrementBy1 (CategoryNo : CARDINAL) ;
(* increment the count for the CategoryNo by 1 *)

PROCEDURE BarChart ;
(* draws a Bar Chart based upon the current values of the counts
associated with the categories being used *)

END Frequencies .

Fig. 6.18.


```
IMPLEMENTATION MODULE Frequencies ;
FROM InOut          IMPORT Write,WriteLn,WriteString ;
FROM MoreInOut      IMPORT WriteLnString ;
CONST
      MaxCategories    = 50 ;
      MaxHeadingLength = 20 ;
VAR
      CharPos          ,
      CategoryNo       ,
      ComponentsInUse  : CARDINAL ;
      FrequencyArray   : ARRAY [1..MaxCategories] OF CARDINAL ;
      Headings         : ARRAY [1..MaxCategories*MaxHeadingLength] OF
                                                      CHAR ;
      Null             : CHAR ;
```

```
PROCEDURE GetStartAndFinishOfCategoryName (CategoryNo : CARDINAL ;
                                           VAR Start,Finish : CARDINAL) ;
BEGIN
 Start := ((CategoryNo–1) * MaxHeadingLength) + 1 ;
 Finish := Start + MaxHeadingLength ;
END GetStartAndFinishOfCategoryName ;

PROCEDURE WriteHeading (CategoryNo : CARDINAL) ;
 VAR
     Pos, LastPos : CARDINAL ;
BEGIN
 GetStartAndFinishOfCategoryName (CategoryNo,Pos,LastPos) ;
 WHILE Pos <> LastPos DO
     Write (Headings[Pos]) ;
     INC (Pos) ;
 END (* WHILE *) ;
END WriteHeading ;

     (* procedures available to other modules *)

PROCEDURE NumberOfCategories (Number : CARDINAL) ;
BEGIN
 IF Number > MaxCategories THEN
     WriteLnString ('Error – Too many categories requested.')
 ELSE
     ComponentsInUse := Number
 END (* IF *)
END NumberOfCategories ;

PROCEDURE Associate (CategoryNo : CARDINAL ;
                     Heading : ARRAY OF CHAR) ;
 VAR
       Pos, ChPos, LastPos : CARDINAL ;
BEGIN
 IF CategoryNo > MaxCategories THEN
     WriteLnString ('Error – Invalid Category Number.') ;
 ELSE
     GetStartAndFinishOfCategoryName (CategoryNo,Pos,LastPos) ;
     ChPos := 0 ;
     WHILE (ChPos <> MaxHeadingLength) AND (ChPos <= HIGH (Heading)) DO
         Headings[Pos] := Heading[ChPos] ;
         INC (ChPos) ;
         INC (Pos) ;
     END (* WHILE *) ;
     WHILE Pos <> LastPos DO
         Headings[Pos] := Null ;
         INC (Pos) ;
     END (* WHILE *) ;
 END (* IF *)
END Associate ;
```

```
PROCEDURE BarChart ;
VAR
    AsteriskCount  ,
    CategoryNo     : CARDINAL ;
BEGIN
  WriteLn ;
  CategoryNo := 0 ;
  WHILE CategoryNo < ComponentsInUse DO
      INC (CategoryNo) ;
      WriteHeading (CategoryNo) ;
      AsteriskCount := 0 ;
      WHILE AsteriskCount <> FrequencyArray[CategoryNo] DO
          INC (AsteriskCount) ;
          Write ('*') ;
      END (* WHILE *) ;
      WriteLn ;
  END (* WHILE *) ;
END BarChart ;

PROCEDURE IncrementBy1 (CategoryNo : CARDINAL) ;
BEGIN
  IF CategoryNo > MaxCategories THEN
      WriteLnString ('Error – Invalid Category Number.')
  ELSE
      INC(FrequencyArray[CategoryNo])
  END (* IF *)
END IncrementBy1 ;

BEGIN          (* Module Body – Initialisation *)
  Null := CHR(0) ;
  ComponentsInUse := 0 ;
  CategoryNo := 0 ;
  WHILE CategoryNo <> MaxCategories DO
      INC (CategoryNo) ;
      FrequencyArray [CategoryNo] := 0 ;
  END (* WHILE *) ;
  CharPos := 0 ;
  WHILE CharPos <> CategoryNo*MaxHeadingLength DO
      INC (CharPos) ;
      Headings [CharPos] := '?' ;
  END (* WHILE *) ;
END Frequencies .
```

Fig. 6.19.

The increased usefulness of Frequencies is illustrated in Fig. 6.20 which shows a main program module to read values of people's income from the keyboard and categorises these to the nearest multiple of 2000.

```modula-2
MODULE IncomeRanges ;
  FROM InOut          IMPORT ReadCard ;
  FROM MoreInOut      IMPORT WriteLnString, WriteStringCard, NewCardValue ;
  FROM Frequencies    IMPORT NumberOfCategories, Associate,
                             IncrementBy1, BarChart ;
  CONST
    Terminator        = 0 ;
  VAR
    Income            : CARDINAL ;

  PROCEDURE AssociateCategories ;
  BEGIN
    Associate ( 1,'£    0–£ 1999 ') ; Associate ( 2,'£ 2000–£ 3999 ') ;
    Associate ( 3,'£ 4000–£ 5999 ') ; Associate ( 4,'£ 6000–£ 7999 ') ;
    Associate ( 5,'£ 8000–£ 9999 ') ; Associate ( 6,'£10000–£11999 ') ;
    Associate ( 7,'£12000–£13999 ') ; Associate ( 8,'£14000–£15999 ') ;
    Associate ( 9,'£16000–£17999 ') ; Associate (10,'£18000–£19999 ') ;
    Associate (11,'£20000—>       ') ;
  END AssociateCategories ;

  PROCEDURE ProcessIncome (Income : CARDINAL) ;
    VAR
      CategoryNo : CARDINAL ;
  BEGIN
    IF Income < 20000 THEN
      CategoryNo := Income DIV 2000 + 1 ;
      IncrementBy1 (CategoryNo) ;
    ELSE
      IncrementBy1 (11) ;
    END (* IF *) ;
  END ProcessIncome ;

BEGIN
  NumberOfCategories (11) ;
  AssociateCategories ;
  WriteLnString ("Type each person's income in £s (ignore pence)") ;
  WriteStringCard ("to indicate the end of the list type ",Terminator,6) ;
  Income := NewCardValue ("Type the next person's Income £ ") ;
  WHILE Income <> Terminator DO
      ProcessIncome (Income) ;
      Income := NewCardValue ("Type the next person's Income £ ") ;
  END (* WHILE *) ;
  BarChart ;
END IncomeRanges .
```

Fig. 6.20.

6.3   IMPORTING OF VARIABLES AND CONSTANTS

Procedures are not the only Modula-2 constructs which can be made available to other modules, but they are amongst the most useful because of the capability of hiding variables within an implementation module thereby protecting them from access by other modules. We have already seen that variables and constants can be declared within an implementation module. Like procedures they also can be made accessible to other modules by declaring them in the definition module. Figure 6.21 shows simplified syntax diagrams relating to definition modules, these specify that constants and variables are objects which can be imported into other modules.

Definition Module :

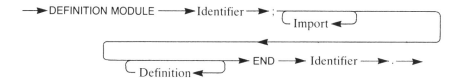

Definition :

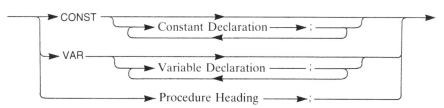

Fig. 6.21.

When variables and constants are declared in a definition module, this automatically makes their declarations available in the corresponding implementation module and these must not be declared again in the implementation module. This is one of the reasons why a definition module has to be compiled before its implementation module. When the definition module is compiled, information regarding variables and constants declared within it is produced which is used later when the implementation module is compiled. If the definition module of Frequencies is altered to that shown in Fig 6.22 then the variable and constant declarations have to be removed from Frequencies' implementation module. Procedures differ from variables and constants as the procedure heading appears in the definition module and also has to be given in the implementation module with the full declaration of the procedure.

Variables and constants which are declared at the outer level of an implementation module have a lifetime of the entire program execution but their scope is restricted to the implementation module. Variables and constants declared in a definition module have a lifetime of the entire program execution but their scope can be extended to any other module which imports them. With the definition module of Frequencies shown in Fig. 6.22 other modules can import any of the procedures, variables and constants and use them. What then are the consequences of doing this? In order to answer this question we will consider the question for variables and constants separately.

```
DEFINITION MODULE Frequencies ;
   (* EXPORT QUALIFIED NumberOfCategories,Associate,IncrementBy1,
                       BarChart,MaxCategories,MaxHeadingLength,
                       CategoryNo,ComponentsInUse,FrequencyArray,
                       Headings ; *)
   (* Module to allow ... (as Fig 6.18) *)

   CONST
       MaxCategories     = 50 ;
       MaxHeadingLength  = 20 ;
   VAR
       CategoryNo        ,
       ComponentsInUse   : CARDINAL ;
       FrequencyArray    : ARRAY [1..MaxCategories] OF CARDINAL ;
       Headings          : ARRAY[1..MaxCategories*MaxHeadingLength] OF
                                                                CHAR ;

   (* procedure headings as Fig 6.18 *)

   END Frequencies .
```

Fig. 6.22.

Importing of Variables

The definition module in Fig. 6.22 makes FrequencyArray visible to other modules. As a consequence it is possible for another module to import this variable and manipulate it in the same way that it can manipulate other variables. So it is possible to write modules such as the one shown in Fig. 6.23.

So what exactly is the problem? Whereas previously these variables were protected from the rest of the program, they can now be accessed without having to go through the procedures provided in Frequencies. The way in which the variable is accessed using the procedures provided by Frequencies and by direct reference to the variable adds to the difficulty in understanding the module. The benefits arising from organising a program into separate mod-

```
MODULE IfYouDoThisYouDeserveAllYouGet ;
FROM Frequencies IMPORT IncrementBy1, BarChart, FrequencyArray,
                        NumberOfCategories, Headings ;
BEGIN
 NumberOfCategories := 6 ;
 IncrementBy1 (1) ;
 Headings[4] := 'hello' ;
 IncrementBy1 (1) ;
 IncrementBy1 (4) ;
 INC (FrequencyArray[4],FrequencyArray[1] + 6) ;
 BarChart ;
END IfYouDoThisYouDeserveAllYouGet .
```

Fig. 6.23.

ules can be undermined if care is not taken when deciding which constructs in an implementation module should be visible outside the module.

This example is extreme because it allows all global variables in Frequencies to be visible to other modules. However it does underline the problems which arise by importing variables into other modules.

As a general rule variables which are crucial to an implementation module should not be made accessible outside the module. All the variables within Frequencies' implementation module are critical to its integrity as a module. Such variables should not be made accessible outside the module. A definition and implementation module pair may safely make variables available outside the implementation module if this does not compromise the integrity of the module. Such variables are typically assigned values within the implementation module but no operation in the implementation module relies upon the variable holding a particular value. It is therefore not critical if other modules alter the values of such variables. QueueModule takes positive measures to protect the variable SizeQueue even though its value is needed by other modules.

A justifiable situation for allowing other modules to import variables is when a module needs to indicate secondary results of computations which will not be required frequently. For example, QueueModule could export a variable whose current value indicates the success of the last of QueueModule's procedures to be called. QueueModule's procedures would then set the value of this variable to indicate success or failure of the procedure in performing its operation. In cases of failure the procedures would not write a message indicating failure, but would set the variable so that other modules can determine how to handle the failure. In general, unless an implementation module has been specifically designed as an input/output module, it should not perform input/output operations particularly for failed operations.

As a further example of the use of importing variables, InOut makes a CHAR variable called termCH available to other modules. termCH holds the value of the character which was typed to terminate a call of ReadString. ReadString has been used on numerous occasions previously without requiring this to be known so this is a secondary result of the procedure which for the most part is not required.

termCH is useful for allowing particular characters, which may terminate a call of ReadString, to have a special meaning. A particular character (e.g. the character whose code is 27 – esc) may be used to indicate that the user wishes to abort the sequence of characters he has just typed and retype them. The procedure MyReadString in Fig. 6.24 achieves this. Notice that the procedure only checks the value of termCH, it does not need to initialise it as on the first call of MyReadString the variable is initialised to a non-committal value by InOut. On subsequent calls of MyReadString termCH will never hold the character whose code is 27. This assumes that all calls of ReadString are made through MyReadString.

```
MODULE ImportingVariablesAndConstants ;
 FROM InOut IMPORT ReadString, termCH, Read, EOL ;
 FROM MoreInOut IMPORT WriteLnString;

 PROCEDURE MyReadString (VAR Reply : ARRAY OF CHAR) ;
 BEGIN
  WHILE termCH = CHR (27) DO
       ReadString (Reply) ;
   END (* WHILE *)
 END MyReadString ;

       (* this procedure is discussed in the following section *)
 PROCEDURE ReadLine (VAR Line : ARRAY OF CHAR) ;
 (* A practical implementation of this procedure would include a check
    on the maximum number of characters in Line. *)
 VAR
    Ch          : CHAR;
    Count       : CARDINAL;
 BEGIN
  Count := 0 ;
  Read (Ch) ;
  WHILE Ch <> EOL DO
       Line [Count] := Ch ;
       Read (Ch) ;
       INC (Count) ;
   END (* WHILE *) ;
  Line[Count] := CHR(0); (* see chapter 8 for a superior method. *)
 END ReadLine ;
```

```
VAR
    Name,NewLine : ARRAY[0..20] OF CHAR;

BEGIN
 MyReadString (Name) ;
 WriteLnString(Name);
 ReadLine (NewLine);
 WriteLnString(NewLine)
 END ImportingVariablesAndConstants.
```

Fig. 6.24.

A variable is only visible to another module if it is imported into this module. A module which does not need to access the variable can avoid compromising the integrity of the implementation module by not importing the variable. If it is necessary to import a variable from another module it should be treated as **read only**, that is to inspect but not alter its value.

In this section we have discussed how variables can be made visible to other modules, and given recommendations on how they should be used.
1.   When writing definition and implementation modules, avoid making a variable accessible outside the implementation module which can allow another module to sabotage the implementation module. Only variables which are not critical to the implementation module should be made available. Typically such variables indicate secondary results of operations.
2.   If you are writing an entire program organised across several modules, write procedures for accessing and updating variables and make these available to other modules rather than make a variable visible to another module.
3.   If you are using modules written by other programmers which make available variables do not import them into your modules unless you have to, and if you do need to import them they should be treated as 'read only' variables. Certain low-level programming problems may need to alter such variables, but these kinds of problem are largely beyond the scope of this book.

Importing of Constants

A definition module can make constants declared in the implementation module available to other modules. For example InOut contains a declaration of a constant for a character denoting the end of line character called EOL which is a character constant whose ordinal value is 30. ReadLine in Fig. 6.24 illustrates how this constant can be used in a procedure for reading a sequence of characters from the keyboard until the return key is pressed. On different computers this key may be associated with a different code but this does not matter. InOut can hide the actual detail of the computer by using a convention that whenever this key is pressed the actual parameter passed to Read is assigned the character whose code is 30. Programs can then be written which check for the return key without needing to be concerned with its character code on different computers.

In QueueModule and Frequencies it would not be unreasonable to make the constants determining the maximum size of the QueueData and FrequencyArray available to other modules. This would then allow programmers writing other modules which use them to cope with the possibilities that the size of the data structures inside the implementation modules may not be adequate for some problems.

Note that the problems associated with the importing of variables do not arise with constants. The problems with variables arise because of the possibility that modules importing them may alter them. By definition this cannot happen with constants as their values cannot be changed. Therefore importing of constants into other modules is entirely safe.

6.4 SUMMARY

Programs written in Modula-2 can be organised into several modules. A program module is considered to have overall control. Definition and implementation modules constitute pairs of modules which each provide some facility. Implementation modules have the capability of hiding objects from the rest of the program thereby localising access to them. However, objects can be made accessible through the corresponding definition module. The relationship between an implementation module, its definition module and other modules which access the module pair can be summarised:

1 Potentially any object (variable, constant or procedure) can be exported from the implementation/definition module pair.

2 The definition module restricts the potentially exportable objects by specifying the objects which can be accessed by other modules.
a In the case of procedures, the entire procedure heading occurs in the definition module so that other modules are able to call the procedure appropriately. The entire procedure declaration, including the procedure heading occurs in the implementation module.
b In the case of variables and constants which are made available to other modules, their declarations occur in the definition module and must not be repeated in the implementation module. Variable and constant declarations which occur in the implementation module are local to that implementation module.

3 A module's import lists further restrict access of objects which are available from an implementation/definition module pair to those listed in the import list.

In this chapter we have considered at some length the use of modules when writing programs. We have stressed the importance of the use of implementation/definition module pairs in organising a complete program. Advantages arise from localising access to variables to the implementation module and of providing access to them through procedures which can be imported into other modules. This increases the reliability of programs by allowing modules to be developed and tested independently of each other. If a fault in the program is discovered the search for cause of the fault can be restricted to identifiable pieces of the program. This helps us to remove faults. These advantages are particularly apparent in large programs, where intelligent program organisation helps during development of the program and in subsequently maintaining and modifying the program. However appropriate program organisation also aids the development and general understandability of smaller programs.

In addition it has been shown that variables and constants can be made accessible from an implementation module to other modules by declaring these in the definition module. In the case of variables this can be dangerous if variables which are critical to the integrity of a module are made visible outside the implementation module. The general advice is not to do this, but to restrict use of this facility to variables which indicate secondary results. Constants can be imported safely into other modules as these cannot be modified.

As we develop the program in a top down manner we decompose the problem into sub-problems. Then we work on the sub-problems individually in a similar manner. At each stage we are assuming that the language will be tailored in the necessary way for achieving that (sub-)problem, and that the necessary data structures and operations which we wish to perform on them will be available. With experience we will be able to recognise sub-problems for which we already have suitable modules to perform the necessary operations. This makes the programming task easier.

Viewed from another perspective this style of programming can be considered as a continual expansion of the programming language. Modula-2 provides several predefined procedures, constants and variables. By writing implementation/definition module pairs which provide facilities which are appropriate to solving the problem at hand, we are effectively tailoring and extending the language to suit the problem. In some cases these will also suit other similar problems and will therefore help during the development of further programs.

TECHNICAL EXERCISES

State which of the following statements are true, and which are false, or partially true (some may be true as far as they go but need further qualification).

1 a module can import procedures from an implementation module.

2 a module can import any variable or constant declared in an implementation module.

3 a module can use any procedure, variable or constant named in a definition module.

4 a module's import lists determine which procedures, variables and constants can be used from other modules.

5 a definition module lists those objects which are available from the corresponding implementation module and can be imported into other modules.

6 a definition module cannot import objects from other modules.

7 a module's import list and definition modules determine which objects the module can access from implementation modules.

8 a module which imports variables from another module cannot alter them.

9 a module which imports variables from another module should not alter them.

10 the module body of a definition module can perform any necessary initialisation.

11 the module body of an implementation module can perform any necessary initialisation.

12 the module body of an implementation module is executed before the execution of the main program module body.

PROGRAMMING EXERCISES

1 Type the definition and implementation modules of Frequencies given in Figs 6.18 and 6.19 into your computer and write a new version of VowelCount which uses this version of these modules.

2 Write a program module CharacterCount which determines the frequency of all alphabetic characters in a text. Avoid using 26 IF statements, instead use the sequencing of characters in the ASCII character set to determine the correspondence between the letter and the category number.

3 Modify the definition and implementation modules of QueueModule so that a BOOLEAN variable Success indicates whether AddToQueue and RemoveFrom-

Queue are successful or not rather than writing out messages from inside the implementation module.

A further useful operation applicable to a queue is to allow other modules to look at the item at the front of the queue without removing it. Include a procedure TopOfQueue which returns the item at the front of the queue without removing it. Remember to consider how this procedure should affect the variable Success.

4 InOut allows a module to import a variable called Done which is set to TRUE if ReadCard or ReadInt reads a valid CARDINAL value or INTEGER value respectively, and FALSE if a CARDINAL or INTEGER value was not correctly read. Rewrite the module IncomeRanges to use Done so that the end of the list of people's salaries is indicated by anything other than a CARDINAL value.

ANSWERS

1 partially true, but only those named in the corresponding definition module can be imported into other modules.

2 false, modules can only import variables and constants declared in a definition module in which case the implementation module must not duplicate the declaration. Variables and constants whose declarations occur in an implementation are accessible only within the implementation module.

3 true.

4 true, assuming that the definition modules list the names occurring in the import lists.

5 true.

6 false, though importing of variables and procedures into definition modules is of little use.

7 true.

8 false, though it is unwise to alter variables imported from other modules as the way in which procedures in the implementation module use them will be hidden.

9 true.

10 false, a definition module does not have a module body.

11 true.

12 true.

Chapter 7

Conditional Statements
and the BOOLEAN Type

In Chapter 3 the IF statement was introduced in its simplest forms, which allow any type of conditional statement to be constructed. However, in many situations the simple forms of the IF statement lead to clumsy code and so Modula-2 provides generalised constructs which are often easier to write, correct and understand. These extra constructs are described in sections 7.2 and 7.3. The first section of the chapter introduces a new data type, BOOLEAN, which is essential to a full understanding of conditional statements.

7.1 THE DATA TYPE BOOLEAN

Modula-2 provides a data type called BOOLEAN. A variable of type BOOLEAN can only have one of two possible values TRUE or FALSE. Three operators are available to act on BOOLEAN variables which give results corresponding to our normal way of thinking when we are trying to be very precise. The operators are

1. NOT (~ is also used to denote NOT)
          NOT TRUE = FALSE   NOT FALSE = TRUE
2. AND (& is also used to denote AND)
          TRUE AND TRUE = TRUE   FALSE AND FALSE = FALSE
          TRUE AND FALSE = FALSE   FALSE AND TRUE = FALSE
3. OR
          TRUE OR TRUE = TRUE   FALSE OR FALSE = FALSE
          TRUE OR FALSE = TRUE   FALSE OR TRUE = TRUE

Notice that in English 'or' is often used to mean one or other, but not both. The OR defined here allows one or other or both.

These operators are used with BOOLEAN variables in BOOLEAN expressions whose results are BOOLEAN values. For example, the declaration

```
VAR
        Large, Middle, Small : BOOLEAN ;
```

declares three BOOLEAN variables. The statements

```
Large := TRUE ;
Small := FALSE ;
```

initialise these to produce the situation illustrated in Fig. 7.1.

197

Large	Small	Middle
TRUE	FALSE	?
BOOLEAN	BOOLEAN	BOOLEAN

Fig. 7.1.

Figure 7.2 shows assignment statements involving BOOLEAN expressions where the result is assigned to Middle.

STATEMENT	RESULT
Middle := Large	TRUE
Middle := Large AND Small	TRUE AND FALSE = FALSE
Middle := Large AND NOT Small	TRUE AND (NOT FALSE) = TRUE AND TRUE = TRUE
Middle := NOT Small AND Large	(NOT FALSE) AND TRUE = TRUE AND TRUE = TRUE
Middle := NOT(Small AND Large)	NOT(FALSE AND TRUE) = NOT(FALSE) = TRUE
Middle := Small AND Large OR Small	(FALSE AND TRUE) OR FALSE = FALSE OR FALSE = FALSE
Middle := Small OR Small AND Large	FALSE OR (FALSE AND TRUE) = FALSE OR FALSE = FALSE

Fig. 7.2.

NOT has highest priority followed by AND and then OR. By studying the syntax diagrams in Appendix 1 it can be seen that NOT is a special high priority operator in Term, AND is a Multiply Operator and OR is an Add Operator.

The general laws of boolean algebra apply to the BOOLEAN expressions of Modula-2, but they are not very useful in the manipulation of program statements. If you wish to know details of the laws you are advised to consult the books in the bibliography under the heading **Logic and Computers**. The following is a brief compilation of some of the more useful formulae.

Boolean Algebra Formulae

The formulae given in Fig. 7.3 can be verified by evaluating all possible cases and showing that they lead to the same result. They are presented here to enable the programmer to simplify certain expressions which may arise while writing programs. Most of them are obvious.

1.	A AND A	= A
2.	A OR A	= A
3.	NOT (NOT A)	= A
4.	A AND B	= B AND A
5.	A OR B	= B OR A
6.	NOT(A AND B)	= NOT A OR NOT B
7.	NOT(A OR B)	= NOT A AND NOT B
8.	(A AND B) OR C	= (A OR C) AND (B OR C)
9.	A OR (B AND C)	= (A OR B) AND (A OR C)
10.	(A OR B) AND C	= (A AND C) OR (B AND C)
11.	A AND (B OR C)	= (A AND B) OR (A AND C)

Fig. 7.3.

BOOLEAN **Expressions: Order of Evaluation**

BOOLEAN expressions are an integral part of conditional and repetitive statements. They form the backbone of the programming process by controlling the execution sequence of statements.

An important feature of Modula-2 is the way a BOOLEAN expression is evaluated. In many other languages the order of evaluation of BOOLEAN expressions is undefined, but in Modula-2 it is very precisely defined. The precedence of the BOOLEAN operators has already been given and the default evaluation of the operands in the expressions is left to right. Figure 7.4 shows a precise statement of how the expression

    Middle := Large AND Small

is evaluated. The important point with this expression is that Small is not evaluated unless Large is TRUE.

    Evaluate Large,
    if Large is FALSE set Middle to FALSE,
    else
        evaluate Small,
        if Small is TRUE set Middle to TRUE,
        else
            set Middle to FALSE.

evaluation of Middle := Large AND Small

Fig. 7.4.

By guaranteeing left to right evaluation and no evaluation, unless it is necessary to determine the result, useful prechecks can be incorporated in IF and WHILE statements to prevent illegal conditions. For example

        IF (Num <> 0) AND (OtherNum DIV Num = Answer) THEN . . . .

guarantees that the division is not carried out when Num is 0.

Though two expressions may be technically equivalent by the rules of Fig. 7.3 there may be a practical difference in their left to right evaluation which is significant in a programming context. Thus the expression

        IF (OtherNum DIV Num = Answer) AND (Num <> 0) THEN . . . .

is not useful, as it does not protect against zero division.

Relational Expressions

The main power of BOOLEAN variables comes in the way they can be used in conjunction with other data types. BOOLEAN variables can be used to store facts about other variables and expressions. This is done by the use of relational expressions which have a result of type BOOLEAN. Relational expressions have already been used in IF statements in Chapter 3. For example, in

        IF Y <> 0 THEN . . . .

The expression (Y <> 0) is a relational expression whose result is a BOOLEAN value. That is

        (Y<>0) = TRUE if Y is not zero,
        (Y<>0) = FALSE if Y is zero.

The result of a relational expression can be assigned to a BOOLEAN variable. For example, if Zerotest is a BOOLEAN variable, the following code fragment is equivalent to the IF statement above

        Zerotest := Y<>0;
        IF Zerotest THEN . . . .

Note that it is not technically incorrect to write

        IF Zerotest = TRUE THEN. . . . . .

but it is poor style. Similarly

        IF ZeroTest = FALSE THEN. . . . .

is normally written

        IF NOT ZeroTest THEN. . . . . . .

BOOLEAN operators may be used in conjunction with relational expressions. For example, the code fragments in Fig. 7.5 each test the same condition.

```
VAR
      Result,Zerotest,Onetest : BOOLEAN;

1.  IF (Y<>0) AND (Z<>1) THEN . . . . . . . . . . .

2.  Zerotest := (Y<>0);
    Onetest := (Z<>1);
    IF Zerotest AND Onetest THEN . . . . . . . .

3.  Zerotest := (Y<>0);
    Onetest := (Z<>1);
    Result := Zerotest AND Onetest;
    IF Result THEN . . . . . . . .

4.  Zerotest := (Y<>0);
    IF Zerotest AND (Z<>1) THEN . . . . . .
```

Fig. 7.5.

The decision about which version to use depends on whether the results
can be used elsewhere in the program. If ZeroTest, OneTest and Result are not
being used elsewhere, the first piece of code is concise and easy to understand
and so should be used. Note that the brackets used in fragment 1 are
necessary since relational operators have the lowest priority of all operators.
The expression

```
Y<>0 AND Z<>1
```

would be interpreted as

```
Y <> (0 AND Z) <> 1
```

which is meaningless because (0 AND Z) is not a BOOLEAN expression and so
causes a compilation error.
    The permissible relational operators are

<	less than,
>	greater than,
<=	less than or equal to,
>=	greater than or equal to,
<> or #	not equal to,
=	equal.

There is a further relational operator called IN, which is discussed in Chapter
10. The syntax chart for an expression is given in Fig. 7.6.

Expression :

Fig. 7.6.

A common use of relational expressions is to test that a number lies within a particular range

```
IF (0 <= Z) AND (Z <= 20) THEN . . . . . . . . . .
```

A common error is to try to write this as

```
IF 0 <= Z <= 20 THEN . . . . . . . . . . .
```

which is not allowed and must be written in the longer form.

The relational operators cannot be used to compare arrays or records (discussed in Chapter 10).

BOOLEAN **Function Procedures**

BOOLEAN values can be returned as the result of function procedures. A procedure declared as

```
PROCEDURE GreaterThanTen (Number : CARDINAL) : BOOLEAN ;
BEGIN
 RETURN Number > 10
END GreaterThanTen ;
```

can be called to provide a BOOLEAN result which can be the test in WHILE and IF statements. For example, assuming that CurrentValue is a CARDINAL variable, the statement

```
IF GreaterThanTen(CurrentValue) THEN (*... ...*) END (* IF *)
```

only executes the statement sequence in the THEN part if GreaterThanTen returns the value TRUE.

7.2 IF **STATEMENTS**

The syntax diagram of the generalised IF statement is defined in Fig. 7.7 and described here in a series of steps.

If Statement :

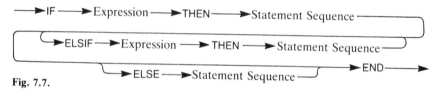

Fig. 7.7.

The most basic versions are

```
IF (*. . BOOLEAN condition . .*) THEN (*. . statement sequence . .*) END (* IF *)
IF (*. . BOOLEAN condition . .*) THEN (*. . statement sequence . .*)
                           ELSE (*. . statement sequence . .*) END (* IF *)
```

which were introduced in Chapter 3. In the former case the statement sequence between THEN and END is only executed if the boolean condition evaluates to TRUE. The ELSE clause is an obvious extension of this to provide another statement sequence which is executed if the boolean condition is FALSE. The statement sequences are called guarded statement sequences, as the BOOLEAN expressions which form the conditions guard entry to the statement sequences (see Fig. 7.8).

```
IF IntegerNum >= 0 THEN
     WriteString('The number ');
     WriteInt(IntegerNum,8);
     WriteString(' is not negative.');
     WriteLn
ELSE (* IntegerNum < 0 *)
     WriteString('The number ');
     WriteInt(IntegerNum,8);
     WriteString(' is negative.');
     WriteLn
END (* IF *)
```

Fig. 7.8.

It is useful to include the conditions under which the ELSE clause is executed as a comment with the ELSE clause. Figure 7.8 can be rewritten, as Fig. 7.9.

```
WriteString('The number ');
WriteInt(IntegerNum,8);
IF IntegerNum >= 0 THEN
     WriteString(' is not negative.')
ELSE (* IntegerNum < 0 *)
     WriteString(' is negative.')
END (* IF *);
WriteLn
```

Fig. 7.9.

The first version seems obviously inferior to the second, but there is often an advantage in treating each of the guarded statement sequences separately during the initial design. After the design is complete, improvements can be made by removing statements that are duplicated in all parts of the IF statement. The first version is more flexible as each of the statement sequences achieves its purpose without the need for succeeding and preceding statements. This is useful at the design stage when the requirements of the program may change or the programmer's ideas may change.

The ELSE version of the IF statement is very useful, but on some occasions it is not sufficiently general. An extra facility is available to allow more than two options. This may be used with or without the ELSE clause. Figure 7.10 shows two skeleton examples to illustrate its forms.

```
IF      (*. . BOOLEAN cond1 . .*)   THEN      IF      (*. . BOOLEAN cond1 . .*) THEN
        (*. . statement seq1 . .*)                    (*. . statement seq1 . .*)
ELSIF   (*. . BOOLEAN cond2 . .*)   THEN      ELSIF   (*. . BOOLEAN cond2 . .*) THEN
        (*. . statement seq2 . .*)                    (*. . statement seq2 . .*)
ELSIF   (*. . BOOLEAN cond3 . .*)   THEN      ELSIF   (*. . BOOLEAN cond3 . .*) THEN
        (*. . statement seq3 . .*)                    (*. . statement seq3 . .*)
ELSE                                          ELSIF   (*. . BOOLEAN cond4 . .*) THEN
        (*. . statement seq4 . .*)                    (*. . statement seq4 . .*)
END (* IF *)                                  END (* IF *)
```

Fig. 7.10.

The boolean conditions guard the corresponding statement sequence, they are evaluated in turn and the statement sequence corresponding to the first to evaluate to TRUE is executed. When one of the guards evaluates to TRUE none of the subsequent guards are evaluated nor are their statement sequences executed. The number of possible ELSIF statements is unlimited. Normally the conditions are designed to be mutually exclusive, but this is not essential. A typical statement is Fig. 7.11.

```
IF (Answer = 'A') OR (Answer = 'a') THEN
    WriteString('This is the correct answer.')
ELSIF (Answer = 'B') OR (Answer = 'b') THEN
    WriteString('This is nearly correct,but not quite.')
ELSIF (Answer = 'C') OR (Answer = 'c') THEN
    WriteString('This is the wrong answer.')
ELSE (* Answer <> 'A','a','B','b','C' or 'c' *)
    WriteString('The answer you have given is invalid.')
END (* IF *)
```

Fig. 7.11.

If the final clause of Fig. 7.11 had a BOOLEAN expression to determine its applicability, an ELSIF clause would have been used instead of the ELSE clause. This allows the possibility that none of the conditions evaluate to TRUE and therefore none of the guarded statement sequences is executed.

When the conditions overlap, the order of evaluation is important. In Fig. 7.12 the ELSIF clauses are not executed if Answer1 equals 20 and Answer2 equals 40.

```
IF (Answer1 = 20) AND (Answer2 = 40) THEN
   WriteString('Both answers are correct')
ELSIF (Answer1 = 20) THEN
   WriteString('The first answer is correct')
ELSIF (Answer2 = 40) THEN
   WriteString('The second answer is correct')
ELSE (* (Answer1 <> 20) AND (Answer2 <> 40) *)
   WriteString('Both answers are incorrect')
END (* IF *)
```

Fig. 7.12.

Example. Interchanging the contents of variables

Given three items in variables A,B,C interchange the items so that

```
A >= B >= C.
```

This problem can be solved in many ways, the solutions here are concerned with demonstrating the use of IF statements. Chapter 5 illustrated a procedure Interchange which swaps the contents of two CARDINAL variables whose procedure heading was

```
PROCEDURE Interchange (VAR Temp1,Temp2: CARDINAL) ;
```

This will be used in the solutions.

Solution 1

Figures 7.13 and 7.14 show a solution to the problem using only IF and ELSE clauses. The comments introduced by (*TRUE indicate assertions which are true at various stages.

```
(*TRUE A,B and C contain any values *)

IF A < B THEN
   InterChange(A,B)
ELSE (* A >= B *)
   (* do nothing *)
END (* IF *);
(*TRUE A >= B with C any value *)

IF B < C THEN
   InterChange(B,C);
   (*TRUE A >= C and B >= C and A,B in either order *)

   IF A < B THEN
      InterChange(A,B)
   ELSE (* A >= B *)
      (* do nothing *)
```

```
END (* IF *)
(*TRUE A >= B >= C *)
```

```
ELSE (* B >= C *)
 (* do nothing *)
END (* IF *)
(*TRUE A >= B >= C *)
```

as IF ELSE clauses

Fig. 7.13.

```
IF A < B THEN
  InterChange(A,B)
END (* IF *);
IF B < C THEN
  InterChange(B,C);
  IF A < B THEN
    InterChange(A,B)
  END (* IF *)
END (* IF *)
```

with redundant ELSE clauses and comments removed

Fig. 7.14.

Solution 2

Figures 7.15 and 7.16 show a solution where A and C are first ordered with respect to each other which establishes that either A or C (or possibly both) already hold their final value. The ELSE clause need not be included in the version in Fig. 7.16, though it is not incorrect to keep it in.

```
(*TRUE A,B and C can contain any values *)
```

```
IF A < C THEN
  InterChange(A,C)
ELSE (* A >= C *)
 (* do nothing *)
END (* IF *);
(*TRUE A >= C *)
```

```
IF A < B THEN (*TRUE A >= C AND B > C *)
  InterChange(A,B)
ELSIF B < C THEN (*TRUE A >= C AND B < A *)
  InterChange(B,C)
ELSE (* A >= B >= C *)
 (* do nothing *)
END (* IF *)
(*TRUE A >= B >= C *)
```

Fig. 7.15.

```
IF A < C THEN                         IF A < C THEN
   InterChange(A,C)                      InterChange(A,C)
END (* IF *);                         END (* IF *);
IF A < B THEN                         IF A < B THEN
   InterChange(A,B)        or            InterChange(A,B)
ELSIF B < C THEN                      ELSIF B < C THEN
   InterChange(B,C)                      InterChange(B,C)
END (* IF *)                          ELSE (* A >= B >= C *)
                                         (* do nothing *)
                                      END (* IF *)
```

Fig. 7.16.

The technique of putting comments to stipulate what should be true before and after IF statements is powerful and general and serves two purposes.

1.   During the design stage such comments specify what the IF statement must achieve as the goal of the statement and what should be true before the IF statement is executed. The IF statement is then designed to ensure that the goal is achieved.

2.   When the code is complete these comments serve to justify the code, especially if they are left in the expanded version of the code, i.e. with the extra ELSE clauses.

The technique of including extra 'do nothing' ELSE or ELSIF clauses is useful at the design stage as it serves to make clear under what conditions the goal has already been achieved and so explicitly states where no action is required.

Nested IF statements

Nested IF statements have been used in previous chapters without comment. Their use, in general, is natural and obvious. The syntax of Modula-2 clearly defines the meaning of IF statements which are embedded within other IF statements, and indentation should be used so as to conform to the meaning. The basic rule is that the word END matches and closes the most recent structured statement which has not yet been closed. Structured statements include WHILE statements and others to be introduced later. Figure 7.17 illustrates the point. When an IF statement is embedded in another IF statement the statement sequence it guards is only executed if the conditions associated with both IF statements are true, Hello is only written if B is greater than A and C. Similarly an IF statement embedded in a WHILE statement is only executed if the statement sequence of the WHILE loop is executed.

```
IF (A < B) THEN                    WHILE ~ EndLoop DO (* ~ means NOT *)
   IF (B > C) THEN                     IF (B < C) THEN
      WriteString('Hello')                B := B+1
   ELSE                                ELSE
      WriteString('GoodBye')              EndLoop := TRUE
   END (* IF *)                        END (* IF *)
END (* IF *)                        END (* WHILE *)

   (a)                                (b)
```

Fig. 7.17.

Indentation and comments do not change the meaning of the statements, they are used to make the meaning clear. If the indentation or the comments are wrong they obscure the program text and may conceal errors! For example, the program fragment of Fig. 7.18 is incorrectly indented, and this obscures the fact that the ELSE and END are attached to the IF statement which tests if (B > C). Unless the programmer has made a bad mistake, there should be an END after the call WriteString('Hello'). The complete program will contain a syntax error due to a missing END.

```
IF (A < B) THEN
   IF (B > C) THEN
      WriteString('Hello')
   ELSE
      WriteString('GoodBye')
   END (* IF *)
```

Fig. 7.18.

7.3   THE CASE **STATEMENT**

The CASE statement can be considered as a special form of the IF statement. The example in Fig. 7.11 can be written as the CASE statement in Fig. 7.19. The essential components of a CASE statement are
1.   an expression which is evaluated (in Fig. 7.19 this is a simple expression to determine the value of Answer), and
2.   a list of ordered cases, each of which consists of a collection of values known as case labels and an associated statement sequence.

The expression is evaluated and tested for equality with the case labels in the order the labels occur. The statement sequence of the first case label which is equal to the result is selected and executed. In contrast with an IF statement, a CASE statement compares the result of the expression for **equality** with a collection of **constant values** (technically, these are the results of constant expressions which are discussed in Chapter 8). A CASE statement can also have an ELSE clause to handle cases not dealt with by the case labels.

```
CASE Answer OF
    'A','a' :    WriteString('This is the correct answer.')|
    'B','b' :    WriteString('This is nearly correct,but not quite.')|
    'C','c' :    WriteString('This is the wrong answer.')
    ELSE        WriteString('The answer you have given is invalid.')
END (* CASE *)
```

Fig. 7.19.

The case labels are restricted to constants of the types CHAR, BOOLEAN, CARDINAL and INTEGER and enumeration types and subrange types (see Chapter 8).

The general form for the CASE statement is given in the syntax diagrams in Fig. 7.20. It should only be used in situations where there is a small fixed number of alternatives, and the ELSE clause should either not be present or should only handle unusual cases like an error. In all other circumstances IF statements should be used.

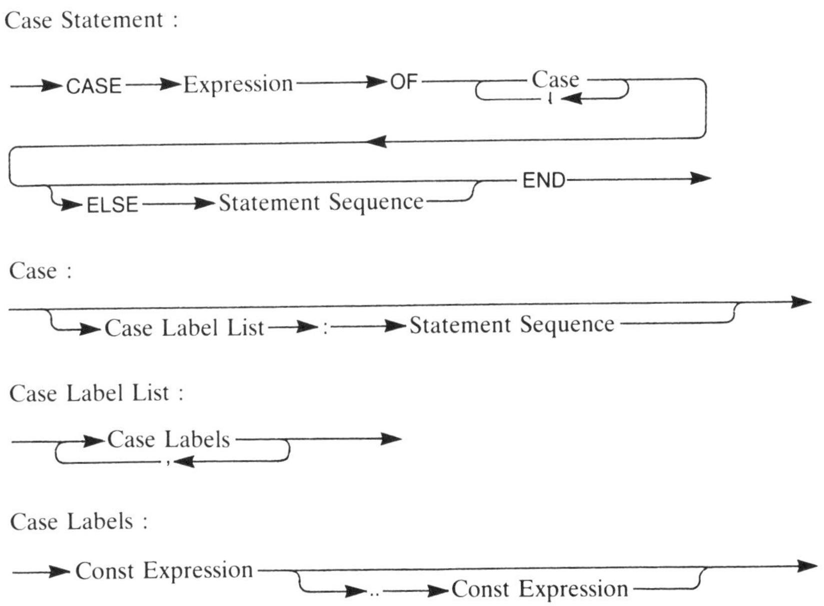

Case Statement :

Case :

Case Label List :

Case Labels :

Fig. 7.20.

When it is suitable the CASE statement is a very concise and clear way of making a selection. The | separates different 'cases' and is allowed to separate a case from a null case. Only one statement sequence is selected and executed when a CASE statement is executed. If there are overlapping labels only the first one which satisfies the equality test with the expression has its corresponding statements executed. In effect this means that it is pointless to have overlapping labels. Note that one of the statement sequences must be executed. A null case label does not match any value of an expression. The ELSE condition acts as a catch-all. If the ELSE clause is omitted and no case label equals the result of the expression then a runtime error is reported. The usefulness of CASE statements is demonstrated in Chapter 8 and the subsequent chapters.

7.4 EXAMPLE. WORD COUNT PROGRAM

This section develops a program which uses BOOLEAN variables and IF statements. A major difficulty when starting to develop a program is understanding precisely the problem to be solved. Consider the following statement of a problem

> Develop a program which reads a sequence of characters, counting the number of words in a line and writing the result to the screen. At the end of the sequence the total number of words counted is written out.

A number of questions need to be answered about this imprecise specification.
1. How is the end of the sequence of characters detected?
2. How is the end of a line indicated?
3. What constitutes a word?

Different answers to these questions can lead to considerable differences in the final program. The answers given here are a little artificial so as to simplify the solution. The answers used are
1. The end of the text is indicated by a special character which will be known inside the program as Terminator. This value can be specified within the module or imported from another module.
2. The end of a line is indicated by the character EOL or the Terminator. EOL is imported from InOut. It is assumed that the Terminator also acts as an end of line signal. Hence it is not necessary for there to be an end of line character terminating the last line as the character marking the end of the text indicates the end of the last line.
3. A word is a collection of characters terminated by a space character, an end of line indicator or an end of text indicator.

An initial formulation of a solution is shown in Fig. 7.21. (An alternative formulation which leads to a simpler solution is shown in the programming exercises at the end of this chapter. Here the solution illustrates the use of nested WHILE statements and more complex BOOLEAN expressions.)

```
MODULE AnalyseText;
  (*. . . declarations . . .*);
BEGIN
  (*. . . initialise variables . . .*);
  WHILE (*. . . not yet the end of the text . . .*) DO
              (*. . . process a line of data . . .*)
  END (* WHILE *);
  (*. . . output the total number of words in the text . . .*)
END AnalyseText.
```

Fig. 7.21.

Notes.

1.   The most important insight is that there is no need for a data structure to store all the words because the only requirement is to count words and this does not require knowledge of what words have been read previously.

2.   It is assumed that the WHILE loop requires some initialisation.

3.   Clearly the most difficult part of the code is processing the line of data, so this is refined first as shown in Fig. 7.22.

```
(*. . . initialise any variables for starting a line . . .*)
WHILE (*. . . not yet end of line . . .*) DO
      (*. . . read a character . . .*);
      IF (*. . . end of a word . . .*) THEN
            (*. . . increment word count . . .*);
            (*. . . indicate that the character is between words . . .*)
      ELSIF (*. . . beginning of a word . . .*) THEN
            (*. . . indicate that a new word has started . . .*)
      END (* IF *)
END (* WHILE *);
(*. . . output the total number of words in the line . . .*)
```

Fig. 7.22.

Notes.

1.   An important design decision here is to choose to read the line as a sequence of characters rather than a sequence of words. The reason for this is that words do not necessarily start or finish a line, there may be spaces at the beginning or end of the line. This makes it slightly more difficult to process a line as a sequence of words.

2.   The word counts are updated at the end of each word, so as to always reflect the number of complete words which have been read at a given moment.

```
MODULE AnalyseText;
(*. . . declarations . . .*);
BEGIN
(*. . . initialise variables . . .*);
WHILE (*. . . not yet the end of the text . . .*) DO
        (*. . . initialise any variables for starting a line . . .*)
        WHILE (*. . . not yet end of line . . .*) DO
                (*. . . read a character . . .*);
                IF (*. . . end of a word . . .*) THEN
                        (*. . . increment word count . . .*);
                        (*. . . indicate that the character is between words . . .*)
                ELSIF (*. . . beginning of a word . . .*) THEN
                        (*. . . indicate that a new word has started . . .*)
                END (* IF *)
        END (* WHILE *);
        (*. . . output the total number of words in the line . . .*)
END (* WHILE *);
(*. . . output the total number of words in the text . . .*)
END AnalyseText.
```

Fig. 7.23.

Figure 7.23 gives the program with the 'process a line of data' refinement included. The most difficult parts of the problem remaining are the decisions about how to record events like 'not yet end of text' or 'not yet end of line' or 'end of word'. These require consideration of what needs to be remembered to ensure correct decisions. We consider how to record whether or not a word is being read first.

Whenever a character has been read the situation is either
1.   a word is being read and the next character indicates whether or not the word is complete.
2.   no word is being read and the next character indicates whether or not a new word starts.

This can be handled by two BOOLEAN variables declared as

```
VAR
        NextCharInWord  ,
        InWord          : BOOLEAN;
```

InWord records whether the previous character is part of a word or part of a sequence of characters between words. NextCharInWord indicates whether the character just read is a character which is part of a word or not.

InWord must be initialised to FALSE at the beginning of each line, and NextCharInWord must be set each time a character is read to indicate whether this character is part of a word or not.

The transition between the two states of currently reading a word and currently reading characters between words can then be determined by the

BOOLEAN expressions

> InWord AND NOT NextCharacterInWord to indicate the end of a word
> NOT InWord AND NextCharacterInWord to indicate the start of a new word

This refinement can be incorporated in the developing program as shown in Fig. 7.24. The current formulation can then be checked to establish that the refinements are correct.

```
MODULE AnalyseText;
CONST
    Space = ' ';
VAR
    InWord,NextCharInWord : BOOLEAN;
(*. . . further declarations . . .*);
BEGIN
(*. . . initialise variables . . .*);
WHILE (*. . . not yet the end of the text . . .*) DO
    (*. . . line has begun . . .*);
    InWord := FALSE;
    WHILE (*. . . not yet end of line . . .*) DO
        (*. . . read a character . . .*);
        NextCharInWord := (*. . . character read is not Space,EOL
                            or Terminator . . .*)
        IF InWord AND ~NextCharInWord THEN
            (*. . . increment word counts . . .*);
            InWord := FALSE
        ELSIF ~InWord AND NextCharInWord THEN
            InWord := TRUE
        END (* IF *)
    END (* WHILE *);
    (*. . . output the total number of words in the line . . .*)
END (* WHILE *);
(*. . . output the total number of words in the text . . .*)
END AnalyseText.
```

Fig. 7.24.

The major problem now remaining is how to recognise the end of a line, the end of the text, and how to update the word counts. First a variable is required to hold the next character read, which can be declared as

```
VAR
    NextChar : CHAR;
```

and does not need initialising. This variable is used in deciding how to terminate the WHILE loops. The value of NextCharInWord can be determined by the assignment statement

```
NextCharInWord := (NextChar <> Space) & (NextChar <> EOL)
                    & (NextChar <> Terminator)
```

Two further variables to flag the end of a line and the end of the text can be declared

```
VAR
      LineEnded,Finish : BOOLEAN;
```

and initialised

```
LineEnded := FALSE
Finish := FALSE
```

These are assigned values by the statements

```
LineEnded := (NextChar = EOL) OR (NextChar = Terminator)
Finish := NextChar = Terminator
```

anywhere after the next character has been read, but the best point is at the end of the line loop. Both are used as loop termination constraints.

Having done this it is straightforward to code the word counts. Two variables are required

```
VAR
      WordsInLine,WordsInText : CARDINAL;
```

the former is initialised to 0 at the start of each line, and the latter at the start of the module. Both must be incremented by 1.

```
(*. . . increment word counts . . .*)
INC(WordsInLine);
INC(WordsInText)
```

These refinements results in the module in Fig. 7.25.

Notes.

1. The code is almost complete and will not be developed further. The output to the screen is straightforward.

2. The definition of a word is very crude and may result in punctuation being treated as a word. It is an interesting exercise to make the specification take account of punctuation.

3. The most interesting question is that of how to perform the input. It is clear that there is no reason to use one particular form of input since the program succeeds for any technique which makes the next character in the sequence available on request. It follows that the input can be carried out by an imported procedure and this allows the program to work for many different styles of input. In fact the program could be redrafted as a procedure and placed in an implementation module for use by other programs This would probably also require the output routines to be imported procedures. Chapters 12 and 13 give the details of the variety of techniques available in

```
MODULE AnalyseText;
(*. . . import EOL and Terminator . . .*);
CONST
      Space = ' ;
VAR
      NextChar                    : CHAR ;
      InWord,NextCharInWord       : BOOLEAN;
      LineEnded,Finish            : BOOLEAN;
      WordsInLine,WordsInText     : CARDINAL;
BEGIN
 WordsInText := 0;
 Finish := FALSE;
 WHILE NOT Finish DO
      WordsInLine    := 0;
      LineEnded      := FALSE;
      InWord         := FALSE;
      WHILE NOT LineEnded DO
           (*. . . read a character . . .*);
           NextCharInWord := (NextChar <> Space) & (NextChar <> EOL)
                                         & (NextChar <> Terminator);
           IF InWord AND ~NextCharInWord THEN
               INC(WordsInLine);
               INC(WordsInText);
               InWord := FALSE
           ELSIF ~InWord & NextCharInWord THEN
               InWord := TRUE
           END (* IF *);
           LineEnded := (NextChar = EOL) OR (NextChar = Terminator);
           Finish := NextChar = Terminator
      END (* WHILE *);
      (*. . . output the total number of words in the line . . .*)
 END (* WHILE *);
 (*. . . output the total number of words in the text . . .*)
END AnalyseText.
```

Fig. 7.25.

Modula-2 for these types of situations. As a matter of interest three possible input routines are mentioned

a.   The input could be accepted from the terminal in which case the input routine would be implemented by calls to Read in InOut.

b.   The input could be accepted from some secondary storage media like magnetic disk. This would require special routines for reading from the media, though usually InOut can be used for such purposes by special techniques.

c.   The input could be accepted from a queue of data. The queue could be added to by some other processor reading data from an external media at the same time as the analysis is being carried out. This could be useful in cases where a computer is being used to control some other piece of equipment. In this case the character reading routine could be using a sophisticated version of the queue module developed in Chapters 5 and 6.

7.5 SUMMARY

1 Tha data type BOOLEAN and BOOLEAN expressions have been discussed. The only values of the type BOOLEAN are TRUE and FALSE. BOOLEAN expressions evaluate to a BOOLEAN value and are an integral part of the IF and WHILE statements.

2 The extended forms of the IF statement involving ELSIF clauses were discussed, these permit an IF statement to consider several alternatives. The CASE statement is specially provided for situations where an expression is to be tested against several alternative constant values, but the case labels of a CASE statement are restricted to constant expressions.

TECHNICAL EXERCISES

1 Evaluate the following expressions

   a FALSE OR TRUE AND TRUE

   b TRUE OR FALSE AND TRUE

   c NOT NOT TRUE

   d NOT FALSE OR TRUE

   e NOT TRUE OR NOT TRUE

   f TRUE AND FALSE OR TRUE

   g NOT(TRUE OR FALSE)

   h NOT(TRUE AND FALSE)

2 Evaluate the following relational expressions

   a $3 < 5$

   b $3 > 5$

   c $3 <> 5$

   d 3 AND 4

   e $3 < 5$ AND $0 = 0$

   f FALSE OR $(3 < 5)$

   g $(3 <> 4)$ AND $(1 > 0)$

   h $\sim(3 < 5)$ OR $(2 = 1)$ OR $(3 > 5)$

3 Given that Ans is a BOOLEAN variable, state its final value after each of the following code fragments has been executed

   a
```
X := 29;
Y := 40;
Ans := X < Y
```

   b
```
X := 29;
Y := 40;
Ans := (X < Y) & (Y = X)
```

   c
```
Ans := FALSE;
Z:= Y + 1;
IF X < Y THEN Ans := X < Z
```

d   WHILE Ans DO
.
.
END (* WHILE *);

....

4 Simplify the program fragment of Fig. 7.11 by using the function procedure CAP so that only upper case characters need to be included in the tests.

5 Without using the standard funtion procedure ABS, write a fragment of code which sets an INTEGER B to the non-negative version of A. For example

A input	B output
3	3
−3	3
0	0

6 Rewrite the following code in a simpler form

```
IF Fred & Joe THEN
    Alf := TRUE
ELSIF Fred & ~Joe THEN
    Alf := FALSE
ELSIF ~Fred & Joe THEN
    Alf := FALSE
ELSIF ~Fred & ~Joe THEN
    Alf := TRUE
END (* IF *)
```

7 Write a fragment of code to do the following

If two numbers Num1 and Num2 are both greater than zero or both less than zero, set Num3 to their product. In all other cases set Num3 to zero.

8 Using comments and indentation, reformat the following program into easily readable form without changing the meaning. Note that the code has no meaning, this is intentional to force you to focus on the structural rules rather than deduce the structure from the meaning.

```
IF MaybeTrue THEN
Num := 0;
IF NotZero THEN
WHILE NotZero DO
IF NotAlwaysTrue THEN
NotZero := CouldBeZero OR IsIt
END;
IsIt := (A < 20);
A := A+1;
END
END
END
```

9 Write a code fragment which takes an INTEGER array Num defined over the range 1 to 20 and adds up all the positive values and stores the answer in a variable PosSum, adds up all the negative values and stores the result in a variable NegSum, and gives the number of zero values in the array in a variable called ZeroNum.

10 Use the syntax diagrams of Fig. 7.19 to say which of the following statements are legal. There is no requirement that they be sensible, the exercise is simply designed to make you aware of what is possible.

a
```
CASE MaybeTrue OF
  TRUE : |
  FALSE : WriteString('Hello')|
  TRUE : WriteString('GoodBye')
END (* CASE *)
```

b
```
CASE Joke OF
  ELSE WriteString ('Silly')
END (* CASE *)
```

c
```
CASE CardNum OF
  0. .20 : WriteString('Less than 21') |
  21. .100 : WriteString('Less than 100,greater than 20') |
END (* CASE *)
```

d
```
CASE NOT Joe AND Fred OF
  TRUE : WriteString('True') |
  FALSE : WriteString('False')
END (* CASE *)
```

e
```
CASE Joe OF
END (* CASE *)
```

11 Rewrite the following code fragment which appears in Fig. 7.25 so that no ELSIF clause is required.

```
IF InWord AND ~NextCharInWord THEN
    INC(WordsInLine);
    INC(WordsInText);
    InWord := FALSE
ELSIF ~InWord & NextCharInWord THEN
    InWord := TRUE
END (* IF *);
```

PROGRAMMING EXERCISES

1 Rewrite QueueModule of Chapters 5 and 6 to implement EmptyQueue and FullQueue as BOOLEAN function procedures.

2 Complete AnalyseText assuming that input is from the keyboard and output is to a screen.

3 Rewrite AnalyseText where a line is defined as ending with EOL and Terminator always follows immediately after an EOL character.

4 Rewrite AnalyseText where only words containing the (upper or lower case) letter e are to be counted.

5 Rewrite AnalyseText of question 4 to use QueueModule. Words read which do not contain the letter e are to be added to the queue. At the end of each line, the words in the queue are to be removed from the queue and written to the screen.

6 An alternative approach to solving the word counting problem is to decide on the actions to be taken for particular characters and to avoid refining the problem to cope with a line at a time in an inner loop. The following pseudo code shows an initial formulation for this approach. Complete the program from this initial formulation.

```
MODULE AnalyseText;
  (*. . . declarations . . .*)
BEGIN
  (*. . . initialise variables . . .*);
  WHILE (*. . . not yet the end of text Terminator . . .*) DO
          (*. . . read next character . . .*)
          IF (*. . . currently part of a word . . .*) THEN
            IF (*. . . new character is a space . . .*) THEN
                        (*. . .          . . .*);
            ELSIF (*. . . new character is EOL or end of text Terminator . . .*) THEN
                        (*. . .          . . .*);
            END (*IF *)
          ELSE (* not currently part of a word *)
            IF (*. . . new character is EOL or end of text terminator . . .*) THEN
                        (*. . .          . . .*);
            ELSIF (*. . . new character is not a space . . .*) THEN
                        (*. . . . . .*);
            END (* IF *)
  END (* WHILE *);
  (*. . . output the total number of words in the text . . .*);
END AnalyseText.
```

ANSWERS

1 **a** FALSE OR TRUE AND TRUE   = FALSE OR (TRUE AND TRUE)
                                      = FALSE OR TRUE
                                      = TRUE
Note that AND has precedence over OR.
   b TRUE OR FALSE AND TRUE   = TRUE OR (FALSE AND TRUE)
                                   = TRUE OR FALSE
                                   = TRUE
   c NOT NOT TRUE   = NOT (NOT TRUE)
                                   = NOT FALSE
                                   = TRUE
   d NOT FALSE OR TRUE   = (NOT FALSE) OR TRUE
                                   = TRUE OR TRUE
                                   = TRUE
   e NOT TRUE OR NOT TRUE   = (NOT TRUE) OR (NOT TRUE)
                                   = FALSE OR FALSE
                                   = FALSE
   f TRUE AND FALSE OR TRUE   = (TRUE AND FALSE) OR TRUE
                                   = FALSE OR TRUE
                                   = TRUE
   g NOT (TRUE OR FALSE)   = NOT TRUE
                                   = FALSE
   h NOT (TRUE AND FALSE)   = NOT FALSE
                                   = TRUE

2 **a** TRUE **b** FALSE **c** TRUE **d** Illegal expression, since neither 3 nor 4 is a BOOLEAN expression as required.
   e $3 < 5$ AND $0 = 0$ = $3 < (5$ AND $0) = 0$
which is an illegal expression since neither 5 nor 0 is a BOOLEAN expression. Note that the common sense interpretation of the statement is not accepted by Modula-2 and brackets round the sub-expressions are needed.
   f FALSE OR $(3 < 5)$ = FALSE OR TRUE
                          = TRUE
   g $(3 <> 4)$ AND $(1 > 0)$ =   TRUE AND TRUE = TRUE
   h FALSE OR FALSE OR FALSE = FALSE

3 **a** TRUE **b** FALSE **c** It depends on the value of X, if it is less than Y then Ans is TRUE, otherwise it is FALSE.
   d Ans must be FALSE since it is not possible to terminate the WHILE loop unless Ans is FALSE. It is of course possible that the loop does not terminate!

4
```
Answer := CAP (Answer);
IF (Answer = 'A') THEN
   WriteString('This is the correct answer.')
ELSIF (Answer = 'B') THEN
   WriteString('This is nearly correct,but not quite.')
ELSIF (Answer = 'C') THEN
   WriteString('This is the wrong answer.')
ELSE
   WriteString('The answer you have given is invalid.')
END (* IF *)
```

5 Two reasonable answers are

```
IF A >= 0 THEN              B := A;
   B := A                   IF A < 0 THEN
ELSE (* A < 0 *)               B := -A
   B := -A                  END (* IF *)
END (* IF *)
```

6 There are many simplified solutions, the common property is that they do not involve an IF statement. For example,

```
Alf := (Fred & Joe) OR (~Fred & ~Joe)
```

or best of all,

```
Alf := (Fred = Joe)
```

7
```
Num3 := Num1*Num2;
IF Num3 < 0 THEN
   Num3 := 0
END (* IF *)
```

The only problem with this solution is that in the first statement Num3 might overflow even though its final value is destined to be zero. If this is a possibility, the answer is to write the obvious longwinded solution

```
IF (Num1 > 0) & (Num2 > 0) OR (Num1 < 0) & (Num2 < 0) THEN
   Num3 := Num1* Num2
ELSE
   Num3 := 0
END (* IF *)
```

8
```
IF MaybeTrue THEN
   Num := 0;
   IF NotZero THEN
      WHILE NotZero DO
         IF NotAlwaysTrue THEN
            NotZero := CouldBeZero OR IsIt
         END (* IF *);
         IsIt := (A < 20);
         A := A+1;
      END (* WHILE *)
   END (* IF *)
END (* IF *)
```

9
```
PosSum := 0;
NegSum := 0;
ZeroNum := 0;
Count := 1;
WHILE Count <> 21 DO
   IF Num[Count] > 0 THEN
      INC(PosSum,Num[Count])
   ELSIF Num[Count] < 0 THEN
      INC(NegSum,Num[Count])
   ELSIF Num[Count] = 0 THEN
      INC(ZeroNum)
   END (* IF *);
   INC(Count)
END (* WHILE *)
```

10 a Legal, but silly! The label TRUE which causes 'GoodBye' to be written out is never considered, since the case where TRUE is associated with a null statement is found first and is executed in preference.

b Legal, but silly! It is perfectly correct only to have an ELSE clause even though technically a 'case' is required, because a 'case' can be the null case.

c Legal, but note that if a number outside the range 0..100 occurred a run time error would be given. One of the clauses of a CASE statement must be executed. It is also true that there is no need for the last ı in the statement, but it is not wrong to put it in as there is a conceptual null case between the ı and the END.

d Legal, there is no problem with this statement!

e Legal, but not useful.

11
```
IF InWord AND ~NextCharInWord THEN
         INC(WordsInLine);
         INC(WordsInText);
   END (* IF *);
   InWord := NextCharInWord
```

Chapter 8

Basic Types, Type Declarations, and Enumeration and Subrange Types

Modula-2 has several predefined basic data types. Three of these types, CARDINAL, CHAR and BOOLEAN have already been considered in detail. This chapter discusses the other basic data types REAL and INTEGER in detail. In addition the relationship between the numeric data types is discussed.

Modula-2 provides an alternative way of declaring literal CHAR constants which is illustrated.

A major advantage of Modula-2 and similar languages is that the programmer can define his own types. Two such classes of programmer-definable types are enumeration and subrange types which are discussed in detail. These and the basic data types form the basis for structured data types, which consist of collections of these types.

8.1 NUMERIC DATA TYPES

It is important to distinguish between the numeric data types, the values of these types, and the way of writing literal constants for these types. The numeric data types REAL, INTEGER and CARDINAL are discussed in this section. Variables of these types can hold values of the respective types, thus INTEGER variables can hold INTEGER values etc. The representation in the computer's memory of these values is largely irrelevant for our current purposes.

The ways of writing numbers of these types in the text of a source program is determined by the syntax diagrams for literal constants of the type. Assuming the declaration

```
VAR  X : CARDINAL ;
```

the assignment statement

```
X := 3
```

states that the literal constant 3 is to be assigned to X. We have already seen many examples of literal whole number constants in declarations, being assigned to CARDINAL variables, and being passed to procedures with formal CARDINAL value parameters.

However, there is not a strict one to one correspondence between the ways that literal constants are written in Modula-2 and the numeric types. The type REAL is discussed first as the way that literal constants for REAL values are written is totally independent of the the way that literal constants for CARDINAL and INTEGER values are written.

Literal REAL Constants

Literal REAL constants are clearly distinguished from literal whole number constants in Modula-2 as they must contain a decimal point. These can be written in two different ways, either with or without a scaling factor. Some examples of valid real constants are

> 10.2   3.0   3.   3.1E3   3.0E3   3.E−1   3.0E−30

The xEy notation indicates the presence of the scaling factor and should be read as 'x ∗ (10 raised to the power of y)'. Thus

> 3.1E3 equals $3.1*10^3$ equals 3100.0

The syntax diagram for literal REAL constants is given in Fig. 8.1. Note that they cannot start with a decimal point and are always decimal numbers.

Literal   REAL   Constant:

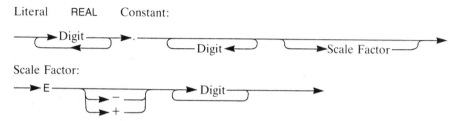

Scale Factor:

where Digit is any of 0,1,2,3,4,5,6,7,8 or 9 (see Fig. 8.6)

Fig. 8.1.

The assignment statements

> X := 23.56
> Y := 4.25E5

assign the literal REAL constant values to the REAL variables X and Y. The representation inside the computer of REAL values is the same for both ways of writing the constants despite their superficial difference.

REAL Values

REAL values typically are not represented precisely within the computer and calculations carried out on them are not guaranteed to be completely accurate. Theoretically, there is an infinity of other real numbers between any two distinct real numbers. However, since computers can only use finite representations, it is impossible to have exact representation. The errors which result are of two related forms, an insufficient number of digits are held in the computer to represent the value, or there is no finite representation of the value. In ordinary arithmetic the latter is demonstrated by the fraction one third which is denoted by a non-terminating number 0.333... . The former is by far the more important since it can lead to serious errors in the calculation of complicated REAL expressions.

Note that the definition of literal REAL constants in Fig. 8.1 does not appear to allow negative values. The syntax diagram indicates that literal constants are unsigned. This does not mean that only non-negative REAL values are allowed in Modula-2, it only means that literal REAL constants are non-negative. The values of variables and constants of appropriate types can be negative but this achieved by using the negating operator (−). It is important not to confuse literal REAL constants with values of the type REAL.

The data type REAL

In Modula-2 the type REAL allows the declaration of variables which can contain REAL values. REAL variables are declared

```
VAR
      Hot,Cold : REAL;
```

A collection of operators and procedures to manipulate REAL values is provided. These are listed and described in Fig. 8.2.

OPERATOR	DESCRIPTION	PRECEDENCE
+	Addition operator, can be used as in A+B, or +A.	1
−	Subtraction operator, can be used as in A−B, or −A.	1
*	Multiplication operator, can be used as in A*B. It cannot be omitted as in some mathematical notation.	2
/	Divide operator, can be used as in A/D.	2
( )	Brackets, can be used as in A*(B+C). They change the order of precedence.	3

Fig. 8.2.

The order of evaluation of REAL expressions involving operators of the same precedence is left to right, for example

20.0 / 4.0 ∗ 5.0 is evaluated as (20.0 / 4.0) ∗ 5.0
5.3 + 3.4 − 2.5 is evaluated as (5.3 + 3.4) − 2.5

In expressions involving operators of different precedences the basic ordering is left to right, but sub-expressions involving operators of higher precedences override this ordering to produce intermediate results when required. For example

20.0 + 5.0 − 4.4 / 2.2 is evaluated as (20.0 + 5.0) − (4.4 / 2.2)

where the sub-expression

4.4 / 2.2

is evaluated to provide the second operand for the subtraction when this value is needed.

The above precedence order corresponds to the normal mathematical notation and the precedence of the corresponding operators for CARDINAL arithmetic discussed in Chapter 3. Assuming the variables of Fig. 8.3a, examples of REAL expressions are shown in Fig. 8.3b with an accompanying commentary.

All variables and constants which appear in REAL expressions must be of type REAL. Thus the constants in the expressions in Fig. 8.3 all contain a decimal point. If they did not, they would not be literal REAL constants and a syntax error would be reported.

Two important procedures, ReadReal and WriteReal, allow the reading and writing of REAL values. They can be imported from a module normally called RealInOut which is distributed with Modula-2.

FROM RealInOut IMPORT ReadReal,WriteReal;

RealInOut contains the procedure headings

```
PROCEDURE ReadReal(VAR x : REAL);
PROCEDURE WriteReal(VAR x : REAL ; n : CARDINAL);
```

In WriteReal the parameter n gives the fieldwidth in which x is to be written out. If fewer character positions than specified for the fieldwidth are needed, leading spaces are written to fill the rest of the fieldwidth. The complete definition module for RealInOut is given in Appendix 4.

First	Second	Third	Fourth
10.2	2.0	3.41	7.0

(a) REAL variables.

First*2.0+3.0   evaluates to 23.4
Left to right evaluation and multiplication has precedence over addition.

3.0+First*2.0   evaluates to 23.4
The answer is the same as in the previous example, because multiplication has a higher precedence than addition which overrides the left to right ordering.

(3.0+First)*2.0   evaluates to 26.4
The brackets cause the addition to be performed before the multiplication.

First/Second+Third   evaluates to 8.51
Division has precedence over addition.

First/Second*Fourth   evaluates to 35.7
Division and multiplication have same the precedence level so they are evaluated left to right.

First/(Second*Fourth)   evaluates to .7285...
The brackets cause the division to be performed after the multiplication. Note that the result is a non-terminating REAL decimal number.

2.0+3.0+Second*First   evaluates to 25.4
2.0 and 3.0 are added and then First and Second are multiplied before the two intermediate results are added.

2.0*First+3.0*Second   evaluates to 26.4
2.0 and First are multiplied, then 3.0 and Second are multiplied and the two results are added.

(b) REAL Expressions.

Fig. 8.3.

Errors in REAL Arithmetic

When writing a program which involves REAL calculations, the programmer should have knowledge of the properties of computer representations of REAL values. The internal representation of REAL values is similar to the scale factor way of indicating a literal constant. See the bibliography under the heading **Elementary Computing** for texts on this subject.

An important reason for errors in calculations is **overflow**. This is the term used when a value is too large for the representation used in the particular Modula-2 implementation. In REAL arithmetic the overflow size tends to be large; typically values between $10E+38$ and $-10E+38$ are valid but you must always check the precise values for any compiler you use. An error is normally reported if overflow occurs since it almost certainly means that the results will be in error. Division by zero, or nearly zero, is a common reason for overflow.

A similar kind of error, termed **underflow**, is caused by a multiplication or division which gives a zero result even though none of the values involved is zero. The reason for underflow is that a value has become too small for the representation. The underflow value tends to be of the order of 10E−38. Underflow nearly always means that the result is in error.

Overflow can sometimes be prevented by apparently superflous bracketing. For example

    Large1∗Large2/Large3

may contain the possibility of overflow because Large1 and Large2 are multiplied first. It is possible that this could be prevented by rewriting the expression in the form

    Large1∗(Large2/Large3),

since the division may help to keep the values relatively small. It is important to know the possible range of value of the variables for the particular problem. In the above example, if it is possible that Large2 is very small, the rewriting might result in underflow where none existed before!

In general, any REAL arithmetic expression has a small error called the **round-off error**. This is caused by the fact that computers can only hold REAL values to a fixed number of significant figures if reasonably efficient calculation is to be maintained. Normally this round-off error is small enough to be ignored. The following examples are chosen to illustrate the dangers which await the unwary.

1.   Subtracting two almost equal values usually leads to a large error relative to the size of the answer. Often a rearrangement of the formula can remove the problem.

2.   Adding a very small value to a very large one may have no effect in a WHILE loop . This is dangerous as ignorance of it can lead to very subtle but important errors in computing results (e.g. in statistical calculations where intermediate results may never be seen).

Figure 8.4 illustrates the latter case. In many implementations of Modula-2 the final value of Large will be the same as its initial value. This is because the difference between the relative magnitudes of Large and Small is so great that the representation of the REAL values is unable to differentiate between the value of Large and the result of Large+Small. Adding Small to Large 10000 times should have a considerable effect, but does not if it is coded in this way.

Figure 8.5 shows an alternative way of writing the program to achieve the same purpose which computes a more accurate result. This version allows Small to have an effect once it is multiplied by a sufficiently large factor. It also avoids the problem of adding a long sequence of values together, which tends to produce a considerable round-off effect. In short, all programs involving REAL arithmetic calculations within loops should be studied carefully for numerical accuracy.

```
MODULE Disappear;
 FROM InOut IMPORT WriteString;
 FROM RealInOut IMPORT WriteReal;
 VAR
       Large,Small  :REAL;
       Count        : CARDINAL;
 BEGIN
  WriteString('Welcome to the disappearing number program');
  Large := 1.0E12; Small := 1.0E2;
  Count := 0;
  WHILE Count < 10000 DO
          Large := Large+Small;
          (*... code which uses value of Large ...*)
          INC(Count)
  END(*WHILE*);
  WriteReal(Large,12);
  END Disappear.
```

Fig. 8.4.

```
MODULE Appear;
 FROM InOut IMPORT WriteString;
 FROM RealInOut IMPORT WriteReal;
 VAR
       Large,NewLarge,Small :REAL;
       Count                : CARDINAL;
 BEGIN
  WriteString('Welcome to the appearing number program');
  Large := 1.0E12; Small := 1.0E2;
  Count := 1;
  WHILE Count <= 10000 DO
      NewLarge := Large + Small*FLOAT(Count);
      (* FLOAT is a procedure function to covert a CARDINAL to a REAL. *)
      (*... code which uses current value of NewLarge ...*)
      INC(Count)
  END(*WHILE*);
  WriteReal(NewLarge,12);
  END Appear.
```

Fig. 8.5.

Literal Whole Number Constants

Literal whole number constants are denoted in three different ways in Modula-2. These are standard decimal (base 10) notation, octal (base 8) and hexadecimal (base 16) notation. If you are unfamiliar with these bases it would be wise to consult the textbooks referenced in the bibliography under the heading **Elementary Computing**. Most literal whole number constants used in this book are decimal. The syntax diagrams for the three kinds of digits, octal, decimal and hexadecimal, are given in Fig. 8.6 and the syntax diagram for literal whole number constants is given in Fig. 8.7. The hexadecimal notation uses the letters A..F as digits, but note that a hexadecimal number may not start with one of these letters. This is to prevent confusion with identifiers, which always start with letters. If a hexadecimal number should start with a letter it is prefixed by 0, for example 0EF23.

Hex Digit :

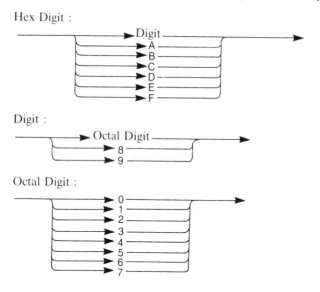

Digit :

Octal Digit :

Fig. 8.6.

Literal Whole Number Constant :

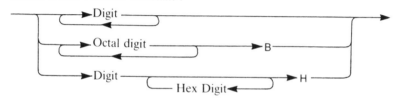

Fig. 8.7.

Some examples of valid literal whole number constants are

Base 10	23		0	023	0023	1045	999	89
Octal	21B	67B	03B	3B				
Hexadecimal	43H	3FH	3H	0B6H	0FFH	03H	3BH	

Note the final example is a hexadecimal constant even though 3B is a valid octal constant if it is written on its own. The final character of the sequence determines whether it is octal or hexadecimal. The hexadecimal digits A to F and the characters B and H indicating octal and hexadecimal constants must be in upper-case.

The data type INTEGER

INTEGER values are positive and negative whole numbers and zero. The range of INTEGER values is much more restricted than REAL values. A typical range on micro-computers is -32768 to $+32767$. However, in contrast to the type REAL, INTEGER values are represented precisely and results of INTEGER arithmetic expressions are entirely accurate.

The operators which act on data of type INTEGER are, $+$, $-$, $*$, DIV and MOD. These have the same precedence rules as for REAL calculations with DIV and MOD replacing the REAL division operator / and acting as in CARDINAL arithmetic. DIV can be thought of as an ordinary division followed by a truncation of the fractional part of the result. Some examples are

```
45 DIV 9 = 5    46 DIV 9 = 5    −46 DIV 9 = −5    46 DIV (−9) = −5
(−46) DIV (−9) = 5
```

MOD can be thought of as giving the remainder resulting from the corresponding DIV operation. It is only defined for positive values of the denominator. If it is important, you should check this in the implementation of Modula-2 you are using as some compilers are non standard in this respect and allow MOD to be used with negative denominators.

Some examples are of calculations using MOD are

```
45 MOD 9 = 0    46 MOD 9 = 1    23 MOD 17 = 6    5 MOD 7 = 5
```

The data type CARDINAL

The type CARDINAL has already been discussed in some detail in Chapter 3, the material presented here is a summary of that information.
1.   CARDINAL values are non-negative whole numbers and are represented accurately within the computer. A typical range for CARDINAL values on a micro-computer are 0 to 65535.

2.   The operators applied to CARDINAL numbers are +, −, ∗, DIV and MOD. These operators have the same properties as those discussed in the section on the type INTEGER.

3.   Care must be taken with CARDINAL arithmetic to ensure that intermediate result of sub-expressions are non-negative values.

INTEGER and CARDINAL Values

The ranges of INTEGER and CARDINAL values overlap as illustrated in Fig. 8.8. Literal whole number constants in the range 0 to the maximum INTEGER value are therefore ambiguous between being INTEGER or CARDINAL values. In practice the type of such numbers is determined from context. If the constant is part of an INTEGER arithmetic expression then the constant is treated as being an INTEGER value; if it is part of a CARDINAL expression then it is treated as a CARDINAL value. Note that this also applies to the declaration of constant identifiers which are similarly ambiguous. For example, assuming the following declarations

```
CONST
      TwentyTwo = 22 ;
VAR
      X : INTEGER ;
      Z : CARDINAL ;
```

both of the following expressions are permitted

```
X := 5 ∗ TwentyTwo
Z := TwentyTwo − 15B
```

Minimum INTEGER value   Maximum INTEGER value

                            0   Maximum CARDINAL value

Fig. 8.8.

In addition, note that octal, decimal and hexadecimal literal constants can be mixed freely in both CARDINAL and INTEGER expressions. They are simply different ways of writing literal constant values of these types.

REAL, INTEGER and CARDINAL : Compatability Questions

The three numeric types, REAL, INTEGER and CARDINAL, cannot be mixed in the same arithmetic expression. This is a considerable restriction and so special facilities are available to reduce the consequences of this restriction.

The types INTEGER and CARDINAL are **assignment compatible** which means that it is possible to assign an INTEGER value to a CARDINAL variable and a CARDINAL value to an INTEGER variable **so long as the values are in the overlapping region of the types** (see Fig. 8.8). However, this does not mean that the two types can be mixed in the same expression.

The following examples illustrate compatible and incompatible cases. Given the declarations

```
VAR
        CAR1,CAR2 : CARDINAL;
        INT1,INT2 : INTEGER;
```

then

```
        CAR1 := INT1
```

is legal if the current value of INT1 lies with in the overlapping region of the two types. If the value does not lie in this region then an error is reported when the program is executed. The assignment statement

```
        CAR1 : = 2*INT1 + INT2
```

is legal as long as the result of the expression is a non-negative value because it is an INTEGER expression and its result can be assigned to a CARDINAL variable. The statement

```
        CAR1 : = 2*INT1 + CAR2
```

is illegal, because the expression consists of a mixture of INTEGER and CARDINAL operands.

Type Transfer and Type Conversion Function Procedures

If it is necessary to mix values of different types in an expression there are special function procedures available to allow an INTEGER value to be interpreted as a CARDINAL value and a CARDINAL value to be interpreted as an INTEGER value. The following two statements are legal

```
        CAR1 := 2*INT1 + INTEGER(CAR2)
        INT1 := 2*CAR1 + CARDINAL(INT2)
```

Note that the name of the function procedure is the same as the name of the required type. These functions rely on the fact that the internal representation of an INTEGER and a CARDINAL are identical over their overlapping region. No calculation takes place, but the function causes the value to be interpreted as being of the named type. These are known as **type transfer** procedures.

When CARDINAL or INTEGER values are passed as parameters either may replace the other as a value parameter. This follows from the fact that INTEGER and CARDINAL values can be directly assigned to variables of either type as long as the values are within the overlapping region. In the case of variable parameters the actual parameter passed must be identical in type with the formal parameter. Assuming the declarations

```
VAR
      Joe : CARDINAL; Fred : INTEGER;
   PROCEDURE TestCase(PosNum : CARDINAL; VAR AnyNum : INTEGER);
```

the following calls of TestCase illustrate the rules

TestCase(Joe,Fred)	Legal, because the actual parameters Joe and Fred are the correct types.
TestCase(Fred,Fred)	Legal, because Fred is assignment compatible with PosNum and identical in type with AnyNum.
TestCase(Joe,Joe)	Illegal, though Joe is identical in type with PosNum, Joe is not identical in type with the variable parameter AnyNum.

The type REAL is not compatible with the other numeric types. REAL values can only be used in CARDINAL and INTEGER expressions through the use of specially provided function procedures. The available function procedures are implementation dependent, but the usual ones available are

```
PROCEDURE TRUNC (x : REAL) : CARDINAL ;
PROCEDURE FLOAT (x : CARDINAL) : REAL ;
```

1. TRUNC(x) converts a real number into a CARDINAL by chopping off any decimal part. For example

```
TRUNC(3.54) = 3
```

2. FLOAT(x) converts a CARDINAL value into a REAL value. For example

```
FLOAT(7) = 7.0
```

These perform conversions between the internal representation of one type to that of another and are therefore known as **type conversion** procedures.

It is important to check the details of your Modula-2 system for the precise facilities it makes available. Frequently there may be some development of FLOAT and TRUNC. Some systems convert to and from INTEGER rather than CARDINAL values to make the handling of negative numbers easier.

Some Additional Numeric Types and Type Manipulation Procedures

Modula-2 recognises that for many programs much larger ranges of numbers may be required than those provided by the types CARDINAL, INTEGER and REAL, so it provides the special types LONGCARD, LONGINT and LONGREAL to cater for this need. These types have the same characteristics as their shorter couterparts except that they cover larger ranges of values. These should only be used when necessary as they use up much more space than the normal types. Some implementations may not make these types available. They are not used further in this book so if they are needed you should consult the details for your particular implementation.

Different implementations on different machines have different ranges for numeric types. It is useful, when writing programs which may be transferred to other computers, to express certain checks in terms of the limits of the range of a type. Modula-2 supplies two standard function procedures to help with this, MIN and MAX. These take a type as a parameter and return the minimum and maximum value respectively of that type. The value returned is of the same type as the actual parameter. For example

> MAX(REAL) returns the REAL value which is the largest possible REAL in the system being used.
> MIN(INTEGER) returns the value which is the smallest possible INTEGER in the system being used.

It is normal for MIN(CARDINAL) to equal 0 and MAX(CARDINAL) to equal 2*MAX(INTEGER)+1.

Some implementations of Modula-2 may not provide MIN and MAX but provide other facilities instead. It is worthwhile checking this point as these function procedures are very useful if they are available.

8.2   A FURTHER WORD ON THE DATA TYPE CHAR

In Chapter 3 the type CHAR was considered in detail. Here we note that there is a practical problem in specifying certain character constants. We have seen many examples of declarations of character constants, such as

```
CONST
    FullStop    = '.' ;
    Terminator  = '*' ;
```

However the ASCII character set contains characters which have no printable form, such as the null character whose character code is 0, and therefore cannot be written as characters in the source program text. In programs so far, we have circumvented this problem by declaring a CHAR variable, Null, and initialising it in a program statement

```
Null := CHR(0) ;
```

even though the variable has been used as though it was a constant.

However, Modula-2 provides an alternative way of writing literal character constants to denote characters. The syntax diagram for literal character constants in Fig. 8.9 shows that these can be written either as the printable form of the character in quotation marks or as their character code. In the latter case the character code is written as an octal number and must finish with the letter C. Null can therefore be declared

```
CONST
      Null = 0C ;
```

and as it is not a variable it does not require the initialisation statement.

Literal Character Constant :

Fig. 8.9.

Literal character constants can also be assigned to variables and can be used in conditions which test a CHAR value. Assuming the declaration

```
VAR
      Ch : CHAR ;
```

then the assignment statement

```
Ch := 27C
```

assigns the escape (esc) character to Ch. An IF statement

```
IF Ch = 65C THEN (*... ...*) END (* IF *)
```

tests if Ch holds the character '5'.

Be careful not to confuse this notation for literal character constants with that for literal whole number constants. 65C is a character value, but 65B is a literal whole number constant. The type of the former is CHAR and will cause a compilation error if attempts are made to assign it to an INTEGER or CARDINAL variable. Similarly an error will be reported if the latter is compared with a CHAR value. Assuming the declarations

```
CONST
      Escape = 27B ;
VAR
      UserReply : CHAR ;
```

the statement

```
IF UserReply = Escape THEN (*... ...*) END (* IF *)
```

is an error because Escape is a numeric constant which is treated either as an INTEGER or CARDINAL value depending on context.

8.3 ANONYMOUS TYPES AND TYPE DECLARATIONS

A major aid in making Modula-2 programs easy to understand and construct is the facility to define new types while maintaining the careful checks on type compatibility that the language provides. The new types are introduced in two ways
1. within a variable declaration,
2. by an explicit type declaration.
The former have been illustrated on several occasions, particularly in the use of arrays. The declaration

```
VAR
    Name : ARRAY [1..20] OF CHAR ;
```

declares Name to be a variable whose type is a twenty-character array. This type does not have an explicit name and therefore such types are called **anonymous types**. Anonymous types are of restricted use as they cannot be referred to again in other variable declarations or formal parameter lists.

However, Modula-2 allows the programmer to explicitly declare types which he wishes to use. The above declaration could be rewritten as

```
TYPE
    NameType = ARRAY [1..20] OF CHAR ;
VAR
    Name : NameType ;
```

any number of variables can then be declared to be of this type. In addition variables of NameType can be passed as a parameter to a procedure whose procedure heading specifies this type for a formal parameter. Both methods are illustrated below, but you are advised to use explicit type declarations unless there are special circumstances.

Simplified syntax diagrams for type declarations are shown in Fig. 8.10. Declarations of new types fall into two broad general classes, those concerned with structured data types (e.g. array types) and enumeration and subrange types. Structured data types are considered in subsequent chapters. Enumeration and subrange types are considered in full in the rest of this chapter.

Type declarations occur, like constant, variable and procedure declarations, as part of module and procedure blocks. A type declaration must textually precede occurrences of its use. Typically a type declaration section precedes a variable declaration section and procedure declarations using these types. Type identifiers obey the same scope rules as identifiers declared in constant or variable declarations.

Type Declaration :

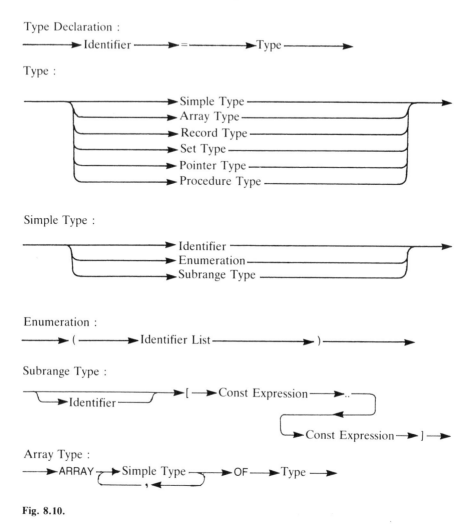

Type :

Simple Type :

Enumeration :

Subrange Type :

Array Type :

Fig. 8.10.

8.4   ENUMERATION TYPES

The declaration of an enumeration type enumerates the values of the type in the declaration. For example, the declarations

```
TYPE
    Science = (Computing,Physics,Chemistry,Biochemistry,Biology,Zoology);
VAR
        Smith,Jones    : Science;
        BoolVal        : BOOLEAN;
```

declare an enumeration type called Science whose values are Computing, Physics, Chemistry, etc. Each of the identifiers listed in the enumeration is implicitly declared as a constant and therefore must be distinct from all other identifiers declared at the same block level. The variables Smith and Jones are declared to be of type Science and can take values in the range defined by the type. The variable BoolVal is of type BOOLEAN which is a standard enumeration type, effectively declared as

```
TYPE
        BOOLEAN = (FALSE,TRUE) ;
```

Values can be assigned to Smith and Jones in assignment statements.

```
Smith := Physics;
Jones := Biology;
Smith := Jones;
BoolVal := Smith < Jones;
```

The last example shows that the relational operators apply to enumeration types. The ordering of the values of an enumeration type is defined to be in ascending order of their enumeration, so Computing is the lowest value of Science and Zoology is the highest. The ordering is determined in a much more precise way because each constant of the type has an ordinal number, of type CARDINAL, associated with it. The first value of the type has an ordinal value of 0 and each subsequent value has an ordinal number one higher than the preceding value. All values in an enumeration type have a unique successor value except the final value which has no successor. The ordinal values associated with the values of Science are

Constant	**Ordinal**
Computer	0
Physics	1
Chemistry	2
Biochemistry	3
Biology	4
Zoology	5

The standard function procedure ORD returns the ordinal value of a constant declared in an enumeration type if it is passed as a parameter. For example

ORD(Computer)

returns the CARDINAL value 0,

ORD(Zoology)

returns 5 and

ORD(Smith)

returns a value between 0 and 5 corresponding to the present value held in Smith.

Similarly, there is a standard procedure to convert an ordinal number into an equivalent value of an enumeration type. This is a function procedure called VAL which takes two parameters, the name of the enumeration type and an ordinal value. For example,

VAL(Science,4)

returns the value Biology. Thus

Smith := VAL(Science,4)

is a valid assignment statement, which assigns Biology to the variable Smith.

VAL is an important procedure which is also applicable to the basic types INTEGER, CARDINAL, and CHAR. In the case of INTEGER and CARDINAL, the result returned is the same as the value passed as the second parameter. For example

VAL(INTEGER,5)

returns 5 as the result.

In general,

VAL(SomeType,ORD(SomeValue))

returns SomeValue as its result if SomeValue is a value of type SomeType. If it is not, then the value returned is the equivalent value in SomeType. An error is flagged if no such value exists.

It is sometimes useful to use each value of an enumeration type in turn, this can be achieved by the program fragment in Fig. 8.11.

This is rather complicated, and in Chapter 9 a considerable simplification becomes apparent. The complication is caused by ensuring that the value of Smith does not go out of the range of the enumeration type. The assignment statement involving VAL and ORD can be replaced by using the familiar procedure INC, as shown in Fig. 8.12.

```
Smith := Computing;
Test := TRUE;
WHILE Test DO
  (*... Carry out the processing required ...*);
  Test := Smith <> MAX(Science);
  IF Test THEN
    Smith := VAL(Science,ORD(Smith) + 1)
  END (*IF*)
END (*WHILE*)
```

Fig. 8.11.

```
Smith := Computing;
Test := TRUE;
WHILE Test DO
  (*... Carry out the processing required ...*);
  Test := Smith <> MAX(Science);
  IF Test THEN
    INC(Smith)
  END (*IF*)
END (*WHILE*)
```

Fig. 8.12.

Both INC and DEC can be used with enumeration types as well as with the types CHAR, CARDINAL and INTEGER.

INC(X)	adds one to the variable X by increasing its ordinal value by one.
INC(X,N)	adds N to the variable X in the sense of increasing its ordinal value by N. N may be any CARDINAL expression.
DEC(X), DEC(X,N)	these are the same as the corresponding INC except that the value is subtracted.

The Use of Enumeration Types

Enumeration types allow the programmer to write code which expresses aptly the meaning of the solution to the problem under consideration. The type Science could be represented by the CARDINAL numbers 0 to 5, but the resulting program would be much harder to understand unless many more comments are added. Figure 8.13 shows two alternative program fragments where Smith is either declared to be of type Science or of type CARDINAL. The first version is more expressive of the problem content and in Modula-2 is the natural one to use.

```
CASE Smith OF                          CASE Smith OF
    Computing      :        |              0 :              |
    Physics        :        |              1 :              |
    Chemistry      :        |              2 :              |
    Biochemistry   :        |              3 :              |
    Biology        :        |              4 :              |
    Zoology        :                       5 :
END (*CASE*)                           END (*CASE*)
```

(a) Smith of type Science.   (b) Smith of type CARDINAL.

Fig. 8.13.

Arrays can be declared so that components of the array are referenced using an enumeration type rather than a CARDINAL or an INTEGER. For example

```
VAR
    University : ARRAY Science OF CARDINAL;
```

or, a type can be explicitly declared. For example

```
TYPE
    NumScientistsType = ARRAY Science OF CARDINAL;
VAR
    University,Polytechnic : NumScientistsType;
```

References to components of University in both situations are of the form

```
University[Biology] := 12
```

One limitation in using enumeration types is that their values cannot be read in or written out using procedures in standard modules supplied with Modula-2. Note particularly that WriteString cannot be used to write out a value of an enumeration type because the constants are not strings of characters. In fact they are stored internally as their ordinal number counterparts. If a message has to be written to indicate the value of an enumeration type then a user declared procedure has to be written. This can use a CASE statement as illustrated above with a call to WriteString for each case,

```
CASE Smith OF
    Computing        : WriteString('Computing') |
    Physics          : WriteString('Physics') |
       (*... etc ...*)
    Zoology          : WriteString('Zoology')
END (*CASE*)
```

A practical advantage of the use of expressive constants in enumeration types is that it makes it much easier for the programmer to notice mistakes. People are very good at picking up mistakes in text which has a rich semantic content. On the other hand, misleading names can help to disguise errors so names have to be chosen with care.

The variables Smith and Jones could have been declared as

Smith,Jones: (Computer,Physics,Chemistry,Biochemistry,Biology,Zoology);

where Smith and Jones are not of type Science, but instead are variables of an anonymous type. Note that it is not possible to declare the type Science and then declare Smith and Jones anonymously as above at the same block level, because this leads to two distinct collections of declarations of the constants in the enumerations which is not allowed.

8.5 SUBRANGE TYPES

It is often the case that the complete range of a type is not needed for a particular variable. For example, a variable called CharsPerLine may be declared as a CARDINAL variable, but only take values between 0 and 80. Modula-2 provides a way of declaring a type to consist of an ordered sequence of values based upon another type. Subranges of any basic type, except REAL, and of any enumeration type or other subrange type can be declared. For example,

```
TYPE
      Range = CARDINAL[0..80];
VAR
      CharsPerLine : Range;
```

or more simply, but not so generally

```
VAR
      CharsPerLine : CARDINAL[0..80];
```

The syntax diagram for a subrange type is given in Fig. 8.14. Usually the type on which the subrange is based has to be specified. In the above example this is CARDINAL. If no base type is specified then the base type is assumed to be INTEGER if the range involves negative numbers, otherwise it is CARDINAL. For example, the declarations

```
VAR
      CharsPerLine   : [0..80];         (* base type CARDINAL *)
      NewChars       : INTEGER[0..80];  (* base type INTEGER *)
      NegRange       : [−5..5];         (* base type INTEGER *)
```

show how the base types CARDINAL and INTEGER are assumed by default. If the range does not involve negative values but the range has to be INTEGER for compatibility with other types, then INTEGER has to be explicitly stated as the base type. The main use of explicitly declared base types is to distinguish INTEGER from CARDINAL subranges.

Subrange Type :

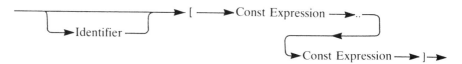

Fig. 8.14.

At first sight there may seem to be little reason to use subrange types, but in fact they are very useful for the following reasons.

1. The subrange is a very useful piece of information for helping a programmer reading the code to see quickly the use to which variables of a given type are to be put.

2. Checks can be made during program execution that the value of a variable has not gone out of range of its expected use. If it does go out of range then an error is reported. The checks can usually be switched off once a program is known to be behaving correctly if efficiency is an important criterion.

3. They are useful in declaring the range of values over which an array can be referenced.

8.6 TYPE COMPATIBILITY

Assignment statements and parameter passing conventions in Modula-2 are determined by an idea of **type compatibility**. It is therefore important to know when two types are compatible. There are two kinds of compatibility, **compatibility** and **assignment compatibility**.

Compatibility

Compatibility is determined by the following rules and is illustrated by the accompanying examples.

1. Two or more types are compatible if they are declared as being equal to each other and are basic types, enumeration types or subrange types. For example,

```
TYPE
     FRED = INTEGER; (* FRED and INTEGER are compatible *);
     JOE = FRED;       (* JOE and FRED are compatible and both are
                          compatible with the basic type INTEGER*);
```

and

```
TYPE
    DaysOfWeek = (Sunday,Monday,Tuesday,Wednesday,Thursday,
                                            Friday,Saturday) ;
    WeekDay = DaysOfWeek ; (* WeekDay is compatible with
                                DaysOfWeek *)
```

2. Two or more types are compatible if one type is a subrange of the other type, or both types are subranges of another common type or are subranges of different types which are themselves compatible. For example

```
TYPE
    Percentage      = [0..100];
    MiddleBand      = [40..60];
    FirstHalf       = [0..50];
    SecondThird     = [33..66];
    SecondHalf      = [51..100];
    Science         = (Computing,Physics,Chemistry,Biochemistry,
                                            Biology,Zoology);
    BioScience      = [Biochemistry..Zoology];
```

Percentage, MiddleBand, FirstHalf, SecondThird and SecondHalf are compatible. FirstHalf and SecondHalf are technically compatible as they are subranges of the same base type, but this of little use as their ranges do not overlap. BioScience is compatible with Science as it is a subrange of it.

3. A string of length 1 (ARRAY [0..0] OF CHAR) is compatible with the type CHAR. This is a special relaxation of the general compatibility rule to make character handling easier. For example, assuming the declarations

```
TYPE
    BigString = ARRAY[0..150] OF CHAR;
VAR
    OneLetter : CHAR;
    LongMessage : BigString;
```

then

```
    LongMessage := OneLetter;
```

is valid as LongMessage can be assigned a string of length 1 and hence a CHAR value. In addition a CHAR value may be passed as a value parameter to a procedure whose corresponding formal parameter is an open array parameter with components of type CHAR.

4. A structured type is only compatible with another type if it is declared as equal to the other type. For example, the declarations

```
TYPE
    UniversityScientists = ARRAY Science OF INTEGER;
    PolytechnicScientists = UniversityScientists;
```

declare UniversityScientists and PolytechnicScientists to be compatible types. However, if these are declared as

```
TYPE
        UniversityScientists = ARRAY[Science] OF INTEGER;
        PolytechnicScientists = ARRAY[Science] OF INTEGER;
```

then UniversityScientists and PolytechnicScientists are incompatible types. This last example explains the language restriction that in formal parameter lists new types cannot be introduced, as this would then be impossible to declare a structured variable which is assignment compatible or identical with the formal parameter.

Assignment Compatibility

This is the same as compatibility except that it also specifies that the types INTEGER and CARDINAL are assignment compatible. The values of types which are assignment compatible can be assigned to variables of the assignment compatible types.

Assignment compatibility determines how different types can be used in assignment statements. It essentially states that a value of one type can be assigned to a variable of a different type if the two types are compatible or the types in question are INTEGER or CARDINAL (or subranges thereof) and the value lies within the overlapping region of their ranges of value.

Compatibility and Parameter Passing

The rules for compatibility also govern how parameters can be passed to procedures.

1. In procedure calls the type of a formal **value** parameter must be compatible with the type of the actual parameter passed to the procedure.

2. The formal and actual parameters of a **VAR** parameter must be identical (at one point in the definition of Modula-2, the rule was that they had to be compatible so it is possible that your compiler satisfies this less restrictive rule; it is wise to check).

8.7 CONSTANT DECLARATIONS AND CONSTANT EXPRESSIONS

Constants were introduced in Chapter 3, and are discussed again here because their types can be any basic type (or set type, see Chapter 10). In addition this section considers the general rules for declaring constants which involve constant expressions. To illustrate constant declarations in some detail, consider the following declarations

```
CONST
        PI = 3.1428;
        Radius = 3.5;
        AreaOfCircle = PI*Radius*Radius;
        Message = 'a literal string constant';
        Length = 5.6;
        AreaOfCylinder = 2.0*AreaOfCircle + Length*2.0*PI*Radius;
```

These examples illustrate a number of points.

1.   A constant that has already been declared can be used in the declaration of another constant. Note carefully that textual ordering is important. If the last two lines of the example are interchanged a syntax error results.

2.   Expressions are allowed in the declaration of a constant as long as the textual ordering restriction is maintained.

3.   WHILE and IF statements are not allowed in declarations of constants, so a lengthy calculation must be written out in full.

4.   A constant expression may only involve other constants. It cannot involve variables.

5.   A constant expression cannot involve function procedure calls.

6.   Structured types such as arrays cannot be declared with constant values.

7.   Constants can be literal strings.

Constant expressions can be used to specify the bounds of ranges of two related types. It might always be the case that one type is an array whose dimension is twice the size of the array of another type. For example

```
TYPE
        DataSize = [0..MaxData];
        SortSize = [0..2*MaxData+1];
        DataTable = ARRAY DataSize OF DataType;
        SortTable = ARRAY SortSize OF DataType;
```

Note that the size of the array is the size of the subrange. The array declarations of Chapter 3 involved the special case where an anonymous subrange type is used in the declaration of the array. For example

```
TYPE DATATABLE = ARRAY[0..MaxData] OF DATATYPE;
        SORTTABLE = ARRAY[0..2*MaxData+1] OF DATATYPE;
```

corresponds to the previous declaration without the creation of explicit subrange types.

Within the same module it is permissible to have many collections of constant declarations. This permits related constant, type, procedure and variable declarations to be grouped together to aid readability. Figure 8.15 is a normal example.

```
MODULE Example;
CONST
  Fundamental = 42;
  Wonders = 7;
  FundamentalWonders = Fundamental DIV Wonders;
VAR
  (*... variable declarations which use these constants ...*)
TYPE
  (*... type declarations using these constants ...*)

(*... procedures which use these variables, types and constants ...*)

CONST
  Kelvin = −273.0;
  DataComplete = TRUE;
VAR
  (*... variable declarations which use these constants ...*)
TYPE
  (*... type declarations using these constants ...*)

(*... procedures which use these variables, types and constants ...*)

BEGIN
        (*... module body ...*)
END Example.
```

Fig. 8.15.

8.8   EXAMPLE. A Definition Module for Multiple Choice Questions

We now develop a definition module using bottom up methods of program development. The experience gained by the bottom up design is used to define an appropriate definition module involving subrange and enumeration types to provide facilities for the solution to the problem. The original specification of the problem is vague because the precise requirements are not yet decided. This is a typical situation where bottom up methods are useful.

Provisional Specification

A procedure called Quest1 is required to write a multiple-choice question to the screen and accept an answer. The answer is verified and a message is given indicating its correctness. If an incorrect answer is given, a limited number of retries are allowed. The question is written to the screen by an assumed procedure Q1WriteScreen and writes out a question as in Fig. 8.16.

Which of the following cities is known as the 'Big Apple'?

A. Paris

B. London

C. New York

D. Bonn

E. Tokyo

Answer one of A,B,C,D or E.

Fig. 8.16.

An outline for Quest1 is shown in Fig. 8.17.

```
PROCEDURE Quest1(VAR ValidAns : BOOLEAN);
  (*... declarations ...*)
BEGIN
  (*... initialisation ...*);
  (*... call Q1WriteScreen ...*);
  (*... accept answer ...*);
  WHILE (*... not yet a valid answer ...*)
              AND (*... not too many tries ...*) DO
      CASE (*... answer ...*) OF
        'A','B','D','E' : (*... write wrong answer message ...*);
                          (*... set valid answer to TRUE ...*)     |
        'C'             : (*... write correct answer message ...*);
                          (*... set valid answer to TRUE ...*)
        ELSE
            (*... write invalid answer message ...*);
            IF (*... number of tries less than maximum allowed ...*) THEN
                (*... write retry message ...*);
                (*... accept answer ...*);
                (*... add 1 to the number of tries ...*)
            END (* IF *)
      END (* CASE *)
  END (* WHILE *)
END Quest1;
```

Fig. 8.17.

The declarations require a constant which specifies the maximum number of tries, and variables to accept the answer and to keep track of the number of tries. These are achieved by the declarations

```
CONST
      MaxTries = 3;
VAR
      NoOfTries    : CARDINAL[0..MaxTries];
      Answer       : CHAR;
```

To complete the procedure the following refinements have to be developed
1. the ELSE part of the CASE statement to handle invalid user replies
2. the incorrect answer clause
3. the correct answer clause
4. the WHILE condition
5. the initialisation section
6. collation of the declarations.

to produce the procedure shown in Fig. 8.18.

```
PROCEDURE Quest1(VAR ValidAns : BOOLEAN);
    (* Analyses a complete question and returns ValidAns as TRUE
       if a sensible answer has been obtained and FALSE otherwise. *)

    (* It is assumed that importing of routines from InOut is performed
       at module level. *)
    CONST
        MaxTries = 3;
    VAR
        NoOfTries : CARDINAL[0..MaxTries];(* subrange expressing the usage *)
        Answer    : CHAR;
BEGIN
    NoOfTries := 0;
    ValidAns := FALSE;
    Q1WriteScreen;    (* Assumed to be available *)
    Read(Answer);
    WriteLn;
    WHILE NOT ValidAns AND (NoOfTries < MaxTries) DO
        CASE Answer OF
           'A','B','D','E':
               WriteString('The answer is incorrect, the correct');
               WriteString(' answer is C - New York');
               ValidAns := TRUE              |
           'C' :
               WriteString('Correct - Well done.');
               ValidAns := TRUE
           ELSE
               WriteString('The answer you have given ') ;
               WriteString('is not in the range A..E.');
               INC(NoOfTries) ;
               IF NoOfTries < MaxTries THEN
                   WriteString(' Please try again ');
                   Read(Answer);
                   WriteLn
               END (* IF *)
        END (* CASE *)
    END (* WHILE *)
END Quest1;
```
Fig. 8.18.

Inspection of this procedure shows that a more general specification can be supported incorporating the following changes.

1. The correct alternative should not be determined inside the procedure.

2. The correct and incorrect messages should not be determined inside the procedure.

3. The question should be asked before the procedure is called rather than by calling another procedure from within it.

The required alterations to the procedure are the removal of the call to Q1WriteScreen, and alterations to the parameter list to allow the correct alternative and the messages in response to correct and incorrect user replies to be passed as parameters to the procedure. In addition the procedure can be reorganised so that validation of the user's reply is separated from the control of input and ouput. These modifications lead to a general procedure for respoding to user replies where there are two alternative system responses as shown in Fig. 8.19.

These two attempts at writing the procedure make it easier to consider the specification and implementation of a module for the validation of user replies to multiple-choice questions and system responses to these replies. Further thought indicates that the provision for only two possible system responses is restrictive. The specification for a more general and useful module can now be more precise.

1. A procedure ValidateAndRespond and supporting types and constants must be made available to other modules.

2. ValidateAndRespond is only concerned with validating user replies and responding to these.

3. The association between possible user replies and system responses must be determined outside the procedure and communicated to it by parameter passing.

4. A maximum number of possible user replies and system responses must be specified. This is arbitrarily determined as 8.

5. A system response is at most 80 characters.

Using these criteria a definition module is defined in Fig. 8.20. Note that types can be exported like other objects. This is discussed in detail in Chapters 10 and 14.

Development of the implemention module is left as an exercise, but the bottom up analysis and the clear specification of the procedure heading and the associated types help.

The planning of this module has lead to the specification of appropriate types for data structures which make the module easy to understand. The following notes are designed to make clear some of the details and suggest possible modifications.

```
TYPE
      Message = ARRAY[0..79] OF CHAR;

PROCEDURE Valid(Ans : CHAR) : BOOLEAN;
BEGIN
  RETURN (Ans >= 'A') & (Ans <= 'E')
END Valid;

PROCEDURE Correct(Ans,WhichAns : CHAR) : BOOLEAN;
BEGIN
  RETURN (Ans = WhichAns)
END Correct;

PROCEDURE Quest2(VAR ValidAns : BOOLEAN; CorrectAns : CHAR;
                              CorrectString,ErrorString : Message);
  CONST
      MaxTries = 3;
  VAR
      NoOfTries : [1..MaxTries];
      Answer :   CHAR;
BEGIN
  NoOfTries := 1;
  Read(Answer);      WriteLn;
  WHILE NOT Valid(Answer) AND (NoOfTries < MaxTries) DO
      WriteString('The answer you have given is not in range.') ;
      WriteString(' Try again : ');
      Read(Answer); WriteLn;
      INC(NoOfTries);
  END (* WHILE *);
  ValidAns := Valid(Answer);
  IF ValidAns THEN
      IF Correct(Answer,CorrectAns) THEN
          WriteString(CorrectString)
      ELSE
          WriteString(ErrorString)
      END (* IF *)
  END (* IF *)
END Quest2;
```

Fig. 8.19.

```
DEFINITION MODULE OutputResponse;
    CONST
        MaxCharsLine = 80;
    TYPE
        (* Declarations of facilities for holding output response messages *)
        Message          = ARRAY[0..MaxCharsLine-1] OF CHAR;
        ResponseType     = [1..8];(* subrange type:
                                    note that 8 = ORD(MAX(AnsType)) *)
        RespTypeTable    = ARRAY ResponseType OF Message;

        (* Declarations of facilities for holding answers and linking
           answers to the required responses. *)
        AnsType          = (A,B,C,D,E,F,G,H); (* enumeration type *)
        AnsRespTable     = ARRAY AnsType OF ResponseType;

        (* Declaration of the procedure which accepts an answer and
           gives a response *)
    PROCEDURE ValidateAndRespond( VAR ValidAns     : BOOLEAN;
                                  VAR NumOfAns      : ResponseType;
                                  VAR AnsResponse   : AnsRespTable;
                                  VAR Responses     : RespTypeTable);

    END OutputResponse.
```

Fig. 8.20.

1.   The restriction of AnsType to eight possibilties is unnecessary, a larger number could have been chosen to ensure that any reasonable number of alternatives could be written to the screen. Perhaps that number **is** eight.

2.   The parameter NumOfAns is used to stipulate how many options are available on the particular question asked. So if the options are A, B and C then NumOfAns has the value 3.

3.   The parameter AnsResponse is a table of the form shown in Fig. 8.21 assuming NumOfAns is 4. This stipulates that if the user's answer to the question is C then system message 2 is written to the screen.

4.   The parameter Responses holds the messages to be printed out. At most 80 characters are allowed for any one response. This could be generalised so that there are many lines of output corresponding to each message.

1	3	2	3	?	?	?	?	Type:ResponseType
A	B	C	D	E	F	G	H	Type:AnsType

Fig. 8.21.

8.9 SUMMARY

This chapter has discussed
1   the numeric types REAL, INTEGER and CARDINAL. The following points are of note.
a The values of numeric types have limited ranges, some implementations provide the types LONGREAL, LONGINT and LONGCARD which represent a larger range of values.
b The numeric types cannot be mixed arbitrarily in arithmetic expressions. The values in a REAL expression must be REAL values, similarly with CARDINAL and INTEGER expressions. Literal REAL constants must contain a decimal point to differentiate them from literal CARDINAL and INTEGER constants.
c The ranges of value for INTEGER and CARDINAL overlap in the range from 0 to the maximum INTEGER value. The types of literal constants in this range are determined from the context in which they are used.
d Special procedures are provided for converting values of one type into values of another and can be used within expressions to convert a value of a different type into the type of the expression.

2   subrange and enumeration types which are useful for making program code more expressive of its purpose, and are of particular use with arrays.

3   the related ideas of compatibility and assignment compatibility which govern special situations where a value of one type can be treated as a value of another type. This is particularly important for the types CARDINAL and INTEGER and subranges of these types, and for passing parameters as value parameters.

TECHNICAL EXERCISES

1   Using the syntax diagrams of Figs 8.6 and 8.7 indicate which of the following are invalid numeric constants and say why they are invalid.

```
0H      −23    23B    23C    68B     23h    A4H
0B      0AFH   67     0FF    56.0    62OH   99C
```

2   Using the syntax diagrams of Fig. 8.1, indicate which of the following are invalid reals and say why they are invalid.

```
3.0         4.    32.2E−03   4.2H   93.E+2  2E+45   56
0.0E−21   +43.2    −2.7      .23E−2  E2      9.5B    10.e2
1.0E2.3
```

3   Given the following REAL variables and their current values, state the results of evaluating the following simple expressions if they are valid, and if they are invalid state the reason.

100.0	20.0	200.0
Temperature	Size	Maximum

a Maximum/Size − 10

b Maximum − Temperature∗0.5

c Maximum − (Temperature∗0.5)

d (Maximum − Temperature)∗0.5

e (Temperature − Maximum∗0.5)

f (Temperature − Maximum)∗0.5

g (Temperature∗Size∗2)

h Temperature∗.2/Size

j Size/Maximum+ Size/Size

k Maximum/Size/10.0

m (Maximum/Size)/10.0

n Maximum/(Size/10.0)

p Maximum/Size−10.0

q (Maximum/Size)−10.0

r Maximum/(Size−10.0)

s Temperature∗2.0∗Size

t Temperature∗2.0/Size

u (Temperature∗2.0)/Size

4 Study the following program and indicate any errors.

```
MODULE ErrorExample;
VAR
     Size1,Size2 : REAL;
BEGIN
  Size1 := 0;
  Size2 := 0.5;
  WHILE Size1 <> 10.0 DO
     Size1 := Size1 + Size2∗Size3
  END
  WriteReal(Size1,10)
END ErrorExample.
```

5 Assuming the following declarations,

```
TYPE
     Science    = (Computing,Physics,Chemistry,Biochemistry,
                                        Biology,Zoology);
     BioScience = [Biochemistry..Zoology];
VAR
     Smith,Jones    : Science;
     Bloggs         : BioScience;
     CardNum1       : CARDINAL;
     CardNum2       : [0..5];
     IntNum1        : INTEGER;
     IntNum2        : INTEGER[0..5];
```

discuss the correctness of each of the following assignment statements for compatibility and correctness.

a Smith := Jones

b Smith := Bloggs

c Bloggs := Jones

d Bloggs := Physics

e Jones := VAL(Science,3)

f CardNum2 := ORD(Chemistry)+ORD(Biology)

g CardNum1 := CardNum2 + IntNum2

h Smith := VAL(Science,CardNum2)

j Smith := VAL(Science,IntNum2)

k IntNum1 := ORD(Chemistry) + ORD(Zoology)

6   Assuming the procedure heading

```
PROCEDURE TestParams(Dalton : Science;VAR Newton : Science);
```

and the declarations in the previous question state which of the following invocations of the procedure are valid.

a TestParams(Biology,Smith)   **d** TestParams(VAL(Science,CardNum2),Jones)
b TestParams(Bloggs,Biology)   **e** TestParams(Jones,VAL(Science,CardNum2))
c TestParams(Physics,Bloggs)   **f** TestParams(Bloggs,Jones)

7   Write type declarations for
   a the suits of a deck of playing cards.
   b chess pieces.
   c the days of the week.
   d the four points of the compass.

8   Assuming the following declaration for MONTH,

```
TYPE
        MONTH = (January,February,March,April,May,June,July,August,
                        September,October,November,December);
```

state whether the following expressions are valid or invalid and for each valid case state the value of the expression.

a January > December   **g** ORD(May)−1 = ORD(April)
b April <= June   **h** VAL(MONTH,2) = March
c April + 1 = May   **j** VAL(MONTH,ORD(December)−4) <=
d January = March OR May < December   VAL(MONTH,ORD(June)+2)
e ORD(May)−1 = April   **k** ORD(March)+VAL(MONTH,3) = June
f ORD(May−1) = April   **l** ORD(February)+ORD(March) = 3

9   Write a procedure which accepts a value parameter of type DaysOfWeek and writes out the day to the console.

PROGRAMMING EXERCISES

1   The procedure Quest1 contains the following code:

```
IF NoOfTries < MaxTries THEN
   WriteString(' Please try again ');
   Read(Answer);
   WriteLn
END(*IF*)
```

Discuss the error which results from omitting the IF .. END (*IF*) while keeping the body of the IF statement in the code.

2 Modify Quest1 to allow it to accept lower case as well as upper case letters in answer to the question. This is good policy unless you are trying to teach some point about precise input.

3 The output of Quest1 can be unsatisfactory on some visual display units. Rewrite it to fit your screen and if a module for direct cursor control is available (procedures like MoveCursor(X,Y:CursPosition)) use these when defining the output to make the layout easy to use.

4 Write the implementation module OutputResponse. Design a suitable test plan for internal and external module testing.

5 Write two procedures to sum the numbers

$$1 + 1/2 + 1/3 + 1/4 \ldots\ldots\ldots + 1/N$$

where N is a CARDINAL value passed as a parameter. The first procedure should sum the values from 1 to 1/N and the second should sum them from 1/N to 1. Predict the result before testing the procedures and explain the difference in behaviour of the two procedures.

6 Use the function procedures ln and exp in MathLib0 (see Appendix 4) to construct a procedure to find the value of a given number to a given power.

7 Using the methods of the BarChart procedure in Chapter 6, or any more sophisticated facilities available as modules, construct a graph of the curve defined by

$$Y = exp(-X)*sin(X)$$

over the range $0 <= X <= 6$. Be careful to choose an appropriate scaling.

8 Ohm's law relates voltage, resistance and current by the formula

Voltage (V) = Current (I) * Resistance (R).

Write a program which accepts three values from the keyboard, corresponding to voltage, current and resistance, and checks and reports whether or not the values are consistent. In addition it should provide a facility for typing a **?** instead of one of the three values, and report the value of the unknown quantity. In developing the program, pay particular attention to making the program easy to use.

ANSWERS

1 –23 No sign is permitted (Modula-2 allows this, but it is not defined as a number in the syntax diagrams).

23C is a literal character constant as defined in Fig. 8.9 and not a literal numeric constant.

68B B indicates that the number is octal, yet it contains the digit 8. This is a contradiction.

23h The hexadecimal indicator must be a capital H.

A4H Hexadecimal numbers must start with a digit. The correct way to write this number is 0A4H.

0FF This is a hexadecimal number with the terminating H missing.

56.0 This is a literal REAL constant, not a literal whole number constant.

62OH The letter **O** has been typed instead of the digit 0. This is a common mistake.

99C This is a literal character constant, in addition it is an invalid character constant because it should be written as an octal number, but contains the digit 9.

2 4.2H Hexadecimal REAL constants are not permitted.

2E+45 There is no decimal point in the number so it cannot be a valid literal REAL constant.

56 There is no decimal point, so its type is CARDINAL or INTEGER.

+43.2 The plus sign is not allowed in the definition of a literal REAL constant. The expression is valid in Modula-2, but it is not simply a literal REAL constant.

–2.7 The minus sign is not allowed for the same reason as in the previous case.

.23E–2 Literal REAL constants may not start with a decimal point.

E2 A scale factor must be preceded by a number which includes a decimal point.

9.5B Octal REAL constants are not allowed.

10e2 The letter e in the scale factor should be capital E.

1.0E2.3 The scale factor cannot contain a decimal point.

3 **a** Invalid, 10 is not a REAL constant.
  b 150.0   **c** 150.0   **d** 50.0   **e** 0.0   **f** –50.0
  g Invalid, 2 is not REAL.
  h Invalid, .2 should be written 0.2.
  j 1.1   **k** 1.0   **m** 1.0   **n** 100.0
  p 0.0   **q** 0.0   **r** 20.0   **s** 4000.0   **t** 10.0   **u** 10.0

4 **a** Size1 is a REAL variable so Size1 := 0 is not a legal statement, it should be
Size1 := 0.0

b Size1 <> 10.0 is a very doubtful expression. The problem is that the slightest round-off error in Size1 will result in the loop never terminating. More useful expressions are

Size1 < 10.0 or ABS(Size1 − 10.0) < 10.0E−10

where ABS is the standard procedural function which returns the absolute value of a number.

c Size3 has not been declared. From the context, it seems likely that it should have been declared as a REAL variable and given an initial value.

d There is a semi-colon missing at the end of the WHILE statement.

e The procedure WriteReal must be imported from the standard module RealInOut. The import lists should contain

FROM RealInOut IMPORT WriteReal;

5 **a** valid

b valid

c compatible, but can be incorrect at execution time if the contents of Jones is outside of the subrange BioScience

d incorrect assignment, but usually only picked up at execution time

e valid

f out of range of the subrange

g mixed expressions are not allowed

h valid

j valid, note that there is no possibility of the conversion producing a value which has no counterpart in the values of the type Science as the possible values for IntNum2 are restricted by the subrange.

k this has no problems as the expression on the right hand side is a CARDINAL expression which is assignment compatible with the data type INTEGER. Note it is not compatible.

6 **a** valid

b invalid, Newton is a VAR prameter and so cannot have a constant passed as a parameter

c invalid, Bloggs is of type BioScience which is not an identical type to Science (some compilers will accept this because they use compatible instead of identical as their criterion, but this is non standard)

d valid

e invalid, the second actual parameter is an expression

f valid

7 The following are possible answers, clearly there are other correct versions.

a Suits = (Clubs,Diamonds,Hearts,Spades);

b Chesspieces = (Pawn,Knight,Bishop,Rook,Queen,King);

c DaysOfWeek = (Sunday,Monday,Tuesday,Wednesday,Thursday,
                     Friday,Saturday);

d CompassPoints= (West,East,South,North);

8 **a** valid, FALSE

b valid, TRUE

c invalid, April+1 involves values of different types.

d invalid, the correct expression is

(January=March) OR (May<November)

which would be TRUE.

e invalid, L.H.S. is a CARDINAL value , the R.H.S. is a value of an enumeration type.

f invalid, MAY − 1 is an invalid expression. In addition the same error as **e**.

g valid, TRUE.

h valid, TRUE.

j valid, TRUE.

k invalid, the results from VAL and ORD are not normally type compatible.

l valid, TRUE.

9 In the import list, the following is required

FROM InOut IMPORT WriteString;

and given that the procedure is part of a larger module it is likely that other routines will also be imported from InOut. The procedure declaration is

```
PROCEDURE WriteDay(Day : DaysOfWeek);
BEGIN
  CASE Day OF
    Sunday     : WriteString('Sunday')        |
    Monday     : WriteString('Monday')        |
    Tuesday    : WriteString('Tuesday')       |
    Wednesday  : WriteString('Wednesday')     |
    Thursday   : WriteString('Thursday')      |
    Friday     : WriteString('Friday')        |
    Saturday   : WriteString('Saturday')
  END(*CASE*)
END WriteDay;
```

A more sophisticated alternative is

```
DEFINITION MODULE WriteOut;
TYPE
      DaysOfWeek = (Sunday,Monday,Tuesday,Wednesday,Thursday,
                                              Friday,Saturday);

PROCEDURE WriteDay(Day: DaysOfWeek);
(* Writes out the day of the week given the equivalent enumeration
      type value. *)
END WriteOut.

IMPLEMENTATION MODULE WriteOut;
FROM InOut IMPORT WriteString;
VAR
      DayChar : ARRAY DaysOfWeek OF ARRAY[0..9] OF CHAR;
      (* This declaration is an array of strings. See Chapter
          10 for details of how to make and use such declarations*)

PROCEDURE WriteDay(Day : DaysOfWeek);
BEGIN
  WriteString(DayChar[Day])
END WriteDay;

BEGIN (*Module initialisation*)
  DayChar[Sunday]       :='Sunday' ;
  DayChar[Monday]       :='Monday' ;
  DayChar[Tuesday]      :='Tuesday' ;
  DayChar[Wednesday]:='Wednesday';
  DayChar[Thursday]     :='Thursday' ;
  DayChar[Friday]       :='Friday' ;
  DayChar[Saturday]     :='Saturday'
END WriteOut.
```

In effect this solution provides a standard format for a module which declares an enumeration type and provides a procedure to write out its the names of the values of the type. The module can be used to provide other useful operations on the type. For example there might be more than one natural ordering on the type and the other could be provided by a procedure in this module.

Chapter 9

Repetitive Statements

The defining characteristic of repetitive statements is that they allow a sequence of other statements to be executed repeatedly. In Chapter 3 the WHILE statement was introduced and in Chapter 7 BOOLEAN expressions were discussed at length. In this chapter the WHILE statement is discussed more fully to illustrate important characteristics of repetitive statements and it is compared with other repetitive statements available in Modula-2.

9.1 THE WHILE STATEMENT

In Chapter 3 we saw that all WHILE statements have the general form shown in Fig. 9.1. The statement sequence is executed repeatedly while the BOOLEAN expression evaluates to TRUE. When the BOOLEAN expression evaluates to FALSE control is passed to the end of the WHILE statement.

WHILE BOOLEAN Expression DO

Statement Sequence

END (∗ WHILE ∗) ;

Fig. 9.1.

When writing a WHILE statement there are three fundamental considerations to be borne in mind
1. eventually it should terminate when a particular goal is achieved, so it is necessary to have a clear idea of the goal which the loop should achieve,
2. there is a reason for the statements of the WHILE loop being executed repeatedly, therefore it is necessary to consider what common properties apply each time the statements are executed,
3. for the loop to terminate the BOOLEAN expression must evaluate to FALSE, therefore it is necessary to consider the exceptional properties which cause the loop to terminate having achieved the goal.

For example, consider a problem where it is necessary to find the position of the first occurrence of a particular character in an array of characters. If it can be guaranteed that the character is in the array, then there exists some currently unknown index into the array which indicates the position of the first occurrence of the character in the array. When the loop terminates this array index will have been found (see Fig. 9.2a). The notation

(*TRUE   comment   *)

is used to indicate that the relationship specified in the comment is known to be true at that point in the code.

The three considerations are reflected in the comments in Fig. 9.2b. From these we can deduce that

1.   the statement sequence must increment Position so that successive components of the array are considered and therefore progress is made towards the goal of finding the first component holding the character,

2.   the BOOLEAN expression is

CharacterArray[Position] <> Ch

which is the inverse of the goal of the loop that

CharacterArray[Position] = Ch

3.   the initialisation for the loop is

Position := 1

so that components are tested starting at the lowest component of the array.

These are incorporated into Fig. 9.2c. The terminating condition is that the character of the array indexed by Position is the same as the character in Ch. In order that progress can be made towards this, the statement sequence increments Position by 1 so that each time the statement sequence is executed successive characters in the array are considered.

Note that the BOOLEAN expression is evaluated before the statement sequence is executed. Therefore, initialisation prior to the WHILE statement is needed to ensure that the BOOLEAN expression is fully defined when it is first tested. In Fig. 9.2 this means that just before entry to the WHILE loop, Ch must hold a particular character and Position must be initialised to a sensible value, i.e the position of the first character in the array.

Figure 9.2c can be paraphrased as

> Initially it is known that somewhere in the array the required character occurs and that there is an index which will reference this character. The WHILE loop starts at the first character in the array and checks each successive character in turn. While the current character under consideration is not the one being searched for, the required index has not been found so Position is incremented. When the loop terminates the character has been found and Position indicates the required index.

Suppose the assumption that the character actually occurs in the array is invalid, the goal of the WHILE statement will have to be modified to allow two possibilities

(*TRUE At least 1 component of the array contains the character
 held in Ch *)
WHILE (*... BOOLEAN Expression ...*) DO
 (*... Statement Sequence ...*) ;
END (* WHILE *) ;
(*TRUE Position is the index of the first component in the array
 holding the same character as in Ch *)

(a)

(*TRUE At least 1 component of the array contains the character
 held in Ch *)
WHILE (*... BOOLEAN Expression ...*) DO
 (*TRUE No character in the array from 1 to the current value
 of Position is the same as the character in Ch *)
 (*... Statement Sequence ...*) ;
END (* WHILE *) ;
(*TRUE Position is the index of the first component in the array
 holding the same character as in Ch *)

(b)

Position := 1 ;
(*TRUE At least 1 component of the array contains the character
 held in Ch *)
WHILE CharacterArray[Position] <> Ch DO
 (*TRUE No character in the array from 1 to the current value
 of Position is the same as the character in Ch *)
 INC (Position) ;
END (* WHILE *) ;
(*TRUE Position is the index of the first component in the array
 holding the same character as in Ch *)

(c)

Fig. 9.2. Development of a WHILE statement.

1. that the character is found,
2. that the character does not occur in the array and Position does not index a
valid position in the array.

These are as shown in Fig. 9.3a. There is no longer a special condition
which has to be true prior to the WHILE statement (see Fig. 9.3b).

Progress towards the goal of the WHILE statement can still be achieved by
incrementing Position, however the BOOLEAN expression must cater for both
possibilities in the goal. The condition

CharacterArray[Position] <> Ch

evaluates to FALSE when the character has been located, and the condition

Position <> ArrayLength+1

evaluates to FALSE when Position is greater than ArrayLength and the character has not been found (see Fig. 9.3c).

```
WHILE (*... BOOLEAN Expression ...*) DO
        (*... Statement Sequence ...*) ;
END (* WHILE *) ;
(*TRUE Position is the index of the first component in the array
        holding the same character as in Ch
    OR  Position = array length + 1 *)
```

(a)

```
WHILE (*... BOOLEAN Expression ...*) DO
        (*TRUE No character in the array from 1 to the current value
                of Position is the same as the character in Ch
            AND  Position is a valid index of the array *)
        (*... Statement Sequence ...*) ;
END (* WHILE *) ;
(*TRUE Position is the index of the first component in the array
        holding the same character as in Ch
    OR  Position = array length + 1 *)
```

(b)

```
Position := 1;
WHILE (Position <> ArrayLength+1) AND
        (CharacterArray[Position] <> Ch) DO
        (*TRUE No character in the array from 1 to the current value
                of Position is the same as the character in Ch
            AND  Position is a valid index of the array *)
        INC (Position) ;
END (* WHILE *) ;
(*TRUE Position is the index of the first component in the array
        holding the same character as in Ch
    OR  Position = array length + 1 *)
```

(c)

Fig. 9.3. Development of a WHILE statement.

With these considerations in mind we can be more precise about the general form of appropriate use of WHILE statements as shown in Fig. 9.4.

It is good practice to determine what should be the case when the WHILE statement terminates, and then to work backwards to consider the common properties which apply at the top of the statement sequence on each iteration. Knowing the goal of the entire statement and what is true inside the statement sequence helps to determine what the BOOLEAN expression should test to ensure the goal is achieved when the loop terminates. Finally, how the statement sequence must influence the variables tested by the BOOLEAN expression to ensure the loop terminates, and how variables should be initial-ised prior to the WHILE statement must be determined.

This approach emphasises the need to define the goals which should be achieved when the repetitive statement terminates, and the need to ensure that the loop will terminate under the appropriate conditions. This can reduce errors which cause infinite loops or loops which can never be executed.

```
(* initialise any variables essential to BOOLEAN Expression *)
WHILE BOOLEAN Expression DO
        (*TRUE some relationship which is true on each iteration *)
```

```
        Statement Sequence executed repeatedly,
        one or more of the statements will affect
        variables involved in the BOOLEAN Expression,
        so that it is possible that the next time it
        is evaluated the result will be FALSE.
```

```
END (* WHILE *) ;
(*TRUE the goal of the WHILE statement has been achieved,
        this includes BOOLEAN Expression being FALSE *)
```

Fig. 9.4.

As a further example, consider a problem where it is necessary to insert a number into an array of numbers which is to be maintained in ascending order. An approach to solving this problem is to move all components of the array whose values are greater than the value to be inserted into the next higher component. This frees the component where the new value should be inserted. A WHILE statement is required to move the larger numbers in the array and to find the position to insert the new number. The new number can then be inserted at its correct position. The solution to this problem is simplified if the number being inserted is held in a component at the low end of the array, OrderedArray[0], which is not included as part of the ordered array. That is, the ordered array extends from component 1 to an index specified by EndOfSortedArray and this variable needs to be incremented when the new number has been included in the array. Figure 9.5a shows an initial formula-tion of the problem.

The property at the top of the statement sequence in Fig. 9.5a must not hold when the goal is achieved and suggests itself as a suitable candidate as the basis for the terminating condition of the BOOLEAN expression.

The call of DEC and the movement of each component after it has been tested are suggested by the goal of the WHILE loop. This results in the code fragment of Fig. 9.5b.

Note that holding the number to be inserted in OrderedArray[0] may result in the BOOLEAN expression testing

OrderedArray[0] < OrderedArray[0]

which causes termination of the loop. This occurs if the number to be inserted is less than all other numbers in the array and has to be inserted in the first position of the ordered array. By holding the number to be inserted in OrderedArray[0], this case can be treated like all other cases. Adding the character in Ch to the end of the character array which was being searched by the program fragment of Fig. 9.3 would have simplified that BOOLEAN expression.

Figure 9.6 shows the code fragments of Fig. 9.5 developed into a procedure Insert, with the detail of how the procedure was developed omitted.

```
(*TRUE OrderedArray is ordered in ascending order *)
Position := EndOfOrderedArray+1 ;
WHILE (*...BOOLEAN Expression...*) DO
        (*TRUE all components whose indexes from Position to
                EndOfOrderedArrayinclusive are greater than
                OrderedArray[0] *)
END (* WHILE *) ;
(*TRUE Position = required position
    AND all components from required position to EndOfOrderedArray
        inclusive have been moved along to the next component *)
OrderedArray[Position] := OrderedArray[0] ;
INC (EndOfOrderedArray) ;
```

(a)

```
(*TRUE OrderedArray is ordered in ascending order *)
Position := EndOfOrderedArray+1 ;
WHILE OrderedArray[0] < OrderedArray[Position−1] DO
        (*TRUE all components whose indexes from Position to
                EndOfOrderedArray inclusive are greater than OrderedArray[0]
            AND all components whose indexes from Position to
                EndOfOrderedArray inclusive have been moved into the next
                higher component *)
        OrderedArray[Position] := OrderedArray[Position−1] ;
        DEC (Position) ;
END (* WHILE *) ;
(*TRUE Position = required position
    AND  all components from required position to EndOfOrderedArray
        inclusive have been moved along to the next component *)
OrderedArray[Position] := OrderedArray[0] ;
INC (EndOfOrderedArray) ;
(*TRUE OrderedArray is an ordered array
    AND OrderedArray[Position] = OrderedArray[0]
    AND EndOfOrderedArray is the index of the next free position in
                        OrderedArray *)
```

Fig. 9.5. (b)

```
PROCEDURE Insert (VAR OrderedArray : ARRAY OF CARDINAL ;
                  VAR EndOfOrderedArray : CARDINAL) ;
(* Inserts a number stored in OrderedArray[0] into its
   appropriate position in the array between component 1
   and component EndOfOrderedArray inclusive if there is room,
   otherwise the procedure does nothing. *)
  VAR
      Position : CARDINAL ;
BEGIN
  IF EndOfOrderedArray <> HIGH(OrderedArray) THEN
      Position := EndOfOrderedArray + 1 ;
      WHILE OrderedArray[0] < OrderedArray[Position - 1] DO
            OrderedArray [Position] := OrderedArray [Position - 1] ;
            DEC (Position) ;
      END (* WHILE *) ;
      OrderedArray [Position] := OrderedArray [0] ;
      INC (EndOfOrderedArray) ;
  ELSE
      (* no room to insert new value, no action *)
  END (* IF *) ;
END Insert ;
```

Fig. 9.6.

9.2 THE REPEAT STATEMENT

Like the WHILE statement, the REPEAT statement involves a statement sequence which is executed repeatedly and a BOOLEAN expression which determines when execution of the loop stops. The general form of the REPEAT statement is shown in Fig. 9.7.

REPEAT

Statement Sequence

UNTIL BOOLEAN Expression
(*TRUE the goal of the REPEAT statement is achieved,
        this includes the BOOLEAN expression being true. *)

Fig. 9.7.

In contrast to the WHILE statement, the REPEAT statement is executed repeatedly while the result of the BOOLEAN expression is FALSE and terminates when it becomes TRUE. Furthermore, the BOOLEAN expression of the REPEAT statement is evaluated at the end of the construct, that is after the statement sequence has been executed. This contrasts with the WHILE statement where the condition is evaluated at the top of the construct and therefore before execution of its statement sequence. The net effect of this distinction is that the statement sequence of a REPEAT statement is executed *at least once*, whereas the statement sequence of a WHILE statement may not be executed if the BOOLEAN expression evaluates to FALSE when it is first tested.

A REPEAT statement is the natural construct to use when it is known that the statement sequence must be executed at least once. This is typically the case when a program communicates with a user to perform an operation repeatedly. Normally the user indicates that a particular operation is to be performed and the program permits the operation to be repeated until the user wishes to stop. The goal of such loops is to elicit a reply from the user to stop repeating the operation. The procedure in Fig. 9.8 illustrates this. GetNewMemberDetails is assumed to request from the user data for one new member. The assumption is that once the user specifies that he wants to perform this operation he will want to perform it at least once.

```
PROCEDURE NewMember ;
BEGIN
 REPEAT
    GetNewMemberDetails ;
    YesNoQuestion ('Do you wish to enter details for another member? ',
                                                      Reply) ;
    UNTIL (Reply = 'N') ;
 END NewMember ;
```

Fig. 9.8.

```
PROCEDURE YesNoQuestion (Question : ARRAY OF CHAR) : CHAR ;
  VAR
     ValidReply    : BOOLEAN ;
     Reply         : CHAR ;
BEGIN
 REPEAT
    WriteLnString (Question) ;
    Read (Reply) ;
    Reply := CAP (Reply) ;
    ValidReply := (Reply = 'Y') OR (Reply = 'N') ;
    IF NOT ValidReply THEN
          WriteLnString ('Type either Y or N. – ') ;
    END (* IF *) ;
 UNTIL ValidReply ;
 WriteLn ;
 RETURN Reply ;
 END YesNoQuestion ;
```

Fig. 9.9.

In Chapter 6, a procedure YesNoQuestion was shown which asked a question of a user and accepted a reply. This procedure treated all characters other than 'Y' and 'y' as negative replies and the dangers of this were pointed out. However, in many situations it is safer to insist that the only valid responses are 'Y', 'y', 'N' and 'n'. As the question has to be asked and a reply accepted at least once, it is natural to formulate this procedure as a REPEAT statement (see Fig. 9.9).

Notice that it is not necessary to initialise Reply before entering the loop as it is given a value by the statement

    Read (Reply)

before the BOOLEAN expression is tested. Variables which are tested by the BOOLEAN expression do not need to be assigned initial values before the REPEAT statement if they are guaranteed to be assigned values within the statement sequence of the REPEAT statement. Note that in situations where this is not the case some initialisation outside the loop may be necessary.

A Comparison of REPEAT and WHILE Statements

It is possible to write any loop as a WHILE statement, however this will be unnatural in many cases. In particular, if the statements of the statement sequence have to be executed at least once then this will require artificially forcing the BOOLEAN expression to evaluate to TRUE for the first iteration or duplicating statements of the statement sequence prior to the WHILE statement in order to guarantee that they are executed once. It is therefore advisable to think very carefully about the kind of repetitive statement to use. At the end of the chapter we give advice on selecting between all the repetitive constructs available in Modula-2. For the present we summarise the similarities and differences between WHILE and REPEAT statements.

1.   WHILE and REPEAT statements both involve a statement sequence which is executed repeatedly until the terminating condition of the construct is satisfied.

2.   The terminating condition is determined by a BOOLEAN expression.

3.   In a WHILE statement the BOOLEAN expression determining the terminating condition is at the top of the construct and is tested **before** the statement sequence is executed. This allows the possibility that the BOOLEAN expression evaluates to FALSE on the first occasion it is tested and therefore prevents the statement sequence from being executed. The statement sequence is executed repeatedly while the BOOLEAN expression evaluates to TRUE, i.e. until it evaluates to FALSE.

4.   In a REPEAT statement the terminating condition is determined by a BOOLEAN expression at the end of the construct which is tested **after** the statement sequence has been executed. This guarantees that the statement sequence is executed at least once. The statement sequence is executed repeatedly until the BOOLEAN expression evaluates to TRUE, i.e. while it evaluates to FALSE.

5.   Where possible it is advisable to make the BOOLEAN expression as strict as possible. With WHILE statements this implies testing for inequality (<>), and with REPEAT statements this implies testing for equality (=), so that in both cases the loops terminate under the strict condition of equality. Using such strict conditions in preference to the weaker conditions of >, <, <= and >= means that if there is a programming error in designing the BOOLEAN expression this will cause the program to go into a non-terminating loop. With the weaker conditions it is more likely that the loop will terminate without achieving the goal. It is easier to recognise and correct a non-terminating loop than it is to find an incorrectly terminating loop.

6.   In both constructs it is essential that the statement sequence alter variables which are involved in the BOOLEAN expression in order that the statement sequence can influence the evaluation of the BOOLEAN expression and thereby cause the loop to terminate.

7.   It is recommended that you develop a habit of designing loops in reverse by determining the goal that should be achieved when the loop has been executed and then determining the terminating condition, the way the statement sequence must influence the terminating condition and any necessary initialisation required before the loop.

Some Common Errors

The most difficult part of using WHILE and REPEAT constructs is determining the appropriate terminating condition which will achieve the required goal and ensuring that this condition can be satisfied. Put a different way, it is often difficult to decide what the BOOLEAN expression at the start or end of the construct should look like and how the statement sequence should make progress towards the goal. Analysing the need for a repetitive statement in terms of the goal to be achieved and looking for the relationship which holds each time around the loop helps tremendously in this respect. However, here we indicate some common types of errors which may help you to quickly diagnose an error in code involving repetitive constructs.

1.   The statement sequence does not influence the BOOLEAN expression. Consider the code fragment of Fig. 9.10a where the terminating condition is that X is greater than 10. This can never be achieved as the statement

```
X := 1 ;
WHILE X <= 10 DO
      Write ('*') ;
END (* WHILE *) ;
```

(a)

```
X := 1 ;
Y := X ;
REPEAT
      Write ('*') ;
      IF X = Y THEN
            INC (X)
      END (* IF *) ;
UNTIL X > 10 ;
```

(b)

```
X := 1 ;
REPEAT
      Write ('*') ;
      INC (X,2) ;
UNTIL X = 10 ;
```

(c)

```
Read (CH) ;
WHILE (Ch <> ' ') OR (Ch <> '.') DO
      Read (Ch) ;
END (* WHILE *) ;
```

(d)

```
Read (Ch) ;
WHILE (Ch < '0') AND (Ch > '9') DO
      Read (Ch) ;
END (* WHILE *) ;
```

(e)

```
WHILE X <= 10 DO
      Write ('*') ;
      INC (X) ;
END (* WHILE *) ;
```

(f)

Fig. 9.10. Some common errors.

sequence does not increment X. This can also appear in more obscure guises, as demonstrated in Fig. 9.10b. The first time around the loop X will equal Y so it will be incremented to 2 but on subsequent iterations X will not equal Y, so X will not be incremented and again the terminating condition will not be achieved.

2. The terminating condition is inappropriate. Consider the code fragment of Fig. 9.10c where the statement sequence increments X by 2 on each iteration and so has the potential of influencing the terminating condition involving X. However as X is initialised to 1, it will always be incremented to an odd number and therefore can never be equal to 10.

3. The starting/terminating condition cannot be achieved. In some situations the BOOLEAN expression associated with a loop construct can become quite complex and error prone. A common error is to confuse AND and OR, and produce a BOOLEAN expression which always evaluates to TRUE or always evaluates to FALSE. For example the BOOLEAN expression in the WHILE statement of Fig. 9.10d always evaluates to TRUE irrespective of the value of Ch. Conversely the BOOLEAN expression of Fig. 9.10e always evaluates to FALSE and so prevents the statement sequence from ever being executed.

4. Appropriate initialisation of variables is omitted. For example, the code fragment of Fig. 9.10f will produce unpredictable results when executed because X is not initialised. In practice X will have a value but this will be any old value which happens to be in the memory location associated with X. If this is greater than 10 the loop will not be executed at all. If it is less than or equal to 10 then the loop will be executed several times.

9.3 THE FOR STATEMENT

Modula-2 has a special repetitive statement for situations when the number of times a statement sequence needs to be executued is known or can be calculated from other known information. This is the FOR statement. Assuming the declarations

```
CONST
        NameLength                  = 40 ;
        Space                       = '' ;
VAR
        Name                        : ARRAY [1..NameLength] OF CHAR ;
        Index                       : CARDINAL ;
```

the following code fragment will initialise an array of characters to spaces

```
FOR Index := 1 TO NameLength DO
        Name [Index] := Space ;
END (* FOR *) ;
```

Similarly a FOR statement is the appropriate construct to use to calculate the factorial of a number as shown in Fig. 9.11.

```
PROCEDURE Factorial (N : CARDINAL) : CARDINAL ;
        (* Assumes that the result is small enough to
            be represented as a CARDINAL value *)
        VAR
        Result,
        J       : CARDINAL ;
BEGIN
    Result := 1 ;
    FOR J := 2 TO N DO
        Result := Result * J ;
    END (* FOR *) ;
    RETURN Result ;
END Factorial ;
```

Fig. 9.11.

There are two forms of the FOR statement. The simpler form shown in Fig. 9.12 is the form that we have already seen and will discuss first.

```
FOR ControlVariable := StartVal TO FinishVal DO
```
```
        Statement Sequence
```
```
END (* FOR *) ;
```

Fig. 9.12.

The control variable is a variable whose type is either INTEGER, CARDINAL, an enumeration type or a subrange of these types. It must not be

1. a component of a structured type (e.g. a component of an array),
2. a variable imported from another module,
3. a formal parameter of a procedure.

The starting and finishing values are expressions whose results must be **compatible** with the control variable. Some implementations only require the expression to be assignment compatible with the control variable but this is non-standard.

The control variable is initialised to a starting value and is then incremented by 1 on each iteration. The statement sequence is executed repeatedly for as long as the control variable lies within the range from the starting value to the finishing value inclusive. If initially the starting value is greater than the finishing value then the statement sequence is not executed. In this respect the FOR statement is more like a WHILE statement than a REPEAT statement.

We can think of the termination of a FOR loop occurring when the control variable is greater than the value of the finishing condition. However, technically this is wrong as the control variable can be an enumeration or subrange type. The lower and upper limits of such types can be used as the starting and finishing values of a FOR statement without the control variable going out of range. For example, assuming the declarations

```
CONST
        NameLength          = 40 ;
        Space               = ' ' ;
TYPE
        NameRange           = [1..NameLength] ;
        NameType            = ARRAY NameRange OF CHAR ;
VAR
        Name                : NameType ;
        Index               : NameRange ;
```

the following code fragment initialises Name to be all spaces

```
FOR Index := 1 TO NameLength DO
        Name [Index] := Space ;
END (* FOR *) ;
```

Compare this with a version using a WHILE statement where Index would be incremented to 41 before the loop terminates and therefore would go out of range of the subrange type NameRange. This would cause an error to be reported when the program runs. This also applies to enumeration types.

```
Index := 1 ;
WHILE Index <= NameLength DO
      Name[Index] := Space ;
      INC (Index) ;
END (* WHILE *) ;
```

Figure 9.13 shows three different ways of initialising an array whose bounds are determined by an enumeration type. The FOR loop provides the simplest way of iterating along the array, the WHILE and REPEAT statements to achieve the same are less natural. In the WHILE and REPEAT versions there is always a problem case with either the first or last member of the enumeration type which has to be treated specially.

A consequence of the definition of the FOR statement, however, is that after a FOR statement terminates the value of the control variable is undefined and should not be used again before being suitably initialised. It may be that you can reason about what you think the value of the control variable should be and find that the compiler you use confirms this, however, as far as the language definition of Modula-2 is concerned, this value can be anything. If you use this 'feature' in a program and compile it on different compilers you may find that it behaves differently when executed.

There are further restrictions on how the control variable should be used in a FOR statement. Its value must not be altered by any of the statements within the statement sequence. This is in stark contrast to WHILE and REPEAT statements where the statement sequence has to influence the evaluation of the terminating condition. In a FOR statement the starting condition and terminating condition should be considered as being calculated prior to the execution of the statement sequence on the first iteration. This does not have to be the case on all compilers, as some may recompute the terminating condition on each iteration. It is therefore important that the statement sequence does not alter variables in a way which would affect the values of the starting and terminating conditions. Despite these restrictions the FOR statement is a very useful construct because the restrictions are designed to tailor the FOR statement for commonly occurring situations.

Figure 9.14 shows the second version of the FOR statement which explicitly specifies the step by which the control variable is incremented. The first version of the FOR statement is effectively an abbreviation for the second version where the increment is 1. However there are situations where a different value for the increment is required. The increment value is a constant expression, that is it must be a constant or must be calculated from other constants. Its type must be either INTEGER or CARDINAL.

```
TYPE
      Suspects = (Fred,George,Annie,Bill,Gill) ;
VAR
      Suspect                 : Suspects ;
      GuiltyProbabilities     : ARRAY Suspects OF REAL ;

FOR Suspect := Fred TO Gill DO
      GuiltyProbabilities [Suspect] := 0.0 ;
END (* FOR *) ;

Suspect := Fred ;
GuiltyProbabilities [Suspect] := 0.0 ;
REPEAT
      INC (Suspect) ;
      GuiltyProbabilities [Suspect] := 0.0 ;
UNTIL Suspect = Gill ;

Suspect := Fred ;
WHILE Suspect <> Gill DO
      GuiltyProbabilities [Suspect] := 0.0 ;
      INC (Suspect) ;
END (* WHILE *) ;
GuiltyProbabilities [Gill] := 0.0 ;
```

Fig. 9.13. Repetitive Statements and Enumeration Types.

```
FOR ControlVariable := StartVal TO FinishVal BY IncrementVal DO
```
```
      Statement Sequence
```
```
END (* FOR *) ;
```

Fig. 9.14.

Figure 9.15 illustrates how this extended version of the FOR statement can be used. The FOR statement of Fig. 9.15a shuffles the names in components 50 to 99 into components 51 to 100, overwriting anything in component 100. In order to shuffle components along in this way it is necessary to start at the end of the array and work backwards. The loop in Fig. 9.15b puts the character in component 50 into all of components 51 to 100 inclusive.

```
TYPE
    Names                   = ARRAY [0..19] OF CHAR ;
VAR
    ArrayOfNames            : ARRAY [1..100] OF Names ;
    J                       : CARDINAL ;

FOR J := 99 TO 50 BY −1 DO
    ArrayOfNames[J+1] := ArrayOfNames[J] ;
END (* FOR *) ;
```

(a)

```
FOR J := 50 TO 99 DO
    ArrayOfNames [J+1] := ArrayOfNames[J] ;
END (* FOR *) ;
```

(b)

Fig. 9.15.

Figure 9.16 illustrates that the starting value, terminating value and increment of the FOR statement can be determined by values read previously from the keyboard. This code fragment allows a user to effectively state 'print every Nth character and their character codes starting from a particular character to the end of the character set'. Notice that the number of repetitions of the FOR loop cannot be determined when the programmer writes the program but can be calculated from the input values once these are known.

```
VAR
    StartingCharacterCode       ,
    EveryNthCharacter           ,
    CharCode                    : CARDINAL ;

ReadCard (StartingCharacterCode) ;
ReadCard (EveryNthCharacter) ;
FOR CharCode := StartingCharacterCode TO 127 BY EveryNthCharacter DO
    IF CharCode < ORD (Space) THEN
        Write (Space) ;
    ELSE
        Write (CHR(CharCode)) ;
    END (* IF *) ;
    WriteCard (CharCode,4) ;
    WriteLn ;
END (* FOR *) ;
```

Fig. 9.16.

It should be noted that the second form of the FOR statement is permitted with enumeration types. For example, a loop

```
FOR Suspect := Fred TO Gill BY 2 DO
    (*... ...*)
END (* FOR *)
```

assigns to Suspect the values Fred, Annie and Gill on successive iterations.

9.4   THE LOOP STATEMENT

The procedure OneDigitNumber in Fig. 9.17 illustrates the final kind of repetitive statement available in Modula-2. Its general form is shown in Fig. 9.18.

```
TYPE
    Digit = [0..9] ;

PROCEDURE OneDigitNumber (Max : Digit) : CHAR ;
VAR
    MaxReply ,
    Reply      : CHAR ;
BEGIN
  MaxReply := CHR (Max + ORD('0')) ;
  LOOP
      WriteLnString ('Select Option – ') ;
      Read (Reply) ;
      IF (Reply >= '0') AND (Reply <= MaxReply) THEN
          EXIT ;
      END (* IF *) ;
      WriteString ('Type a number between 0 and ') ;
      Write (MaxReply) ;
  END (* LOOP *) ;
  WriteLn ;
  RETURN Reply ;
END OneDigitNumber ;
```

Fig. 9.17.

```
LOOP
```

Statement Sequence

```
END (* LOOP *) ;
```

Fig. 9.18.

The statement sequence of the LOOP statement is executed indefinitely, unless it is terminated by an EXIT statement from within the statement sequence. The EXIT statement passes control directly to the end of the LOOP statement and terminates the statement. This can be used in conjunction with an IF statement to terminate the LOOP statement as in OneDigitNumber. If the character read is a numeric character in the permitted range then control is passed to the end of the LOOP statement and the loop terminated. In this case, this is also the end of the procedure so control is automatically passed back to where the procedure was called with the value of Reply returned as the result.

The LOOP statement should be considered as a construct to be used in exceptional circumstances. Both WHILE and REPEAT statements can be reformulated as LOOP statements in conjunction with an IF statement and an EXIT statement. Figure 9.19 illustrates each of these reformulations as LOOP statements.

```
LOOP
        IF NOT BOOLEAN Expression THEN EXIT END (* IF *) ;

        ┌─────────────────────────┐
        │  Statement Sequence     │
        └─────────────────────────┘
END (* LOOP *) ;
```

                (a) a WHILE statement recast as a LOOP statement

```
LOOP
        ┌─────────────────────────┐
        │  Statement Sequence     │
        └─────────────────────────┘
        IF BOOLEAN Expression THEN EXIT END (* IF *) ;
END (* LOOP *) ;
```

                (b) a REPEAT statement recast as a LOOP statement

Fig. 9.19.

These are inappropriate uses of the LOOP construct and the WHILE or REPEAT version is preferred. With a LOOP statement, EXIT statements can appear at any point within the statement sequence. Therefore, even having located an IF statement and an EXIT statement at the top or the bottom of the statement sequence, it is still possible that other EXIT statements may appear in the statement sequence. If this is the case then the LOOP statement does not correspond directly to a REPEAT or WHILE statement. Conversely, the conditions which determines the way REPEAT and WHILE statements terminate appears in a predetermined syntactic position which makes locating them easy.

Why, then, is this construct provided and how should it be used?

Modula-2 is a general purpose programming language for writing many kinds of programs. Certain types of programs are written such that they never terminate. For example, an **operating system** runs whenever a computer is switched on and provides numerous useful facilities to allow other programs to run. You may not have cause to write an operating system but you may find yourself in a position of writing a program which runs other programs. If, say, a small business runs only a few programs and asks you to provide an easy way of running these, you may then write a non-terminating program such as the program fragment shown in Fig. 9.20. Later in the book you will see more advanced programs which involve sections of program code consisting of non-terminating LOOP statements.

When EXIT statements are used with LOOP statements there should be a good reason for not using a WHILE or REPEAT statement. In some cases the speed at which the program runs is critical to the problem being solved and the EXIT statement can speed up execution by quickly passing control out of a LOOP statement. On some occasions the BOOLEAN expression of a WHILE or REPEAT statement can become complex and the program may be easier to read and understand if a LOOP statement and EXIT statements are used.

```
LOOP
    WriteLnString ('Only switch the machine off when this message') ;
    WriteLnString ('is displayed.') ;
    WriteLn ;
    Reply := MenuReply ('Accounts/Pay Roll/Debtors/') ;
    CASE Reply OF
        '0' : Run(Accounts) |
        '1' : Run(PayRoll) |
        '2' : Run(Debtors)
    END (* CASE *) ;
END (* LOOP *) ;
            (* n.b. it would be pointless having statements after this LOOP
            statement as they would never be executed. *)
```

Fig. 9.20.

It should be noted that when a LOOP statement is within a procedure a RETURN statement inside the statement sequence of the LOOP statement causes the procedure to return control at that point. This provides an alternative way of exiting LOOP statements.

9.5 NESTED LOOPS

The WHILE, REPEAT, FOR and LOOP statements each involve a statement sequence in the construct, any of which may themselves be loop constructs thereby allowing loops to be contained in other loops. In such situations it is said that one loop is **nested** inside another. Consider the code fragment in Fig. 9.21a which involves one FOR statement nested inside the statement sequence of another FOR statement. The outer loop will be executed three times and each time the outer loop is executed the inner loop will be executed four times. In total the inner loop will be executed twelve times giving the output shown in Fig. 9.21b.

The inner loop separates pairs of numbers by a six space gap, and the outer loop separates groups of pairs by forcing a new line to be started. Each pair of numbers is produced by executing the inner loop once and each row is produced by executing the outer loop once.

```
WriteString(' X Y      X Y      X Y      X Y') ;
FOR X := 1 TO 3 DO      (* Outer loop *)

        FOR Y := 1 TO 4 DO      (* Inner loop *)
              WriteCard (X,2) ;
              WriteCard (Y,2) ;
              WriteString ('      ') ;
        END (* FOR Y *) ;

        WriteLn ;
END (* FOR X *) ;
```

(a) nested FOR statements

X	Y		X	Y		X	Y		X	Y
1	1		1	2		1	3		1	4
2	1		2	2		2	3		2	4
3	1		3	2		3	3		3	4

(b) output of the nested FOR loops

Fig. 9.21.

This ability to nest one loop inside another gives great flexibility. Figure 9.22 shows a definition module for displaying a list of options on a visual display screen from which a user can select one of the options by typing a number corresponding to the option. MenuReply is called by passing to the procedure a list of options in an array of characters and returns the character corresponding to the selected option.

DEFINITION MODULE Menus ;

PROCEDURE MenuReply (Options : ARRAY OF CHAR) : CHAR ;
  (∗ writes the sequence of characters in Options but for every
  occurrence of '/' in the array a new line is started.
  The '/' character is used to separate a list of options
  to be printed on the screen, each option is numbered starting
  at 0 for the first option. A maximum of 10 options is permitted.
  A new line is written before the first option and '/' should not
  precede it, the '/' after the final option is obligatory.
  Returns as its result the numeric character associated with the
  selected option OR '∗' if Options is empty. ∗)

END Menus .

Fig. 9.22.

MenuReply can be called by passing a string constant to the procedure, such as

    Reply:=MenuReply('Exit/Enter Details/Amend Details/Delete Details/')

or by declaring a variable whose type is an array of characters

    VAR
        Menu : ARRAY [0..79] OF CHAR ;

then initialising it and passing it to the procedure

    Menu   := 'Exit/Enter Details/Amend Details/Delete Details/' ;
    Reply   := MenuReply (Menu) ;

In either case WriteMenu will display

    0 : Exit
    1 : Enter Details
    2 : Amend Details
    3 : Delete Details

The implementation module for Menus is given in Fig. 9.23. In order to list the options WriteMenu uses two repetitive statements one nested within the other. The outer loop writes the successive options and the inner loop writes the sequence of characters for an option name. These are both achieved by WHILE statements in WriteMenu.

OneDigitNumber allows the user to select any of these options by typing the number corresponding to the option. Note that WriteMenu assigns the number of options written to its variable parameter NoOfOptions so that this value can be passed onto OneDigitNumber in order to restrict the user to option numbers displayed on the screen.

```
IMPLEMENTATION MODULE Menus ;
    FROM InOut              IMPORT Write,WriteLn,WriteString,WriteCard,Read ;
    FROM MoreInOut          IMPORT WriteLnString ;

    PROCEDURE WriteMenu (VAR Options : ARRAY OF CHAR ;
                         VAR NoOfOptions : INTEGER) ;
        (* Hidden. writes out the options and returns the number of options
        written in NoOfOptions. *)
    VAR
        StringPos, LastChPlus1 : CARDINAL ;
    BEGIN
     StringPos          := 0 ;
     NoOfOptions        := -1 ;
     LastChPlus1        := HIGH (Options) ;
     WriteLn ;
     WHILE (StringPos <> LastChPlus1) AND (Options[StringPos] <> 0C) DO
        INC (NoOfOptions) ;
        WriteCard (NoOfOptions,1) ;
        Write (' ') ;
        WHILE (StringPos <> LastChPlus1) AND
              (Options[StringPos] <> '/') DO
            Write (Options[StringPos]) ;
            INC (StringPos) ;
        END (* WHILE *) ;
        INC (StringPos) ;
        WriteLn ;
     END (* WHILE *) ;
    END WriteMenu ;


    TYPE
        Digit = [0..9] ;


    PROCEDURE OneDigitNumber (Max : Digit) : CHAR ;
        (* Hidden. as in Fig 9.17 *)
    END OneDigitNumber ;


    PROCEDURE MenuReply (Options : ARRAY OF CHAR) : CHAR ;
     VAR
        NoOfOptions : INTEGER ;
    BEGIN
     WriteMenu (Options,NoOfOptions) ;
     IF NoOfOptions < 0 THEN
        RETURN '*' ;
     ELSE
        RETURN OneDigitNumber (NoOfOptions) ;
     END (* IF *) ;
    END MenuReply ;


    END Menus .
```

Fig. 9.23.

9.6 ADVICE ON WHICH REPETITIVE STATEMENT TO USE

Figure 9.24 summarises the criteria to use when deciding which type of repetitive statement to use. Note that these should be taken as guidelines, as other factors will influence the decision to use particular constructs. In particular, speed of execution may on occasions indicate that the LOOP statement is appropriate for fast exits from inside a statement sequence. Where possible and where the program code does not become unreadable REPEAT and WHILE loops are preferable and should be used rather than LOOP statements. In practice the WHILE statement is the most widely used repetitive construct and this is why it was introduced in Chapter 3.

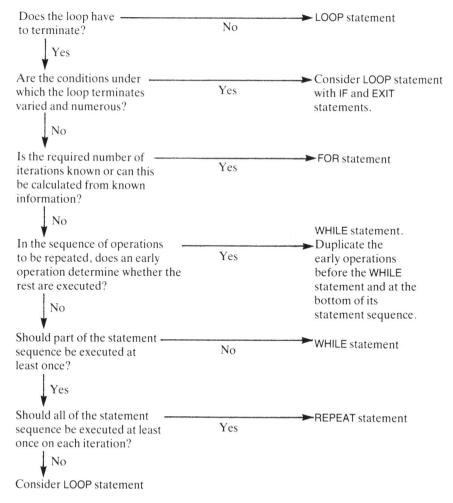

Fig. 9.24. Guidelines to Use of Repetitive Statements.

9.7 SUMMARY

In this chapter the four repetitive statements have been discussed. These are the WHILE, REPEAT, FOR and LOOP statements.

1 The WHILE and REPEAT statements allow repeated execution of a statement sequence and termination is achieved through the result of a BOOLEAN expression. The REPEAT statement guarantees that the statement sequence is executed once. The test associated with a WHILE statement is performed before the statement sequence is executed and therefore allows the possibility that the statement sequence will not be executed.

2 The FOR statement uses a control variable to determine the number of times the statement sequence is executed. A starting value and a terminating value are specified for the control variable. The statement sequence is executed while the value of the control variable lies within the range specified by the starting value and the terminating value, and the control variable is automatically incremented at the end of each iteration. If no increment value is specified this is assumed to be 1. If the increment value is negative then the control variable is effectively decremented at the end of each iteration. If the increment value is positive and the starting value is greater than the terminating value then the statement sequence is not executed. Similarly if the increment value is negative and the starting value is less than the finishing value then the statement sequence is not executed. The starting value and finishing value can be arbitrarily complex expressions but their types must be CARDINAL, INTEGER, enumeration types or subranges of these types. The increment value is a constant expression which means that this value has to be a constant or has to be calculated from other constants currently in scope.

3 The LOOP statement allows non-terminating repetition.

4 In conjunction with IF and EXIT statements, the LOOP statement permits termination of the statement sequence from any point within the sequence. It is advised that other repetitive statements be used in preference to this statement where this does not lead to overly complex code, or other factors such as speed of execution, do not suggest otherwise.

TECHNICAL EXERCISES

1 For the following problems state which of a FOR, REPEAT, WHILE or LOOP statement is most appropriate.

    a Read 10 CARDINAL values from the keyboard and compute their average.

    b Read an indefinite number of CARDINAL values from the keyboard and compute their average and allow the user to indicate when the sequence of values is finished.

c calculate the value of a number raised to the power N by repeated multiplication where N is a CARDINAL value.

2 **a** Rewrite the procedure YesNoQuestion (Fig. 9.9) using a LOOP statement.
b Rewrite the procedure OneDigitNumber (Fig. 9.17) using a REPEAT statement.
c Rewrite both procedures using WHILE statements.
d Comment on the readability and appropriateness of each version.

3 Consider the following loops and indicate whether they will terminate appropriately or not, and if not state what alterations are required to correct them.

```
(* to write 10 asterisks *)
FOR X := 1 TO 10 DO
    Write ('*') ;
    INC (X) ;
END (* FOR *) ;
```

(a)

```
(* to write 10 asterisks *)
WHILE J > K DO
    Write ('*') ;
    K := K + 1 ;
END (* WHILE *) ;
```

(b)

```
(* to write 10 asterisks *)
LOOP
    INC (J) ;
    Write ('*') ;
    IF J = 11 THEN
        EXIT
    END (* IF *) ;
END (* LOOP *) ;
```

(c)

```
(* to write 10 asterisks *)
J := 0 ;
REPEAT
    Write ('*') ;
UNTIL J = 10 ;
```

(d)

```
J := 1 ;
REPEAT
    Read (Ch) ;
    IF Ord(Ch) > ORD (' ') THEN
        NAME[J] := Ch ;
        INC (J) ;
    END (* IF *) ;
UNTIL ORD (Ch) <= ORD (' ') ;
```

(e)

```
J := 1 ;
LOOP
    Read (Ch) ;
    IF ORD(Ch) <= ORD(' ') THEN
        EXIT
    END (* IF *) ;
    Name[J] := Ch ;
    INC (J) ;
END (* LOOP *) ;
```

(f)

4 State whether the following FOR statements are valid or not, and if not state why they are not valid. Assume an import list

FROM AnotherModule IMPORT T,U,Programming,DocumentingProgram,Work ;

(∗ where T is a CARDINAL and U an INTEGER variable and
Programming, DocumentingProgram and Work are procedures
which take no parameters ∗)

and the declarations

```
TYPE Days  = (Mon,Tue,Wed,Thur,Fri,Sat,Sun) ;
VAR  Day   : Days ;
     X     : CARDINAL ;
     Y,Z   : INTEGER ;
     Q     : REAL ;
     WorkHoursPerDay : ARRAY Days OF CARDINAL ;
```

a   FOR X := 1.0 TO 3.0 DO   **b**   FOR Day := Fri TO Mon DO
            Write ('∗') ;   Work ;
        END (∗ FOR ∗) ;   END (∗ FOR ∗) ;

c   FOR Day := Sun TO Sat DO   **d**   FOR Day := Mon TO Sun DO
            Work ;   Work ;
        END (∗ FOR ∗) ;   END (∗ FOR ∗) ;

e   FOR Day := 1 TO 7 DO
            Work ;
        END (∗ FOR ∗) ;

f   FOR T := 1 TO 5 DO   **g**   FOR U := –5 TO 5 DO
            Write ('∗') ;   Write ('∗') ;
        END (∗ FOR ∗) ;   END (∗ FOR ∗) ;

h   FOR WorkHoursPerDay[Mon] := 9 TO 12 DO
            Programming ;
        END (∗ FOR ∗) ;

j   PROCEDURE Afternoon (Time : CARDINAL) ;
        BEGIN
          FOR Time := 1 TO 5 DO
              DocumentingProgram ;
          END (∗ FOR ∗) ;
        END Afternoon ;

5   For each of the following loops state the value of J and what will have
    happened to the array after the loop has terminated.

a   J := 1 ;   **b**   FOR J := 1 TO 20 BY 2 DO
        WHILE J < 20 DO   Name[J] := ' ' ;
            Name[J] := ' ' ;   END (∗ FOR ∗) ;
            INC (J,2) ;
        END (∗ WHILE ∗)

c   J := 1 ;
        WHILE J <> 21 DO
            Name[J] := ' ' ;
            INC (J,2) ;
        END (∗ WHILE ∗) ;

6 Consider the following program fragment

```
PROCEDURE Insert (VAR ArrayToSearch : ARRAY OF CARDINAL ;
                  VAR NoOfComponents : CARDINAL) ;
VAR
      Top,Bottom,Middle : CARDINAL ;
BEGIN
  Bottom := 1 ;
  Top := NoOfComponents ;
  REPEAT
    Middle := (Bottom + Top) DIV 2 ;
    IF ArrayToSearch [Middle] <> ArrayToSearch [0] THEN
           Bottom := Middle + 1
    ELSE
           Top := Middle – 1
    END (* IF *) ;
  UNTIL (Top <> Bottom) ;
  FOR J := NoOfComponents TO Bottem BY –1 DO
             ArrayToSearch [J+1] := ArrayToSearch [J] ;
  END (* FOR *) ;
  ArrayToSearch [Bottom] := ArrayToSearch [0] ;
  INC (NoOfComponents) ;
END Insert ;
```

a State what will be the case when the REPEAT statement terminates.
b What assumption is made about the problem in order that a REPEAT statement is used?
c What must be true of the array in order that this works?

PROGRAMMING EXERCISES

1 Write a version of FindPosition (Figs 9.2 and 9.3) in which the formal parameter CharacterArray is an open array parameter.

2 Write a procedure MatchCharSequences which compares two arrays of characters for equality. The procedure should use open array parameters. (If the arrays are not the same size then they cannot be equal.)

3 Write a function procedure Palindrome which has a formal open array parameter, CharacterSequence, and returns TRUE if the character sequence reads the same forward as it does backwards and FALSE otherwise.

4 Look at the WHILE statements in Figs 6.4, 6.16, 6.19, 6.20, 6.24, 7.25, 8.18 and 8.19 and rewrite those which would be more appropriately written using repetitive constructs other than WHILE statements.

5 Using technical exercise 6 as a basis, write an efficient procedure (in contrast to that of Fig. 9.3) to

a find a particular value in the array and return the index of the component which holds the matching value.

b or reports that the value is not in the array if the value is not found.

Efficiency has not been a major concern in the chapter, but devise a way to compare the efficiency of this procedure with that of Fig. 9.3 especially for larger arrays.

ANSWERS

1 **a** FOR statement as the number of iterations is known.

b the most appropriate way of formulating this is as a WHILE loop. Using InOut, an initial call of ReadCard outside the loop so that the BOOLEAN condition can test Done.

```
Total := 0 ;
NoOfValues := 0 ;
ReadCard (Number) ;
WHILE Done DO
        INC (Total,Number) ;
        INC (NoOfValues) ;
        ReadCard (Number) ;
END (* WHILE *) ;
IF NoOfValues <> 0 THEN
        Average := Total DIV NoOfValues
ELSE
        Average := 0
END (* IF *) ;
```

c FOR statement as the number of iterations is known

```
Result := 1 ;
FOR Count := 1 TO N DO
        Result := Result * Number
END (* FOR *) ;
```

2 **a** PROCEDURE YesNoQuestion (Question : ARRAY OF CHAR) : CHAR ;
```
        VAR
                Reply : CHAR ;
        BEGIN
        LOOP
                WriteLnString (Question) ;
                Read (Reply) ;
                Reply := CAP (Reply) ;
                IF (Reply = 'Y') OR (Reply = 'N') THEN
                        WriteLn ;
```

```
                RETURN Reply ;
          END (* IF *) ;
          WriteLnString ('Type either Y or N. – ') ;
    END (* LOOP *) ;
  END YesNoQuestion ;


b   PROCEDURE OneDigitNumber (Max : Digit) : CHAR ;
      VAR
            ValidReply : BOOLEAN ;
            MaxReply ,
            Reply      : CHAR ;
      BEGIN
        MaxReply := CHR (Max + ORD('0')) ;
        REPEAT
            WriteLnString ('Select Option – ') ;
            Read (Reply) ;
            ValidReply := (Reply >= '0') AND (Reply <= MaxReply) ;
            IF NOT ValidReply THEN
                WriteLnString ('Type a number between 0 and ') ;
                Write (MaxReply) ;
            END (* IF *) ;
        UNTIL ValidReply ;
        WriteLn ;
        RETURN Reply ;
      END OneDigitNumber ;


c   PROCEDURE YesNoQuestion (Question : ARRAY OF CHAR) : CHAR ;
      VAR
            ValidReply : BOOLEAN ;
            Reply      : CHAR ;
      BEGIN
        ValidReply := FALSE ;
        WHILE NOT ValidReply DO
            WriteLnString (Question) ;
            Read (Reply) ;
            Reply := CAP (Reply) ;
            ValidReply := (Reply = 'Y') OR (Reply = 'N') ;
            IF NOT ValidReply THEN
                WriteLnString ('Type either Y or N. – ') ;
            END (* IF *) ;
        END (* WHILE *) ;
        WriteLn ;
        RETURN Reply ;
      END YesNoQuestion ;
```

```
PROCEDURE OneDigitNumber (Max : Digit) : CHAR ;
   VAR
      ValidReply : BOOLEAN ;
      MaxReply ,
      Reply      : CHAR ;
BEGIN
 MaxReply := CHR (Max + ORD('0')) ;
 ValidReply := FALSE ;
 WHILE NOT ValidReply DO
      WriteLnString ('Select Option – ') ;
      Read (Reply) ;
      ValidReply := (Reply >= '0') AND (Reply <= MaxReply) ;
      IF NOT ValidReply THEN
         WriteLnString ('Type a number between 0 and ') ;
         Write (MaxReply) ;
      END (* IF *) ;
 END (* WHILE *) ;
 WriteLn ;
 RETURN Reply ;
END OneDigitNumber ;
```

d As the repetitive statements are reasonably short the LOOP statement versions seem to have the edge. They do not require the introduction of a BOOLEAN variable as in the WHILE and REPEAT versions. The BOOLEAN variables are introduced into these versions to avoid evaluating the same BOOLEAN expression twice in the IF statements and then in the terminating condition of the loop. The REPEAT versions are more appropriate than the WHILE statements as part of the loop has to be executed at least once. If the procedures were longer the REPEAT versions would be easier to understand than the LOOP versions as the terminating condition is more obvious in this construct.

3 a Inside a FOR statement the control variable is incremented automatically and therefore must not be incremented by a call to INC. If this is removed it will write 10 asterisks.

b J and K must be suitably initialised before the WHILE statement, for example

```
J := 10 ;
K := 0 ;
```

c J must be initialised to 1 before the LOOP statement.

d This is an infinite loop as J is not incremented, include INC(J) inside the statement sequence of the REPEAT statement.

e This is fine as long as Name is an array whose lower bound is 1, and as long as the number of characters typed does not exceed the number of components in the array. It would be safer to include a further condition to stop the REPEAT statement when the number of characters which the array can hold is exceeded.

f This is the same problem as **e** but cast as a LOOP statement, the same comments made in **e** apply here.

4   **a** invalid the starting and terminating conditions cannot be REAL values.

  b valid, though silly as the loop can never be executed because the starting value is greater than the terminating value.

  c valid — ditto.

  d valid.

  e invalid Day is not compatible with CARDINAL values.

  f invalid, the control variable of a FOR statement cannot be imported from another module.

  g ditto.

  h invalid, the control variable of a FOR statement cannot be a component of an array.

  j invalid, the control variable of a FOR statement cannot be a parameter.

5   **a** J will be 21.

  b J will be undefined.

  c J will be 21.

In all cases the components of the array with odd indexes between 1 and 19 inclusive will be set to the character space.

6   **a** When the REPEAT statement terminates

    Bottom = Top + 1

holds. In addition, Bottom and Top effectively divide the array into two parts such that

(i) all components of the array between Bottom and NoOfComponents are greater than or equal to the item to be inserted,

(ii) all components between 1 and Top are less than the item to be inserted.

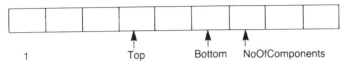

This REPEAT statement performs what is called a binary search or binary chop to find the position to insert an item in an ordered array. The loop repeatedly deals with a partition of the array which includes the position at which the new item is to be inserted. On each iteration the one of Top or Bottom is updated to make the partition smaller. Eventually the partition disappears with Top and Bottom dividing the array into the two parts indicated above.

Note that if the item to be inserted is already in the array then Bottom indexes the array at its position. A test

IF ArrayToSearch[Bottom] <> ArrayToSearch[0] THEN

can be used to prevent insertion of duplicate items into the list.

b (*TRUE Top >= Bottom *) initially, that is that the ordered array is not empty.

c The components of array between 1 and NoOfComponents must be ordered. Additionally, it is assumed that there is a vacant component NoOfComponents+1 to allow the components between Bottom and NoOfComponents inclusive to be moved along into the next higher component.

Chapter 10

Structured Types and Files

The types of variables discussed to date are predeclared basic types, such as INTEGER, CARDINAL and REAL, and user-defined types such as enumerated types and array types. These have proved sufficient to enable a rich variety of Modula-2 constructs to be demonstrated and for us to develop solutions to reasonably complex problems. In part, this is because arrays are a powerful and flexible data structure which can be used to build many other more complex structures. However, Modula-2 provides further types which can be used to declare other data structures. These provide powerful aids to thinking, when trying to solve difficult programming problems involving data of different forms. The structures discussed in this chapter are records, sets, advanced features of arrays and an introduction to the idea of a file.

At the end of the chapter many of these structures are used to solve a problem of creating and processing a file of student data.

10.1 RECORDS AND THE WITH STATEMENT

An array essentially groups together many variables of the same type into a structure which can be manipulated in its entirety. Often it is useful to be able to combine data items of **different types** into one unit which can be manipulated as a whole. Records are collections of data of differing types packaged together as a whole. For example, the declarations

```
TYPE
     BookReference = RECORD
                    Title           : ARRAY [0..50] OF CHAR ;
                    Author          : ARRAY [0..40] OF CHAR ;
                    YearPublished   : CARDINAL ;
                    Price           : REAL
                    END ;
VAR
     FirstBook, SecondBook: BookReference ;
```

declare two variables each of which consist of two arrays of characters, a CARDINAL value and a REAL value. The data held within a record usually has a common characteristic, in this case the data associated with a book is collected together within a record variable.

The individual data items in a record are referred to as the fields of the record. Variables of type BookReference consist of four fields called Title, Author,

YearPublished and Price. Individual fields of a record are referenced using the notation

```
FirstBook.Title := 'Little Dorrit'
FirstBook.Author := 'Charles Dickens'
```

The field name selects the particular field of the record.

In addition to accessing individual fields, a record can be referenced and manipulated in its entirety. For example the assignment statements

```
SecondBook := FirstBook
```

copies all the fields of FirstBook into the corresponding fields of SecondBook. In particular, a record can be passed as a parameter to a procedure. For example a procedure InitialiseBook can be written with a procedure heading

```
PROCEDURE InitialiseBook (VAR ThisBook : BookReference) ;
```

and can then be called by the statement

```
InitialiseBook (FirstBook)
```

Note that if the data is not organised as a record this procedure would require four parameters. One of the advantages of record structures is manifest in the simplification of procedure declarations and calls.

Records cannot be compared using the relational operators, thus an IF statement

```
IF FirstBook = SecondBook THEN (*... ...*) END (* IF *)
```

is illegal.

Figure 10.1 shows simplified syntax diagrams for elementary record types.

Record Type :

Field List Sequence :

Field List :

Fig. 10.1.

A record declaration can include a field whose type is another record. This is illustrated in Fig. 10.2 where OneStudent is declared as a variable of type StudentDetailType and its field StudentName is itself a record consisting of two fields, Surname and Forename, both of which are arrays of characters. Figure 10.3 illustrates diagrammatically the structure of OneStudent. Records can be embedded within other records to any depth.

```
CONST
        MinCourse       = 0 ;
        MaxCourse       = 20 ;
TYPE
        CourseType      = [MinCourse..MaxCourse] ;
        SingleName      = ARRAY [0..19] OF CHAR ;
        NameType        = RECORD
                            Surname  : SingleName ;
                            Forename : SingleName ;
                          END ;
        StudentDetailType = RECORD
                            StudentName : NameType ;
                            Course      : CourseType ;
                            Deleted     : BOOLEAN ;
                          END ;
VAR
        OneStudent      : StudentDetailType ;
```

Fig. 10.2.

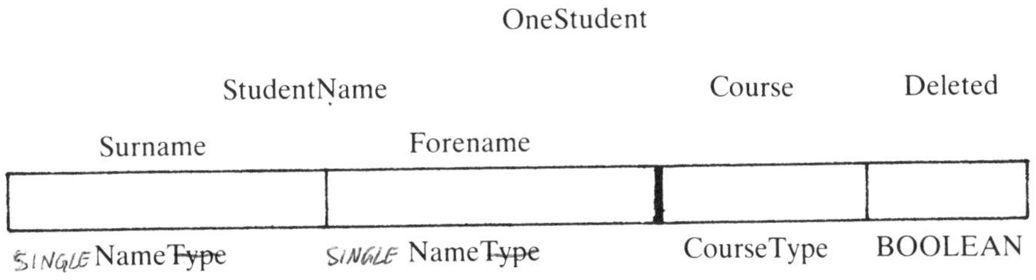

Fig. 10.3.

A problem with this kind of structure is the complexity of referring to individual data items in the record. For example, the following sequence of statements initialises all of the fields included in OneStudent

```
OneStudent.StudentName.Surname  := 'Other' ;
OneStudent.StudentName.Forename := 'Anne' ;
OneStudent.Course    := 1 ;
OneStudent.Deleted   := FALSE ;
```

In the second statement, the string 'Anne' is assigned to the array in the Forename field of the record in the StudentName field of the variable OneStudent. The problems of keeping track of such references are alleviated by the WITH statement.

The WITH Statement

A special construct called the WITH statement is provided for use when a large number of items have to be referred to in the same record structure. The above initialisation of OneStudent can be written more concisely as

```
WITH OneStudent DO
      StudentName.Surname := 'Other' ;
      StudentName.Forename := 'Anne' ;
      Course          := 1 ;
      Deleted         := FALSE ;
END (* WITH *)
```

or alternatively

```
WITH OneStudent.StudentName DO
      Surname  := 'Other' ;
      Forename : = 'Anne' ;
END (* WITH *) ;
WITH OneStudent DO
      Course          := 1 ;
      Deleted         := FALSE ;
END (* WITH *) ;
```

Simplified syntax diagrams relevant to the WITH statement are shown in Fig. 10.4. Such a statement refers to a particular record structure at the top of the statement and within the statement sequence references to fields of the record structure can be abbreviated to the field name. The definition of Designator allows the selected record to be embedded within other record or array structures. Notice that inside the statement sequence the dot (.) before a field name is omitted.

With Statement :

```
────────►WITH─►Designator ─►DO──►Statement Sequence ────────►END──►
```

Designator :

```
────────►Identifier ──────────┬────────────────────────────►
                          ┌────┴──►·──►Identifier─┐
                          └──►[ ──►Exp List ──►] ─┘
                                    ◄──────────
```

Fig. 10.4.

A word of warning is in order concerning the WITH statement. If an identifier inside a WITH statement can refer to a field of the structure named by the designator then this is how it is interpreted *irrespective of any other use that the name may have in its own right*. For example, if a program processing records of type StudentDetailType contains a variable called Course then within the statement

```
WITH OneStudent DO
      Course := Course ;
END (* WITH *) ;
```

both references to Course are to the field of OneStudent. In this case the WITH statement creates a hole in the scope of the variable Course. More generally a WITH statement creates a hole in the scope of any variable which has the same name as the fields of the record referenced by the designator. Undisciplined use of the WITH statement can render a program more difficult to read as it allows references to fields of a record which look like references to normal variables. It is therefore recommended to restrict the extent of a WITH statement to a few lines of the program text and to avoid such statements extending over several pages.

Example. Use of records in QueueModule

In QueueModule in Chapter 6 four data items are used to represent a queue data structure
1. the array QueueData,
2. the variable HeadQueue,
3. the variable EndQueue,
4. the variable SizeQueue.
The representation of a queue can be specified by a declaration of a record type

```
TYPE
      Queue = RECORD
                  QueueData : QueueType;
                  HeadQueue : CARDINAL;
                  EndQueue  : CARDINAL;
                  SizeQueue : CARDINAL
                  END (* RECORD *);
```

Variables to represent queues are then declared

```
VAR
      FirstQueue,SecondQueue : Queue;
```

Records are most useful when there is a requirement for many records of the same type. So an array of records is a useful and common data structure. This permits a generalisation of QueueModule to cater for problems where more than one queue is required. The data structure internal to QueueModule can be an array of queues

```
TYPE
      QueueStructure = ARRAY[1..MaxNoQueues] OF Queue;
```

This is particularly interesting since the record itself contains an array. As noted above there is no restriction on the number of levels of nesting of one data structure within another.

In the original design of QueueModule the type of the items in the queue is CARDINAL, however it is more likely that the items in the queue will be record structures. A more realistic representation of a collection of queues is shown in Fig. 10.5.

```
TYPE
        QueueRange          = [0..MaxQueue] ;
        ItemType            = RECORD
                                QueueItem1 : CARDINAL;
                                QueueItem2 : INTEGER
                                END (* RECORD *);
        Queue               = RECORD
                                QueueData : ARRAY[1..MaxQueue] OF ItemType ;
                                HeadQueue ,
                                EndQueue ,
                                SizeQueue : QueueRange ;
                                END (* RECORD *);
        QueueStructure      = ARRAY[1..MaxNoQueues] OF Queue;
VAR
        Queues              : QueueStructure;
```
Fig. 10.5.

10.2 VARIANT RECORDS

The requirement that all variables of a particular record type contain exactly the same fields can be overstrong so a special kind of record is available which allows record variables to use different collections of fields in the record. These kinds of records are known as variant records as different variations of the structure of the record are possible. The variant part of a record type is constructed using a declaration whose syntactic structure corresponds closely to the CASE statement. CASE statements are then used to determine which variant of a record is being used. An ELSE part is allowed in the variant as in the CASE statement.

Figure 10.6 shows the declaration of a variant record Vehicle which allows variations of the record to represent different kinds of vehicles. For a car the fields of the record are Registration, Transport, NoOfPassengers, Length, and Height. A record to represent a bus has the same fields except that it has no NoOfPassengers field, but instead has two other fields called NoOfSittingPassengers and NoOfStandingOfPassengers. The variants are determined by the field Transport which is a normal field of the record. This field can be assigned a value like any other field and this value determines which variant is applicable for a particular record.

Figure 10.7 illustrates how a particular Vehicle record might be initialised, and Fig. 10.8 shows a procedure for processing all of the variants of Vehicle. This tests the value of Transport using a CASE statement so that a particular record can be processed appropriately. If FordEscort is passed to it as a parameter the processing associated with a car because its Transport field's current value is Car. Transport is a **tag field** and VehicleType its **tag field type**. WriteVehicleDetails assumes a further procedure WriteVehicleType for writing the values of the enumerated type.

A record declaration can involve any number of variants and they can be embedded within each other.

```
TYPE
      VehicleType = (Car,Bus,Van);
      Vehicle     = RECORD
                        RegistrationNumber : ARRAY[0..6] OF CHAR;
                        CASE Transport : VehicleType OF
                            Car   : NoOfPassengers          : CARDINAL    |
                            Bus   : NoOfSittingPassengers   : CARDINAL ;
                                    NoOfStandingPassengers  : CARDINAL    |
                            Van   : MaxTonnage              : REAL
                        END (* CASE *);
                        Length : REAL;
                        Height : REAL
                   END (* RECORD *);
```

Fig. 10.6. A variant record.

```
VAR
      FordEscort : Vehicle ;

WITH FordEscort DO
      RegistrationNumber    := 'GLW496T';
      Transport             := Car;
      NoOfPassengers        := 4;
      Length                := 159.8 ; (* inches *)
      Height                := 55.1 ; (* inches *)
END (* WITH *);
```

Fig. 10.7. Initialising a variant record.

```
PROCEDURE WriteVehicleDetails (ThisVehicle : Vehicle) ;
BEGIN
  WITH ThisVehicle DO
      WriteLnString ('Registration ') ;
      WriteString (RegistrationNumber) ;
      WriteLnString ('Vehicle type ') ;
      WriteVehicleType (Transport) ;
      CASE Transport OF
          Car : WriteStringCard ('Seats ',NoOfPassengers,2) |
          Bus : WriteStringCard ('Seats ',NoOfSittingPassengers,3) ;
              WriteStringCard ('Standing ',NoOfStandingPassengers,3) |
          Van : WriteLnString ('Max load ') ;
              WriteReal (MaxTonnage,8) |
      END (* CASE *);
      WriteLnString ('Length ') ;
      WriteReal (Length,5) ;
      WriteLnString ('Height ') ;
      WriteReal (Height,5) ;
  END (* WITH *) ;
END WriteVehicleDetails ;
```

Fig. 10.8. Processing variant records.

It is possible to omit the tag field and only specify the tag field type. Figure 10.9 shows a record type declaration including the line

```
CASE : CustDetType OF
```

(some compilers only accept CASE CustDetType OF but this is non standard). In such situations it is assumed that the program can deduce when to use different variants without requiring a tag field to explicitly indicate which variant to use. This has obvious dangers and should be used with great care. Figure 10.9 illustrates an example of its possible use. It is assumed that the fields of the variant MainRec are normally adequate to hold all the data for a customer, but occasionally the data to be placed in the CustomerDetail field is too large and the data needs to overflow into continuation records which are dealt with as the variant ContRec. The value in NoOfContinueRec of a MainRec variant is used to determine how many of the immediately following records in CustomerArray are to be treated as ContRec variants before the next record to be treated as a MainRec variant is met.

There are two points of special interest in the CustomerDetails declaration
1.   The variants of the record have no fields in common. This is a common case in programs written for business applications.
2.   The tag field type is a enumeration type declared especially for the variants of the record.

```
TYPE
    LineOfDetail              = ARRAY[0..40] OF CHAR;
    PersonnelDetail           = ARRAY[1..3] OF LineOfDetail;
    ContPersonnelDetail       = ARRAY[1..4] OF LineOfDetail;
    CustDetType               = ( MainRec,ContRec );
    CustomerDetails           =
                RECORD
                CASE : CustDetType OF
                    MainRec :    Surname,Forename      : LineOfDetail;
                                 CustomerDetail        : PersonnelDetail;
                                 NoOfContinueRec       : CARDINAL          |
                    ContRec:     ContCustomerDetail    : ContPersonnelDetail
                END (* CASE *);
                END (* RECORD *);
    CustomerArray             = ARRAY[1..1000] OF CustomerDetails;
```

Fig. 10.9.

The complete syntax diagrams for the Field List including variant parts is given in Fig. 10.10.

Field List :

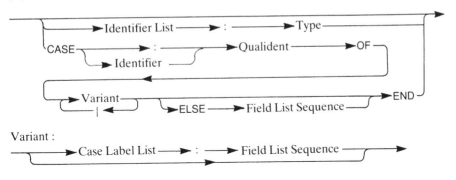

Variant :

Fig. 10.10.

10.3   SETS

Sets are a further useful structured type which correspond to the mathematical idea of a set. Set declarations have to stipulate the type of the set elements, just as arrays have to specify the type of their components. For example, the declarations

```
TYPE
    CardSet = SET OF CARDINAL[0..20];
VAR
    SetVar : CardSet;
```

declare a variable SetVar to be a set of a subrange of CARDINAL values. The syntax diagram for the specification of a set type is shown in Fig. 10.11.

Set Type :

—————→SET OF—————→Simple Type —————→

Fig. 10.11.

The Simple Type in Fig. 10.11 determines the domain of the set. This can be any subrange of CARDINAL values, non-negative INTEGER values or an enumeration type. There are normally quite severe implementation restrictions on the maximum size of the domain. You should check carefully what the restriction is in the implementation you are using. In practice, this means that set element types are declared as subranges of the basic types. Later in this chapter a type CharSet is used for demonstration purposes, but it may not be permitted in some implementations of Modula-2 due to restrictions on the size of sets.

In mathematics a constant set is denoted by the notation

{1,2,3..7}

which is a set with the elements 1,2,3,4,5,6 and 7 as members. In Modula-2 a set is denoted in a similar way except that the type of the set precedes the list of members. In this example it can be written

CardSet{1,2,3..7}

Constant sets can be used within statements like other constants. Unlike other structured types, set constants can be declared in a constant declaration, for example

CONST
    Elements1To7 = {1..7};

The empty set is denoted as {}. The syntax diagrams for references to sets in declarations and statements are given in Appendix 1.

Set Operations

A collection of operators for manipulating sets according to the normal mathematical conventions are provided. Descriptions of the mathematical rules for manipulating sets are given in Fig. 10.12 with an explanation of how the operation is carried out in Modula-2. For further details consult the texts recommended in the bibliography under the heading **Logic and Computers**.

Relational Set Operations

The relational expressions of arithmetic have equivalents for comparing two sets. A further operator IN is available for testing whether a particular element is a member of a set. These all evaluate to a BOOLEAN result. They are summarised in Fig. 10.13.

The test for set membership is a commonly needed operation. For example

```
7 IN SetVar
```

takes the value TRUE if 7 is a member of SetVar and FALSE otherwise. This is very useful in IF and WHILE statements, especially when the element is a variable and the set is a constant. For example

```
IF SomeNum IN CardSet{0..20} THEN ..... END (* IF *)
```

is a more readable way of writing the equivalent statement

```
IF (SomeNum >=0) AND (SomeNum <= 20) THEN ..... END (* IF *).
```

The saving can be considerable if there are a number of subranges to be tested. If the same subrange is used frequently, it is useful to define a constant set

```
CONST
    ZeroToTwenty = CardSet{0..20};
```

and test for membership of this set by

```
IF SomeNum IN ZeroToTwenty THEN ..... END (* IF *)
```

Two standard procedures, INCL and EXCL, are provided for updating set variables. These require two parameters.

```
PROCEDURE INCL(Set,Element);
PROCEDURE EXCL(Set,Element);
```

INCL adds an element to an existing set. For example

```
INCL(SetVar,7)
```

includes the element 7 in the set SetVar. If 7 is already in SetVar no change occurs. The first parameter can be any valid set type and the second parameter must be an element of the same type as the set's elements. EXCL removes an element from a set. For example

```
EXCL(SetVar,7)
```

excludes the element 7 from the set SetVar. If 7 is not an element of SetVar, no change occurs. The parameters are identical to INCL. The second actual parameter can be a variable, thus the following calls of INCL and EXCL are permitted

Union.   +

   CardSet{0..5,7} + CardSet{7..12}   equals CardSet{0..5,7..12}
   SetVar + CardSet{}   equals SetVar

The union of two sets is the set of all elements in one or other of the sets or both. It is represented by +. The union of a set and the empty set is just the original set.

Intersection.   *

   CardSet{0..5,7} * CardSet{7..12}   equals CardSet{7}
   SetVar * CardSet{}   equals CardSet{}

The intersection of two sets is a set containing all the elements common to both sets. It is denoted by *. The intersection of a set and the empty set is the empty set.

Difference.   −

   CardSet{0..5,7} − CardSet{7..12}   equals CardSet{0..5}

The difference of two sets is the set of elements in the first set but not in the second set. It is denoted by −.

Symmetric Difference.   /

   CardSet{0..5,7} / CardSet{7..12}   equals CardSet{0..5,8..12}

The symmetric difference of two sets is the set of elements in one or other of the sets, but not both. It is denoted by /.

The precedence of these operators is the same as the precedence of their counterparts in arithmetic expressions.

Fig. 10.12. Set Operations.

Membership.   IN
   Something IN SetVar1   TRUE if Something is a member of SetVar1
                                   otherwise FALSE
IN is used to determine if a particular value is a member of a set.

Equality.   =
   SetVar1 = SetVar2   TRUE if SetVar1 contains precisely the
                                   same elements as SetVar2, otherwise FALSE

Inequality.   <> or #
   SetVar1 <> SetVar2   TRUE if one of the sets contains one or more
   SetVar1 # SetVar2   elements not contained in the other,
                                   otherwise FALSE

Inclusion.   <= or >=
   SetVar1 <= SetVar2   TRUE if all the members of SetVar1 are
   SetVar2 >= SetVar1   members of SetVar2, otherwise FALSE

Fig. 10.13. Relational Set Operations.

```
INCL(SetVar,VarElement)
EXCL(SetVar,VarElement)
```

which include and exclude the current contents of the variable VarElement in the set SetVar respectively.

The BITSET Type

Modula-2 provides a standard set type called BITSET whose characteristics are useful for low level programming (which is discussed more fully in Chapter 14).

BITSET Variables are declared in the normal way, for example

```
WordRepresentative : BITSET;
```

If a constant is specified without a preceding type identifier then it is assumed to be of type BITSET. For example

```
{0,3,7..12}
```

is a set of type BITSET. All normal set operators apply to BITSET sets.

The importance of BITSET is that variables of this type are defined to occupy one word of the computer's memory. BITSET is effectively declared as

```
TYPE
    BITSET = SET OF [0..WordLength-1];
```

where WordLength is the number of bits in the computer's standard word. A statement such as

```
WordRepresentative := {0,3,7}
```

initialises WordRepresentative with bits 0,3 and 7 set in the memory location representing WordRepresentative.

The operations on variables and constants of type BITSET can be implemented using the logical operators of the computer's machine code. This guarantees a highly efficient implementation of the operators and, in conjunction with facilities described in Chapter 14, powerful access to machine characteristics which are normally only available when writing in assembler languages. For this reason BITSET is the default type of set constants.

10.4 MULTI-DIMENSIONAL ARRAYS

Arrays are flexible and powerful data structures which can be used for many different tasks. They have been widely used throughout the book and are summarised here in their most general form, along with some of their special properties. The usual way to declare an array type is

```
TYPE
        ArrayType = ARRAY SomeType OF OtherType;
```

where SomeType is a basic type and OtherType can be any basic or structured type.

In the example programs developed in previous chapters OtherType has been restricted to basic types, however the components of arrays can be structured types. For example, the declarations

```
TYPE
        SubRange1 = CARDINAL[10..20];
        SubRange2 = CARDINAL[22..24];
        Vector1   = ARRAY SubRange1 OF INTEGER;
        Table1    = ARRAY SubRange2 OF Vector1;
VAR
        Vec1 : Vector1;
        Tab1 : Table1;
```

declares two variables, Vec1 which is an array of INTEGER values, and Tab1 which is an array of arrays of INTEGER values. Arrays of arrays are usually called tables or two-dimensional arrays. Tab1 can be visualised as illustrated in Fig. 10.14. Figure 10.14a corresponds closely to the way the array is represented internally within the computer's memory, Fig. 10.14b corresponds more closely to the way that we usually think about tables when they are used in commercial programs.

When processing Tab1 the following assignment statements are permitted

```
Tab1[22]        := Vec1
Vec1            := Tab1[22]
Tab1[24][15]    := Vec1[18]
```

the first assigns the entire array in Vec1 to the subarray Tab1[22], and the second assigns the entire contents of the subarray Tab1[22] to Vec1. The third copies the value in the component Vec1[18] into component 15 of the subarray Tab1[24]. In Fig. 10.14b the subarrays correspond to the rows.

References to structures within structures keep a consistent left to right ordering when determining the part of the structure being referenced. Thus Tab1[22] refers to the structure of type Vector1 and therefore is compatible with Vec1. Similarly Tab1[23][20] refers to component 20 of Tab1[23] so its type is INTEGER.

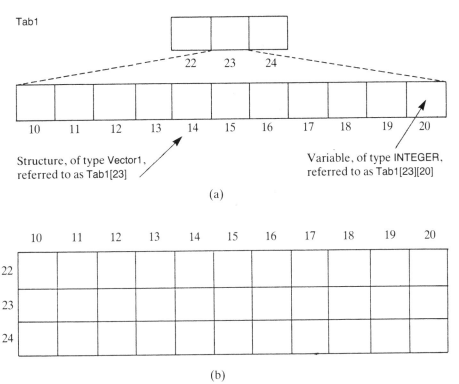

Fig. 10.14.

Figure 10.14b is misleading in one important respect. Whilst the rows correspond to the subarrays Tab1[22], Tab1[23] etc, the columns do not correspond to subarrays. There is no subarray Tab1[14] in this example, and an assignment statement

```
Tab1[14] := SomeVariable
```

is invalid. This is because the declaration of Tab1 specifies that its primary index is Subrange1. The table, however, could have been declared with its indexes the other way about

```
TYPE
        SubRange1 = CARDINAL[10..20];
        SubRange2 = CARDINAL[22..24];
        Vector2   = ARRAY SubRange2 OF INTEGER;
        Table2    = ARRAY SubRange1 OF Vector2;
VAR
        Vec2 : Vector2;
        Tab2 : Table2;
```

Tab2 is an array of 11 subarrays each with 3 components. The declaration of arrays with more than one dimension should be carefully thought out to determine which dimension is of more importance and this should be made the primary index of the array.

The components of arrays can be other structured types besides arrays. For example, the declarations

```
TYPE
        Colour              = (White,Black) ;
        Pieces              = (King,Queen,Rook,Knight,Bishop,Pawn) ;
        BoardPosition       = RECORD
                                Occupied      : BOOLEAN ;
                                OccupyingPiece : Pieces ;
                                PieceColour    : Colour
                              END ;
        BoardRow            = ARRAY [1..8] OF BoardPosition ;
        ChessBoard          = ARRAY [1..8] OF BoardRow ;
VAR
        Board               : ChessBoard ;
```

declare a two-dimensional array of records which can be used to represent a chess board in a chess playing program.

There is no restriction on the depth of nesting of one data structure within another. Thus complex structures can be built, which can be referenced at many different levels of detail. Assume in addition to the above declarations of Table1, Vector1, Tab1 and Vec1 the following declarations

```
TYPE
        TableAndCounter   = RECORD
                              Counter        : CARDINAL;
                              ManyItems      : Table1
                            END (* DataRecord *);
        RecArray          = ARRAY[1..100] OF TableAndCounter;
VAR
        Rec1              : TableAndCounter;
        Arr1              : RecArray;
```

then Arr1 is an array of 100 components each of which consists of a record with two fields, the first a CARDINAL value and the second a two-dimensional array. The following assignment statements maintain type compatibility and therefore are all valid.

```
Rec1.ManyItems := Tab1
Rec1.ManyItems[22][12] := Tab1[24][20]
Arr1[50].Counter := 23
Arr1[50].ManyItems[22] := Vec1
```

In general, the types which are arrays of arrays are important special cases corresponding to the handling of tables and more general mathematical structures. To cater for this, special shorthand notations are available. The idea is that the declaration

```
TYPE
        ThreeDTable = ARRAY [1..20] OF ARRAY [1..10] OF
                                        ARRAY [1..5] OF CHAR ;
```

can be written

```
TYPE
        ThreeDTable = ARRAY [1..20] [1..10] [1..5] OF CHAR ;
VAR
        SomeTab      : ThreeDTable ;
```

and that statements such as

```
SomeTab [15][9][4] := 'A'
```

can be written

```
SomeTab [15,9,4] := 'A'
```

This is a convenient shorthand and it corresponds closely to matrix notation used in mathematics.

A note on compatibility

In declaring arrays, anonymous types can be introduced within the declaration, but as always with anonymous types this prevents other variables of the type being declared. For example, the declarations

```
TYPE
        Table = ARRAY [1..10] OF ARRAY [1..50] OF INTEGER;
VAR
        Tab3  : Table;
        Vec3  : ARRAY [1..50] OF INTEGER;
```

have the consequence that Tab3[3] and Vec3 are incompatible. They are of completely different types and are not even assignment compatible. Thus the statement

```
Tab3[3] := Vec3
```

generates a syntax error at compile time. In fact Vec3 is not compatible with any other variable, though the components of Vec3 are compatible with any INTEGER variable. Tab3[5] is only compatible with other components of type Table, which permits a statement such as

```
Tab3[5] := Tab3[10]
```

This, of course, is a special case of the rule that two different structured types are never compatible. That is,

```
TYPE
      Newtable = ARRAY [1..10] OF ARRAY [1..50] OF INTEGER;
```

is a completely different type to Table and is not compatible with it.

10.5 OPEN ARRAY PARAMETER PASSING

In Chapter 4 open array parameters were discussed. They are a mechanism allowing an array of any length to be passed as an actual parameter to a procedure. It is useful in many situations and has been used on many occasions throughout the book, especially in passing arrays of characters to procedures. There is a restriction on open array parameters, they only apply to one dimension of an array. A typical example is

```
PROCEDURE TestArray (AnyArrayOfSomeType : ARRAY OF SomeType);
```

which allows the actual parameter to be any array whose elements are of type SomeType, with no restriction on the number of elements in the array. If SomeType is itself an array type, then it must have been previously declared with a fixed number of elements. This means that matrix manipulation routines cannot be written easily for arbitrary sized matrices using open array parameters.

Another facility is available which relaxes Modula-2's restrictions on type compatibility. It is based on a type WORD which can be imported from the special module SYSTEM. The type WORD is a representation of the underlying computer's word, similar to the type BITSET. However, a formal parameter of type WORD in a procedure declaration turns off the normal type checking. Any actual parameter whose physical representation in the computer's memory is one word is a valid parameter for a WORD formal parameter.

Even more significantly, a formal parameter of type ARRAY OF WORD is compatible with any actual parameter whatever its type. Special facilities are available within Modula-2 to manipulate such arrays, these are dealt with in Chapter 14. It is sufficient at present to understand that the facility is available and to recognise that a declaration of the form

```
PROCEDURE Example(VAR AnyVar : ARRAY OF WORD);
```

allows any variable to be passed to the procedure.

10.6 FILES

The amount of main memory in a computer is usually small compared with overall memory requirements and its contents are lost when the power is switched off, so it is inadequate for long term storage requirements. Thus, permanent storage for storing programs and data is needed. In the past magnetic tapes were used for this purpose, and at present magnetic disks are widely used. These kinds of storage media are also called secondary storage. Access to such permanent data storage media is normally very much slower than to main memory.

When accessing secondary storage it is usually more efficient to read a reasonably large amount of data in a single step. When using magnetic tape this is essential, but in the case of disks it is simply more efficient. These features have had a large influence on the abstract view taken of accessing data from secondary storage.

The method of input and output which we have used to date has been restricted to output to the visual display screen and input from the keyboard. These have many similarities to secondary storage in the methods of communication even if the actual storage structure (normally the user's brain) is somewhat different.

The data structure used to represent external storage media is the **file**. It comes in many guises only two of which are discussed here. The first is the **serial file** which is based on the characteristics of magnetic tape. The logical view of such files is illustrated in Fig. 10.16.

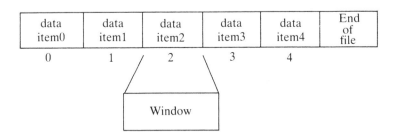

Fig. 10.16.

The window indicates the part of the file which is currently available to the program. Reading the data viewed in the window automatically moves the window to the next data item. A serial file is read from the beginning, one data item at a time, until all the data required is read or the end of file marker is read. The window views the next item to be read and is undefined after the end of file marker is read. Construction of a serial file merely requires writing the data items in order followed by an end of file marker. Console output and keyboard input are normally thought of as serial files of ASCII characters.

The second kind of file is the random access file. This allows direct access to any element of the file for writing, reading or both. The access is normally by the data item number. This kind of access is not supported by magnetic tapes, but it is supported by magnetic disk units though this is still relatively slow compared to accessing an array in main memory. Figure 10.16 is appropriate for random access files, but the positioning of the window is achieved by an explicit instruction rather than by being automatically moved by one unit as a result of reading a data item.

As the underlying logical model of serial and direct access files are the same it is possible to access a file in either way. The basic kinds of file processing considered in this chapter fall into one of the following categories

1. a new file is created and data is written to it sequentially.

2. a file is read sequentially from beginning to end. A second file can be created and the data from the first file can be written to the second file with some modifications. This is a traditional method of updating a large file.

3. data is appended to the end of a file which already exists. The new data is written sequentially at the current end of the file.

4. a file is accessed at random positions in the file in order to read data at arbitrary positions in the file. There need be no specific ordering of the required data items.

5. a file is accessed at random positions in the file in order to write data at arbitrary positions in the file.

Typical data items in a file are individual characters, values of basic types or records. Usually all the data items in a particular file are the same type, though clearly in the case of records with variant parts this is quite a flexible criterion. Two kinds of file data items are particularly important in practical computing

1. files of characters, often called text files. Such files are constantly used in all aspects of computing, as they correspond closely to printed documents. The standard module InOut is an example of the usefulness of text input from the keyboard and output to the visual display screen. As indicated in detail in the next section InOut can be redirected to a file and used to handle text from disk or other input or output media. Such files can only be accessed serially.

2. files of records. These form the basis of standard commercial computing applications. An example is a file of customer's accounts consisting of a record for each customer of the company. In many applications such files are processed as serial files. The records are held in a specific order to make them

easy to update. Serial files held in this fashion are often referred to as sequential files. If necessary, they can be processed as direct access files.

10.7 REDIRECTION OF INPUT AND OUTPUT THROUGH InOut

The standard module InOut provides facilities to input sequences of characters from the keyboard and output sequences of characters to the visual display screen. This effectively treats the keyboard as a file of characters from which input can be accessed sequentially and the visual display screen as a file of characters to which sequences of characters can be written sequentially. These input and output channels can be redirected to files on secondary storage media to process text files sequentially.

A text file is essentially a sequence of characters which can contain two special characters, an end of file character and an end of line character. Thus, it can be considered to be a sequence of lines of characters. Clearly this is a most important form of communication between people and computers and for storing information to be read by people. The end of file character is used to indicate the end of a text file, whose counterpart when accepting input from the keyboard is a character reserved so that the user can indicate the end of the input data. The end of line character is very useful in handling text from both the keyboard and files on secondary storage media.

InOut makes available

1. a constant EOL which can be imported into other modules and used to test whether the current character is the end of line character.

2. a BOOLEAN variable Done which is set to TRUE if one of InOut's reading procedures successfully reads data and FALSE otherwise. The latter often indicates that the read procedure has read the end of file marker.

Essentially, InOut has one input and one output channel which default to the keyboard and visual display screen, but which can be attached to files on other input and output devices. Redirection of the channels is achieved by four other procedures provided in InOut. The procedure headings of these are

```
PROCEDURE OpenInput  (DefaultExtension : ARRAY OF CHAR);
PROCEDURE OpenOutput (DefaultExtension : ARRAY OF CHAR);
PROCEDURE CloseInput;
PROCEDURE CloseOutput;
```

1. OpenInput and OpenOutput attach InOut's input and output channel respectively to files available from other devices. Often this is to a physical file on secondary storage media. Both procedures generate a request to the visual display screen for the user to type the name of the file to which input or output is redirected. Their parameters allow a default file extension to be

specified for file names where the user omits an extension. Such defaults are dependent upon the computer which is being used and may vary in different implementations of Modula-2. If these operations are performed successfully then Done is set to TRUE, otherwise Done is set to FALSE.

2.   CloseInput and CloseOutput. CloseInput closes the current input file and redirects the channel to accept subsequent input from the keyboard; CloseOutput closes the current output file and redirects the output channel to the visual display screen.

For details of all the facilities provided by InOut consult the definition module in Appendix 4.

A very simple but useful example of processing text files is given in Fig. 10.17.

```
MODULE CopyFile;
  FROM InOut IMPORT (* VAR *) Done,
                (* PROCEDURE *) OpenInput,OpenOutput,Read,Write,
                                CloseInput,CloseOutput;
(* Copies an input file to an output file.An opportunity is given to
    stipulate the input and output files. If no filenames are given
    the program defaults to the console. If the console is used for input
    the user must know the ASCII character which represents end of file.
*)
  VAR
       Ch : CHAR;
  BEGIN
  OpenInput('');           (* requests filename to be input at the keyboard *)
  IF Done THEN             (* checks that input file opened *)
          OpenOutput('');
          IF Done THEN (* checks that output file is opened *)
                  WHILE Done DO (* Done = FALSE now checks for end of file *)
                          Read(Ch);
                          Write(Ch)
                  END (* WHILE *);
                  CloseOutput;
          END (* IF *);
          CloseInput;
  END (* IF *);
  END CopyFile.
```

Fig. 10.17.

The file handling facilities of InOut are limited. There is only one input and output channel available so when input is redirected to a file no input can be accepted from the keyboard using InOut's reading procedures until the channel is redirected to the keyboard. Similarly redirecting the output to a file prevents output being sent to the screen until the channel is redirected. In addition, InOut only permits sequential access of one input and one output file at any one time which is restrictive for most commercial applications. For these reasons it is essential to have file handling modules which do not affect input from the keyboard and output to the screen and permit flexible accessing of multiple files.

10.8 IMPORT AND EXPORT OF TYPES AND SIMPLE FILE HANDLING

As has been noted already, input from the keyboard and output to the screen are not provided as part of the Modula-2 language, but are achieved through modules provided with the compiler or written by the user. File input and output is also handled through a separate module. At present there is no agreed collection of file handling facilities in the various implementations of the language, though there are strong moves to standardise the modules provided. In any case the modules supplied for handling files tend to be complex because of the sophisticated low level facilities they provide, so we present here a simple file handling module which can easily be written in any of the available implementations by an experienced Modula-2 programmer. This has the advantage of allowing files to be treated at a high level. The module is required to provide both sequential and direct access to any given file.

This module involves some important organisational facilities

1. A logical filename within the program must be associated with a physical file on disk (or wherever). This is necessary because it is normal to run a program many times with different data from different physical files.

2. A file must be opened before reading or writing data to the file is permitted and the method of opening must stipulate the kind of access (i.e sequential access or random access). This is important in commercial applications as it helps to secure the integrity of files. Similarly, a file must be closed when processing of its data is complete or before it is opened for a different kind of access. These properties help to prevent dangerous events like one program reading a file while another one overwrites it. Such events are possible because the physical files are held on secondary storage which may be accessible to more than one program.

3. As files are held on external storage media it is always possible that some perfectly normal access to data will fail. Only a very simplified version of protection from this type of event is given in the module.

Import and Export of Types

The file handling module has to make available a type so that other modules are able to perform input and output on as many files as they need. The definition module in Fig. 10.18 makes available two types, FILE and FileCategory, which other modules can import and use in the same manner as other types.

The type FILE is exported as an **opaque type** whose representation details are not provided. FileCategory is said to be exported **transparently** because the details of the type are made available to other modules. FileCategory is an enumerated type and the constants of the enumerated type are also available to other modules.

Any type can be exported transparently by including its declaration in a definition module, just as in Chapter 6 we saw that variables and constants can be made available to other modules. A type which is exported opaquely requires special arrangements between the implementation module and the definition module which exports it. These are discussed in detail in Chapter 14. For the present it is sufficient to note that opaque types are used in importing modules in the same way that standard and user-defined types are used, except that the operations which can be performed on variables of the type are restricted to the procedures provided for manipulating the type.

The Design of SimpleFile

The following comments give details of the design of SimpleFile.

1   Connect,DisConnect

Connect associates an internal FILE variable with a physical file. The internal file name is termed the logical file name (often simply termed the logical file) to distinguish it from a physical file name associated with an actual file which exists on the secondary storage media. If the physical file does not exist, a new one is created if possible. There will be a failure to connect if the FILE variable is already connected to a file. DisConnect is used to free the FILE variable for connection to another file. If the attached physical file has not been closed DisConnect closes it before performing the disconnection.

2   Opening and closing files

The various procedures for opening a file cause FILE variables, and the physical files to which they have been attached, to be prepared for the appropriate mode of access. Each procedure provides a different mode of access.

a. OpenRead

This initialises the file for sequential reading starting at the beginning of the file.

b. OpenWrite

This initialises the file for sequential writing. For this procedure to succeed, the connected file must be a new one. This is to prevent an existing file being overwritten by mistake.

c. OpenAppend

This initialises the file for sequential writing to a file starting at the present end position of the file. This allows extra data to be written to the end of an existing file.

d. OpenUpdate

This initialises the file for direct access to a positionally specified data item. The item can be read or written to as required by specifying the position of the item in the file. The item must exist otherwise an error occurs.

The Close procedure terminates the current method of access on the file, but it does not disconnect the FILE variable from the physical file. So the file can be opened for some other mode of access, for example having written a file, it may then be necessary to then read it.

3   ReadFromFile,WriteToFile

These process a file sequentially. Each call of ReadFromFile reads the data item currently in the window and updates the window to the next data item. When the end of the file is reached the window contains the end of file marker. When this is read, the function procedure EOF will return a value TRUE when called. After a successful read of a normal data item EOF returns FALSE. When writing, the window is always looking at the next free space. A file opened using OpenWrite or OpenAppend has an end of file marker written at the end of the file when it is closed. In order to use these procedures

a.the file variable specified in procedure calls must have been connected to a physical file using Connect,

b. the file must have been opened in the correct mode. In order to call ReadFromFile the file must have been opened by a call to OpenRead, and to use WriteToFile the file must have been opened by a call to either OpenWrite or OpenAppend.

4   EOF,Success

These are flags which are available to modules using the file module. EOF
is a BOOLEAN function procedure which returns the value TRUE whenever
data has not been successfully read in sequential mode even though the
call to the read routine was valid. In particular it returns TRUE when the
end of file marker is read. Thus it is typically used as illustrated by the
program fragment

```
Connect(SomeFile,'afilename',SomeRec);
OpenRead(SomeFile);
ReadFromFile(SomeFile,SomeRec);
WHILE NOT EOF(SomeFile) DO
        (*... process data read from file ...*) ;
        ReadFromFile(SomeFile,SomeRec)
END (* WHILE *)
```

Success is a BOOLEAN variable which has the value FALSE whenever a
procedure call is not completed successfully. The precise meaning of
successful completion is given in the annotated comments accompanying
each procedure in the definition module.

5   ReadDirect, WriteDirect

These are used to give direct access to individual items of a file. For
example

```
ReadDirect(SomeFile,0,SomeItem)
```

reads the first item of the physical file connected to the file variable
SomeFile and puts it in SomeItem. A call

```
ReadDirect(SomeFile,6,SomeItem)
```

reads the seventh item of the file. A call of WriteDirect

```
WriteDirect(SomeFile,5,SomeItem)
```

overwrites the sixth item in the file with the contents of SomeItem. In order
to use these procedures
a. the specified file variable must have been connected to a physical file by
a call to Connect,
b. the file must have been opened by a call of OpenUpdate.

```
DEFINITION MODULE SimpleFile;
 FROM SYSTEM IMPORT WORD;
 TYPE
     FileCategory = (Closed,ORead,OWrite,OAppend,OUpdate);
   (* FileCategory is used to check the present access mode of a
     logical file. *)
     FILE;
   (* FILE is a type to be used in declaring logical file variables.*)
 VAR
     Success : BOOLEAN;
   (* Success is used to indicate whether or not a procedure call has
     carried out its task. *)

 PROCEDURE Connect(VAR FileVar : FILE;
                          FileName : ARRAY OF CHAR;
                   VAR SampleRec : ARRAY OF WORD);
 (* A file cannot be used unless a physical filename is attached to a
     program filename of type FILE. SampleRec should be a variable of the
     type to be read and written to the file.
     Success = the file has been properly connected. *)

 PROCEDURE OpenRead(VAR FileVar : FILE);
 (* Opens a file for sequential reading. The file can only be read from
     the beginning.
     Success means that the file is opened for reading.
     NOT Success means that the file is not opened for reading, possibly
     because it is already open in some other mode. *)

 PROCEDURE OpenWrite(VAR FileVar : FILE);
 (* Opens a file for sequential writing. The file can only be written
     if no physical file with the same name exists.
     Success means that the file is opened for writing.
     NOT Success means that the file is not opened for writing, possibly
     because it is already open in some other mode. *)

 PROCEDURE OpenAppend(VAR FileVar : FILE);
 (* Opens a file for appending onto the end of the current file.
     Success means that the file is opened ready to add data to the end
     of the file.
     NOT Success means that the file is not open for appending, possibly
     because it is already open in some other mode. *)

 PROCEDURE OpenUpdate(VAR FileVar : FILE);
 (* Opens a file for updating an item specified by its item number.
     The first item on the file is item 0.
     Success means that the file is opened ready to reference any item
     directly.
     NOT Success means that the file is not open for updating, possibly
     because it is already open in some other mode. *)
```

PROCEDURE ReadFromFile(VAR FileVar : FILE;
                              VAR Record : ARRAY OF WORD);
(* Performs a sequential read from the specified file. The window is
   updated to the next item.
   Success means that the read has been successful.
   NOT Success means that the file is not open for reading.
   If an end of file marker is read the function procedure EOF will
   return the value TRUE. *)

PROCEDURE WriteToFile(VAR FileVar : FILE;
                              VAR Record : ARRAY OF WORD);
(* Performs a sequential write to the specified file. The window is
   updated to the next item.
   Success means that the write has been successful.
   NOT Success means that the file is not open for writing. *)

PROCEDURE ReadDirect(VAR FileVar : FILE;
                              RecNum : CARDINAL;
                              VAR Record : ARRAY OF WORD);
(* Reads an item from the specified file into the variable Record.
   The item is specified by its number relative to the beginning of
   the file. The first item has a number 0.
   Success means that the item has been read.
   NOT Success means that the item has not been read either because
   the item size is incorrect, the item number is beyond the end of
   the file or the file is not open for update. *)

PROCEDURE WriteDirect(VAR FileVar : FILE;
                              RecNum : CARDINAL;
                              VAR Record : ARRAY OF WORD);
(* Writes the contents of the variable Record into an item of the
   specified file. The item is specified by its number relative to the
   beginning of the file. The first item has a number 0.
   Success means that the item has been written.
   NOT Success means that the item has not been written either because
   the item size is incorrect, the item number is beyond the end of
   the file or the file is not open for update. *)

PROCEDURE EOF(VAR FileVar : FILE) : BOOLEAN;
(* EOF means that the end of file has been read, or a hardware error
   has occurred.
   NOT EOF means that the end of file has not yet been read. *)

PROCEDURE Close(VAR FileVar : FILE);
(* Causes the specified logical file to be closed for the present type
   of access. That is, the file access mode is Closed. The file may now
   be opened again in any access mode.
   An end of file marker is written after the last data item for
   files opened using OpenWrite and OpenAppend. *)

```
PROCEDURE DisConnect(VAR FileVar : FILE);
(* Causes the logical file to be disconnected from the physical file. No
   actions may be taken without a call to connect. *)

PROCEDURE Status(VAR FileVar : FILE) : FileCategory;
(* Returns the current access mode of a file. It should not be used
   unless the logical file has been connected to a physical file by
   a call to Connect. *)

END SimpleFile.
```

Fig. 10.18.

10.9 EXAMPLE. Use of the SimpleFile Module: StudentFileHandling

This section illustrates the use of SimpleFile to provide higher level procedures to carry out file creation, update and maintenance for a commercial style application. The problems encountered here are typical, though simplified, versions of the problems in the development of commercial systems. Since a high proportion of computer programming is related to commercial applications, these ideas are interesting and important.

Specification

A computer laboratory computer reservation system requires a single file of student records. Each record contains details about a student including the student's computer user number. Each student is issued with a card with his computer user number on it. This card and number give permission for the student to use computer facilities, and in particular to book time on a computer.

A module, StudentFileHandling, is required which makes available a record type for student details and file handling operations relating to groups of student records and individual student records. In particular the detail of file accessing modes should be hidden and there should be minimum interaction between the individual procedures.

The required operations are
1. create the file of student details (CreateStudentFile),
2. close and disconnect the student file (DisconnectStudentFile),
3. append further student records at the end of the file (ExtendStudentFile),
4. print out the details of all current students (WriteCurrentStudentList),
5. print out the details of all deleted students (WriteDeletionList),
6. print out the details of a particular student passed to the procedure (WriteOutStudentDetail),

7. return the student record corresponding to a given student number (ExtractStudent),

8. print out the details of a student determined by a given student number (SupplyStudentDetail),

9. update a particular record in the file determined by a given student number (UpdateStudentRecord),

10. delete a particular student from the file determined by a given student number (DeleteStudent),

11. restore a deleted student within the file determined by a given student number (RestoreStudent).

The names in brackets are the names of procedures to be provided in the module.

CreateStudentFile opens the file and initialises it to represent an empty file ready for new students to be appended to the empty file using ExtendStudentFile.

DisconnectStudentFile closes and disconnects the file so that it is no longer available for use. This must always be called at the end of a program to ensure that the file is left in a well-defined state.

ExtendStudentFile, WriteCurrentStudentList and WriteDeletionList are operations which are performed on groups of student records.

The remaining operations are performed on a single student record determined by a student number or student record which is passed as the parameter to the procedures. DeleteStudent and RestoreStudent are left as a programming exercise (see programming exercise 4) and are not discussed further here.

The Logical Structure of the Student Details File

Modules using StudentFileHandling treat the file as a sequence of records of type StudentRecordType whose declaration is shown in Fig. 10.19 and which StudentFileHandling makes available to other modules by including it in its definition module.

Student details include a name, a course and a BOOLEAN flag to indicate whether or not the student number is still valid. The existence of this flag implies that StudentFileHandling remembers students who have been deleted. This allows a check to be kept on students who have had their authorisation withdrawn, but still own a card. It also allows a deleted student to be restored easily.

```
TYPE
    StudentDetailType  = RECORD
                          StudentName    : NameType;
                          Course         : CourseType;
                          Deleted        : BOOLEAN
                         END (* RECORD *);
    StudentRecordType = RECORD
                          StudentNumber  : StudentRange;
                          StDetail       : StudentDetailType
                         END (* RECORD *);
```

Fig. 10.19.

A definition module for StudentFileHandling is given in Fig. 10.20. The procedures allow relatively simple access to the student record file. Note that the only way to add new student records to the file is by appending a group of new student details (which may be just one student's details) using Extend-StudentFile. However, the facility for updating provided by UpdateStudentRecord allows any existing record to be altered. This is a dangerous facility if misused, but is essential because a student's details may need updating or a mistake may have been recorded on his details. The danger is reduced by allowing importing modules to update only by reference to an existing student number rather than a physical record number. It would be a serious mistake to permit updating by reference to physical record numbers as this would confuse the implementation detail of the module with the student record handling as seen by importing modules.

A careful study should be made of Fig. 10.20 to understand the facilities provided before a detailed analysis is made of the particular implementation. The exercises suggest further improvements of the abstraction of the student file provided here, so the definition module should be studied with an eye to how it can be improved.

```
DEFINITION MODULE StudentFileHandling;

CONST
    MinCourse  = 0;    MaxCourse = 20;
    MinStudent = 0;    MaxStudent = 2000;

TYPE
    CourseType            = [MinCourse..MaxCourse];
    StudentRange          = [MinStudent..MaxStudent];
    SingleName            = ARRAY [0..19] OF CHAR;
    ForenameList          = ARRAY[0..1] OF SingleName;
```

```
NameType                     = RECORD
                                 Surname    : SingleName;
                                 Forenames  : ForenameList
                             END(*RECORD*);
StudentDetailType            = RECORD
                                 StudentName: NameType;
                                 Course     : CourseType;
                                 Deleted    : BOOLEAN
                             END(*RECORD*);

StudentRecordType            = RECORD
                                 StudentNumber  : StudentRange;
                                 StDetail       : StudentDetailType
                             END(*RECORD*);
VAR
  FileError                  : BOOLEAN;
```
(* On initialisation FileError is set to FALSE if there is an
   error on opening the student file. ExtendStudentFile sets
   it to TRUE if there is an error extending the file. In all
   other procedures it is checked for a device error. If a device
   error occurs then the program is aborted. The files will then
   be in an undefined state and backup files should be restored. *)

PROCEDURE WriteOutStudentDetail(StudRec : StudentRecordType);
  (* Given a student's record as input, writes out the details to InOut's
     output channel. That is, normally to the console. *)

PROCEDURE WriteCurrentStudentList;
  (* Writes out the list of current students with their details in
     ascending order of student number to InOut's output channel which
     is normally redirected to a file or printer before calling this
     procedure. *)

PROCEDURE WriteDeletionList;
  (* Writes out the list of students, with their details in ascending
     order of student number, who have been part of the student list, but
     are no longer current members. the list is written to InOut's
     output channel which is normally redirected to a file or printer
     before calling this procedure. *)

PROCEDURE CreateStudentFile;
  (* Creates the student file ready for adding students.If attempts
     are made to use the file before it exists unpredictable results
     will be obtained.
     FileError = the connected file existed before the program's
     execution. *)

PROCEDURE DisconnectStudentFile;
  (* Closes and disconnects the student file. This must be called before
     the program using the student file terminates or the file will be
     left in an undefined state. *)
```
```

PROCEDURE UpdateStudentRecord(StRec   : StudentRecordType;
                           VAR OutOfRange : BOOLEAN);
(* Writes a student record to an already existing record. The record
    number is determined by the student number. This is a simple routine
    which does no checking. If you require checking you must do it by
    reading the record, validating your update and then writing the
    record back to the file.
    OutOfRange = the student number supplied has no corresponding data
    on the file. *)

PROCEDURE ExtractStudent(StNumber   : StudentRange;
                  VAR Student   : StudentRecordType;
                  VAR OutOfRange : BOOLEAN);
(* Returns in Student a copy of the student record corresponding to the
    student with number StNumber.
    OutOfRange = the student number supplied has no corresponding data
              on the file. *)

PROCEDURE SupplyStudentDetails(StNumber   : StudentRange;
                        VAR OutOfRange : BOOLEAN);
(* Writes to the default output file (the console) a student's details.
    A warning is written if the student has a deleted number.
    OutOfRange = the student number supplied has no corresponding data
              on the file. *)

PROCEDURE ExtendStudentFile;
(* Adds new students to the student file by taking details of a student
    from the console. A file of additions is created, under the name
    StudAdd.Dat, as a permanent record. This file is used in making the
    additions to the student file.
    FileError = StudAdd.Dat exists already. It should always be renamed
              or deleted before calling this procedure. *)

PROCEDURE DeleteStudent (StNumber   : StudentRange;
                  VAR OutOfRange : BOOLEAN);
(* Logically deletes the specified student from the file. The student
    can be reinstated as a logical member of the student file by using
    RestoreStudent.
    OutOfRange = the student number supplied has no corresponding data
              on the file. *)

PROCEDURE RestoreStudent (StNumber   : StudentRange;
                  VAR OutOfRange : BOOLEAN);
(* Logically restores the specified student from the file. This undoes
    the DeleteStudent operation.
    OutOfRange = the student number supplied has no corresponding data
              on the file. *)

END StudentFileHandling.

Fig. 10.20.

The Physical Structure of the Student Details File

To simplify file access within StudentFileHandling the student's user number can correspond to the number of the record in the file which holds the student's details. If a student's details are placed in record 25 in the file, the card issued has the number 25 and the record can be accessed by a call to ReadDirect in SimpleFile with the student number as its parameter. (Technically the user number is redundant information in the file, but it is useful as a check and means that if a design change is made later in the life of the module, which removes the correspondence between user number and record number, the internal changes are not too radical.)

StudentFileHandling's implementation module has to maintain the file and consequently needs additional information to be stored in the file for maintenance purposes. This information can be hidden from other modules. The physical file which StudentFileHandling creates and maintains consists of a sequence of StFileRecordType records whose declaration is

```
TYPE
    RecKind              = (Header,Rest);
    StFileRecordType     = RECORD
                              CASE :   RecKind OF
                              Header : LengthOfFile : CARDINAL      |
                              Rest   : AStudent      : StudentRecordType
                              END (* CASE *)
                           END (* RECORD *);
```

The use of a variant record is a standard file processing technique. The first record of the file is used for holding data about the physical file and is usually called the header record. The other records of the file contain the student data. In this case the first record, record 0, holds the record number corresponding to the highest student number in use. In this implementation, this number also corresponds to the number of students who have been allocated numbers because computer user numbers are allocated in strict ascending order. By checking the header record, requests for direct access to a particular student record (via the student number) can be checked to see that the student number is valid and therefore corresponds to a record in the file.

Records for deleted students are not physically deleted from the file but are indicated by setting the field Deleted in the student's details to TRUE. The record is said to have been logically deleted as procedures accessing the file are not normally permitted to find and return deleted students. This is an important technique used in commercial systems. Often data which is not required for one purpose is used for other purposes. For example, the deleted student records may be included in reports on usage, or to reinstate the student if an error has been made, or to provide information on students who are no longer computer users as with WriteDeletionList. Note that an alternative implementation might remove the details of deleted students from the file and store them in a separate deleted students file.

The Implementation Module

An implementation module for StudentFileHandling is given in Fig. 10.22. The relationships between procedures in the module are illustrated in Fig. 10.21. The procedure ChangeStudentFileStatus alters the mode of access to the file when necessary, thereby guaranteeing that the file is open in the correct mode for each of the procedures. The current mode is remembered in the variable CurrentAccessMode.

Within the implementation module the procedures which operate on a single student record, UpdateStudentRecord, ExtractStudent and SupplyStudentDetails, access the file as a random access file. Those applicable to groups of students, WriteCurrentStudentList, WriteDeletionList and ExtendStudentFile, access the file sequentially. The latter operation also causes the file to be accessed randomly via the call to AddToStudentFile. This accesses the file as a random access file in order to retrieve the header record and determine how many students' details are currently in the file. It also updates the header record with the new number of students' details in the file after the file has been extended. However, the process of extending the file is carried out by sequentially appending new records to the end of the file. A careful study of the procedures in Fig. 10.22 gives an appreciation of file handling in both the sequential and direct access modes.

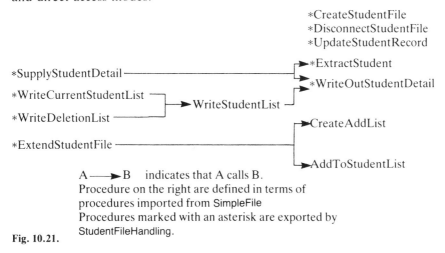

Fig. 10.21.

A———►B   indicates that A calls B.
Procedure on the right are defined in terms of procedures imported from SimpleFile
Procedures marked with an asterisk are exported by StudentFileHandling.

```
IMPLEMENTATION MODULE StudentFileHandling;
 FROM SimpleFile IMPORT
   (* TYPE *)              FILE,FileCategory,
   (* VAR *)               Success,
   (* PROCEDURE *)         Connect,OpenRead,OpenWrite,OpenAppend,OpenUpdate,
                           ReadFromFile,WriteToFile,ReadDirect,WriteDirect,EOF,
                           Close,DisConnect,Status;
 FROM MoreInOut IMPORT
   (* PROCEDURE *)         WriteLnString,NewCardValue,WriteStringCard;
 FROM InOut IMPORT
   (* PROCEDURE *)         WriteLn,WriteString,ReadString,ReadCard,Read;

 TYPE
   RecKind          = (Header,Rest);

   StFileRecordType = RECORD
                         CASE (*:*) RecKind OF
                           Header : LengthOfFile : CARDINAL |
                           Rest   : AStudent : StudentRecordType
                         END (* CASE *)
                       END (* RECORD *);
 VAR
   StudentFile  : FILE;
   SampleRecord : StFileRecordType;
   CurrentAccessMode : FileCategory ;

 PROCEDURE WriteOutStudentDetail(StudRec : StudentRecordType);
   (* exported procedure: also used internally *)
 BEGIN
   WITH StudRec DO
     WriteStringCard('STUDENT NUMBER: ',StudentNumber,6);
     WITH StDetail DO
       WriteLn;
       WriteLnString('STUDENT NAME: ');
       WITH StudentName DO
         WriteLnString(Forenames[0]);
         WriteString(' ');
         IF Forenames[1][0] <> 0C THEN
           WriteString(Forenames[1]);
           WriteString(' ')
         END (* IF *);
         WriteString(Surname)
       END (* WITH *);
       WriteLn;
       WriteStringCard('COURSE TYPE: ',Course,3);
     END (* WITH *)
   END (* WITH *)
 END WriteOutStudentDetail;
```

```
PROCEDURE CloseStudentFile(Complete : BOOLEAN);
 (* exported procedure *)
BEGIN
 IF CurrentAccessMode <> Closed THEN
    Close(StudentFile)
 END (* IF *);
 IF Complete THEN
    DisConnect(StudentFile)
 END (* IF *);
 FileError := ~ Success;
END CloseStudentFile;


PROCEDURE DisconnectStudentFile;
 (* exported procedure *)
BEGIN
 CloseStudentFile(TRUE)
END DisconnectStudentFile;


PROCEDURE ChangeStudentFileStatus (NewMode : FileCategory);
 (* hidden procedure *)
BEGIN
 IF CurrentAccessMode <> NewMode THEN
    CloseStudentFile(FALSE);
    CASE NewMode OF
     Closed    : Close(StudentFile)|
     ORead     : OpenRead(StudentFile)|
     OWrite    : OpenWrite(StudentFile)|
     OAppend  : OpenAppend(StudentFile)|
     OUpdate   : OpenUpdate(StudentFile)|
    END (* CASE *);
    FileError := ~ Success;
    IF ~ FileError THEN
       CurrentAccessMode := NewMode
    ELSE
       WriteLnString ('Device error — restore backup files.');
       HALT    (* HALT terminates program *)
    END (* IF *);
 END (* IF *);
END ChangeStudentFileStatus;


PROCEDURE CreateStudentFile;
 (* exported procedure *)
 VAR
    StudRec : StFileRecordType;
BEGIN
    ChangeStudentFileStatus(OWrite);
    StudRec.LengthOfFile := 0;
    WriteToFile(StudentFile,StudRec);
    ChangeStudentFileStatus(Closed);
END CreateStudentFile;
```

```
PROCEDURE WriteStudentList(ListKind : BOOLEAN);
 (* hidden procedure
    ListKind = TRUE writes out all valid student numbers with the
                      corresponding details.
    Listkind = FALSE writes out all invalid student numbers and the
                      corresponding details. *)
 VAR
    StRec : StFileRecordType;
BEGIN
 ChangeStudentFileStatus(ORead);
 ReadFromFile(StudentFile,StRec);
 ReadFromFile(StudentFile,StRec);
  WHILE NOT EOF(StudentFile) DO
    IF ListKind & ~ StRec.AStudent.StDetail.Deleted
       OR
       ~ ListKind & StRec.AStudent.StDetail.Deleted
    THEN
       WriteOutStudentDetail(StRec.AStudent)
    END (* IF *);
    ReadFromFile(StudentFile,StRec);
  END (* WHILE *);
 ChangeStudentFileStatus(Closed);
END WriteStudentList;

PROCEDURE WriteCurrentStudentList;
  (* exported procedure – this routine is only practical if InOut's
    output channel is redirected to some other output device
    e.g. a printer. *)
BEGIN
 WriteStudentList(TRUE);
END WriteCurrentStudentList;

PROCEDURE WriteDeletionList;
  (* exported procedure – this routine is only practical if InOut's
    output channel is redirected to some other output device
    e.g. a printer. *)
BEGIN
 WriteStudentList(FALSE);
END WriteDeletionList;

PROCEDURE ExtractStudent(StNumber      : StudentRange;
                         VAR Student   : StudentRecordType;
                         VAR OutOfRange : BOOLEAN);
  (* exported procedure: also used internally *)
 VAR
    StRec : StFileRecordType;

 PROCEDURE CopyDetails;
 BEGIN
  ReadDirect(StudentFile,0,StRec);
```

```
    IF (StNumber > 0) AND (StNumber <= StRec.LengthOfFile) THEN
      ReadDirect(StudentFile,StNumber,StRec);
      Student := StRec.AStudent;
      OutOfRange := FALSE
    ELSE
      OutOfRange := TRUE
    END (* IF *)
  END CopyDetails;


BEGIN (* ExtractStudent *)
 ChangeStudentFileStatus(OUpdate);
 CopyDetails;
END ExtractStudent;




PROCEDURE SupplyStudentDetails(StNumber        : StudentRange;
                               VAR OutOfRange : BOOLEAN);
  (* exported procedure *)
  VAR
    OneStudent : StudentRecordType;
BEGIN
 ExtractStudent(StNumber,OneStudent,OutOfRange);
 IF ~ OutOfRange THEN
    WriteOutStudentDetail(OneStudent);
    IF OneStudent.StDetail.Deleted THEN
      WriteLnString('                  WARNING                    ');
      WriteLnString('THIS STUDENT NUMBER IS NOW INVALID.')
    END (* IF *);
  END (* IF *)
END SupplyStudentDetails;

PROCEDURE UpdateStudentRecord(StRec              : StudentRecordType;
                              VAR OutOfRange : BOOLEAN);
  (* exported procedure *)
  VAR
    TempRec : StFileRecordType;
BEGIN
 ChangeStudentFileStatus(OUpdate);
 ReadDirect(StudentFile,0,TempRec);
 IF (StRec.StudentNumber > 0) AND
    (StRec.StudentNumber <= TempRec.LengthOfFile) THEN
    OutOfRange       := FALSE;
    TempRec.AStudent := StRec;
    WriteDirect(StudentFile,StRec.StudentNumber,TempRec)
 ELSE
    OutOfRange := TRUE
 END (* IF *);
END UpdateStudentRecord;
```

```
PROCEDURE ExtendStudentFile;
 (* exported procedure *)

 PROCEDURE CreateAddFile;
   (* creates a file of student details ready to be added to the student
      file using AddToStudentFile. The file created is called StudAdd.Dat
      and must not exist before this procedure is used. Any previous file
      which requires to be kept for reasons of data integrity should be
      renamed. *)

   PROCEDURE ReadStudentName(VAR WholeName : NameType);
   BEGIN
     WITH WholeName DO
        WriteLnString('Please type SURNAME : ');
        ReadString(Surname);
        WriteLnString('Please type first name : ');
        ReadString(Forenames[0]);
        WriteLnString('Please type middle name : ');
        ReadString(Forenames[1])
     END (* WITH *)
   END ReadStudentName;

   PROCEDURE NoMoreStudents() : BOOLEAN;
    TYPE
       CHARSET = SET OF CHAR;
    CONST
       ValidAns = CHARSET{'Y','y','N','n'};
       NegAns  = CHARSET{'N','n'};
    VAR
       OneCh : CHAR;
    BEGIN
     WriteLnString('Do you wish to record more students? Y/N ');
     LOOP
        Read(OneCh);
        IF OneCh IN ValidAns THEN
           EXIT
        END;
        WriteLnString('Please type Y or N: try again ')
     END (* LOOP *);
     RETURN OneCh IN NegAns
    END NoMoreStudents;

   PROCEDURE ReadCourse(VAR SubjectNumber : CourseType);
    VAR
       Number : CARDINAL;
    BEGIN
     LOOP
        WriteLnString(' Please type the subject number of the student : ');
        ReadCard(Number);
        IF (MinCourse <= Number) & (Number <= MaxCourse) THEN
```

```
        EXIT
      END (* IF *);
      WriteLnString('Invalid subject number, please try again.')
    END (* LOOP *);
    SubjectNumber : = Number;
  END ReadCourse;

  VAR
    StudDetail  : StudentDetailType;
    AddFile     : FILE;

BEGIN (* CreateAddFile *)
  Connect(AddFile,'StudAdd.Dat',StudDetail);
  OpenWrite(AddFile);
  FileError := ~ Success;
  IF ~ FileError THEN
    WITH StudDetail DO
      REPEAT
        ReadStudentName(StudentName);
        ReadCourse(Course);
        Deleted := FALSE;
        WriteToFile(AddFile,StudDetail)
      UNTIL NoMoreStudents()
    END (* WITH *)
  END (* IF *);
  Close(AddFile);
  DisConnect(AddFile)
END CreateAddFile;

PROCEDURE AddToStudentFile;
  (* AddFile has records of type StudDetails. The procedure takes
     AddFile, a file of students to be added to the main student file
     and appends them to the end of the file allocating student numbers
     at the time. *)
  VAR
    StRec      : StFileRecordType;
    StudDetail : StudentDetailType;
    NextNum    : StudentRange;
    AddFile    : FILE;

BEGIN
  ChangeStudentFileStatus(OUpdate);
  ReadDirect(StudentFile,0,StRec);
  NextNum := StRec.LengthOfFile + 1;

  ChangeStudentFileStatus(OAppend);
  Connect(AddFile,'StudAdd.Dat',StudDetail);
  OpenRead(AddFile);
  ReadFromFile(AddFile,StudDetail);
  WHILE NOT EOF(AddFile) DO
```

```
        WITH StRec.AStudent DO
          StudentNumber := NextNum;
          StDetail       := StudDetail;
          INC(NextNum);
        END (* WITH *);
        WriteToFile(StudentFile,StRec);
        ReadFromFile(AddFile,StudDetail)
      END (* WHILE *);

      ChangeStudentFileStatus(OUpdate);
      StRec.LengthOfFile := NextNum − 1;
      WriteDirect(StudentFile,0,StRec);
      ChangeStudentFileStatus(Closed);

      Close(AddFile);
      DisConnect(AddFile);
    END AddToStudentFile;

  BEGIN (* ExtendStudentFile *)
   CreateAddFile;
   IF ~ FileError THEN
      AddToStudentFile
   END (* IF *)
  END ExtendStudentFile;

  PROCEDURE DeleteStudent (StNumber        : StudentRange ;
                                 VAR OutOfRange : BOOLEAN) ;
  BEGIN
   WriteLnString ('Not yet implemented.') ;
  END DeleteStudent;

  PROCEDURE RestoreStudent (StNumber        : StudentRange ;
                                 VAR OutOfRange : BOOLEAN) ;
  BEGIN
   WriteLnString ('Not yet implemented.') ;
  END RestoreStudent;

BEGIN
 Connect(StudentFile,'StudentDat.Dat',SampleRecord);
 CurrentAccessMode := Closed;
 FileError := ~ Success;
 IF FileError THEN
   WriteLnString('ERROR CONNECTING STUDENT FILE.');
 END (* IF *);
END StudentFileHandling.
```

Fig. 10.22.

10.10 SUMMARY

This chapter has introduced the structured types records and sets and has discussed multi-dimensional arrays. In addition files were introduced.

1 Records consist of collections of items which can be of differing types. The WITH statement is specially provided for use with records so that fields can be referenced without having to repeat the record variable name. These are an important structure in commercial applications especially when used in conjunction with files.

2 Sets closely correspond to the mathematical concept of sets. The usefulness of sets is dependent upon the particular Modula-2 compiler and its limitation on the number of elements which can be represented in a set.

3 Arrays have been introduced previously. In this chapter it was noted that arrays can be multi-dimensional and that two-dimensional arrays are often used to represent tables in commercial applications.

4 Files are collections of data stored on secondary storage media. They are not provided as part of the language but are supported by standard modules provided with Modula-2 compilers. They allow information to be stored permanently and provide a mechanism for accessing and updating this information. Two kinds of files were discussed, sequential and direct access files. Input from the keyboard and output to the screen is similar to input from and output to sequential files of characters, and the procedures in InOut can be redirected to text files on secondary storage media. A module for performing sequential and direct access to a file of records was presented to illustrate typical file processing operations and the use of records.

It is of special note that sets can be compared using the relational operators. Arrays and records cannot be compared using relational operators and if these operations are required then procedures have to be written to perform them.

TECHNICAL EXERCISES

1 Given the declarations

```
TYPE
    DetailData =        RECORD
                        DataList        : ARRAY[1..20] OF CARDINAL;
                        EntryPoint      : CARDINAL;
                        END (* RECORD *);
    PrimaryData =       RECORD
                        Item1           : INTEGER;
                        Item2           : CARDINAL;
                        Message         : ARRAY[0..40] OF CHAR;
                        ExtraData       : ARRAY[1..30] OF DetailData;
                        END (* RECORD *);
VAR
    FirstRec,SecondRec          : PrimaryData;
    SubRec1,SubRec2             : DetailData;
```

state which of the following statements are syntactically correct and explain the errors in any incorrect statements.

a FirstRec := SecondRec

b SubRec1.EntryPoint := FirstRec.Item1

c SubRec1 := ExtraData[23]

d PrimaryData.Message := 'Good Morning'

e SubRec2.DataList := SubRec1.DataList

f WITH FirstRec DO

ExtraData.DataList[20] := SecondRec.Item2;

ExtraData := SubRec2

END (* WITH *)

2 Explain with examples the difference between a variant record with an explicit tag and one with an implicit tag.

3 Is it permissible to have one variant record inside another variant record?

4 Assuming the constant set declarations

```
CONST
    First       = CardSet{1,3,5,7,9} ;
    Second      = CardSet{2,4,6,8} ;
    Third       = CardSet{3,4,7,8,9} ;
```

state the results of the following set expressions.

a First + Third   **b** First − Second   **c** First − Third   **d** First * Second

e First * Third   **f** Second − Third   **g** First/Second   **h** First/Third

j Third − First   **k** Second/First   **l** Third/First   **m** First + First

5 Given the declarations

```
TYPE
      GraphNodes = [0..20];
      SetNode     = SET OF GraphNodes;
      SetGraph    = ARRAY GraphNodes OF SetNode;
CONST
      CorrectRange  = SetNode{0..5,10..15};
VAR
      Graph1,Graph2 : SetGraph;
      Alpha,Beta    : GraphNodes;
      Gamma         : SetNode;
```

state which of the following statements are syntactically correct and explain the errors in any incorrect statements.

a IF Alpha IN CorrectRange THEN ..... END (* IF *)

b IF Gamma IN Graph1[4] THEN ..... END (* IF *)

c INCL(Beta,Graph2)

d WHILE Alpha IN CARDINAL{3..8} DO ..... END (* WHILE *)

e Graph1 := Graph2

f Graph1[0] := Graph1[20] + Graph2[3]

g Count := 0 ;
```
      WHILE (Count <= 20) AND (Gamma <= CorrectRange) DO
        Gamma := Gamma*Graph1[Count];
        INC(Count)
      END (* WHILE *)
```

PROGRAMMING EXERCISES

1 Look at the module Frequencies in Chapter 6 and rewrite it so that the headings are held in an array of character arrays.

2 Design and implement a program which includes a two dimensional array of CARDINAL values to represent a 3 by 3 magic square, and which allows the user to enter values into each component in order to try and complete the magic square. The program must be able to tell the user whether he has completed the square correctly. (A magic square is a two dimensional matrix of values in which the sum of values in each row, column and diagonals from corner to corner are the same.)

Adapt the program to cope with a 5 by 5 magic square.

3 The procedure DisconnectStudentFile serves two purposes. Redesign the definition and implementation modules so that a separate procedure is provided to carry out each function.

4 The procedures in the implementation module of StudentFileHandling for deleting and restoring a student's details are incomplete. Write the code required to logically delete a student from the file and to restore the student if his details are subsequently required again.

5 The procedure UpdateStudentRecord only permits one update for each call of the procedure. Write a higher level procedure which allows a user to update many student records directly. Automatic opening and closing of the file should be provided.

6 The module StudentFileHandling is based on using StudentRecordType. Redesign the module to base it on the use of the record type StudentDetail and the type StudentRange. There should be no mention of the type StudentRecordType in the definition module.

7 In StudentFileHandling, the sequential file handling procedures carry out very specific tasks, but the direct access procedures are mainly rather general. Rewrite the module (exercises 3 and 4 are a help) so that all the provided procedures are for specific tasks, with a lower level module available to carry out more general tasks.

8 After consulting texts on commercial batch master/transaction file updates, write a classical update program in Modula-2.

ANSWERS

1 **a** Correct.   **b** Correct INTEGER and CARDINAL are assignment compatible.
   c Correct.   **d** Error, PrimaryData is a type not a variable.
   e Correct.   **f** Error, FirstRec.ExtraData is an array of DetailData items.

2 An explicit tag is one which is part of the record and can be tested in a program to see what type of record is available normally using a CASE statement. An example is

```
AccountType = (Supplier,Customer);
Account = RECORD
            CASE AccountVar  : AccountType OF
                  Supplier   : (* Supplier details *) |
                  Customer : (* Customer details *)
            END (* CASE *)
          END (* RECORD *);
```

The AccountVar field can be referenced to establish whether this is a supplier or customer record.

An implicit tag is one which which has no variable to reference and so the user program must have some other means of knowing the record's type. An example is

```
Account = RECORD
            CASE : AccountType OF
              Supplier      : (* Supplier details *) |
              Customer      : (* Customer details *)
            END (* CASE *)
          END (* RECORD *);
```

3 Yes, there is no problem about having one variant inside another one. In fact the variant could go many levels deep. For example, an array inside a variant part of a record might have records as elements and these elements could have variant parts.

4 All sets are of type CARDINAL.
   a {1,3,4,5,7,8,9} **b** {1,3,5,7,9} **c** {1,5} **d** {} **e** {3,7,9} **f** {2,6}
   g {1,2,3,4,5,6,7,8,9} **h** {1,4,5,8} **j** {4,8} **k** same as **g** **l** same as **h**.
   m {1,3,5,7,9}

5 **a** Correct. **b** Error, 'element IN set' is valid, 'set IN set' is invalid. The correct way of doing this is the expression Gamma <= Graph1[4].
   c Error, the parameters are in the wrong order and Graph2 is an array of sets. **d** Error, CARDINAL {3,8} is a literal set value based on the type CARDINAL, not a set value based on the type GraphNodes.
   e Correct. **f** Correct, + means union.
   g Correct. Either the loop is not entered (if Gamma is not a subset of CorrectRange), or it is executed 21 times and computes the union of Gamma and all the sets in the array of sets in Graph1. A better way of writing this is

```
IF (Gamma <= CorrectRange) THEN
  Count := 0 ;
  WHILE (Count <= 20) DO
    Gamma := Gamma*Graph1[Count];
    INC(Count)
  END (* WHILE *)
END (* IF *)
```

Chapter 11

Pointer Types, Dynamic Data Structures and Multiple Data Structures

In Chapter 10 the structured types, arrays, records and sets are discussed. These are known as static structures because their sizes and structure have to be stated when the program is written and remain the same while it runs. In this chapter **pointer types** are introduced and their use for creating and manipulating dynamic structures is illustrated. Dynamic data structures can change their size and structure as the program executes.

In comparison with structured types, pointer types are a lower level facility allowing the programmer to create and manipulate data structures which are not provided directly in the language. In order to do this pointer types embody a high degree of flexibility, but this is purchased at the cost of increased programming complexity and difficulty of finding errors in programs using pointers. The safest way to use pointer types is to hide the data structures for which they are required in implementation modules which have been thoroughly tested.

In addition this chapter shows how multiple versions of a data structure can be made available to other modules.

11.1 POINTER TYPES AND POINTER VARIABLES

This section is concerned only with the mechanics of using pointer types. Pointers are not easy to learn and use, therefore the examples are artificially simplified to help you to become familiar with declaring and manipulating pointer variables. The subsequent sections concentrate on their use in manipulating dynamic data structures.

Declaration of Pointer Types and Pointer Variables

Pointer types and pointer variables are declared in the same way as other types and variables. The essence of a pointer variable is that it is a variable which points to a **node** which can hold a value of another type. Whereas normal variables are containers for values, the values of pointer variables are signposts to a container. An analogy with the rooms of a building can be made. Normal variables can be thought of as rooms with names on their doors and access to the room is achieved by referring to the name of the room. Nodes can be considered as rooms which have numbers rather than names and pointer variables as signposts around the building giving directions to rooms by room numbers.

The declaration of a pointer variable or a user-defined pointer type must state the type of the node which will be pointed at. For example, the declarations

```
TYPE
    CardinalPointer          = POINTER TO CARDINAL ;
    IntegerPointer           = POINTER TO INTEGER ;
VAR
    A   : CardinalPointer ;
    B   : IntegerPointer ;
    C   : POINTER TO BOOLEAN ;
```

declare two user defined types, CardinalPointer and IntegerPointer and three pointer variables, A,B and C. The declarations of CardinalPointer and IntegerPointer declare a pointer type and the type of the node which variables of the pointer type can point at. The declaration of C states that it is a pointer variable which can point at a node which holds a value of type BOOLEAN. The general form of a pointer type specification is shown in Fig. 11.1. **Type** indicates the type of the node and can be any basic type or a user-defined type currently in scope.

Pointer Type :

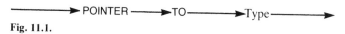

POINTER ──────── TO ──────── Type ────────

Fig. 11.1.

The declarations of A,B and C state that they are pointer variables. They can be pictured as shown in Fig. 11.2. The arrows indicate that the pointers point at something which is unknown, the values of such pointer variables are said to be undefined until they are initialised with meaningful values.

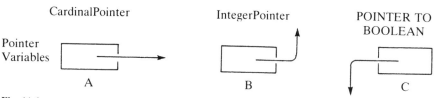

| CardinalPointer | IntegerPointer | POINTER TO BOOLEAN |

Pointer Variables   A   B   C

Fig. 11.2.

Creation and Deletion of Nodes

Declarations of pointer variables do not involve the creation of the node which is to be pointed at by the variable. Creation of nodes is under the explicit control of the programmer who creates and deletes nodes by the standard procedures NEW and DISPOSE.

Nodes are created by NEW. It allocates space for the node and in addition assigns a value to a pointer variable to make it point at the newly created node. Given the above declarations

    NEW (A)

creates a node for a variable which can hold a CARDINAL value and assigns a value to A to make it point to this node. NEW uses information associated with A's declaration in determining the type of the node. If NEW is called with B as its parameter then it creates a node to hold an INTEGER value and makes B point to this new node. The consequences of calling NEW twice with A and B as its parameter on subsequent calls is illustrated in Fig. 11.3.

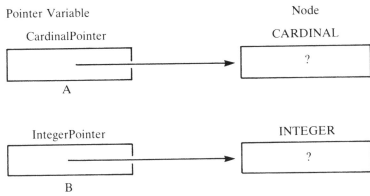

Fig. 11.3.

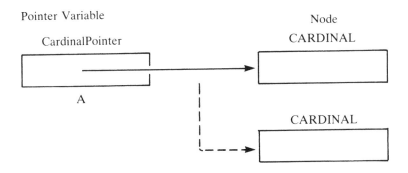

The dotted line indicates that A pointed at this node prior to the call of NEW (A), and the solid line indicates that A points to the new node after the call.

Fig. 11.4.

Each time NEW is called it allocates memory for another node and makes the pointer variable point at this node. If the call

NEW (A)

is performed again another area of memory is allocated for a node and A is made to point to this node as illustrated in Fig. 11.4. Note that if A already pointed to a node then after the call to NEW it no longer points at that node, and that node is then inaccessible unless another pointer points at it.

The inverse operation of destroying a node is achieved by the standard procedure DISPOSE. A call of

DISPOSE (A)

releases the memory for the node and leaves the pointer variable A undefined.

Figure 11.5 shows a module illustrating the use of NEW and DISPOSE. The following points are noteworthy

1.   in order to use NEW and DISPOSE it is necessary to import two procedures ALLOCATE and DEALLOCATE from a module called Storage supplied with Modula-2. Note that the procedures NEW and DISPOSE are not imported, however they call ALLOCATE and DEALLOCATE which have to be imported.

2.   the pointer variables A,B and C are global to the module and exist while the program is running, but at times the values in the pointer variables are undefined.

3.   the nodes which are pointed at by A,B and C exist between a call to NEW and a subsequent call of DISPOSE. The periods at which A,B and C point to a node are indicated on the right hand side of the module.

```
MODULE NewAndDispose ;
  FROM Storage IMPORT ALLOCATE, DEALLOCATE ;
  TYPE
      IntegerPointer          = POINTER TO INTEGER ;
      CardinalPointer         = POINTER TO CARDINAL ;
  VAR
      A       : IntegerPointer ;
      B       : CardinalPointer ;
      C       : POINTER TO BOOLEAN ;
  BEGIN
  NEW (A) ;
  NEW (B) ;
  NEW (C) ;
  DISPOSE (B) ;
  DISPOSE (C) ;
  NEW (B) ;
  DISPOSE (A) ;
  DISPOSE (B)
  END NewAndDispose .
```

Fig. 11.5.

Assignment and Pointer Variables

In the previous section it was seen that a call of NEW would assign a value to a pointer variable so that it points to the node created by NEW. It is also possible to assign values directly to pointer variables. For example, assuming the declarations

```
TYPE
      CardinalPointer = POINTER TO CARDINAL ;
      IntegerPointer  = POINTER TO INTEGER ;
VAR
      A,B    : CardinalPointer ;
      C,D    : IntegerPointer ;
      E      : POINTER TO CARDINAL ;
```

the following sequence of statements is possible

```
NEW (A) ;
B := A ;
```

The effect of the assignment statement is to make B point to the node which A currently points to. The situation after these statements is illustrated in Fig. 11.6a. Similarly Fig. 11.6b shows the effects of the statement sequence

```
NEW (C) ;
NEW (E) ;
D := C ;
```

Note that the following assignment statements are not permitted

```
D := A
B := E
```

because in each case the types of the pointers are not assignment compatible. In particular, though an INTEGER variable is assignment compatible with a CARDINAL variable, a **pointer** to an INTEGER variable is not assignment compatible with a **pointer** to a CARDINAL variable. Hence

```
D := E
```

also is not a permissible assignment statement.

It is also possible to compare two pointer variables. For example

```
IF A = B THEN
      (*... ...*)
END (* IF *) ;
```

compares the pointer variables A and B and evaluates to TRUE if the variables point to the same node and FALSE otherwise. Note that this compares the two pointers and determines whether they point at the same node but it does not compare two nodes to see if they hold the same value.

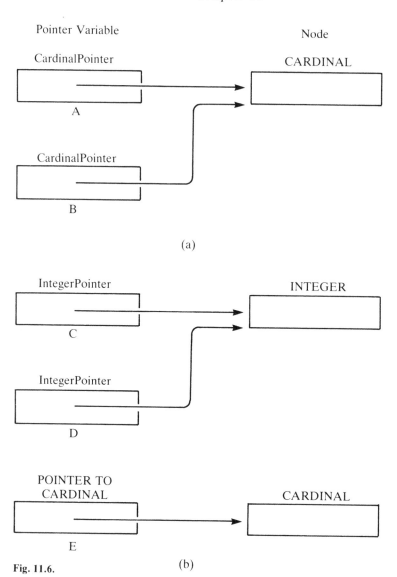

Fig. 11.6.   (b)

References to nodes

The nodes created by calls of NEW have no names of their own, so all references to them have to be made via the pointer variables which point at the nodes. In effect it is necessary to refer to the node as 'the node A points at'. This is done with the **dereferencing** operator ∧. For example the assignment statement

    A∧ := 6

assigns 6 to the node pointed to by A. Similarly an assignment statement

```
B∧ := 3
```

puts the value 3 in the node pointed at by B.

Pointer variables can therefore be used in assignment statements in two ways. An assignment statement

```
B := A
```

makes B point at the node which A points at, whereas a statement

```
B∧ := A∧
```

puts the value in the node which A points at into the node pointed at by B. Figure 11.7 summarises the difference between a pointer variable and the node it points at, and the way to refer to each.

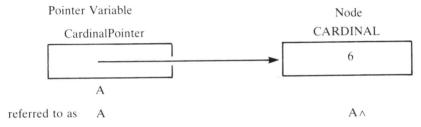

Pointer Variable   Node

CardinalPointer   CARDINAL

                         6

            A

referred to as   A   A∧

Fig. 11.7.

The value inside a node can be tested within a BOOLEAN expression by referring to it using the dereferencing operator

```
IF A∧ <> 10 THEN
    (*... ...*)
END (* IF *)
```

Given the following declarations

```
VAR
    Fred : POINTER TO CARDINAL ;
    Joe  : POINTER TO INTEGER ;
```

and two calls of NEW to create nodes

```
NEW (Fred) ;
NEW (Joe) ;
```

Fred cannot be made to point at the node which Joe points at because Fred and Joe are not assignment compatible, so

```
Fred := Joe
```

is invalid. However Fred∧ holds a CARDINAL value and Joe∧ holds an INTEGER value, therefore Fred∧ is assignment compatible with Joe∧ and the following assignment statement is permitted

```
Fred∧ := Joe∧
```

The value NIL

Like other variables, pointer variables need to be initialised with sensible values before they are used. If attempts are made to use a pointer variable before it has been given an intelligible value then the effect is undefined, unpredictable and usually disastrous.

For such situations a special pointer value is provided called NIL. This value can be assigned to any pointer variable irrespective of its node type, and can be interpreted as 'points at nothing'. It is often necessary to initialise pointer variables before they are used. The assignment statement

```
B := NIL
```

achieves this. However, it is not necessary to initialise a pointer variable to NIL if NEW is immediately called with it as a parameter. For example,

```
A := NIL ;
NEW (A) ;
```

assigns NIL to A and then immediately overwrites the contents of A with the pointer to the new node.

In Fig. 11.8a it is essential to initialise A to NIL. This code fragment reads CARDINAL values until a value which is less than 11 is input, then A is made to point to a node which can hold a CARDINAL value. At this stage it no longer holds the value NIL and therefore the WHILE statement terminates.

It is often necessary to assign the value NIL to a pointer variable after DISPOSE has been called

```
DISPOSE (A) ;
A := NIL ;
```

so that any subsequent check on whether the variable points at anything is sensible. Figure 11.8b shows the code fragment of Fig. 11.8a expanded so that when a number between 0 and 5 is entered, A is made to point to a new node which is then released in the second IF statement. By resetting A to NIL the WHILE statement is repeated until a value in the range 6 to 10 inclusive is entered.

Summary

1 Pointer variables are variables which can point at nodes.

2 The specification of a pointer type involves two types, a type for the pointer variable and a type of the node which the pointer variable can point at.

3 Nodes are created and destroyed by calls to the standard procedures NEW and DISPOSE. In order to use these, a module has to include in its import list

   FROM Storage IMPORT ALLOCATE,DEALLOCATE ;

4 Nodes can only be referenced via pointer variables, using the dereferencing symbol ∧. A∧ can be read as 'the node pointed to by A'.

5 NIL is a special value to be interpreted as 'does not point at anything'. It can be assigned to any pointer variable.

```
A := NIL ;
WHILE A = NIL DO
     T := NewCardValue ('Type a number – ') ;
     IF T <= 10 THEN
          NEW (A) ;
          ...
     END (* IF *) ;
END (* WHILE *) ;
```
                (a)

```
A := NIL ;
WHILE A = NIL DO
     T := NewCardValue ('Type a number – ') ;
     IF T <= 10 THEN
          NEW (A) ;
          ...
     END (* IF *) ;
     IF T <= 5 THEN
          DISPOSE (A) ;
          A := NIL ;
     END (* IF *) ;
END (* WHILE *) ;
```
                (b)

Fig. 11.8.

11.2 POINTERS AND STRUCTURED TYPES

In section 11.1 the types of all nodes are basic types. In general there are few occasions when pointers to nodes of these types are useful. The major use of pointers is with structured types and in particular with records. Pointers can be used with arrays in two ways; pointers to arrays and arrays of pointers are both permitted. However the use of pointers with records is of fundamental importance because this permits the programmer to build flexible data structures whose size is indeterminate when the program is written, or whose theoretically maximum size may exceed the capacity of the computer being used. At the cost of some additional complexity, pointers permit the programmer to create complex data structures whose structure can be controlled and tailored to cope with the demands made on the program.

The first point of note is that the type of a field in a record can be a pointer type. It is therefore permissable to make the following declarations

```
TYPE
    NodePntr    = POINTER TO Node ;
    Node        = RECORD
                     Value      : CARDINAL ;
                     NextNode   : NodePntr
                  END ;
VAR
    A,B         : NodePntr ;
```

A and B are pointer variables that point to nodes which are records with two fields. The declarations of NodePntr and Node illustrate the one exception to the scoping rule that types have to be declared before they are referred to by other declarations. The declaration of NodePntr refers to the type Node which is declared after it. Within declarations, the position following the words POINTER TO is the only place where a type identifier that has yet to be declared can occur.

If NEW is now called with A as its parameter, memory is allocated for a node with two fields whose types are CARDINAL and NodePntr, and A is made to point at the node as illustrated in Fig. 11.9. The record can be referenced via the pointer variable with the pointer dereferencing operator as A∧.

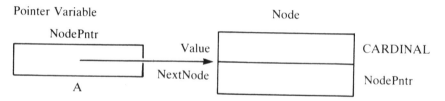

Fig. 11.9.

The usual notation for referring to a field of a record by a dot before the fieldname is followed, so the way to refer to 'the Value field of the node pointed to by A' is a concatenation of the way to refer to the node (A∧) and to a field (.Value)

```
A∧.Value
```

and similarly for the NextNode field

```
A∧.NextNode
```

This allows us to access individual fields and perform the normal operations associated with the type of the field. For example,

```
A∧.Value := 0 ;
A∧.NextNode := NIL ;
```

is a way of initialising fields of the node. Alternatively the WITH statement can be used to state which record to deal with and the fields can be referenced inside the WITH statement in the normal manner

```
WITH B∧ DO
    Value    := 0 ;
    NextNode := NIL
END (* WITH *)
```

Figure 11.10 shows a code fragment which creates two nodes, one pointed at by A and the other pointed at by B, and initialises the fields of each. The final two assignment statements have important consequences for the way that pointers are used. The first of these statements makes the NextNode field of the record A∧ point at B. The second makes B point at nothing. However, A now points to a node which points to another node. In effect A points to the first of a list of two nodes. Figure 11.11 illustrates the situation before and after these two assignment statements.

```
NEW (A) ;                        (* create two nodes. *)
NEW (B) ;

WITH A∧ DO                       (* initialise the fields of each. *)
    Value       := 0 ;
    NextNode    := NIL
END (* WITH *) ;
WITH B∧ DO
    Value       := 0 ;
    NextNode    := NIL
END (* WITH *) ;

A∧.NextNode := B ;               (* make the node which A points at *)
B := NIL ;                       (* point to the node which B points at. *)
```

Fig. 11.10.

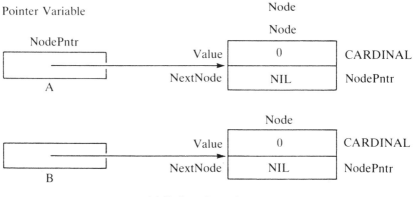

(a) Before the assignment statements.

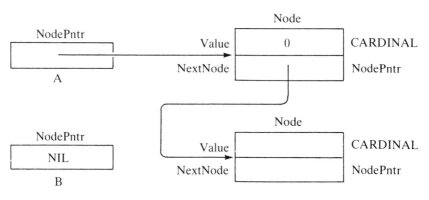

(b) After the assignment statements.

Fig. 11.11.

This list can be extended to have three nodes in it by calling NEW with B as a parameter and then making the second node point to this new node

```
NEW (B) ;
WITH B∧ DO
     Value := 0 ;
     NextNode := NIL ;
END (* WITH *) ;
A∧.NextNode∧.NextNode := B ;
B := NIL ;
```

Alternatively NEW could be called with A∧.NextNode∧.NextNode as its parameter thereby making this field point to the newly created node in one step. The fields of the new node can then be initialised in a WITH statement

```
NEW (A∧.NextNode∧.NextNode) ;
WITH A∧.NextNode∧.NextNode DO
      Value     := 0 ;
      NextNode := NIL ;
END (* WITH *) ;
```

It is unusual to have references to nodes as complex as

A∧.NextNode∧.NextNode

as this can only ever refer to the NextNode field of the second node to which A gives access. Usually the number of nodes in a list is not known, and it is necessary to be able to refer to a node at any position in a list of nodes. A general way of finding and referring to a node in a list is needed.

11.3 LINKED LISTS

The kind of structure which we have started to build is known as a **linked list**; 'list' because the entire structure is capable of holding a sequence of values and 'linked' because it uses pointers. Arrays are a kind of list but they are not linked structures. Lists in general have several operations which are normally associated with them. Typical operations which are performed on lists are

1. add a new item to a list,
2. delete an item from a list,
3. alter an item in a list,
4. access an item in a list,
5. request the number of items in a list.

Special kinds of lists restrict these operations in particular ways. For example, a queue is a special kind of list which restricts addition of new items to one end of the list and removal of items at the other end.

Different ways of implementing data structures make certain operations easier to perform than others. Arrays are essentially fixed length lists which are very good for giving quick access to an item in a list whose position is known. They are less good for other kinds of operations such as inserting an item into the middle of an array which requires other items to be shuffled along to make a component available into which the new item can be inserted. Linked lists are not so good at giving quick access to any particular item in a list, but make insertion and deletion of items from lists much easier and efficient than arrays. The following discussion concentrates on how to insert, delete and locate items in a linked implementation of a list.

Insertion of an Item in a Linked List

Assume that List is a pointer variable of type NodePntr

```
VAR
      List : NodePntr ;
```

and that it has been initialised to NIL

```
List := NIL
```

If new nodes need only be inserted at the front of the list then it is only necessary to
1.   create a new node,
2.   make its NextNode field point at whatever List currently points at,
3.   and make List point to the new node which has just been created.
The following statement sequence does this

```
NEW (NewNode) ;
NewNode∧.NextNode := List ;
List := NewNode;
```

This statement sequence can be written as a procedure which will insert a new item into the front of a list as shown in Fig. 11.12.

```
PROCEDURE InsertHead (Item : CARDINAL ;
                      VAR List : NodePntr) ;
VAR
      NewNode : NodePntr ;
BEGIN
 NEW (NewNode) ;
 WITH NewNode∧ DO
      Value := Item ;
      NextNode := List
 END (* WITH *) ;
 List := NewNode
END InsertHead ;
```

Fig. 11.12.

If the list is empty then List holds the value NIL, so the statement

```
NewNode∧.NextNode := List ;
```

initialises the NextNode field of the new node with the NIL value. List is then made to point at the new node (see Fig. 11.13). If List currently points to a list of nodes then the NextNode field of the new node is made to point at the first node of this list, and List is made to point at the new node (see Fig. 11.14). This latter situation is always the case if the list contains any nodes. Once the new node has been incorporated into the list NewNode need no longer point at the node.

A program fragment

```
List := NIL ;
FOR Count := 1 TO 10 DO
       InsertHead (Count,List)
END (* FOR *) ;
```

creates the list shown in Fig. 11.15.

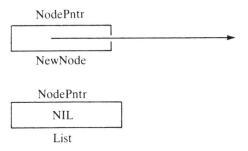

(a) Before the statement sequence.

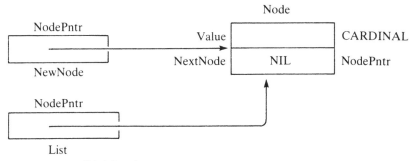

(b) After the statement sequence.

Fig. 11.13.

If items are to be inserted at the end of the list it is necessary to
1. find the node which is currently at the end of the list
2. and then make its NextNode field point to the new node.
    Finding the node at the end of a list can be done with a WHILE loop which
looks for a node whose NextNode field has a value NIL

```
CurrentNode := List ;
WHILE CurrentNode∧.NextNode <> NIL DO
       CurrentNode := CurrentNode∧.NextNode
END (* WHILE *)
```

Note that to do this it is necessary to have another pointer variable so that successive nodes can be referenced without losing the pointer to the original list. Pointers used in this way are often called **travelling pointers**.

The case where List refers to an empty list has to be treated as a special case, for in this situation List must be made to point at the new node. The procedure InsertTail in Fig. 11.16 inserts a new node at the end of a list.

Pointer Variable   Node

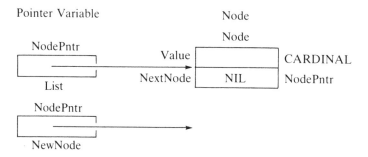

(a) Before the statement sequence.

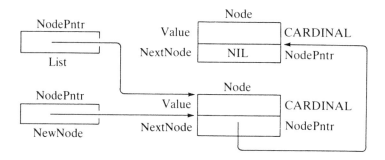

(b) After the statement sequence.

Fig. 11.14.

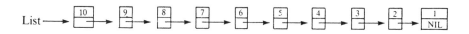

Fig. 11.15.

```
PROCEDURE InsertTail (Item : CARDINAL ;
                      VAR List : NodePntr) ;
  VAR
      CurrentNode,NewNode : NodePntr ;
  BEGIN
   NEW (NewNode) ;
   WITH NewNode ∧ DO
          Value        := Item ;
          NextNode     := NIL
   END (* WITH *) ;
   IF List = NIL THEN
          List := NewNode ;
   ELSE
          CurrentNode := List ;
          WHILE CurrentNode ∧ .NextNode <> NIL DO
                CurrentNode := CurrentNode ∧ .NextNode
          END (* WHILE *) ;
          CurrentNode ∧ .NextNode := NewNode
   END (* IF *)
  END InsertTail ;
```

Fig. 11.16.

Ordered Lists

A third possibility is that an item has to be inserted in the middle of a list. It is often necessary for the items in a list to be in some order. This can be achieved by always inserting new items such that the modified list is still ordered correctly. For example, a program may require that a list of product descriptions be created with the descriptions ordered alphabetically so that the list may be written in alphabetical order to a file. The problem may be analysed as shown in Fig. 11.17.

This analysis suggests that the data structure holding the product descriptions can be hidden within another module. However, careful consideration has to be given to the interface between the module for reading and displaying the product descriptions and the module concerned with maintaining the product list.

Reading and creating the list requires a procedure for inserting an item into the list (Insert).

Writing the list to file needs a way of keeping track of the product description which is currently being written and a way of moving on to the next. In addition this requires a way of determining when the end of the list has been reached. These requirements can be met if it is assumed that the module maintaining the list provides a notion of a 'current' item in the list and

```
MODULE ProductDescriptions ;
  (*... Read the product descriptions and store them in a list in
         alphabetical order ...*)   ;
  (*... Print list of product descriptions ...*)
END ProductDescriptions .
```

(a) Initial analysis of the product decriptions problem.

```
MODULE ProductDescriptions ;

  PROCEDURE ReadDescriptions ;
  BEGIN
   (*... Read a product description ...*) ;
   WHILE (*... not finished ...*) DO
       (*... insert the description into the product list
                        at its correct position ...*) ;
       (*... read the next description ...*) ;
   END (* WHILE *)
  END ReadDescriptions ;

  PROCEDURE WriteDescriptions ;
  BEGIN
   (*... initialise the file for writing ...*) ;
   WHILE (*... not end of product list ...*) DO
       (*... print the current product description ...*) ;
       (*... move on to the next product description ...*) ;
   END (* WHILE *) ;
   (*... close the file ...*)
  END WriteDescriptions ;

BEGIN
  ReadDescriptions ;
  WriteDescriptions ;
END ProductDescriptions .
```

(b) Refinements of reading and writing product descriptions.

Fig. 11.17.

provides procedures for
1. retrieving the current item (ContentsOfCurrent),
2. moving the current item on to the next item in the list (NextCurrent),
3. setting the current item to be the item at the start of the list (InitialiseCur-rent),
4. testing for a situation where there is no current item (CurrentExists).

Figure 11.18 shows the definition module for OrderedList which provides procedures for performing the required operations for inserting items into the list and for accessing items in the list.

```
DEFINITION MODULE OrderedList ;
    CONST
        ItemLength              = 30 ;
    TYPE
        ItemType                = ARRAY [0..ItemLength–1] OF CHAR ;

    PROCEDURE Insert (NewItem : ItemType) ;
        (* Inserts NewItem into the list at the correct position. *)

    PROCEDURE ContentsOfCurrent (VAR Item : ItemType) ;
        (* Returns in Item the item in the current node. *)

    PROCEDURE CurrentExists () : BOOLEAN ;
        (* Returns TRUE if a current item exists,
            otherwise FALSE if InitialiseCurrent has not been called or
                            if NextCurrent has been called so that the
                            end of the list has been reached.*)

    PROCEDURE InitialiseCurrent ;
        (* Sets the current node to be the first in the list if the list
            is not empty. *)

    PROCEDURE NextCurrent ;
        (* if the current node exists then it is set to be the next
            node in the list. When the end of the list has been reached
            CurrentExists will return FALSE. *)

    END OrderedList .
```

Fig. 11.18.

Assuming that these procedures are available the module ProductDescriptions can be completed as shown in Fig. 11.19.

It now remains for the implementation module of OrderedList to be developed so as to hide the list for the product descriptions from the program module. Two pointer variables global to the module, List and CurrentNode, are needed in the module to maintain the list and support the required operations.

The purpose of CurrentNode is to point at the current node in the list, and its position in the list is determined by the procedures InitialiseCurrent and NextCurrent.

1. InitialiseCurrent sets CurrentNode to point to the front of the list,

2. NextCurrent moves the current node on to the next node in the list by assigning to CurrentNode the value in the NextNode field of the node it currently points at, assuming that CurrentNode references a valid item in the list.

```
MODULE ProductDescriptions ;
    FROM OrderedList              IMPORT Insert,ContentsOfCurrent,CurrentExists,
                                         NextCurrent,InitialiseCurrent,
                                         ItemType ;
    FROM SimpleFile               IMPORT FILE, Connect, OpenWrite, WriteToFile,
                                         Close, DisConnect ;
    FROM InOut                    IMPORT ReadString ;
    FROM MoreInOut                IMPORT WriteLnString ;

    VAR
        ProductFile : FILE ;

    PROCEDURE ReadDescriptions ;
     VAR
        Product : ItemType ;
     BEGIN
      WriteLnString ('Type product descriptions, type RETURN after each.') ;
      ReadString (Product) ;
      WHILE Product[0] <> '' DO
         Insert (Product) ;
         ReadString (Product) ;
      END (* WHILE *) ;
     END ReadDescriptions ;

    PROCEDURE WriteDescriptions ;
     VAR
        Product : ItemType ;
     BEGIN
      Connect (ProductFile,'products.dat',Product) ;
      OpenWrite (ProductFile) ;
      InitialiseCurrent ;
      WHILE CurrentExists () DO
         ContentsOfCurrent (Product) ;
         WriteToFile (ProductFile,Product) ;
         NextCurrent ;
      END (* WHILE *) ;
      Close (ProductFile) ;
      DisConnect (ProductFile) ;
     END WriteDescriptions ;

   BEGIN
    ReadDescriptions ;
    WriteDescriptions
   END ProductDescriptions .
```

Fig. 11.19.

The function procedure CurrentExists can be defined simply as a check that
CurrentNode refers to a valid node; that is that CurrentNode's value is not NIL.

ContentsOfCurrent need only return the value of the item held in the node referred to by CurrentNode.

The variable List always refers to the first node in the list if one exists, otherwise it holds the value NIL.

These are apparent in the completed module in Fig. 11.24.

Insertion of Items in an Ordered List

Insertion of a new item into the list requires locating the appropriate position in the list to insert the new item, creating a new node and adjusting pointers to include the new node in the list. If the ordering of the list is alphabetical then the item can be inserted immediately before the first item in the list which is alphabetically after the item to be inserted. This position can be found using a WHILE loop

```
ThisNode := List ;
WHILE (ThisNode <> NIL) AND LessThan(NewItem,ThisNode ∧ .Item) DO
      ThisNode := ThisNode ∧ .NextNode ;
END (* WHILE *) ;
```

The situation when this WHILE statement terminates is illustrated in Fig. 11.20. The product description is shown here as one character, however the principle is the same for longer sequences of characters.

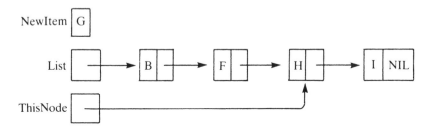

Fig. 11.20.

In order to insert G into the list it is necessary to make F's node point at the node created for G, and to make the new node point to H's node. The WHILE loop has found the wrong node, for the node that enables the list to be updated correctly is the previous node. Note that ThisNode is useful in comparing the value in a node and the value to be inserted. The WHILE loop can be rewritten to use a **trailing pointer**, which is another pointer variable which points at the node immediately prior to that pointed at by ThisNode

```
ThisNode := List ;
PreviousNode := NIL ;
WHILE (ThisNode <> NIL) AND LessThan(NewItem,ThisNode∧.Item) DO
    PreviousNode := ThisNode ;
    ThisNode := ThisNode∧.NextNode ;
END (* WHILE *) ;
```

Figure 11.21 illustrates the situation when the appropriate position in the list is found.

Once this situation has been reached the list can be updated by the statements

```
    (* create the new node *)
NEW (NewNode) ;
NewNode∧.Item := NewItem ;
    (* update the pointers *)
NewNode∧.NextNode := ThisNode ;
PreviousNode∧.NextNode := NewNode ;
```

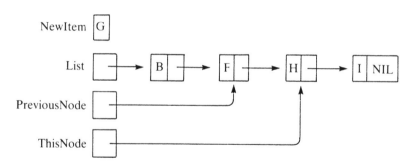

Fig. 11.21.

It is necessary to check that this formulation works in the boundary cases when the item is to be inserted at the front or at the end of the list. If the new item to be inserted is A then this WHILE loop will terminate in the situation illustrated in Fig. 11.22. In this case

1. the new node has to be updated to point to the previous first item in the list,
2. and List should be made to point to the new node.

Whenever PreviousNode holds the value NIL, the special case of inserting an item at the front of the list requires updating List to point to the new node. This requires the code which updates the pointers to be altered to that shown in Fig. 11.23. We leave it to you to check that this code fragment inserts an item at the end of the list correctly.

The completed implementation module for OrderedList incorporating this code in the procedure Insert is shown in Fig. 11.24. Note that Insert uses a procedure FindPosition which returns in its variable parameters the two nodes between which the new node is inserted. It is possible to write these procedures so that FindPosition only returns the value for PreviousNode as ThisNode can always be determined from the pointer in PreviousNode. Returning both pointers helps us to think about the insertion in a clearer way. Note also that Insert inserts an item into the list even if it is already in the list. See programming exercise 2 for suggested improvements to FindPosition and avoiding inserting duplicate items.

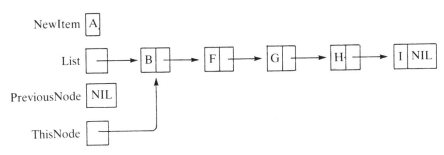

Fig. 11.22.

```
        (* create the new node *)
NEW  (NewNode) ;
NewNode∧.Item := NewItem ;
        (* update the pointers *)
NewNode∧.NextNode := ThisNode ;
IF PreviousNode = NIL THEN
        List := NewNode
ELSE
        PreviousNode∧.NextNode := NewNode ;
END (* IF ELSE *) ;
```

Fig. 11.23.

```
IMPLEMENTATION MODULE OrderedList ;
 FROM Storage IMPORT ALLOCATE, DEALLOCATE ;
 TYPE
      NodePntr          = POINTER TO Node ;
      Node              = RECORD
                            Item         : ItemType ;
                            NextNode     : NodePntr
                          END ;
 VAR
      List
      CurrentNode       : NodePntr ;

 PROCEDURE LessThan (Item1,Item2 : ItemType) : BOOLEAN ;
     (* returns TRUE if Item1 is less than Item2, FALSE otherwise. *)
 VAR
     CharPos : CARDINAL ;
BEGIN
  CharPos := 0 ;
  WHILE (CharPos <> ItemLength) AND
        (Item1[CharPos] = Item2[CharPos]) DO
     INC (CharPos) ;
  END (* WHILE *) ;
  RETURN (CharPos <> ItemLength) AND (Item1[CharPos] < Item2[CharPos])
END LessThan ;

 PROCEDURE FindPosition (VAR Item : ItemType ;
         VAR PreviousNode,ThisNode : NodePntr) ;
BEGIN
  ThisNode := List ;
  PreviousNode := NIL ;
  WHILE (ThisNode <> NIL) AND LessThan(ThisNode∧.Item,Item) DO
     PreviousNode := ThisNode ;
     ThisNode := ThisNode∧.NextNode ;
  END (* WHILE *) ;
END FindPosition ;


                  (* procedures available to other modules. *)
 PROCEDURE CurrentExists () : BOOLEAN ;
BEGIN
  RETURN CurrentNode <> NIL
END CurrentExists ;

 PROCEDURE InitialiseCurrent ;
BEGIN
  CurrentNode := List
END InitialiseCurrent ;

 PROCEDURE NextCurrent ;
BEGIN
  IF CurrentExists () THEN
```

```
        CurrentNode := CurrentNode ∧ .NextNode
    END (* IF *)
END NextCurrent ;

PROCEDURE ContentsOfCurrent (VAR Item : ItemType) ;
BEGIN
  IF CurrentExists () THEN
      Item := CurrentNode ∧ .Item
  END (* IF *) ;
END ContentsOfCurrent ;

PROCEDURE Insert (NewItem : ItemType) ;
  VAR
        NewNode , ThisNode , PreviousNode    : NodePntr ;
BEGIN
  FindPosition (NewItem,PreviousNode,ThisNode) ;
  NEW (NewNode) ;
  NewNode ∧ .Item := NewItem ;
  NewNode ∧ .NextNode := ThisNode ;
  IF PreviousNode = NIL THEN
    List := NewNode
  ELSE
    PreviousNode ∧ .NextNode := NewNode ;
  END (* IF *) ;
END Insert ;

BEGIN
  List := NIL ;
  InitialiseCurrent ;
END OrderedList .
```

Fig. 11.24.

Deleting Items from Linked Lists

Similar considerations arise when an item is to be deleted from a list. This involves finding the appropriate node in the list and then altering pointers to exclude the item from the list. When deletion is restricted to the beginning or end of a list the problem of locating the item is straightforward, we leave these as exercises at the end of the chapter.

In order to delete an item at any position in a list it is necessary to protect the list from the consequences of trying to delete a non-existent item. The following code fragment locates the position at which the item should occur using FindPosition, and then checks that ThisNode contains the item to be deleted. A function procedure Equals is assumed to compare two items of type ItemType for equality.

```
FindPosition (ItemToDelete,PreviousNode,ThisNode) ;
IF (ThisNode <> NIL) AND Equals(ThisNode∧.Item,ItemToDelete) THEN
      (* delete item *)
END (* IF *) ;
```

Note that if the item does not occur in the list, then PreviousNode references a node whose item is less than the item to be deleted or holds the value NIL, and ThisNode references a node whose item is greater than the item to be deleted or holds the value NIL.

Figure 11.25 shows a typical situation determined by FindPosition. In order to remove H from this list it is be necessary to make the node pointed at by PreviousNode point at the node which ThisNode's NextNode field points at, and then to DISPOSE ThisNode.

```
PreviousNode∧.NextNode := ThisNode∧.NextNode ;
DISPOSE (ThisNode) ;
```

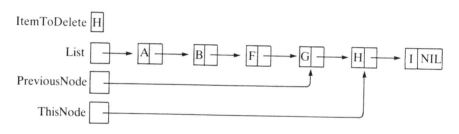

Fig. 11.25.

Figure 11.26 illustrates the situation when the first item in the list is to be deleted. Again this is a special case as PreviousNode holds the value NIL. This signals that the pointer variable List should be updated

```
IF PreviousNode = NIL THEN
      List := ThisNode∧.NextNode
ELSE
      PreviousNode∧.NextNode := ThisNode∧.NextNode
END (* IF *) ;
DISPOSE (ThisNode) ;
```

We again leave it to you to check that the case of deleting the last item in the list is catered for by the normal case.

Figure 11.27 shows a procedure Delete which can be included within the ProductList module for extensions of the problem requiring items to be deleted.

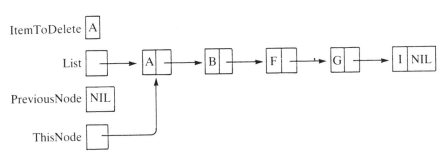

Fig. 11.26.

```
PROCEDURE Delete (ItemToDelete : ItemType) ;
VAR
      ThisNode,PreviousNode : NodePntr ;
BEGIN
  FindPosition (ItemToDelete,PreviousNode,ThisNode) ;
  IF (ThisNode <> NIL) AND Equals(ThisNode∧.Item,ItemToDelete) THEN
     IF PreviousNode = NIL THEN
            List := ThisNode∧.NextNode
     ELSE
            PreviousNode∧.NextNode := ThisNode∧.NextNode
     END (* IF *) ;
     DISPOSE (ThisNode) ;
  END (* IF *) ;
END Delete ;
```

Fig. 11.27.

11.4 STRUCTURE SHARING

In the previous sections there have been situations where two or more pointers point at the same node. If other nodes are linked from this node then both pointers allow access to the same list of nodes. In other situations one pointer points at a node in the middle of a list of nodes pointed at by another pointer. In such situations the pointers are said to **structure share** because they both point at the same structure or sub-structure and thereby share this structure.

Structure sharing is essential in some situations. It is useful on a temporary basis for travelling and trailing pointers, and on a permanent basis in the way that CurrentNode provides a reference into a list of nodes. Some data structures, such as graphs, require multiple pointers to the same sub-structure. For such data structures structure sharing is essential and advanced techniques for memory management are required.

However, permanent structure sharing is dangerous and should be used with care and discretion. In particular it is important not to inadvertently introduce structure sharing in programs. Structure sharing is caused as a result of

1. assignment statements,
2. value parameters.

Assignment between pointer variables has a different meaning to assignment between variables of other types. For example, in the case of variables of basic types, arrays and records

```
Var1 := Var2
Array1 := Array2
Record1 := Record2
```

the assignment statement means copy the contents of one variable into another variable. In the case of arrays and records the entire structure is copied and multiple copies of the same structure exist.

However, with pointers

```
List1 := List2
```

only copies the pointer and not the structure being pointed at. This does not make List1 point at a copy of the structure pointed at by List2, but makes List1 point at the same structure. Any subsequent alterations to the structure accessed through List1 will cause the same changes to be apparent when the structure is accessed through List2. This can cause difficulties when trying to understand a program and should be avoided.

Unfortunately structure sharing can lead to utter disaster. If the list referenced by List1 is destroyed (by calls to DISPOSE) and List1 is reset to NIL, this has dire consequences for Lists2 if it is left pointing at a list of nodes which no longer exist! Any attempts to reference the nodes pointed at by List2 would then cause unpredictable errors in the program.

Parameter passing can lead to unintended structure sharing. If a pointer variable is passed as a variable parameter to a procedure then the pointer is passed directly to the procedure and alterations to the formal parameter cause the same alterations to the actual parameter. If a pointer variable is passed as a value parameter then a new memory location is allocated for the formal parameter and the pointer is copied into the formal parameter. As always with pointers this only means that the pointer is copied and not that the entire structure being pointed at is copied. The formal parameter and the actual parameter therefore share the same structure. If inside the procedure the structure is destroyed and the formal parameter is set to NIL, the actual parameter is left pointing at a structure which no longer exists.

We recommend that structure sharing be avoided where possible, and kept under strict control where it is unavoidable. Multiple pointer variables pointing at the same structure should be used with discretion. Pointer variables should always be passed as variable parameters to procedures unless there are good reasons otherwise, such as using a formal value parameter as a temporary travelling pointer in a procedure which does not alter the data structure.

11.5   LINKED IMPLEMENTATION OF QueueModule

The implementation module of QueueModule in Chapters 5 and 6 use a fixed length array to hold the items in the queue. This has the limitation that the maximum number of items to be held in the queue has to be determined when the module is compiled and before the program using the module is run. For many programs the maximum number of items cannot be determined before it is run, or the theoretical maximum number of items may exceed the available main memory of the machine though the maximum required in practice may be within the machine's capabilities. In such situations a linked representaion of a queue is more appropriate.

Note that a linked implementation of a queue holding a certain number of items requires more memory compared with an array of the same size because the pointers have to be held in main memory. However linked representations do not reserve memory to hold items which are not being used in the way that arrays do.

A linked representation of a queue can be implemented using the techniques discussed for linked lists but with insertion of nodes restricted to the end of the linked list and removal of nodes restricted to the start of the list. The implementation module of QueueModule in Fig. 11.29 embodies procedures AddToQueue and RemoveFromQueue which manipulate pointers in a way that is now familiar. This module makes available more than one queue using the techniques discussed in the following section.

11.6   MULTIPLE HIDDEN DATA STRUCTURES

Some problems require more than one data structure to be made available by another module. For example, a program may require several queues. One way of providing a fixed number of data structures is for the implementation module to contain an array of pointers to several data structures. The definition module for a module which provides a fixed number of queues is shown in Fig. 11.28. It makes available a type Queue to other modules which can declare variables of type Queue. The type Queue is a user-defined sub-range type which is used to uniquely identify particular queues hidden in the implementation module. All the procedures in the module have to be modified to take an extra parameter to indicate the queue on which the operation is to be performed.

Figure 11.29 shows a possible implementation module, it contains an array of pointers to queues. Variables of type Queue declared in importing modules are used to index this array.

When CreateQueue is called a queue is created by using the next available element of the array, and the Queue variable parameter is assigned the value which indexes the array to select this queue. QueuesInUse keeps track of the current highest valued element of the array so that the next available element is provided by incrementing this variable.

DeleteQueue deletes the queue but the component of QueueArray is not made available for reuse, so this component cannot be used in the creation of other queues (see technical exercise 8).

The module's body initialises the array of pointers so that procedures in the module can use ExistsQueue to check whether they are being used appropriately.

11.7 SUMMARY

1 Pointer types are contructs which, in conjunction with records, allow programs to create flexible and dynamic data structures. The mechanics of pointers are summarised at the end of section 11.1.

2 Some of these data structures are linked lists, ordered lists and linked implementations of queues. The advantage of linked representations over implementations based upon fixed size arrays is that the maximum number of items to be included in the list does not have to be determined before a program runs. There are standard algorithms for creating and manipulating linked structures which you can consult (see the Bibliography under the heading **Data Structures**). More complex linked structures are discussed in Chapter 13.

3 Definition and implementation module pairs can provide multiple data structures by using an array of pointers to a dynamic data structure. Procedures provided by the module require a parameter indicating which data structure to use, this is the used as an index into the array of pointers to determine the appropriate data structure.

DEFINITION MODULE QueueModule;

CONST
    MinQNo = 1;
    MaxQNo = 10;
    MaxNoQueues = MaxQNo – MinQNo + 1;
VAR
    Success : BOOLEAN;
    (* All procedures indicate their success or failure by setting Success
      to TRUE if the operation has been performed, otherwise it is set to
      FALSE. *)
TYPE
    ItemType   = ... (* whatever type the user requires *)
    Queue   = [MinQNo..MaxQNo];

PROCEDURE CreateQueue (VAR ThisQueue : Queue);
(* Initialises ThisQueue to be a new queue ready for use. If no new queues
  are available Success is set to FALSE and ThisQueue remains
  uninitialised *)

PROCEDURE DestroyQueue (VAR ThisQueue : Queue);
(* Destroys ThisQueue if the queue is currently empty. If it is not empty
  Success is set to FALSE and the queue still exists.*)

PROCEDURE AddToQueue (VAR ThisQueue : Queue; Data : ItemType);
(* Adds Data to the end of the queue ThisQueue. *)

PROCEDURE RemoveFromQueue (VAR ThisQueue : Queue; VAR Data : ItemType);
(* Returns the item at the head of the queue ThisQueue and removes it from
  the queue. If the queue is empty Success is set to FALSE and Data is
  undefined. *)

PROCEDURE TopOfQueue (VAR ThisQueue : Queue; VAR Data : ItemType);
(* Returns the item at the head of the queue ThisQueue without removing it
  from the queue. If the queue is empty Success is set to FALSE and Data
  is undefined. *)

PROCEDURE FullQueue (VAR ThisQueue : Queue) : BOOLEAN;
(* Returns TRUE if the queue ThisQueue is full, otherwise FALSE. *)

PROCEDURE EmptyQueue (VAR ThisQueue : Queue) : BOOLEAN;
(* Returns TRUE if the queue ThisQueue is empty, otherwise FALSE. *)

PROCEDURE LengthOfQueue (VAR ThisQueue : Queue) : CARDINAL;
(* Returns a value representing the number of items currently in the queue.
  If ThisQueue does not represent a valid queue Success is set to FALSE. *)

END QueueModule.

Fig. 11.28.

```
IMPLEMENTATION MODULE QueueModule;
  FROM Storage IMPORT ALLOCATE,DEALLOCATE;

  TYPE
      QueueItemPointer        = POINTER TO QueueItem;
      QueueItem               = RECORD
                                   Item        : ItemType;
                                   NextItem    : QueueItemPointer
                                   END (* RECORD *);
      QueuePoint              = POINTER TO QueueRecord;
      QueueRecord             = RECORD
                                   HeadQueue,
                                   EndQueue    : QueueItemPointer;
                                   SizeQueue   : CARDINAL
                                   END;
      QueueArray              = ARRAY Queue OF QueuePoint;
  VAR
      QueuesInUse         : [0..MaxNoQueues];
      Queues              : QueueArray;

  PROCEDURE ExistsQueue (VAR ThisQueue : Queue) : BOOLEAN;
  BEGIN
    RETURN (ThisQueue <= QueuesInUse) AND (Queues[ThisQueue] <> NIL)
  END ExistsQueue;

(* ALL PROCEDURES FROM THIS POINT ARE AVAILABLE VIA THE DEFINITION MODULE
*)

  PROCEDURE CreateQueue(VAR ThisQueue : Queue);
  BEGIN
    IF QueuesInUse <> MaxNoQueues THEN
        Success := TRUE;
        INC(QueuesInUse);
        ThisQueue := QueuesInUse;
        NEW (Queues[ThisQueue]);
        WITH Queues[ThisQueue]^ DO
              HeadQueue := NIL;
              EndQueue := NIL;
              SizeQueue  := 0
        END (* WITH *);
    ELSE
        Success := FALSE
    END (* IF *)
  END CreateQueue;

  PROCEDURE DestroyQueue(VAR ThisQueue : Queue);
  BEGIN
    IF Queues[ThisQueue]^.SizeQueue = 0 THEN
      Success := TRUE;
      DISPOSE (Queues[ThisQueue]) ;
```

```
      Queues[ThisQueue] := NIL
  ELSE
      Success := FALSE
  END (* IF *)
END DestroyQueue;

PROCEDURE AddToQueue(VAR ThisQueue : Queue; Data : ItemType);
  VAR
      NewItem : QueueItemPointer;
BEGIN
  IF ExistsQueue(ThisQueue) THEN
      NEW(NewItem);
      WITH NewItem∧ DO
          Item := Data;
          NextItem := NIL
      END (* WITH *);
      WITH Queues[ThisQueue]∧ DO
          IF HeadQueue = NIL THEN
              HeadQueue := NewItem
          ELSE
              EndQueue∧.NextItem := NewItem
          END (* IF *);
          EndQueue := NewItem;
          INC(SizeQueue)
      END (* WITH *);
      Success := TRUE
  ELSE
      Success := FALSE
  END (* IF *)
END AddToQueue;

PROCEDURE RemoveFromQueue(VAR ThisQueue : Queue; VAR Data : ItemType);
  VAR
      OldItem : QueueItemPointer;
BEGIN
  IF ExistsQueue(ThisQueue) THEN
      WITH Queues[ThisQueue]∧ DO
          IF HeadQueue <> NIL THEN
              OldItem := HeadQueue;
              Data    := HeadQueue∧.Item;
              HeadQueue := HeadQueue∧.NextItem;
              IF HeadQueue = NIL THEN
                  EndQueue := NIL
              END (* IF *);
              DEC(SizeQueue);
              DISPOSE(OldItem);
              Success := TRUE
          ELSE
              Success := FALSE
          END (* IF *)
```

```
        END (* WITH *);
    ELSE
        Success := FALSE
    END (* IF *)
END RemoveFromQueue;


PROCEDURE TopOfQueue(VAR ThisQueue : Queue; VAR Data : ItemType);
    VAR
        OldItem : QueueItemPointer;
BEGIN
    IF ExistsQueue(ThisQueue) THEN
        WITH Queues[ThisQueue] ∧ DO
            IF HeadQueue <> NIL THEN
                Data     := HeadQueue ∧ .Item;
                Success := TRUE
            ELSE
                Success := FALSE
            END (* IF *)
        END (* WITH *);
    ELSE
        Success := FALSE
    END (* IF *)
END TopOfQueue;


PROCEDURE FullQueue(VAR ThisQueue : Queue) : BOOLEAN;
BEGIN
    IF ExistsQueue(ThisQueue) THEN
        Success := TRUE;
        RETURN FALSE
    ELSE
        Success := FALSE;
        RETURN TRUE
    END (* IF *)
END FullQueue;


PROCEDURE EmptyQueue(VAR ThisQueue : Queue) : BOOLEAN;
BEGIN
    IF ExistsQueue(ThisQueue) THEN
        Success := TRUE;
        RETURN Queues[ThisQueue] ∧ .SizeQueue = 0
    ELSE
        Success := FALSE;
        RETURN TRUE
    END (* IF *)
END EmptyQueue;


PROCEDURE LengthOfQueue(VAR ThisQueue : Queue) : CARDINAL;
BEGIN
    IF ExistsQueue(ThisQueue) THEN
        Success := TRUE;
```

```
        RETURN Queues[ThisQueue]∧.SizeQueue
    ELSE
        Success := FALSE;
        RETURN 0
    END (* IF *)
    END LengthOfQueue;

 BEGIN (* initialise the pointers to the queues to NIL
            and set QueuesInUse. *)
    FOR QueuesInUse := 1 TO MaxNoQueues DO
            Queues[QueuesInUse] := NIL
    END (* FOR *);
    QueuesInUse := 0
 END QueueModule.
```

Fig. 11.29.

TECHNICAL EXERCISES

Assuming the declarations

```
    TYPE
            IntegerPointer      = POINTER TO INTEGER ;
            CardinalPointer     = POINTER TO CARDINAL ;
            RealPointer         = POINTER TO REAL ;
    VAR
            A,B                 : IntegerPointer ;
            C,D                 : CardinalPointer ;
            E                   : POINTER TO CARDINAL ;
            x,y                 : INTEGER ;
            z                   : CARDINAL ;
```

1 State which of the following calls of NEW are valid and which are invalid

  a NEW (C)

  b NEW (x)

  c NEW (C∧)

2 If only the following calls to NEW have been executed

```
    NEW (C)
    NEW (D)
```

state which of the following calls of DISPOSE are valid and which invalid

  a DISPOSE (C∧)

  b DISPOSE (C)

  c DISPOSE (D)

  d DISPOSE (B)

  e DISPOSE (x)

3 If only the following calls of NEW have been executed

    NEW (A)
    NEW (C)

state which of the statements in the following statement sequence are valid (assuming that valid statements are executed and invalid statements are ignored).

a B := A ;

b A = C ;

c A := x ;

d A∧ := x ;

e A∧ := z ;

f z := C∧ ;

g z := A∧ ∗ B∧ ;

h A∧ := B∧ + C∧ ;

j E := C ;

k E∧ := C∧ ;

l A := NIL ;

m x := NIL ;

n C∧ := NIL ;

4 Assuming the above declarations and an initial situation of

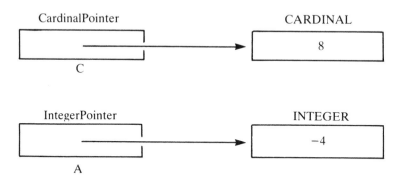

with all other pointer variables initialised to NIL draw a diagram to illustrate the situation after the following statement sequence has been executed.

```
NEW (B) ;
B∧ := A∧ * A∧ ;
D := C ;
D∧ := D∧ + C∧ ;
DISPOSE (C) ;
C := NIL ;
NEW (E) ;
E∧ := ABS (B∧) ;
NEW (C) ;
```

5   State what if anything is wrong with the following module

```
MODULE Pointers ;
TYPE
      IntPntrPntr      = POINTER TO POINTER TO INTEGER ;
VAR
      A,B              : IntPntrPntr ;
BEGIN
  NEW (A) ;
  NEW (A∧) ;
  A∧∧ := 6 ;
  NEW (B) ;
  B∧ := A∧ ;
END Pointers .
```

6   Comment on the validity of the following groups of declarations

a   TYPE
           A = POINTER TO B ;
           B = RECORD
               C : INTEGER ;
               D : A
               END ;

b   TYPE
           X = RECORD
               Y : INTEGER ;
               Z : W
               END ;
           W = POINTER TO X ;

7   Write a procedure DisposeList to be included in the OrderedList module which uses DISPOSE to release all the nodes in a linked list and resets the module variables to represent an empty list.

8   QueueModule makes available 10 queues to other modules, however it does not guarantee that 10 queues will be available all the time. Why is this so? How could the module be modified to guarantee that 10 queues are always available?

PROGRAMMING EXERCISES

1   Write an implementation and definition module pair called StackModule which provides 10 stacks for use by other modules. Inside the definition module implement a stack as a linked structure. The operations to be included in the stack module are

Push — which adds a new item given as a parameter at the front of a particular stack.

Pop — which removes the item at the front of the stack and returns this in a variable parameter.

Empty — which returns TRUE if there are no items in the stack, otherwise FALSE.

ContentsOfTop — which returns the contents of the item on the top of a stack in a variable parameter without removing it from the stack.

CreateStack — which creates and initialises a new stack.

DestroyStack — which destroys a particular stack if there are no items in it.

Build checks into the implementation module to prevent modules using it incorrectly.

Design a set of test data to test that the module works correctly and write a test program to show that the program module works correctly.

2   Rewrite the procedure FindPosition in Fig. 11.24 so that its procedure heading is

```
PROCEDURE FindPosition (VAR Item : ItemType ;
           VAR PreviousNode,ThisNode : NodePntr ;
                VAR AlreadyInList : BOOLEAN) ;
```

so that AlreadyInList is set to TRUE if the item is already in the list, that is ThisNode references a node which already contains the item being searched for, and FALSE otherwise.

Modify Insert to use this procedure and provide further procedures

a InsertIfNotInList whose procedure heading is

```
PROCEDURE InsertIfNotInList (NewItem : ItemType ;
                VAR DoneIt : BOOLEAN) ;
```

which does not insert the item if it is already in the list and sets DoneIt to TRUE if the item has been inserted, otherwise FALSE.

b DeleteIfInList whose procedure heading is

```
PROCEDURE DeleteIfInList (ItemToDelete : ItemType ;
                VAR DoneIt : BOOLEAN) ;
```

to delete a specified item from a list if it is in the list. DoneIt is set to TRUE if the item was in the list and has been deleted, otherwise it is set to FALSE.

Write a program module which reads the list of product names created by the program in Fig. 11.19 and accepts an indefinite number of descriptions typed at the keyboard which should be deleted from the list if they are in it. The program should then write out the modified list to another file.

3 Modify the OrderedList module so that it provides 10 ordered lists for use by other modules.

Write a program which accepts a list of names and an indication of whether a name is that of a male or female, and inserts the names into one of two lists, one for names of males and the other for names of females. When all names have been entered the program should write the names to two files one for males and one for females, and additionally writes all the names to a third file with all names of females ordered alphabetically followed by all names of males ordered alphabetically.

Write a test program which reads back each of these files and displays their contents on the video display screen to check that the files have been created correctly.

4 Implement QueueModule so that there is no limit on the number of queues available to other modules, by holding existing queues in a linked list instead of in a variable of type QueueArray.

ANSWERS

1 **a** valid.

b invalid — x is not a pointer variable.

c invalid — C∧ is not a pointer variable, it is a node holding a CARDINAL value.

2 **a** invalid — C∧ is not a pointer variable.

b valid.

c valid.

d this will not cause a compilation error as B is a pointer variable, however B does not point to a valid node so the consequences of trying to dispose of a non-existent node is unpredictable and will cause an execution error.

e invalid — as x is not a pointer variable.

3 **a** valid.

b invalid — as A and C are of different types.

c invalid — as A is a pointer variable and x is an INTEGER variable and therefore are not the same type.

d valid.

e valid.

f valid.

g valid.

h invalid — as B∧ is an INTEGER value and C∧ is a CARDINAL value and operands of mixed types are not permitted in arithmetic expressions.

j invalid — as A and E are not pointer variables of the same type.

k again this will not cause a compilation error but as E does not reference a valid node it cannot be assigned a value, therefore an execution error is to be expected.

l valid.

m invalid — as x is not a pointer variable.

n invalid — as C∧ is not a pointer variable, but a node which can hold a CARDINAL value.

4

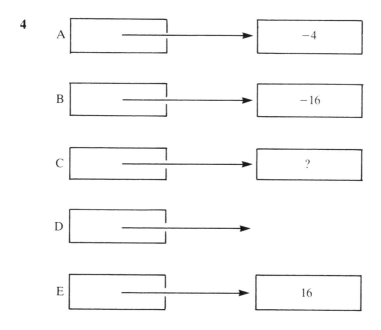

The structure sharing which occurs between C and D is of concern as, when C is DISPOSEd, D is left pointing at a node which does not exist.

5 In order to use NEW, ALLOCATE must be imported from Storage. Otherwise, there is techinically nothing wrong with the module, though the declaration of IntPntrPntr is unusual. After the last statement the situation is

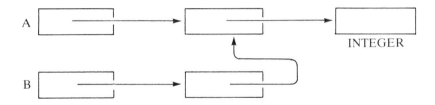

6 a valid.

b invalid — the only place where forward references to types which are declared later is in the declaration of pointer types, not within records.

7
```
PROCEDURE DisposeList ;
VAR
      TempNode : NodePntr ;
BEGIN
WHILE List <> NIL DO
      TempNode := List ;
      List      := List∧.NextNode ;
      DISPOSE (TempNode) ;
END (∗ WHILE ∗) ;
CurrentNode := NIL ;
END DisposeList ;
```

8 The module does not guarantee that 10 queues are always available as it does not make available for reuse queues which have been destroyed. To remedy this some mechanism for recycling queues is needed, for example the array of pointers to queues in the implementation module could be replaced by a queue of 10 pointers to queues. CreateQueue would then remove the queue at the front of the queue of queue pointers and Destroy-Queue would replace a queue pointer at the end of the queue of queue pointers. This involves QueueModule making use of one of its own queues internally, which can be initialised in the module body.

Chapter 12

Local Modules and Program Design

The primary organisational constructs in Modula-2 are the module and the procedure. By using a judicious combination of these any programming problem can be broken down into units, each of which is logically separate from the rest of the system. The art and science of program design involves choosing units with simple comprehensible interfaces to other units. A sign that this is happening effectively comes from definition modules, which should consist of objects each of whose existence is a natural consequence of other objects in the definition module. QueueModule is an example of a consistent logical whole with a clean interface.

In this chapter a more detailed study is made of the modularisation facilities within Modula-2 and their consequences for the way a programmer thinks about program construction. In particular this chapter introduces local modules.

The essence of a module is that it provides a facility with a precisely defined and comprehensible interface to other modules. The interface between any two modules is defined by the objects which one of the modules allows to be exported from it, and the objects which the other module chooses to import from it. A definition module defines all those objects which may be used by other modules and hence it defines the objects which it and its implementation module partner export. A module's import lists state those objects exported by other modules which are required by this module.

The complete list of objects which can be exported or imported under the appropriate conditions is

1. procedures
2. types
3. variables
4. constants
5. modules.

Importing and exporting of procedures, variables and constants is discussed at length in Chapter 6. Types can be imported and exported in a similar manner as illustrated in Chapter 10. In the case of types there is a special facility for exporting a type without giving any details about it. This is known as opaque export and the type FILE in the file handling module of Chapter 10 is an example of how such types are used. Opaque types are discussed in more detail in Chapter 14. When modules are imported and exported they obey the same rules as other objects. This chapter discusses how objects are imported into and exported from local modules, and the consequences for the scope rules of the language.

The chapter concludes with an example program which uses local modules and illustrates the rules for importing and exporting objects.

12.1 LOCAL MODULES

Modules which have been shown to date have all been separately compiled modules, either main program modules or definition and implementation module pairs. However, not all modules need to be compiled separately from other modules. Modula-2 provides a further kind of module which has the advantages associated with an implementation module of being able to hide data structures and the implementation detail of procedures within them, but without having to store them in separate files. Undoubtedly the ability to compile modules separately from each other has advantages. In particular it allows a module to be reused in many programs. However, the benefits of localising program objects within modules is applicable in parts of a program which are specific to a particular problem and where there is little likelihood of the module being of use in other programs. Local modules allow a module to be constructed from modules declared internal to it.

Modules are constructs allowing the design and development of software building blocks. That is, they are an important technique in the control of complexity. This is true of both general purpose modules which can take advantage of separate compilation, and system specific pieces of code which have their own logical existence within the system as a whole. To allow many different and flexible methods of design, modules can be declared within other modules to any level of nesting. Modules may even be declared within procedures and are then subject to the lifetime restrictions of the procedures.

Local modules are declared in the declaration section of a block with constants, types, variables and procedures. As with other kinds of modules, a local module provides a protective skin around its contents. A local module, however, does not require a definition module. Instead it has an export list which lists the objects which are accessible outside of it. Figure 12.1 illustrates how local modules are declared. This should not be read as an example of good style but as an example of what is permitted.

```
MODULE LocalModulesExample ;
 IMPORT (* separately compiled MODULES *) MoreInOut, Menus, Utilities ;
 FROM  InOut  IMPORT WriteString, ReadString ;

 MODULE Genders ;
  IMPORT Menus ;
  IMPORT WriteString ;
  FROM  MoreInOut  IMPORT WriteLnString ;
  EXPORT (* TYPE *) Gender, (* PROCEDURES *) GetGender, WriteGender ;
  TYPE
     Gender  = (Male,Female) ;

  PROCEDURE GetGender (VAR ThisGender : Gender) ;
   VAR
     Reply : CHAR ;
   BEGIN
    Reply := Menus.MenuReply ('Male/Female/') ;
    IF Reply = 1 THEN
          ThisGender := Male
    ELSE
          ThisGender := Female
    END (* IF *) ;
   END GetGender ;

  PROCEDURE WriteGender (ThisGender : Gender) ;
   BEGIN
    WriteLnString ('Gender is ') ;
    CASE ThisGender OF
      Male    : WriteString ('Male ') |
      Female : WriteString ('Female ') |
    END (* CASE *) ;
   END WriteGender ;
 END Genders ;

 MODULE Names ;
  IMPORT ReadString, WriteString ;
  IMPORT MoreInOut ;
  EXPORT QUALIFIED (* TYPE *) Name,
                    (* PROCEDURES *) ReadName, WriteName ;
  TYPE
     Name      = ARRAY [0..19] OF CHAR ;

  PROCEDURE ReadName (VAR ThisName : Name) ;
   BEGIN
    MoreInOut.WriteLnString ('Please type the name – ') ;
    ReadString (ThisName) ;
    END ReadName ;

  PROCEDURE WriteName (VAR ThisName : Name) ;
   BEGIN
```

```
      MoreInOut.WriteLnString (' The name is - ') ;
      WriteString (ThisName) ;
    END WriteName ;
  END Names ;

  TYPE
      Person = RECORD
                OnesName   : Names.Name ;
                OnesGender : Gender ;
                END (* RECORD *) ;
  VAR
      People : ARRAY [1..10] OF Person ;
      Count  : CARDINAL ;

BEGIN
  FOR Count := 1 TO 10 DO
      Names.ReadName (People[Count].OnesName) ;
      GetGender (People[Count].OnesGender) ;
  END (* FOR *) ;
  WITH Utilities DO
      Sort (People) ;
  END (* WITH *) ;
  FOR Count := 1 TO 10 DO
      WITH People[Count] DO
          Names.WriteName (OnesName) ;
          WriteGender (OnesGender) ;
      END (* WITH *) ;
  END (* FOR *) ;
END LocalModulesExample .
```

Fig. 12.1.

The following points are of note

1. a local module is declared in exactly the same way that an implementation module is declared, except

    a. the word IMPLEMENTATION is omitted,

    b. the module terminates with a semi-colon rather than a full stop,

    c. it lists in its export list the objects declared within it that can be accessed from outside the module.

    Note that a local module is allowed an optional module body though neither of Genders or Names has one.

2. The module's export list determines those objects which can be accessed from outside the module and this can be specified in two ways

    a. unqualified export. The names of the objects are listed after the word EXPORT and these objects are then available in the surrounding module, in this case the program module. Thus GetGender, WriteGender and Gender are available for use in the main module.

b. qualified export. By adding the word QUALIFIED after EXPORT references to the exported objects from outside the module have to be prefixed with the module name. Thus ReadName is referred to as Names.Read-Name.

3. A local module can only access objects outside the module which are explicitly imported into the module. Thus Genders cannot access the array People or use the type Person as they are not imported into the module.

4. There are several different ways for a module to state that objects are to be imported into it

a. selectively importing the objects required. This is the method of importing objects from definition and implementation module pairs which we have used to date, using FROM to specify the module and IMPORT to select the objects required. This is called unqualifying import as it is not necessary to qualify references to the objects with the prefix of the module name from which they are imported.

b. importing objects which are in scope in the surrounding module. Both Genders and Names import WriteString from the main program module simply by including the procedure name in the import lists because it is in scope in the surrounding module. Names additionally imports ReadString. Both ReadString and WriteString are themselves imported into the main module from InOut, however this is irrelevant as far as the importing local modules are concerned. The array People could have been imported into either module (or both) by including it in their import lists.

c. importing the entirety of another module. For example, Genders imports the entirety of the Menus module, which is a separately compilable module imported in its entirety by the program module. Inside Genders, objects in this module have to be referred to using the prefix of the module name. Thus Menus.MenuReply refers to the procedure MenuReply from the Menus module. This is really a special case of case b. as far as importing an object is concerned in that the module which is imported is in scope in the surrounding module and can therefore be imported into local modules. However, it has the ramification that references to objects in the imported module have to be qualified by the module name.

5. Qualified reference to objects within modules is syntactically the same as references to fields within records. As a consequence the WITH statement can be used so that qualification is not required within the WITH's statement sequence.

6. Finally, the way that the main module imports objects from definition module and implementation module pairs affects how these objects can be referenced in the main module. The modules MoreInOut and Menus are imported in their entirety to allow the local modules either to import the

entire module or to select the objects that they require. The main module itself does not use objects from these modules but it must import them for the local modules. Local modules cannot import anything which is not in scope in the surrounding module. A module Utilities is assumed to provide various utility procedures, one of which is Sort. As the main module imports the entire module, it must refer to the Sort procedure by qualifying it with the module's name.

If the above description has seemed difficult do not overly worry, most people find this topic difficult. So let us summarise these points in a different way.

12.2   SCOPE RULES REVISITED

Chapter 6 described the scope rules of Modula-2, or rather the scope rules of the part of the language discussed up to that point. However, local modules require additional rules.

Scope Rule 5

A module block cannot reference objects declared in surrounding blocks except for those permitted through Scope Rule 6.

This effectively states that a module is a self contained entity and objects in surrounding blocks cannot be accessed as non-local objects in the way that procedures can access such objects. Figure 12.2 illustrates the scope of the local module within a global module.

```
MODULE Global;

    MODULE Local;                          Scope of objects
                                           in the normal
        Scope of objects declared in       scope of Global
        Local, plus any objects imported   plus any objects
        from the scope of Global. This     exported from
        can include objects imported       the local module
        from other modules into Global.    Local.

    END Local;

END Global.
```

Fig. 12.2.

12.3 IMPORT AND EXPORT LISTS

Scope Rule 6

> A module can only access objects which are external to it if they are listed in its import lists.

This applies to program modules and to implementation and definition modules as well as local modules. There are slight differences in the way that local modules import objects compared with the way that modules which are compiled separately can import objects from definition modules. Figure 12.3 summarises the methods of importing for all modules.

Scope Rule 7

> A local module can extend the scope of a local object by including it in its export list.

Objects which are included in a local module's export list are then available for use in the surrounding module. This effectively enlarges the scope of the object to be that of the surrounding module. The export list of a local module can have two forms, unqualified export or qualified export. In the former case references to objects in the surrounding module can optionally qualify references to the objects by using the prefix of the module name or just refer to the object directly. Objects which are exported using qualified export must be referred to using the prefix of the module name.

As local modules can declare other local modules within them, modules themselves can be exported from a local module by either qualified or unqualified export. Figure 12.4 shows the possibilities for exporting objects from a local module. Note that a module which imports another module in its entirety can only access objects which the latter exports in qualified mode.

Note that
1. when a local module exports objects, the surrounding module must not include these objects in its import list. Import lists are used to import objects into a module from a larger scope only,
2. care must be taken when using unqualified export that the identifier names are not already in use in the surrounding module as this will cause an error,
3. undisciplined export of objects from local modules using unqualified export can render it difficult to locate the declaration of the object in a large module, as references to the object need not indicate the module name,
4. the WITH statement can be used to temporarily unqualify references to objects in local modules.

Import into a compilation unit from a definition module M.

main module's import lists	references to objects
IMPORT M ;	M.x M.y M.z
FROM M IMPORT x,y,z ;	x y z

The objects which can be imported are procedures, types, constants and variables. Note that local modules in the implementation module cannot be listed in the definition module and therefore cannot be imported into other modules.

Import into a local module from the surrounding module.

local module's import list	references to objects from within the local module
IMPORT x,y,z ;	x y z M.x M.y M.z
IMPORT M ; ´	M.x M.y M.z ***
FROM M IMPORT x,y,z ;	x y z

where M is a module which is in scope in the surrounding module.

*** If M is a local module then x,y and z must be
     exported in qualified mode.

The objects which can be imported are procedures, types, constants, variables and modules. A local module can import an entire module (local or global) which is in scope in the surrounding module.

Fig. 12.3.

As qualified and unqualified export modes provide two different ways of referring to exported objects, you may be wondering about objects which are exported from separately compiled modules. These are automatically exported in qualified mode. The early definition of Modula-2 required this to be explicitly stated in definition modules, as was indicated in comments in the definition modules shown in Chapter 6. However, as objects could not be exported in unqualified mode from definition modules, the redundant export list in a definition module was removed from the language.

As there are several possibilities for importing and exporting objects, it is usual to adopt some conventions on the way that objects are imported and exported in programs. We suggest

1. when a main module or implementation module imports objects for use in the module these are imported using the FROM form of the import list notation.

2. when a module has to import objects for use exclusively by its local modules, it imports the entire module so that its local modules can use the FROM form of an import list to select the objects it needs from the imported module.

3. objects should be exported from local modules into surrouding modules so that it is obvious where the objects originate. If the origin of the objects is not obvious from their names then QUALIFIED export should be used.

Exporting objects from a local module M into the surrounding module.

Assuming the module structure

```
MODULE Main ;
   MODULE M ;
      (* declarations of x,y and z as local objects of M *)
      MODULE N ;
         (* declarations of a,b and c as local objects of N,
            and export of a,b and c in qualifed mode *)
      END N ;
   END M ;
END Main.
```

M's export list	references to the objects in M from the surrounding module					
EXPORT x,y,z ;	x	y	z	M.x	M.y	M.z
EXPORT QUALIFIED x,y,z ;	M.x	M.y	M.z			
EXPORT N ;	N.a	N.b	N.c	M.N.a	M.N.b	
EXPORT QUALIFIED N ;	M.N.a	M.N.b	M.N.c			

Fig. 12.4.

12.4   THE LIFETIME OF LOCAL MODULES AND THEIR LOCAL OBJECTS

The scope of an object declared in a local module is the local module, unless its scope has been extended by being exported. However, the lifetime of the object is that of the surrounding block. This is because the lifetime of a local module is that of its surrounding block.

Most local modules are declared to be local to another module and therefore their lifetime normally corresponds to the entire execution of the program. However, if you study the syntax diagram for a procedure declaration in Appendix 1, you will see that modules can be declared locally to a procedure. Such modules have a lifetime corresponding to the invocations of the procedure. This means that the body of the local module is executed every time the enclosing procedure is called. In effect the following procedure

```
PROCEDURE Protected;
   MODULE InsideAProcedure;
      (* module declarations *)
   BEGIN (* initialisation statements *)
   END InsideAProcedure;
END Protected;
```

is like a normal procedure, except that the module body can only refer to those objects outside the module which are explicitly imported into the module. The initialisation statements of the module act like the body of a normal procedure because they are executed each time the procedure is called. In other words this is a way of constructing a procedure whose scope rules are restricted to those of a module. An important consequence of this is that no objects can be exported to the outer module (this is not true if the procedure has a normal procedure body), so the only ways of returning results are

1. by parameter passing, but remember the parameters to Protected have to be imported into InsideAProcedure,

2. by importing a variable from the surrounding module and then altering its value. This effectively requires the module inside the procedure to select the set of non-local objects it references.

Modules local to a procedure are not used a great deal in practice and are not discussed further.

SUMMARY

The scope and lifetime rules for local modules are

1 Any object in the scope of the block immediately surrounding a local module can be imported into the local module. This includes objects which may have been imported into the surrounding module.

2 Any object in the scope of a local module can be exported to the block containing the declaration of the local module. The object can be exported in qualified or unqualified mode.

3 A local module has a lifetime corresponding to the lifetime of the block in which it is declared.

12.5   SEPARATE COMPILATION

As local modules introduce an alternative to separately compiled modules the design of a program involves decisions as to whether to write a module as a separate compilation unit or as a local module. The advantages of separately compiled modules are

1.   They can be used in many different programs if they carry out a general task. InOut and QueueModule are examples of general modules of this type.

2.   If an implementation module is recompiled, there is no need to recompile any other part of the system.

3.   If an implementation module is found to have unsatisfactory characteristics, it can be rewritten without affecting the rest of the program. This is an important factor in the development of large systems, because it allows a

programmer to design a prototype implementation module to be used in testing other parts of the system. Meanwhile a final version of the implementation module can be developed which may, for example, be required to meet precise efficiency criteria.

4. Once a definition module has been defined, other modules can be developed before the implementation module is available. Testing is possible using a skeleton implementation module which merely makes the calls to the procedures legal. Thus a design can be carried out by defining a series of definition modules before any implementation modules are written. This is true top down analysis.

An important factor that comes out of the analysis of the advantages of separately compiled modules is the necessity for very precisely defined definition modules. A programmer must know how the objects exported from a module will behave in all relevent circumstances. Mathematical methods of specifying behaviour are useful to provide the precise definitions, but are beyond the scope of this book.

When using separately compiled modules the development of definition modules is crucial. The following points are of note

1. If a definition module is altered then other modules have to be recompiled. Definition modules should be designed with great care so that the need to recompile them is avoided. The definition modules are the interfaces between different building blocks of the system and a misdesign of an interface is a costly mistake.

2. The purpose of the module as given in the definition module cannot change. There is no point keeping a definition module syntactically the same if alterations to the implementation module result in changes to the behaviour of the module.

3. The art of designing definition modules requires a lot of talent and experience. It is all too easy to create a large number of definition modules which prove to be impractical when the implementation modules are developed. Thus a certain amount of bottom up analysis may be necessary by investigating methods of implementation before creating definition modules. The modularisation and the necessity to develop definition modules has the advantage of forcing the bottom up development to take place within narrow design limits. The module QueueModule gives an elementary example of the difficulties of designing the definition module even in very simple situations. If the first implementation is known to apply only to small queues and is to use pointer types it is easy to forget to provide a procedure in the definition module for testing whether a queue is full. Once the consequences of changing the definition module of a widely used module are understood, program-

mers tend to think very carefully about the design of definition modules. To give a feeling for the effect, imagine that a substantial change is made to InOut after you have been using Modula-2 for five years!

4.   During the development of a large or medium sized program it is essential that the interfaces between modules are consistent. Modula-2 automatically checks that this is so by referring to definition modules when modules which import objects from it are compiled and when their corresponding implementation modules are compiled.

Organisational features play an important part in the control of separately compiled modules. It has already been noted that alterations to definition modules require recompilation of the implementation module and modules which use the definition and implementation module pair. Thus an alteration to a definition module can have severe repercussions in an environment where numerous programs and modules have to be recompiled.

Most Modula-2 compilers allow a working program to link the compiled modules together to produce an executable program, which is not linked each time the program is run. In this case, if changes are made to modules, there may be no requirement to change the working program. However, this is dangerous if used lightly, as the working program can become out of step with the current modules and when eventually it becomes necessary to modify this program a lot of work may be needed to incorporate all the alterations. The standard Modula-2 approach is to link the modules together each time a program is executed. This is a powerful check that all the current modules are logically consistent.

It is not possible to have circular importation at the definition module level. Figure 12.5 demonstrates what is not possible since each definition module would have to be compiled before the other.

```
DEFINITION MODULE Fred;          DEFINITION MODULE Joe;
  FROM Joe IMPORT ConstB ;         FROM Fred IMPORT TypeA ;
     (*... ...*)                       (*... ...*)
END Fred.                        END Joe.
```

Fig. 12.5.

It is legitimate for implementation modules to import in this circular fashion as the definition modules can be compiled before the implementation modules. This is not to say that it is good practice. Circular references should be considered the exception. Note that definition and implementation modules are separate when it comes to considering importation. If the same object is required in both the definition and implementation module, it must be imported into both.

12.6 EXECUTION OF MODULE BODIES

The body of a separately compiled module is executed before the body of the importing module. This is to guarantee the essential requirement that the imported objects have been initialised properly before they are used in the importing module. However this cannot be guaranteed if there are circular importations, such that two or more modules each require that the other module(s) are initialised before its body is executed. In such situations the order of execution of the module bodies is undefined. This is a good reason for avoiding circular importations, and ensuring that implementation module bodies only reference procedures and variables declared internal to the module.

In the case of local modules at the same level of nesting the module bodies should be considered as being executed in the sequence of their textual occurrence. You are, however, strongly advised to make the order of execution of local module bodies irrelevent by prohibiting their bodies from doing anything other than initialise objects which are local to the module. This is a fairly natural restriction since local modules should be largely self contained.

12.7 THE DESIGN OF MODULES

The design and construction of modules is intimately connected with the method of top down analysis. The two extreme types of modules are the general purpose module and the program specific module. InOut is a typical example of the first and StudentFileHandling in Chapter 10 is a typical example of the second. The philosophy of Modula-2 is that a large class of general purpose modules can be developed which help in the development of more specific modules. These modules can be shared by many Modula-2 programmers and, as time goes on, modules are available for developing programs to solve other problems more quickly and more easily.

When efficiency is an overriding criterion it may be necessary to design very specific modules to carry out certain operations. Typical examples of such operations are

> complex mathematical procedures (e.g. to solve differential equations)
> sorting and searching large data structures
> real number applications
> disk access procedures.

Such modules tend not to use other modules unless they are known to be extremely efficient. If a separately compiled module has been designed to be particularly efficient in some respect then the definition module should state its performance criteria in terms of space and time. Note that efficiency is normally a matter of the method chosen to solve the problem rather than the details of the coding, though it is possible that poor coding can produce an inefficient program from an efficient algorithm. It is part of any programmer's normal duty to ensure that his code is written in a clear and efficient manner even if the algorithm could be more efficient.

When efficiency is less important, it is normal to build programs by making as much use of existing modules as possible. If an individual programmer, or organisation, is working on developing programs in a specific field, there is a major opportunity to increase productivity by the design of suites of modules to carry out standard tasks within the field. This phenomena has occurred in the previous generation of programming languages (for example, scientific packages in FORTRAN), but Modula-2 provides exactly the facilities needed to ensure the success of such techniques.

The module StudentFileHandling, developed in chapter 10, is a suitable example of a separately compiled module for analysis. The following list considers the features of the module, before a critical appraisal is carried out

1. It uses the module SimpleFile and totally protects other modules from the details of this file handling module. A completely different file handling module could be used without changing the definition module.

2. The physical record structure of the file on disk is not known to other modules, which see a simple logical model of the student record file provided through the definition module and the available procedures for manipulating the file. In the actual implementation module the difference between the logical and physical file is slight, essentially only the existence of a header record. However, the differences could be more substantial. It is possible to construct a physical implementation which does not include the student number on the file. If this modification to the physical file is made no alterations to the definition module are required.

3. Procedures are provided which enable all likely operations on individual student records and groups of student records.

The above points indicate that the module is a coherent whole, which can be used by a programmer writing modules which use the student record file. Despite these points the module design can be improved. One criticism is that the procedures of the definition module are not all at the same design level. The procedures CreateStudentFile, ExtendStudentFile, WriteCurrentStudentList and WriteDeletionList carry out high level operations on groups of student records.

Conversely, the procedures ExtractStudent, UpdateStudentRecord and SupplyStudentDetails are lower level procedures which operate on a specified student record. These groups of procedures perform operations at different logical levels and a better design is to separate the logical levels. Two different modules can be provided. One can provide lower level operations on a specified record and the other can make available higher level procedures that do not require knowledge of the underlying structure of student records. This module can make available procedures which manipulate groups of student records but hide the underlying structure of the records. Possible procedure headings for the higher level module are given in Fig. 12.6 and can be included within a definition module. The corresponding implementation module will require the lower level module to support these operations. Each of these high level procedures performs a specific operation and requires very little knowledge of files. Only the procedure DisconnectStudentFile is typical of general file handling procedures. As the redesigned module carries out very specific operations, it is only of use in very specific situations. If other operations on the student file are required then the lower level module must be used.

A further criticism of the procedures suggested in Fig. 12.6 and the original StudentFileHandling module is that they only act on one particular named file. This is easily modified by providing an initialisation procedure which allows the physical file name to be read from the keyboard or another file.

(* Procedures which analyse groups of student records in ascending order
   of student number. *)

PROCEDURE WriteCurrentStudentList;
(* Writes out the list of current students with their details in ascending
   order of student number. *)

PROCEDURE WriteDeletionList;
(* Writes out the list of students, with their details in ascending order
   of student number, who have been part of the student list, but are no
   longer current members. *)

PROCEDURE CreateStudentFile;
(* Creates the student file ready for adding students to the file using
   ExtendStudentFile. Attempts to use other procedures before the file has
   been created will produce unpredictable results.
   FileError = the connected file existed before the program's execution. *)

PROCEDURE DisconnectStudentFile;
(* Closes and disconnects the student file. This must be called before the program using the
   student file terminates or the file will be left in an undefined state. *)

PROCEDURE ExtendStudentFile;
(* Adds new students to the student file by taking details of a student from the keyboard. A file of
    new students is created in the file StudAdd.Dat
    which are then appended to the student file. StudAdd.Dat is retained as
    a permanent file.
    FileError = StudAdd.Dat exists already. It should always be renamed or
                      deleted before calling this procedure. *)

(* Procedures which manipulate particular details of students. *)

PROCEDURE ChangeStudentNames;
(* Accepts a student number from InOut's default input channel and requests
    a change to the present name. The corresponding student details are then
    updated. The process can be repeated for any number of students. *)

PROCEDURE ChangeStudentCourses;
(* Accepts a student number from InOut's default input channel and requests
    a change to the present course. The corresponding student details are then
    updated. The process can be repeated for any number of students. *)

PROCEDURE DeleteStudents;
(* Accepts a student number from InOut's default input channel and
    logically deletes it from the file. The process can be repeated for
    any number of students. *)

PROCEDURE RestoreStudents;
(* Accepts a student number from InOut's default input channel and
    restores the student details. The process can be repeated for any
    number of students. *)

Fig. 12.6. Possible procedures for high level file access.

12.8   EXAMPLE. Lilliput University Laboratory Control System

This example is designed to illustrate the use of local and separately compiled
modules. Much of the system is grossly simplified to enable a complete
solution to be presented in the text. The most difficult part of designing such a
system is discovering what is required of the system. This is known as systems
analysis and is beyond the scope of this book. The requirements of the system
are assumed to have been determined already. The analysis which determines
the current implementation is presented purely for explanatory purposes and
in no sense constitutes a system analysis.

Lilliput Scenario

Lilliput University has one microcomputer laboratory and a resource problem regarding this equipment. There are usually more students wishing to use a microcomputer than there are microcomputers available. A supervisor has been appointed to ensure that fair play is maintained. Waiting students form a queue and whenever a student leaves a computer, the supervisor allocates it to the next student in the queue. A number of problems have arisen

1.   The supervisor finds it difficult to establish whether or not a student has the right to use the laboratory (for example, students who persistently attempt to jump the queue may be banned for a period).

2.   The students complain of wasting a lot of time queueing.

3.   Despite the efforts of the supervisor some students stay on a computer most of the day.

To improve matters Lilliput has developed the following remedies

1.   Each student is issued with a computer user number and a card with this number which gives the holder rights to use the laboratory. A file of student details (see Chapter 10 and the previous section) is held on a disk with a special flag to indicate that a student has had his access rights withdrawn. The supervisor has access to this file on a microcomputer provided for his use.

2.   A nearby room has been set aside as a study room where students can wait for a computer to become free. A student registers with the supervisor when he arrives and when a computer is available the supervisor provisionally books him to a computer and calls him. If the student does not claim the computer within a set time this provisional booking is cancelled. The queue of students is controlled from the supervisor's microcomputer by the program reporting to the supervisor the next student waiting and the number of the next available computer. Whilst a student is using a computer he temporarily gives up his card to the supervisor. This is returned to the student when he leaves the computer.

3.   When other students are waiting, a maximum time limit is set for a student to remain booked on a computer. When a student's time expires a message is automatically generated at the supervisor's microcomputer informing him that a student's time is up and that another student is waiting. The supervisor can then decide what action to take. This includes the possibility of disabling the maximum time check. The check can be enabled at any time.

The problem is to implement a suitable program to assist the supervisor. The techniques used here suffice to produce a prototype version of the complete system. The solution uses the design methods and Modula-2 constructs discussed so far.

Bottom Up Considerations

Initially, some bottom up design is in order to consider what modules are currently available and potentially useful for the solution. These include

InOut, MoreInOut	Standard input from keyboard and output to screen
StudentFileHandling	The module developed in Chapter 10 can check the validity of the student number on a student's card
QueueModule	The queue module developed in Chapter 11 can be used for two queues
	a. student's waiting for a computer
	b. unused computers waiting for a student.

At least one other separately compiled module is required to control the timing of the system. All versions of Modula-2 provide some method of doing this, but there is no standard module. Instead we postulate a definition module to supply the necessary timing procedures and assume that they are provided in the corresponding implementation module using the specific timing techniques provided by the particular Modula-2 compiler. The proposed definition module is shown in Fig. 12.7.

```
DEFINITION MODULE Timer;
            (* uses units of 10 seconds *)
    CONST
        MaxTime          = 7200; (* 20 hours *)
        MaxTimePlus      = MaxTime + 1;
        BookingTime      = 360; (* 1 hour for a student booked on a micro *)
        ConfirmationTime = 12; (* 2 minutes for a provisional booking *)
    TYPE
        Time             = [0..MaxTimePlus];

    PROCEDURE ReturnTime() : Time;
      (* Returns the difference between the current time and starting time
         in units of 10 seconds. *)

    PROCEDURE RestartTime;
      (* Initialises the starting time to zero. *)

    END Timer.
```

Fig. 12.7.

It can be argued that the timing module should be more general with the constants declared in the main module. The alternative view is taken here that this timing module is specific to this system and that all timing related data appears in this module. Note that if any change is made to the timing constants this requires recompiling the definition module and the extra re-compilations which follow from recompiling a definition module. An alternative is to declare variables rather than constants and initialise the variables in the module body of the implementation module so that altering their values only requires recompiling the implementation module. A further possibilty is to read the values for the variables from a file as part of the implementation module's body so that modifying the values only requires modifying the data in the file and no recompiling. A procedure to modify the values held in the file can be included as part of the definition module.

After establishing the facilities which are potentially useful, the solution to the problem is developed in a top down manner so as to utilise these facilities where appropriate.

Top Down Considerations

The first design decision is that the program module will be concerned with the dialogue between the program and the supervisor to provide the control for all the different aspects of the system. The only exception to this is the use of SupplyStudentDetail from StudentFileHandling which requests information from the supervisor on its own behalf. There are three main aspects to be considered in controlling the booking of student to computers

1. keeping track of students waiting for a computer.
2. keeping track of computers available to be booked to students.
3. keeping track of which computer has been booked to which student. This also involves the problem of the provisional booking of a computer to a student, and the possibility that the student may not turn up. It is important that a student is not made to leave a computer until the student provisionally booked to the computer arrives and claims his place.

Each of these sub-problems is best considered in isolation. However, there are relationships between the sub-problems. For example, a computer cannot be booked to a student whose booked time has not expired and be in the pool of available computers at the same time. Maintaining these relationships is considered to be the concern of the main module.

The isolation of the sub-problems is a natural consequence of thinking in modular terms and immediately makes the overall solution seem easier. The solution for each sub-problem can be isolated in a local module to provide the protection necessary from other parts of the solution. The modules are

1. StudentWaitPool: a group of students waiting for computers who are serviced on a first come first served basis
2. MicroPool: a pool of computers available for use. The order in which

computers are allocated is not crucial, however the wear and tear on each computer should be approximately the same.

3.   Bookings: to keep track of which student is booked to which computer and at what time the booking occurred. It also records provisional bookings and allows them to be changed to confirmed bookings if the student arrives within the time allowed for taking up a provisional booking.

The complication of the two stages when a computer is booked to a student leads to the following points.

1.   A computer can only be provisionally booked when a student is registered as waiting for a computer and one is available. Subsequently the booking can be confirmed when the student reports to the supervisor to take up the booking. If a computer is already available when the student informs the supervisor that he wants to use a computer, it can be provisionally booked and converted to a confirmed booking immediately.

2.   A computer is first provisionally booked even if no-one is currently using it. Separating provisional from confirmed bookings is important as a student using a computer may leave before the student who has been provisionally booked to it arrives.

3.   When a student, who is provisionally booked on a computer, arrives and it is still occupied by the student whose booked time has expired, the arriving student is registered as booked to the computer. When the previous occupant claims his card and the supervisor checks it in the system, a message is returned that the computer is not currently booked to that student. This is a weakness in the system (see programming exercise 7 for a proposed improvement). The weakness is in the automated part of the system; the supervisor copes easily by keeping the entitlement cards in two different groups, those allocated and those asked to leave.

A particular computer can be in one of four states
a. available (no provisional and no confirmed booking),
b. not in use and provisionally booked to a student yet to arrive (provisional booking only),
c. in use by a student whose booked time has not expired (confirmed booking only),
d. in use by a student whose booked time has expired and it is provisionally booked to another student yet to arrive (confirmed booking and provisional booking).

Figure 12.8 shows these states, the possible transitions from one state to another and the conditions under which the transitions occur. For example, a computer can be provisionally booked to a waiting student when it is booked to a student whose booked time has run out (transition 4). If the student who is provisionally booked to the computer fails to turn up in time to confirm the booking then the provisional booking is cancelled (transition 6).

The sole concern of the body of the program module is to determine what action, if any, is required. Actions may be necessary because some particular event has occurred or because the supervisor requests a particular operation.

The conditions which require continual monitoring so that the program can invoke actions to deal with them are

1.   a computer is now available to be provisionally booked to a student and the supervisor must be informed so that he can inform the student (IfPossiblePprovisionallyBookMicroToStudent),

2.   a student has not taken up his booking within the time limit (CheckForStudentNonArrival),

3.   when students are waiting to use computers, the supervisor has to be informed of the expiry of a student's time on a computer (IfNecessaryReviseBookings).

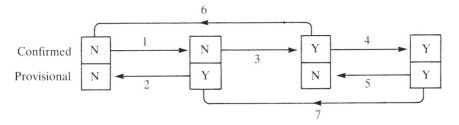

Transition	Condition
1	student arrives and available computer
2	student fails to arrive to take up provisional booking in time allowed
3	provisionally booked student arrives to take up computer
4	student's booked time expires & other students waiting
5	student fails to take up provisional booking in time allowed & booked student whose time has expired is still at the computer
6	student leaves before booked time expires
7	student leaves after booked time expires but before provisionally booked student arrives

Fig. 12.8.

In addition the supervisor has to be able to invoke operations to

1.   record a request by a student to use a computer (NewRequestForMicroByStudent),

2.   record the arrival of a provisionally booked student to take up the booking (ConfirmBooking),

3.   record the departure of a student (StudentLeavingMicro),

4.   switch on the timing out of students when others are waiting (EndUnlimitedTime),

5.   switch off the timing out of bookings when special circumstances require it (handled as a part of IfNecessaryReviseBookings).

The first four of these requests are handled by the supervisor typing single character commands at the keyboard which are read by a procedure called BusyRead. This procedure is supplied in a standard module called Terminal (see Appendix 4). It reads a character from the keyboard if one has been typed, but if no character has been typed at the keyboard it returns the null character without waiting for a character to be typed. Compare this procedure with Read which is also used in the program module for questions which insist that the supervisor replies to a question.

Figure 12.9 shows the relationship between these procedures and the transitions of Fig. 12.8. Note that the situation where a student's booked time has expired and there are other students waiting for computers (transition 4) is handled by a sequence of two procedures. IfNecessaryReviseBookings puts the computer into the pool of available computers but allows Bookings to reflect that the timed out student is still occupying the computer. IfPossibleProvisionallyBookMicroToStudent removes the computer from the pool when it is provisionally booked to the next student. In this way all provisional bookings are made from the pool of available computers without confusing operations of the Bookings module with those of the MicroPool module. The design is much cleaner if the hidden data structures and associated procedures are provided in separate modules and only used by the program module. The data structures of MicroPool and Bookings are logically separate; the existence of each does not affect the other. Thus they should not know about each other. The connection between them is via the requirements of the program module. Each can be implemented differently according to changing requirements without requiring alterations to the other.

The module Bookings must maintain a representation for the bookings of computers and provide procedures so that the progam module can achieve these state transitions for each computer. The operations which are required of the module are

Transition	Procedures in Lilliput
1	IfPossibleProvisionallyBookMicroToStudent
2	CheckForStudentNonarrival
3	ConfirmBooking
4	IfNecessaryReviseBookings
	IfPossibleProvisionallyBookMicroToStudent
5	CheckForStudentNonarrival
6	StudentLeavingMicro
7	StudentLeavingMicro

Fig. 12.9.

1. provisionally book a student to a particular computer (MakeProvisional-Booking),

2. update a booking from a provisional to a confirmed booking for a particular computer (MakeBooking),

3. cancel a provisional booking (CancelProvisionalBooking),

4. determine whether there are any bookings which have expired and if so return the student and the computer of the earliest booking (CheckForNextTimedOutBooking),

5. determine whether there are any provisional bookings which have expired and if so return the student and computer of the earliest provisional booking (CheckForNextTimedOutProvBooking),

6. terminate a confirmed booking (TerminateBooking),

7. indicate if a particular computer is currently booked (ExistsBooking),

8. indicate if a particular computer is provisionally booked for another student (ExistsProvisionalBooking).

Figure 12.10 shows how these procedures can support the required transitions.

Transition	Procedures in Bookings
1	MakeProvisionalBooking
2	CheckForNextTimedOutProvBooking
	CancelProvisionalBooking
3	MakeBooking
4	CheckForNextTimedOutBooking
	TerminateBooking
	MakeProvisionalBooking
5	CancelProvisionalBooking
6	TerminateBooking
7	TerminateBooking

Fig. 12.10.

The ability to switch on and off the timing out of confirmed bookings suggests a further local module to control this. Figure 12.11 shows a local module ControlTimingOut which provides procedures for suspending and restarting timing out of bookings, and to check whether bookings are currently being timed out or not. The implementation of this module is simplistic here, however more sophisticated alternatives can be handled inside the module.

```
MODULE ControlTimingOut;
  EXPORT RestartTimingOut,SuspendTimingOut,TimingOut;
  VAR
      TimingOutFlag : BOOLEAN; (* A flag to determine whether or not
                                   student bookings are to be terminated
                                   because other students are waiting. *)

  PROCEDURE RestartTimingOut;
  BEGIN
   TimingOutFlag := TRUE;
  END RestartTimingOut;

  PROCEDURE SuspendTimingOut;
  BEGIN
   TimingOutFlag := FALSE;
  END SuspendTimingOut;

  PROCEDURE TimingOut() : BOOLEAN ;
  BEGIN
   RETURN TimingOutFlag;
  END TimingOut;

BEGIN
  TimingOutFlag := TRUE;
END ControlTimingOut;
```

Fig. 12.11.

The program module is given in Fig. 12.12. The local modules have still to be developed, however their export lists are included in Fig. 12.12. The procedure headings of each procedure must be determined so that they can be called appropriately and are shown in the Figures indicated. The program module and its procedures also assume a separately compiled module Global-Dec which contains declarations of the types MicroRange and StudentRange. The full specification of this module is left until any further global declarations are determined. Note the advantage of using descriptive (if long) names; very few comments are required if they are chosen carefully.

```
MODULE Lilliput;
 FROM GlobalDec IMPORT (* TYPE *) MicroRange,StudentRange;
 FROM InOut IMPORT WriteLn,WriteString,Read,ReadCard,WriteCard;
 FROM MoreInOut IMPORT WriteLnString,NewCardValue,WriteStringCard;
 FROM Terminal IMPORT BusyRead;
 FROM StudentFileHandling IMPORT      (* CONST *) MaxStudent,
                              (* PROCEDURE *) SupplyStudentDetails;
 CONST
   ESC        = 33C;
   NoOfMicros = 4;
 VAR
   Ch : CHAR;


 MODULE MicroPool;
  EXPORT AvailableMicro,AddMicroToPool,NextAvailableMicro;
                  (* AS IN FIG 12.15 *)
 END MicroPool;


 MODULE StudentWaitPool;
  EXPORT AddStudentToPool,NextStudent,StudentIsWaiting,
         NoOfStudentsWaiting;
                  (* AS IN FIG 12.16 *)
 END StudentWaitPool;


 MODULE Bookings;
  EXPORT CheckForNextTimedOutBooking,  CheckForNextTimedOutProvBooking,
         TerminateBooking,             CancelProvisionalBooking,
         MakeBooking,                  MakeProvisionalBooking,
         ExistsBooking,                ExistsProvisionalBooking;
                  (* AS IN FIG 12.13 *)
 END Bookings;


 MODULE ControlTimingOut;
  EXPORT RestartTimingOut,SuspendTimingOut,TimingOut;
                  (* AS IN FIG 12.11 *)
 END ControlTimingOut;


 PROCEDURE NewRequestForMicroByStudent;
  VAR
     StudentNumber : StudentRange;
     Ans           : CHAR;
     Error         : BOOLEAN;
  BEGIN
   REPEAT
     StudentNumber := NewCardValue('Please type the student number ');
     SupplyStudentDetails(StudentNumber,Error);
     IF Error THEN
       WriteLnString('Invalid student number. ');
       Ans := 0C;
     ELSE
```

```
            WriteLnString('Is this correct? Type C or c if the answer is ');
            WriteLnString('correct, otherwise type any other character.');
            Read(Ans)
        END (* IF *);
      Ans := CAP(Ans);
      IF Ans <> 'C' THEN
        REPEAT
            WriteLnString('Do you wish to try again? Y/N ');
            Read(Ans);
            Ans := CAP(Ans);
        UNTIL (Ans = 'Y') OR (Ans = 'N');
      END (* IF *);
  UNTIL (Ans = 'C') OR (Ans = 'N');
  IF Ans = 'C' THEN
    AddStudentToPool(StudentNumber);
    IF ~AvailableMicro() THEN
      WriteLnString('The size of the student waiting list is ');
      WriteCard(NoOfStudentsWaiting(),4)
    END (* IF *)
  END (* IF *)
END NewRequestForMicroByStudent;


PROCEDURE IfNecessaryReviseBookings;
  VAR
    StudentNumber  : StudentRange;
    MicroNumber    : MicroRange;
    Ans            : CHAR;
    BookedTimeUp   : BOOLEAN;
BEGIN
  IF TimingOut() & StudentIsWaiting() & ~AvailableMicro() THEN
    CheckForNextTimedOutBooking(BookedTimeUp,StudentNumber,MicroNumber);
    IF BookedTimeUp THEN
      REPEAT
        WriteLnString("Students are waiting and a student's time is up.");
        WriteLnString("Cancel the student's booking? Y/N ");
        Read(Ans);
        Ans := CAP(Ans)
      UNTIL (Ans = 'Y') OR (Ans = 'N');
      IF Ans = 'Y' THEN
        AddMicroToPool(MicroNumber);
        WriteStringCard('Student on micro number ',MicroNumber,6);
        WriteString(' should be told to expect next student')
      ELSE
        SuspendTimingOut;
        WriteLnString('Unlimited time allowed until e or E is pressed.')
      END (* IF *)
    END (* IF BookedTimeUp *)
  END (* IF *)
END IfNecessaryReviseBookings;
```

```
PROCEDURE StudentLeavingMicro;
  (* The student chooses to leave a micro. If the booking has
     automatically been cancelled, the student is flagged as
     not being booked to the micro.*)
  VAR
      StudentNumber  : StudentRange;
      MicroNumber    : MicroRange;
      Retry,Correct  : BOOLEAN;
      Ans            : CHAR;
BEGIN
 REPEAT
      StudentNumber := NewCardValue('Type No. of the student leaving ');
      MicroNumber   := NewCardValue('Type No. of the micro vacated ');
      TerminateBooking(StudentNumber,MicroNumber,Correct);
      IF Correct THEN
          Retry := FALSE;
          WriteLnString("The student's booking has been cancelled.");
          IF ~ExistsProvisionalBooking(MicroNumber) THEN
              AddMicroToPool(MicroNumber);
          ELSE
              WriteLnString('The micro is still provisionally booked.')
          END (* IF *)
      ELSE
          WriteLnString('This student is not booked this micro.');
          REPEAT
              WriteLnString('Do you wish to repeat or quit? (R/Q)');
              Read(Ans);
              Ans := CAP(Ans);
          UNTIL (Ans = 'R') OR (Ans = 'Q');
          Retry := Ans = 'R'
      END (* IF Correct *)
 UNTIL NOT Retry
END StudentLeavingMicro;


PROCEDURE IfPossibleProvisionallyBookMicroToStudent;
 VAR
     StudentNumber  : StudentRange;
     MicroNumber    : MicroRange;
BEGIN
 IF StudentIsWaiting() & AvailableMicro() THEN
      StudentNumber := NextStudent();
      MicroNumber   := NextAvailableMicro();
      MakeProvisionalBooking(MicroNumber,StudentNumber);
      WriteStringCard('Announce that student number ',StudentNumber,5);
      WriteStringCard('is provisionally booked to micro number',
                                            MicroNumber,5);
      WriteString('.')
 END (* IF *)
END IfPossibleProvisionallyBookMicroToStudent;
```

```
PROCEDURE CheckForStudentNonarrival;
 VAR
    StudentNumber  : StudentRange;
    MicroNumber    : MicroRange;
    TimeOut        : BOOLEAN;
BEGIN
 CheckForNextTimedOutProvBooking(TimeOut,StudentNumber,MicroNumber);
 IF TimeOut THEN
       CancelProvisionalBooking(StudentNumber,MicroNumber);
       IF ~ExistsBooking(MicroNumber) THEN
          AddMicroToPool(MicroNumber)
       END (* IF *);
       WriteStringCard('Student number ',StudentNumber,6);
       WriteStringCard('has not been booked to micro number ',
                                              MicroNumber,6);
       WriteLnString('due to lack of confirmation within the time limit.')
 END (* IF *)
END CheckForStudentNonarrival;

PROCEDURE ConfirmBooking;
 VAR
    StudentNumber  : StudentRange;
    MicroNumber    : MicroRange;
    Found          : BOOLEAN;
BEGIN
 StudentNumber:=
       NewCardValue('Type student No. to complete the confirmation.');
 MakeBooking(StudentNumber,MicroNumber,Found);
 IF Found THEN
    WriteStringCard('The student is booked micro number ',MicroNumber,6)
 ELSE
    WriteLnString('The student is not booked, check the student number.')
 END (* IF *)
END ConfirmBooking;

PROCEDURE EndUnlimitedTime ;
BEGIN
 RestartTimingOut;
 WriteLnString('Normal cancellation of bookings whose times ');
 WriteString('are up will now occur.')
END EndUnlimitedTime ;

BEGIN (* Lilliput body *)
 LOOP
          (* check for a supervisor invoked action *)
     BusyRead(Ch);
     Ch := CAP(Ch);
     IF Ch = 'N' THEN
          NewRequestForMicroByStudent
```

```
        ELSIF Ch = 'L' THEN
            StudentLeavingMicro
        ELSIF Ch = 'C' THEN
            ConfirmBooking
        ELSIF Ch = 'E' THEN
            EndUnlimitedTime
        ELSIF Ch = ESC THEN
            EXIT
        END (* IF *);

            (* checks for system invoked action *)
        IfPossibleProvisionallyBookMicroToStudent;
        CheckForStudentNonarrival;
        IfNecessaryReviseBookings
    END (* LOOP *)
END Lilliput.
```

Fig. 12.12.

The Bookings **module**

The choice of a suitable representation for bookings requires some thought. If it is the case that students always use a computer until their booked time expires then the next booking to be timed out is the one which started the earliest. The behaviour required of the booking module would be that of a queue of booked computers. However, as students may leave the laboratory before their booked time expires (transition 6) and students may not arrive to confirm provisional bookings (transitions 2 and 5), the required behaviour must be more sophisticated. The data structure used in Bookings is a two-dimensional array which associates computers with students. The primary dimension of the array is the number of the computer and the second dimension is the kind of booking, provisional or confirmed. Other representations are possible which do not require that Bookings know of all computers in the laboratory when the program is compiled. The provision of a pool of available computers permits more flexible representations in Bookings to be concerned only with provisionally booked and booked computers. In this alternative framework computers can be removed from the system and further computers can be included within the system by inclusion in the pool of available computers.

Figure 12.13 shows the module Bookings. The procedure AnyStudentTimeUp linearly searches the array to find the confirmed booking or provisional booking which started earliest and then determines whether the booking should be timed out. In addition, Bookings assumes that the program module imports the separately compiled module Timer and a constant MaxMicros available in GlobalDec as well as objects already available in the program module so that Bookings can import these from the surrounding scope.

```
MODULE Bookings;
FROM Timer IMPORT      (* CONST *) MaxTime,MaxTimePlus,BookingTime,
                                   ConfirmationTime,
                       (* TYPE *)  Time,
                       (* PROCEDURE *) ReturnTime;
IMPORT (* GlobalDec *) (* CONST *) MaxMicros,
                       (* TYPE *) StudentRange,MicroRange;
IMPORT (* InOut *) WriteLn,WriteString,Read,ReadCard,WriteCard;
IMPORT NoOfMicros;
EXPORT CheckForNextTimedOutBooking,   CheckForNextTimedOutProvBooking,
       TerminateBooking,             CancelProvisionalBooking,
       MakeBooking,                  MakeProvisionalBooking,
       ExistsBooking,                ExistsProvisionalBooking;
CONST
  NoStudent      = 0; (* for the case of no student being booked. *)
  MicroNotInUse  = 0; (* for the case of a micro not being booked. *)
TYPE
  BookingKind       = (Confirmed,Provisional);
  StudentAndTime    = RECORD
                        StNumber     : StudentRange;
                        TimeAllocated : Time
                      END (* RECORD *);
  MicroBooking      = ARRAY BookingKind OF StudentAndTime;
  MicroLabBookings  = ARRAY [1..MaxMicros] OF MicroBooking;
VAR
  LabBookings    : MicroLabBookings;
  ECounter       : BookingKind;
  Counter        : CARDINAL;


(* PROCEDURES RELATED TO TIME SPENT ON A COMPUTER. *)


PROCEDURE AnyStudentTimeUp(VAR TimeUp     : BOOLEAN;
                           VAR StudNum    : StudentRange;
                           VAR MicroNum   : MicroRange;
                           WhichBooking   : BookingKind;
                           TimeLimit      : Time          );
(* Hidden procedure. Checks all bookings to find the next student
   whose booked time is up. If there is more than one, the one booked
   for the longest time is returned.
   WhichBooking = Confirmed, checks time up for confirmed bookings.
                = Provisional, checks time up for provisional
                              bookings.
   Check all bookings if provisional bookings are being considered.
   Check only bookings which do not have a provisional booking if
   confirmed bookings are being considered. *)
```

```
VAR
    PresentTime,MostTime    : Time;
    MostMicro               : MicroRange:
    Student                 : StudentRange;
    Count                   : CARDINAL;
BEGIN
    MostTime    := MaxTimePlus;
    MostMicro   := MicroNotInUse;
    Student     := NoStudent;
    FOR Count   := 1 TO NoOfMicros DO
        IF (WhichBooking = Provisional) OR
           (LabBookings[Count,Provisional].StNumber = NoStudent) THEN
            WITH LabBookings[Count,WhichBooking] DO
                IF MostTime > TimeAllocated THEN
                    MostTime  := TimeAllocated;
                    MostMicro := Count;
                    Student   := StNumber
                END (* IF *)
            END (* WITH *)
        END (* IF *)
    END(*FOR*);
    StudNum     := Student;
    MicroNum    := MostMicro;
    TimeUp := (Student <> NoStudent) &
              ((ReturnTime() - MostTime) > TimeLimit)
END AnyStudentTimeUp;

PROCEDURE CheckForNextTimedOutBooking(VAR TimeUp : BOOLEAN;
                                      VAR StudNum : StudentRange;
                                      VAR MicroNum : MicroRange    );
(* Exported procedure. *)
BEGIN
    AnyStudentTimeUp(TimeUp,StudNum,MicroNum,Confirmed,BookingTime)
END CheckForNextTimedOutBooking;

PROCEDURE CheckForNextTimedOutProvBooking(VAR TimeUp   : BOOLEAN;
                                          VAR StudNum  : StudentRange;
                                          VAR MicroNum : MicroRange);
(* Exported procedure. *)
BEGIN
    AnyStudentTimeUp(TimeUp,StudNum,MicroNum,Provisional,ConfirmationTime)
END CheckForNextTimedOutProvBooking;

(* PROCEDURES WHICH DEFINE BOOKINGS OF STUDENTS TO MICROS. *)

PROCEDURE InitStudentAndTime (VAR ThisRecord: StudentAndTime);
(* Hidden procedure. *)
BEGIN
    WITH ThisRecord DO
        StNumber := NoStudent;
```

```
    TimeAllocated := MaxTimePlus;
  END (* WITH *);
END InitStudentAndTime;


PROCEDURE CheckBooking(StudNum        : StudentRange;
                       MicroNum        : MicroRange;
                       WhichBooking  : BookingKind) : BOOLEAN;
(* Hidden procedure. TRUE: The named student is booked on the named
   micro. FALSE: Otherwise. WhichBooking determines whether the
   booking is provisional or confirmed. *)
BEGIN
  RETURN LabBookings[MicroNum,WhichBooking].StNumber = StudNum
END CheckBooking;


PROCEDURE TerminateBooking(StudNum        : StudentRange;
                           MicroNum        : MicroRange;
                           VAR Success : BOOLEAN);
(* Exported procedure. Cancels a confirmed booking of a specified
   student from a specified micro.
   Success = TRUE, if the student was booked to the micro.
           = FALSE, otherwise. *)
BEGIN
  Success := CheckBooking(StudNum,MicroNum,Confirmed);
  IF Success THEN
    InitStudentAndTime (LabBookings[MicroNum,Confirmed]);
  END (* IF *)
END TerminateBooking;


PROCEDURE CancelProvisionalBooking(StudNum : StudentRange;
                                   MicroNum : MicroRange);
(* Exported procedure. A provisional booking for a named student is
   cancelled. *)
BEGIN
  InitStudentAndTime(LabBookings[MicroNum,Provisional]);
END CancelProvisionalBooking;


PROCEDURE ExistsBooking (MicroNum : MicroRange) : BOOLEAN;
  (* Exported procedure. Returns TRUE if the specified micro is
     currently booked and in use, otherwise FALSE. *)
BEGIN
  RETURN LabBookings [MicroNum,Confirmed].StNumber <> NoStudent ;
END ExistsBooking;


PROCEDURE ExistsProvisionalBooking (MicroNum : MicroRange) : BOOLEAN;
  (* Exported procedure. Returns TRUE if the specified micro is
     provisionally booked to a student, otherwise FALSE. *)
BEGIN
  RETURN LabBookings [MicroNum,Provisional].StNumber <> NoStudent ;
END ExistsProvisionalBooking;
```

```
PROCEDURE MakeBooking(StudNum        : StudentRange;
                          VAR MicroNum : MicroRange;
                          VAR Exists      : BOOLEAN);
(* Exported procedure. Converts a provisional booking to a
   confirmed booking. Returns the number of the micro booked
   to the student, if it exists.
   Exists = TRUE, if the student was provisionally booked on a micro.
          = FALSE, otherwise. *)
  VAR
    Count : MicroRange;
BEGIN
  Exists      : = FALSE;
  Count       : = 0;
  WHILE (Count < NoOfMicros) & (~ Exists) DO
    INC(Count);
    WITH LabBookings[Count,Provisional] DO
      IF StNumber = StudNum THEN
        Exists := TRUE;
        LabBookings[Count,Confirmed].StNumber := StNumber;
        LabBookings[Count,Confirmed].TimeAllocated := TimeAllocated;
        StNumber := NoStudent;
        TimeAllocated := MaxTimePlus;
        MicroNum := Count
      ELSE
        Exists := FALSE
      END (* IF *)
    END (* WITH *)
  END (* WHILE *)
END MakeBooking;


PROCEDURE MakeProvisionalBooking(MicroNum : MicroRange;
                                   StudNum : StudentRange);
(* Exported procedure. Provisionally books the specified micro
   to the specified student. *)
BEGIN
  WITH LabBookings[MicroNum,Provisional] DO
    StNumber      := StudNum;
    TimeAllocated := ReturnTime()
  END (* WITH *)
END MakeProvisionalBooking;


BEGIN (* Bookings initialisation *)
  FOR Counter := 1 TO NoOfMicros DO
    FOR ECounter := Confirmed TO Provisional DO
      InitStudentAndTime(LabBookings[Counter,ECounter]);
    END (* FOR *)
  END (* FOR *);
END Bookings;
```

Fig. 12.13.

The StudentWaitPool, MicroPool **and** GlobalDec **Modules**

StudentWaitPool and MicroPool can be constructed using QueueModule of Chapter 11. There is a problem in allowing both MicroPool and StudentWaitPool to use queues in QueueModule as each requires its queue to hold different types of items from the other but the queues in QueueModule have to be the same types. Creating two separate copies of QueueModule would be rather extravagent and instead variant records are used to provide a solution. The declaration of the variant record is shown in the separately compiled module GlobalDec in Fig. 12.14. These objects can be imported into StudentWaitPool and MicroPool so that each can use the appropriate variant of the record for the type of items in their respective queues. Note that the variant record does not need a tag field as each module knows which variant it uses. A completely different solution to the problem of allowing a module such as QueueModule to permit queue items of different types is presented in Chapter 14.

GlobalDec has a completely dummy implementation module as all the information about the module is contained in the definition module which is shown in Fig. 12.14. Any recompilation of this module forces a recompilation of almost every module in the system.

```
DEFINITION MODULE GlobalDec;
  FROM StudentFileHandling IMPORT (* CONST *) MaxStudent;
  CONST
      MaxMicros = 100;
  TYPE
      StudentRange   = [0..MaxStudent];
      MicroRange     = [0..MaxMicros];
      WhichQueue     = (Wait,Free);
      ItemType       = RECORD
                          CASE      : WhichQueue OF
                            Wait : MicroN : MicroRange        |
                            Free : Stud    : StudentRange
                          END (* CASE *)
                       END (* RECORD *);
  END GlobalDec.
```

Fig. 12.14.

The modules MicroPool and StudentWaitPool provide the specialised procedures to operate on their respective queues. These are straightforward and their detail can be readily understood from Figs 12.15 and 12.16.

```
MODULE MicroPool;
(* Uses a queue structure as a method of controlling the micro pool. *)
 FROM QueueModule IMPORT (* TYPE *) Queue,
                     (* PROCEDURES *) AddToQueue,RemoveFromQueue,
                                 EmptyQueue,CreateQueue;
 IMPORT (* GlobalDec *) ItemType,MicroRange;
 IMPORT (* CONST *) NoOfMicros;
 EXPORT AvailableMicro,AddMicroToPool,NextAvailableMicro;
 VAR
    FreeQueue : Queue;

 PROCEDURE AddMicroToPool(MicroNum : MicroRange);
  VAR
    TempMicro : ItemType;
 BEGIN
  TempMicro.MicroN := MicroNum;
  AddToQueue(FreeQueue,TempMicro);
 END AddMicroToPool;

 PROCEDURE NextAvailableMicro() : MicroRange;
  VAR
    TempMicro : ItemType;
 BEGIN
  RemoveFromQueue(FreeQueue,TempMicro);
  RETURN TempMicro.MicroN
 END NextAvailableMicro;

 PROCEDURE AvailableMicro() : BOOLEAN;
 BEGIN
  RETURN NOT EmptyQueue(FreeQueue)
 END AvailableMicro;

 VAR
    Count : MicroRange;
 BEGIN
  CreateQueue(FreeQueue);
  FOR Count := 1 TO NoOfMicros DO
     AddMicroToPool(Count)
  END(*FOR*)
 END MicroPool;
```

Fig. 12.15.

```
MODULE StudentWaitPool;
(* Uses a queue structure as a method of controlling the student pool. *)
  FROM QueueModule IMPORT (* TYPE *) Queue,
                  (* PROCEDURES *) AddToQueue,RemoveFromQueue,
                                   EmptyQueue,LengthOfQueue,CreateQueue;
  IMPORT (* GlobalDec *) ItemType,StudentRange;
  EXPORT AddStudentToPool,NextStudent,StudentIsWaiting,
         NoOfStudentsWaiting;
  VAR
     WaitQueue : Queue;

  PROCEDURE AddStudentToPool(StudNum: StudentRange);
   VAR
     TempStudent : ItemType;
  BEGIN
   TempStudent.Stud := StudNum;
   AddToQueue(WaitQueue,TempStudent)
  END AddStudentToPool;

  PROCEDURE NextStudent() : StudentRange;
   VAR
     TempStudent : ItemType;
  BEGIN
   RemoveFromQueue(WaitQueue,TempStudent);
   RETURN TempStudent.Stud
  END NextStudent;

  PROCEDURE StudentIsWaiting() : BOOLEAN;
  BEGIN
   RETURN NOT EmptyQueue(WaitQueue)
  END StudentIsWaiting;

  PROCEDURE NoOfStudentsWaiting() : CARDINAL;
  BEGIN
   RETURN LengthOfQueue(WaitQueue)
  END NoOfStudentsWaiting;

BEGIN
 CreateQueue(WaitQueue)
END StudentWaitPool;
```

Fig. 12.16.

Figure 12.17 shows the module structure of the program module and its
local modules and their import and export lists which indicate the relationship
between modules. When the completed modules are substituted for these
abbreviated modules, the completed program is a modular solution to a
non-trivial problem.

```
MODULE Lilliput;
  IMPORT Timer;          (* For Bookings *)
  IMPORT QueueModule;  (* For MicroPool and StudentWaitPool *)
  FROM GlobalDec IMPORT (* CONST *) MaxMicros,
                        (* TYPE *) MicroRange,StudentRange,ItemType;
  FROM InOut IMPORT WriteLn,WriteString,Read,ReadCard,WriteCard;
  FROM MoreInOut IMPORT WriteLnString,NewCardValue,WriteStringCard;
  FROM Terminal IMPORT BusyRead;
  FROM StudentFileHandling IMPORT (* CONST *) MaxStudent,
                        (* PROCEDURE *) SupplyStudentDetails;
CONST
  ESC       = 33C;
  NoOfMicros = 4;
VAR
  Ch : CHAR;

MODULE MicroPool;
  FROM QueueModule IMPORT (* TYPE *) Queue,
                  (* PROCEDURES *) AddToQueue,RemoveFromQueue,
                                   EmptyQueue,CreateQueue;
  IMPORT (* GlobalDec *) ItemType,MicroRange;
  IMPORT (* CONST *) NoOfMicros;
  EXPORT AvailableMicro,AddMicroToPool,NextAvailableMicro;
                  (* AS IN FIG 12.15 *)
END MicroPool;

MODULE StudentWaitPool;
  FROM QueueModule IMPORT (* TYPE *) Queue,
                  (* PROCEDURES *) AddToQueue,RemoveFromQueue,
                                   EmptyQueue,LengthOfQueue,CreateQueue;
  IMPORT (* GlobalDec *) ItemType,StudentRange;
  EXPORT AddStudentToPool,NextStudent,StudentIsWaiting,
          NoOfStudentsWaiting;
                  (* AS IN FIG 12.16 *)
END StudentWaitPool;

MODULE Bookings;
  FROM Timer IMPORT (* CONST *) MaxTime,MaxTimePlus,BookingTime,
                                ConfirmationTime,
                  (* TYPE *) Time,
                  (* PROCEDURE *) ReturnTime;
  IMPORT (* GlobalDec *) (* CONST *) MaxMicros,
                        (* TYPE *) StudentRange,MicroRange;
  IMPORT (* InOut *) WriteLn,WriteString,Read,ReadCard,WriteCard;
  IMPORT NoOfMicros;
  EXPORT CheckForNextTimedOutBooking,  CheckForNextTimedOutProvBooking,
          TerminateBooking,             CancelProvisionalBooking,
          MakeBooking,                  MakeProvisionalBooking,
          ExistsBooking,                ExistsProvisionalBooking;
                  (* AS IN FIG 12.13 *)
```

```
END Bookings;

MODULE ControlTimingOut;
  EXPORT RestartTimingOut,SuspendTimingOut,TimingOut;
                    (* AS IN FIG 12.11 *)
  END ControlTimingOut;
                    (* AS IN FIG 12.12 *)
  END Lilliput.
```

Fig. 12.17.

The solution to this problem utilises existing modules and data structures for some sub-problems, and the development of problem specific modules and data structures such as Bookings for other sub-problems. This is typical. Most problems are solved by a combination of already developed code and some specialised code.

Testing Lilliput

The testing of Lilliput is an interesting exercise. A proposed testing sequence is
1. test StudentWaitPool using techniques from Chapters 5 and 6,
2. test MicroPool similarly,
3. test Bookings in the following steps
   a. test that the timing procedures work by writing a special test program to use them,
   b. test the booking procedures using the timing procedures.
   Note that these tests can be carried out by treating Bookings as a main module.
4. test the complete module in stages. In the main module body a suitable ordering of tests is the natural ordering of events in the system
   a. students arriving
   b. students leaving
   c. confirmation of a provisional booking
   d. a student leaving
   e. all computers in use
   f. a queue of waiting students formed
   g. a student leaves
   h. time out of a student
   j. computers are freed for further bookings by non-confirmation or a student leaving.

It is an interesting exercise to design a sequence of events to test each of these cases.

12.9 SUMMARY

This chapter has introduced the important construct of the local module. Local modules are a structuring construct with the advantages of implementation modules for hiding objects within them and only exporting the necessary detail to the other parts of the program. Local modules, however, are embedded within other modules and therefore cannot be compiled separately. They are important for modularising a program where there appears to be no benefit from compiling the modules separately.

Local modules have implications for the scope rules of the language. Essentially the scope rules for local modules prohibit a local module from referencing objects declared outside of it except those listed in its import lists. In addition, a local module may increase the scope of objects which are in scope in the module to the surrounding block by including them in its export list. The export list of a local module serves a similar purpose as the definition module of an implementation and definition module pair. However, because a local module is embedded within a module which uses it, the export list does not have to give full details of the object's declaration as in a definition module.

Import and export lists have several forms which determine how objects which have been imported or exported can be referenced. These are summarised in Figs 12.3 and 12.4.

The program Lilliput provides a prototype solution to Lilliput University's utilisation of their computer laboratory. Though the program tackles only a subset of the difficulties that can occur, it is the most important program in this book. It exemplifies the advantages of modules as the major structuring construct of Modula-2.

TECHNICAL EXERCISES

1   Decide whether or not the following statements are true, and in the case of false statements say why they are false.

a Local modules can automatically use any object which is scope in the block containing the module's declaration.

b A module can automatically use objects declared within a module local to it.

c A local module can use any object in scope in the surrounding module.

d Two local modules declared within the same module and at the same level cannot use objects declared in the other.

e Implementation modules can declare local modules.

f A local module can contain an implementation or definition module.

g A local module can import a separately compiled module even though its surrounding scope does not use the module.

h If an object is exported in qualified mode the object has to be qualified to reference it.

j An object exported from a local module can be referenced in qualified or unqualified mode.

PROGRAMMING EXERCISES

1   Write and incorporate into the program Lilliput procedures which allow the supervisor to determine how many computers are free at a given time and how many students are waiting for computers.

2   As it stands the system allows the same student to be booked to many computers. This is only prevented by the manual card system. Implement an upgraded system which restricts each student to one computer and does not allow the student to be simultaneously booked a computer and be in the queue of students waiting for a computer.

3   Develop a facility for the supervisor to be able to change the booked time for any particular computer. The supervisor should be able to extend or curtail a particular student's stay at a micro.

4   The modules MicroPool and StudentWaitPool are almost identical. Take advantage of this to rewrite the program so that both modules are replaced by one module to do both jobs by declaring the procedures it provides to take an extra parameter determining which queue to use. Do you prefer this solution?

5   It is a mistake to assume that all computers work all the time. Implement facilities for the supervisor to be able to specify that certain computers are unavailable.

6   If the maximum time that a student can provisionally book a computer is reasonably long, it is prudent to allow cancellation of a provisional booking. Implement a facility to allow the supervisor to cancel provisional bookings at the request of a student. If the student is also allowed to cancel a request for a computer, consider the changes needed to the design.

7   A flaw in the design is pointed out in the text. It appears when a student has been automatically deallocated from a computer and then comes to reclaim the entitlement card. Try correcting this by using the ordered list

module of Chapter 11 to hold a list of students who have been automatically deallocated and have not yet collected their card. Reconsider your solution after reading the next chapter.

8 Lilliput's rival is Brobdingnag University which is implementing a similar system. The main difference is that a typical laboratory contains 2000 microcomputers. Redesign the module Bookings to permit efficient searching of a data structure representing a large number of computers. (Chapter 13 suggests some sophisticated data structures that may help if you cannot think of appropriate solutions currently.)

9 An alternative starting point in developing a solution for Lilliput's problem is to orient the solution around the state that a student is in at any given moment rather than the present orientation around the bookings of computers. Design a solution to the problem using this idea.

ANSWERS

1 **a** false, the objects must be explicitly imported into the module.
b false, the objects must be explicitly exported from the local module.
c true, if the object is explicitly imported into the local module.
d false, they can if they are exported from one local module to the surrounding module and then imported into the other local module.
e true, but the definition module cannot make local modules available to other modules in their entirety.
f false, declarations of separately compiled modules are at the same scope level as the main module.
g true, but the separately compiled module must be imported into the surrounding module even though this does not use it. A local module cannot import from a separately compiled module without the module being imported into the module surrounding the local module.
h true, unless a FROM version of an import list unqualifies it or a WITH statement is used to temporarily allow unqualified reference inside its statement sequence.
j true, unless it was exported in qualified mode.

Chapter 13

Recursion and Advanced
Use of Procedures

Chapter 11 discussed the use of pointers for creating and maintaining dynamic data structures. The focus was on the data structure called a **linked list**. In this chapter the idea of **recursion** is introduced and the discussion uses linked lists to illustrate recursive data structures. A further recursive data structure known as a **tree** is discussed.

The chapter also introduces facilities allowing procedures to be stored in variables and for passing them as parameters to other procedures.

13.1 RECURSION

The abstract idea of a list can be characterised as consisting of either
a.   an empty list, denoted by [],
b.   a pair comprising a head and a tail. The head is the value of the first item in the list and the tail is a sublist consisting of the remaining items in the list. We denote this pair as [head tail].
For example

 [5 [8 [12 [10 []]]]]

denotes a list of four numbers. The head of the entire list is the value 5, and the tail is the sublist

 [8 [12 [10 []]]]

which consists of a head, the value 8, and a tail, the sublist

 [12 [10 []]]

The tail of this sublist consists of a head which is the value 10 and a tail which is an empty list.

This characterisation of a list embodies the fundamental ideas of a recursive definition. The part of the definition that states that the tail of the list is itself a list refers to its own definition. In order that such a definition is not entirely circular there must be a terminating property. In the above definition this is the characterisation of an empty list which is not defined in terms of other characteristics of lists, but in terms of a particular value which indicates the end of a list. As the study of infinite structures is outside the scope of this book there will always be some value to indicate the end of a recursive structure.

We have already seen an example of a recursive definition in Chapter 11, where pointers were used to implement a list as a linked structure. The linked list data structure involved the following type declaration

```
TYPE
    NodePntr    = POINTER TO Node ;
    Node        = RECORD
                    Value    : ItemType ;
                    NextNode : NodePntr
                  END ;
```

The type Node is defined in terms of itself through the NextNode field which is a pointer to another object of type Node. By declaring a variable of type NodePntr

```
VAR
    OneList : NodePntr ;
```

and by using the predefined procedure NEW, a sequence of nodes can be created and organised into the list illustrated in Fig. 13.1. The recursive nature of this structure can be made more explicit if the above declarations are rewritten as

```
TYPE
    LIST    = POINTER TO Node ;
    Node    = RECORD
                Head : ItemType ;
                Tail : LIST
              END ;
```

so that it is explicitly stated that the Tail field of the node also refers to a list.

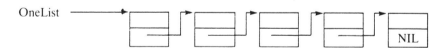

OneList

Fig. 13.1.

The essentials of a recursive definition are

1.   that the thing is defined in terms of itself. In the case of this linked implementation of a list, a list is defined as a value and a pointer to a further list,

2.   a terminating value, which can be used to indicate the end of a recursive structure. In the case of Modula-2 dynamic data structures implemented as pointers, this is the value NIL. In effect, NIL represents the empty list in a linked implementation of a list.

The second requirement prohibits the following declaration

```
TYPE
      InvalidList = RECORD
                         Head : ItemType ;
                         Tail : InvalidList
                         END ;
```

as no value can be stored in Tail to indicate the end of the list. In Modula-2 recursive data structures must be declared in terms of pointers so that NIL can be used to indicate the end of a recursive structure.

Data structures which have a recursive definition can be processed by **recursive procedures**. A recursive procedure is one which includes within the body of the procedure a call to itself. Typically, a recursive procedure looks like

```
PROCEDURE RecursiveProc (Any,Parameters : WhateverType) ;
BEGIN
  (*... ...*) ;
  RecursiveProc (Some,Parameters) ;
  (*... ...*) ;
 END RecursiveProc ;
```

For example, if a procedure is required to write out the value of each item in a list then this can be formulated recursively as a procedure which writes out the value in the head of the list and then calls itself to write out the tail of the

```
PROCEDURE WriteOut ( ( *... list ...*) ) ;
BEGIN
  IF (*... the list is not empty ...*) THEN
      (*... Write out the value of the head of the list ...*) ;
      WriteOut ( ( *... the tail of the list ...*) ) ;
  END (* IF *) ;
END WriteOut ;
```

(a)

```
PROCEDURE WriteOut (VAR ThisList : LIST) ;
BEGIN
  IF ThisList <> NIL THEN
      WriteCard (ThisList∧.Head,10) ;
      WriteOut (ThisList∧.Tail)
  END (* IF *)
END WriteOut ;
```

(b)

Fig. 13.2.

list. Figure 13.2 shows a recursive procedure WriteOut to write out a list of CARDINAL values. WriteOut calls itself recursively to write out the tail of each sublist. Each call of the procedure treats the sublist it is given as a list in its own right, writes out the value of the Head field of the first node and then calls itself to write out the sublist referenced by the Tail field. Eventually one of the calls of WriteOut is given an empty list to write out, the value of the actual parameter is NIL, and no further recursive calls are made.

Figure 13.3b shows the sequence of recursive procedure calls when WriteOut is used to write out the values of the list and sublists shown in Fig. 13.3a. The notation for the abstract list is used to denote the lists passed to calls of the procedure, though in reality only the pointers to (sub-)lists are actually passed to the procedure. In Fig. 13.3b indentation is used to indicate that execution of the procedure is restarted on a new list. The recursive calls terminate on a 'last to start first to finish' basis, so that the order in which recursive calls terminate is the reverse of the order in which they started.

Just as recursive definitions of the data structure require a terminating value, a recursive procedure requires a terminating condition to prevent the procedure calling itself forever. In this case the terminating condition is when ThisList references an empty list indicated by the value NIL. In order that the procedure eventually stops recursively calling itself, it is necessary that each recursive call makes some progress towards this terminating condition. In this example WriteOut is called on the tail of the list passed as the formal parameter so that eventually the terminating condition is achieved.

The recursion in WriteOut is known as **tail recursion** because the recursive call occurs as the last statement executed in WriteOut. Tail recursive procedures can usually be written easily as iterative procedures using a repetitive construct. An iterative version of WriteOut is shown in Fig. 13.4. SubList is a travelling pointer which references each of the nodes of the list in turn.

In the recursive version of the procedure the parameter ThisList provides access to the list. When the recursive version calls itself the previous value for ThisList is not lost. The previous values of ThisList are automatically held on a stack by the Modula-2 run-time system, so that when an inner call of the procedure is finished the appropriate value of ThisList for the calling block is accessible. This has little consequence for tail recursive procedures. However, consider the procedure ReverseWriteOut in Fig. 13.5 where the recursive call is made before the value of the node is written out. The effect of this procedure is for the recursive calls to dive down to the end of the list and then to write out the value in each node as each of the recursive calls comes to

[5 [8 [12 [10 []]]]]

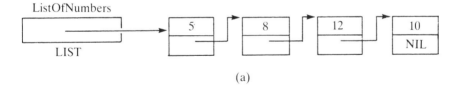

ListOfNumbers

(a)

WriteOut ([5 [8 [12 [10 []]]]]) ;

    WriteCard (5,10) ;
    WriteOut ([8 [12 [10 []]]]) ;

        WriteCard (8,10) ;
        WriteOut ([12 [10 []]]) ;

            WriteCard (12,10) ;
            WriteOut ([10 []]) ;

                WriteCard (10,10) ;
                WriteOut ([]) ;

                ThisList = [] so
                  do nothing
            WriteOut returns control to place where it was called
         WriteOut returns control to place where it was called
      WriteOut returns control to place where it was called
   WriteOut returns control to place where it was called
WriteOut returns control to place where it was called

(b) Recursive calls of WriteOut.

Fig. 13.3.

```
PROCEDURE IterativeWriteOut (VAR ThisList : LIST) ;
VAR
    SubList : LIST ;
BEGIN
 SubList := ThisList ;
 WHILE SubList <> NIL DO
     WriteCard (SubList∧.Head,10) ;
     SubList := SubList∧.Tail
 END (* WHILE *)
END IterativeWriteOut ;
```

Fig. 13.4.

completion. As a consequence the values in the list are written out in reverse order. Figure 13.6 shows this diagramatically, again the parameters are represented by the abstract representation of the list rather than the actual pointers.

```
PROCEDURE ReverseWriteOut (VAR ThisList : LIST) ;
BEGIN
    IF ThisList <> NIL THEN
        ReverseWriteOut (ThisList∧.Tail) ;
        WriteCard (ThisList∧.Head,10) ;
    END (* IF *)
END ReverseWriteOut ;
```

Fig. 13.5.

ReverseWriteOut ([5 [8 [12 [10 []]]]]) ;

    ReverseWriteOut ([8 [12 [10 []]]]) ;

        ReverseWriteOut ([12 [10 []]]) ;

            ReverseWriteOut ([10 []]) ;

                ReverseWriteOut ([]) ;

                    ThisList = [] so
                    do nothing
                ReverseWriteOut returns control to where it was called

            WriteCard (10,10) ;
            ReverseWriteOut returns control to where it was called

        WriteCard (12,10) ;
        ReverseWriteOut returns control to where it was called

    WriteCard (8,10) ;
    ReverseWriteOut returns control to where it was called

WriteCard (5,10) ;
ReverseWriteOut returns control to where it was called

    Recursive calls of ReverseWriteOut preceding calls to WriteCard

Fig. 13.6.

In Chapter 11 the module OrderedList contained a procedure Insert for inserting an item into a list at its correct position. Figure 13.7 shows a recursive procedure, InsertInList, which performs the same operation. InsertInList calls itself recursively until the appropriate position is found in the list. Further recursive calls are prevented if

1. the head of the list given as the parameter is less than the item to be inserted
2. the end of the lists is found.

For example, assume that ItemType is declared to be the type CARDINAL and that a variable ListOfNumbers currently references an ordered list of CARDINAL values which is equivalent to the abstract list [5 [8 [10 [12 []]]]]. A call

> InsertInList (9,ListOfNumbers)

creates a new node to hold the value 9 and incorporates this node in the list between the nodes holding the values 8 and 10. Figure 13.8 shows the sequence of calls of InsertInList as this is achieved. The variable parameter ThisList is indicated by a broken arrow to the variable or field of a record to which it gives direct access. Each time the procedure is called a new copy of ThisList is created which holds a pointer to a particular node in the structure. Thislist gives direct access back to the pointer to the entire list on the first call and to the Tail fields of nodes on subsequent recursive calls. Note that when the appropriate position has been found and the new node has been created, the assignment to the formal **variable** parameter ThisList updates the pointer to the (sub-)list in order to incorporate the new node in the list. This relies on Thislist being a variable parameter.

```
PROCEDURE InsertInList (Item : ItemType ; VAR ThisList : LIST) ;
VAR
      NewList : LIST ;
BEGIN
  IF (ThisList = NIL) OR NOT(LessThan (ThisList∧.Head,Item)) THEN
      NEW (NewList) ;
      WITH NewList∧ DO
            Head := Item ;
            Tail := ThisList ;
      END (* WITH *) ;
      ThisList := NewList ;
  ELSE
      InsertInList (Item,ThisList∧.Tail) ;
  END (* IF *) ;
END InsertInList ;
```

Fig. 13.7.

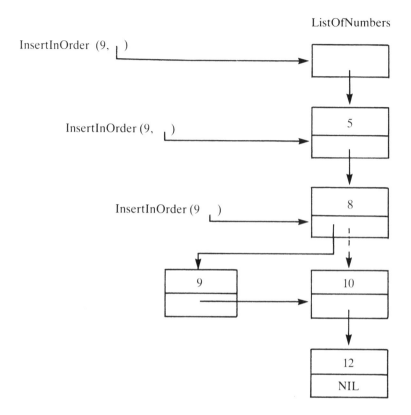

InsertInOrder returns control to place where it was
called with new item inserted in list

InsertInOrder returns control to place where it was called

InsertInOrder returns control to place where it was called

Fig. 13.8.

To summarise,

1. recursive data structures are data structures which are defined in terms of themselves. They require a terminating value which indicates the end of the structure. In Modula-2 these can be implemented as structures using pointers with the value NIL as the terminating value.

2. a recursive procedure is one which calls itself. The procedure must include a terminating condition which prevents it calling itself forever. Each recursive call must pass as actual parameters some modified version of its formal parameters so that progress is made towards the terminating condition.

13.2 RECURSIVE DATA STRUCTURES — TREES

Lists are the most straight forward example of a recursive data structure, and recursive procedures which operate upon them can normally be easily re-formulated as iterative procedures using repetitive statements. Other classes of recursive data structures are more complex and recursive procedures to operate upon them are both more natural and easier to formulate than iterative versions. One such class of data structure is known as a **tree**. A tree is a data structure where each node has only one other node which refers to it, but which may refer to several other nodes. The node which gives access to another node is known as its parent node, and the nodes which it gives access to are known as its children nodes (see Fig. 13.9). A linked list can be viewed as a special kind of tree where each node has only one child node.

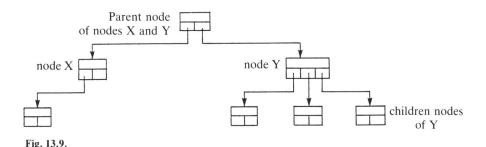

Fig. 13.9.

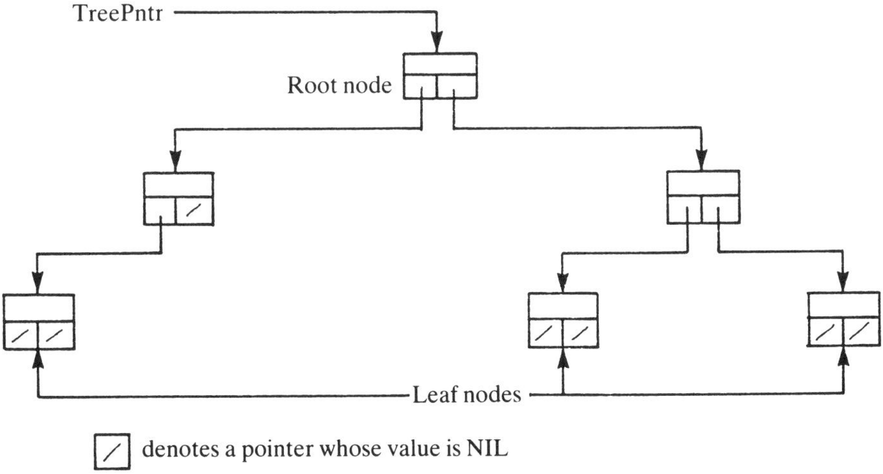

Fig. 13.10.

Discussion will be limited to trees where each node has at most two branches leading from it. Such trees are called **binary trees** (see Fig. 13.10). A tree has one special node known as the **root** of the tree which provides access into the entire tree. Nodes which have no branches leading from them are called **leaf nodes**. Like the special case of the empty list there is a special case of an empty tree which is a tree which does not have a root node. By convention the root is drawn at the top and leaf nodes at the bottom.

Binary trees are constructed using recursive type declarations such as those in Fig. 13.11. The LeftSubTree and RightSubTree fields of a node point to nodes which can be viewed as root nodes of subtrees. Leaf nodes are merely subtrees without any further subtrees hanging from them. An empty tree is represented by a pointer variable or field holding the value NIL.

```
TYPE
        TREE            = POINTER TO Node ;
        Node            = RECORD
                            Item            : ItemType ;
                            LeftSubTree     ,
                            RightSubTree  : TREE
                          END ;
VAR
        OneTree       : TREE ;
```

Fig. 13.11.

One use of a binary tree is to maintain an ordered list efficiently. Recall that a problem with linked lists is how to insert a new item. If the list is ordered then finding the appropriate position can be an expensive operation in terms of computation time. Locating the appropriate position in a binary tree is usually more efficient, though this cannot be guaranteed as the order in which items are inserted affects the efficiency.

One common way of maintaining a tree as an ordered list is to insist that, at all times

1.   all the items in the left subtree hanging from a node are less than or equal to the item in the node,

2.   all the items in the right subtree hanging from a node are greater than the item in the node.

If this is true of all nodes in the tree then the tree is ordered such that nodes down LeftSubTree pointers have priority over the information in a particular node which in turn has priority over nodes down RightSubTree pointers (see Fig. 13.12).

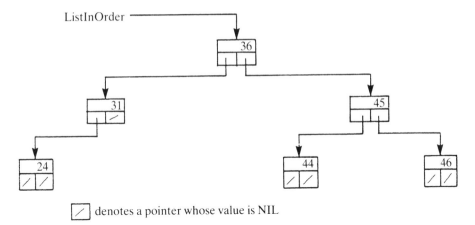

ListInOrder

△ denotes a pointer whose value is NIL

Fig. 13.12.

Insertion of an item into the tree requires
a. finding the position in the tree where the new node is to be inserted
b. creating a new node
c. altering the pointers in the tree to include the new node in the tree.

The position in the tree at which a new item is inserted is determined by the rules
1. if the subtree is empty then
    create a node for the new item
    and hang it from the subtree
2. if the new item = the item in this node in the tree then
    handle case where the item is already in the tree
3. if the new item < the item in this node in the tree then
    insert the new item in the subtree hanging from
            this node's LeftSubTree field
4. if the new item > the item in this node in the tree then
    insert the new item in the subtree hanging from
            this node's RightSubTree field

Figure 13.13 shows the development of these rules into a procedure InsertInTree which inserts an item in its correct position in an ordered tree. It assumes the declaration

    TYPE
        ItemType = CARDINAL ;

and the declaration of a variable which accesses a valid tree which can be passed to it

VAR
    ListInOrder : TREE ;

InsertInTree relies on the pointer to a (sub)tree being passed as a variable parameter so that, when the (sub)tree is found to be empty, assignment of a value to the formal parameter by the call of NEW causes the corresponding actual parameter to point at the newly created subtree. The reason NewItem is a variable parameter is to prevent multiple copies of the item being created, one each time InsertInTree is called. With some modifications which are discussed in following sections InsertInTree is incorporated in the module OrderedList shown in Figs 13.22 and 13.23.

```
PROCEDURE InsertInTree (VAR ThisTree : TREE ;
                        VAR NewItem : ItemType) ;
BEGIN
 IF ThisTree = NIL THEN
  (*... create a node for the item
      and hang it from ThisTree ...*)
 ELSIF NewItem = ThisTree∧.Item THEN
  (*... cope with duplicate ...*)
 ELSIF NewItem < ThisTree∧.Item THEN
      InsertInTree (ThisTree∧.LeftSubTree,NewItem)
 ELSE (* NewItem > ThisTree∧.Item *)
      InsertInTree (ThisTree∧.RightSubTree,NewItem)
 END (* IF *)
END InsertInTree ;
```

(a)

```
PROCEDURE InsertInTree (VAR ThisTree : TREE ;
                        VAR NewItem : ItemType) ;
BEGIN
 IF ThisTree = NIL THEN
      NEW (ThisTree) ;
      WITH ThisTree∧ DO
          Item                := NewItem ;
          LeftSubTree     := NIL ;
          RightSubTree    := NIL ;
      END (* WITH *) ;
 ELSIF NewItem = ThisTree∧.Item THEN
      (* cope with duplicate *)
 ELSIF NewItem < ThisTree∧.Item THEN
      InsertInTree (ThisTree∧.LeftSubTree,NewItem)
 ELSE (* Item > ThisTree∧.Item *)
      InsertInTree (ThisTree∧.RightSubTree,NewItem)
 END (* IF *)
END InsertInTree ;
```

(b)

Fig. 13.13.

13.3 PROCEDURE TYPES AND PROCEDURE VARIABLES

In Modula-2 procedure types can be declared and variables can be declared to hold procedures. In addition, procedures can be passed as actual parameters to other procedures. This later facility allows a procedure which takes a procedural parameter to be passed different procedures and so use different procedures on different invocations. These facilities allow procedures to be manipulated in very flexible ways.

Procedure types are declared by a type specification which looks similar to a procedure heading but with the names of the procedure and parameters omitted. For example

```
TYPE
    ProcCard1 = PROCEDURE (CARDINAL) ;
```

declares ProcCard1 to be the type for all procedures which have one formal CARDINAL value parameter.

Variables can be declared to hold procedures in the usual ways, either by using a type identifier or by specifying the type in full in the variable declaration, for example

```
VAR
    Fred    : ProcCard1 ;
    Joe     : PROCEDURE (CARDINAL,CARDINAL) ;
    Bill    : PROCEDURE (VAR CARDINAL,REAL) ;
    Bob     : PROCEDURE (TREE) : TREE ;
```

Fred is a variable which can hold a procedure that has one formal value parameter whose type is CARDINAL. Joe is a variable which can hold a procedure which has two formal value parameters of type CARDINAL. Bill is a variable which can hold a procedure which has two formal parameters, the first is a CARDINAL variable parameter and the second a REAL value parameter. Bob is a variable which can hold a function procedure with one formal parameter of type TREE and this returns a result of the same type. The syntax diagrams for procedure type specifications are shown in Fig. 13.14. Note that in the specification of a procedure type, procedure and parameter names do not occur.

Once variables for holding procedures have been declared, assignment statements can be used to store procedures in variables. The procedure which is stored in a variable must conform with the type of the variable in terms of the numbers and types of parameters, and whether it returns a result or not. Assuming the declarations in Fig. 13.15a the assignment statements in Fig.

Procedure Type :

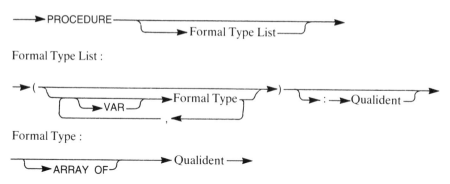

Formal Type List :

Formal Type :

Fig. 13.14.

13.15b are valid whereas that shown in Fig. 13.15c is invalid because SquareR-
oot has one REAL formal parameter and returns a REAL result but Pete can only
hold a function procedure which has one CARDINAL formal parameter and
returns a CARDINAL result.

```
TYPE
      FuncCard1 = PROCEDURE (CARDINAL) : CARDINAL ;
VAR
      Pete       : FuncCard1 ;

PROCEDURE Square (X : CARDINAL) : CARDINAL ;
BEGIN (*... ...*)
END Square ;

PROCEDURE Cube (X : CARDINAL) : CARDINAL ;
BEGIN (*... ...*)
END Cube ;

PROCEDURE SquareRoot (X : REAL) : REAL ;
BEGIN (*... ...*)
END SquareRoot ;
```

(a)

```
Pete := Square                    Pete := SquareRoot
Pete := Cube
```

(b)   (c)

Fig. 13.15.

A procedure stored in a procedure variable can be called by reference to the variable, for example

```
X := Pete (3)
```

calls the procedure currently held in Pete with 3 as the actual parameter and assigns the result of the function procedure to X. Assuming that Pete holds the procedure Square this causes Square to be called and 9 to be assigned to X. The statement sequence

```
Pete := Square ;
WriteCard (Pete (3),6) ;
Pete := Cube ;
WriteCard (Pete (3),6) ;
```

writes out the square of 3 and then the cube of 3.

It is an error to try to call a procedure via a procedure variable before a procedure has been assigned to the variable.

The assignment statement

```
Pete := Square
```

does not call the procedure Square, it simply assigns it to the variable Pete. A call of a function procedure which has no formal parameters requires an empty actual parameter. This distinguishes a call of a function procedure from assignment of a procedure to a procedure variable. For example

```
X := RandomNumber ()
```

calls the function procedure RandomNumber, whereas

```
ProcVar := RandomNumber
```

stores the procedure in ProcVar, assuming that it has been suitably declared.

The procedure type PROC is a standard type defined in the language for a parameterless procedure and is equivalent to

```
TYPE
      PROC = PROCEDURE ;
```

Procedure variables which can hold procedures that have an open array formal value parameter are very useful. For example a variable declaration

```
VAR
      ProcOnArrayOfChars : PROCEDURE (ARRAY OF CHAR) ;
```

can hold any procedure which requires an array of characters to be given as its actual parameter, such as WriteString or WriteLnString.

13.4 PROCEDURAL PARAMETERS AND REVISIONS TO OrderedList

In this section the OrderedList module of Chapter 11 is reconsidered. The major modifications to the module are that the idea of a current node is removed and that programming techniques using recursion, procedure variables and procedural parameters are used instead. In addition, the OrderedList module of Chapter 11 is less useful than it might be, because it is oriented towards the product description problem. This problem itself has been over-simplified by declaring the data associated with a product description to be a character array. It is more usual in such problems for the data to be represented by a record with several fields of different types. For example, the type ItemType is more realistically illustrated in Fig. 13.16.

```
TYPE
    ItemType        = RECORD
                        Description      : ARRAY [0..29] OF CHAR ;
                        Code             : ARRAY [0..5] OF CHAR ;
                        QuantityInStock  ,
                        ReorderLevel     : CARDINAL ;
                        Supplier         : ARRAY [0..49] OF CHAR ;
                      END (* RECORD *) ;
```

Fig. 13.16.

Use of Procedure Variables

In the previous formulation, procedures which insert an item in the data structure embody a test to determine where the item should be inserted, but this test is dependent upon the types of the values stored in the nodes. In the case of ProductDescriptions the list is maintained as an alphabetical ordering of descriptions and the test has to compare two character arrays. If the list consisted of CARDINAL values then the required test would be a CARDINAL 'less than' test. This problem can be overcome by

1. writing InsertInTree to call a procedure held in a procedure variable to determine the ordering. This allows the ordering procedure to be changed without altering the code of InsertInTree.

2. providing a further procedure in OrderedList to assign to the procedure variable a procedure declared in the importing module. In this way InsertInTree becomes part of a general ordering module where the required ordering is determined by the importing module.

The rest of this chapter is devoted to demonstrating how this can be achieved in practice.

Assume the declaration of a procedure type in OrderedList's definition module

```
TYPE
      Proc2ItemsBool = PROCEDURE (VAR ItemType,
                                  VAR ItemType) : BOOLEAN ;
```

and a variable Ordering declared in OrderedList's implementation module

```
VAR
      Ordering        : Proc2ItemsBool ;
```

InsertInTree can be defined to call the procedure stored in Ordering to determine if one item is ordered before another as shown in Fig. 13.17a.

```
PROCEDURE InsertInTree (VAR ThisTree : TREE ;
                             VAR Item : ItemType) ;
BEGIN
  IF  ThisTree = NIL  THEN
      NEW (ThisTree) ;
      WITH ThisTree ∧ DO
              Item                := NewItem ;
              LeftSubTree      := NIL ;
              RightSubTree     := NIL ;
      END (∗ WITH ∗) ;
  ELSIF  Ordering (Item,ThisTree ∧ .Item)  THEN
      InsertInTree (ThisTree ∧ .LeftSubTree,Item)
  ELSE
      InsertInTree (ThisTree ∧ .RightSubTree,Item)
  END (∗ IF ∗)
END InsertInTree ;
```

(a)

```
PROCEDURE  Insert  (NewItem : ItemType) ;
BEGIN
 InsertInTree (ListInOrder,NewItem)
END Insert ;
```

(b)

Fig. 13.17.

InsertInTree has to be given a tree as a parameter so that it can pass subtrees to recursive calls of itself. This means that InsertInTree cannot be made available outside the module because initially it must be passed ListInOrder which is local to the implementation module. Consequently a further procedure is needed which is available outside the module and which is only passed the item as a parameter. This procedure then calls InsertInTree passing the pointer to the root node as the parameter (see Fig. 13.17b).

It is also of note that Insert's formal parameter is a value parameter so that it creates a copy of the actual parameter thereby permitting constants as well as variables to be passed to be inserted in the tree. However, InsertInTree's formal parameter NewItem is a variable parameter providing a reference back to the variable created for Insert's formal parameter NewItem, thus avoiding creating multiple copies of the item during recursive calls.

Procedural Parameters

In order to allow Ordering to hold a procedure declared outside of the OrderedList's implementation module, it is necessary to provide another procedure which can take a procedure as a parameter and assign this to Ordering.

Procedures are allowed to accept other procedures as actual parameters. This is achieved by specifying a formal parameter to be a procedural type as illustrated in SetOrdering in Fig. 13.18. SetOrdering assigns to Ordering the procedure passed to it is as an actual parameter.

This procedure also assumes a BOOLEAN variable OrderingSet which can prevent SetOrdering from being called more than once. OrderingSet can also be used to prevent Insert being used before the procedure determining the ordering has been initialised.

```
PROCEDURE SetOrdering (OrderingProcedure : Proc2ItemsBool) ;
BEGIN
  IF NOT OrderingSet THEN
      Ordering          := OrderingProcedure ;
      OrderingSet       := TRUE ;
      Success           := TRUE ;
  ELSE
      Success := FALSE ;
  END (* IF *) ;
END SetOrdering ;
```

Fig. 13.18.

Figure 13.19a shows procedure definitions for two procedures, OrderOnStock-Level and OrderOnSupplier, and Fig. 13.19b shows alternative calls to SetOrdering which enable the ordering of the items in the list to be based on different criteria. The variable OrderingSet ensures that the ordering procedure can only be set once in any given program, thus preventing the use of two different ordering procedures in the same program. However differing programs may order the data differently.

```
PROCEDURE OrderOnSupplier (VAR Item1,Item2 : ItemType) : BOOLEAN ;

  PROCEDURE LessThan (VAR Name1,Name2 : ARRAY OF CHAR) : BOOLEAN ;
  (* returns TRUE if Name1 is ordered before Name2, otherwise FALSE *)
  VAR
      Finish,CharPos : CARDINAL;

BEGIN
  CharPos := 0 ;
  IF HIGH (Name1) < HIGH (Name2) THEN
    Finish := HIGH (Name1) + 1 ;
  ELSE
    Finish := HIGH (Name2) + 1 ;
  END (* IF *) ;
  WHILE (CharPos <> Finish) AND
         (Name1[CharPos] <> 0C) AND (Name2[CharPos] <> 0C) AND
         (Name1[CharPos] = Name2[CharPos]) DO
            INC(CharPos) ;
  END (* WHILE *) ;

  IF (CharPos = Finish) THEN
    IF HIGH(Name1) = HIGH(Name2) THEN
      RETURN TRUE
    ELSE
      RETURN (HIGH(Name2) > HIGH(Name1)) AND (Name2[CharPos] <> 0C)
    END (* IF *)
  ELSE
      RETURN Name1[CharPos] < Name2[CharPos]
  END (* IF *)
  END LessThan ;


BEGIN (* OrderOnSupplier *)
  RETURN LessThan (Item1.Supplier,Item2.Supplier)
END OrderOnSupplier ;

PROCEDURE OrderOnStockLevel (VAR Item1,Item2 : ItemType) : BOOLEAN ;
BEGIN
  RETURN Item1.QuantityInStock < Item2.QuantityInStock
END OrderOnStockLevel ;
```

(a)

```
        SetOrdering (OrderOnStockLevel)
        SetOrdering (OrderOnSupplier)
```

(b)

Fig. 13.19.

Procedural parameters can also be used in writing procedures which perform general tasks but which vary part of the sequence of operations from one call of the procedure to another. This is achieved by passing different procedures as the actual parameters on different calls.

With trees and linked lists it is often necessary to process each item in the data structure in an identical manner. In the OrderedList module of Chapter 11 this was made possible by the idea of a current node which could be moved forward and reset, however this requires the module to contain repetitive statements to iterate down the list. This module provided a primitive though useful way of processing each item.

In the case of tree structures there are **tree walking** algorithms which allow each item of a tree to be processed and which are typically recursive. The action to be performed at each node of the tree is usually provided as a procedural parameter. For example InOrderTreeWalk in Fig. 13.20 visits each node in a tree so that it writes out all the information in a node's left subtree, then writes out the information in the node and then writes out the information in its right subtree. This order of priorities is known as an **inorder tree traversal** and corresponds to the ordering of the nodes determined by the way that InsertInTree inserts them into the tree.

```
PROCEDURE InOrderTreeWalk (VAR ThisTree : TREE) ;
BEGIN
  IF ThisTree <> NIL THEN
     InOrderTreeWalk (ThisTree ∧ .LeftSubTree) ;
     WITH ThisTree ∧ DO
           WriteLnString (Description) ;
           WriteString (Code) ;
           WriteCard (QuantityInStock,10) ;
           WriteCard (ReorderLevel,10) ;
           WriteString (Supplier) ;
        END (* WITH *) ;
        InOrderTreeWalk (ThisTree ∧ .RightSubTree) ;
  END (* IF *)
END InOrderTreeWalk ;
```

Fig. 13.20.

The action performed on each item can be determined by a procedure which is external to InOrderTreeWalk. Figure 13.21 illustrates a procedure ProcessEachItem which takes a procedural parameter of type Proc1Item. By declaring InOrderTreeWalk local to ProcessEachItem the procedural parameter is in scope and available for use inside InOrderTreeWalk. InOrderTreeWalk applies ProcessEachItem's procedural procedure to each of the nodes of the tree in order.

Recall that the scope rules prevent procedures which are local to other procedures being exported from the surrounding module. In any case, InOrder-TreeWalk would not be made available outside the OrderedList module as it has to be passed the hidden tree. ProcessEachItem can be made available to other modules.

```
TYPE
      Proc1Item = PROCEDURE (VAR ItemType) ;


PROCEDURE ProcessEachItem (Process : Proc1Item) ;

  PROCEDURE InOrderTreeWalk (VAR ThisTree : TREE) ;
  BEGIN
   IF ThisTree <> NIL THEN
      InOrderTreeWalk (ThisTree∧.LeftSubTree,Process) ;
      Process (ThisTree∧.Item) ;
      InOrderTreeWalk (ThisTree∧.RightSubTree,Process) ;
   END (* IF *)
  END InOrderTreeWalk ;

BEGIN
  InOrderTreeWalk (ListInOrder) ;
END ProcessEachItem ;
```

(a) ProcessEachItem has a procedural parameter.

```
PROCEDURE WriteDescription (VAR Item : ItemType) ;
BEGIN
  WriteLnString (Item.Description) ;
END WriteDescription ;

PROCEDURE WriteItemToFile (VAR Item : ItemType) ;
BEGIN
  Write (OutputFile,Item) ;
END WriteItemToFile ;
```

(b) Two possible procedures which can be passed to ProcessEachItem.

```
ProcessEachItem (WriteDescription) ;
ProcessEachItem (WriteItemToFile) ;
```

(c) Calls of ProcessEachItem.

Fig. 13.21.

Figures 13.22 and 13.23 show new definition and implementation modules for OrderedList which include the modifications discussed in this chapter.

```
DEFINITION MODULE OrderedList ;
VAR
    Success : BOOLEAN ;
            (* set to FALSE if Insert is called before SetOrdering
              set to FALSE if attempt made to call SetOrdering more
                        than once *)
TYPE
    DescriptionType        = ARRAY [0..29] OF CHAR ;
    CodeType               = ARRAY [0..5] OF CHAR ;
    SupplierType           = ARRAY [0..49] OF CHAR ;
    ItemType               = RECORD
                                Description     : DescriptionType;
                                Code            : CodeType;
                                QuantityInStock ,
                                ReorderLevel    : CARDINAL ;
                                Supplier        : SupplierType;
                             END (* RECORD *) ;
    Proc1Item              = PROCEDURE (VAR ItemType) ;
    Proc2ItemsBool         = PROCEDURE (VAR ItemType,
                                        VAR ItemType) : BOOLEAN ;

PROCEDURE SetOrdering (OrderingProcedure: Proc2ItemsBool) ;
        (* initialises OrderingProcedure to be used in conjunction with
          Insert. OrderingProcedure determines the comparison of one
          item with another and the position which an item will be
          inserted into the ordered list, it defines the ordering on items
          held in the ordered list.
          The procedure specified as the OrderingProcedure must return
                TRUE if its first parameter is to be ordered before the
                second, otherwise FALSE. *)

PROCEDURE Insert (NewItem : ItemType) ;
        (* Inserts NewItem into the list at the correct position. *)

PROCEDURE ProcessEachItem (Process : Proc1Item) ;
        (* Executes the procedure passed to it on each item in the ordered
          list. *)

END OrderedList .
```

Fig. 13.22.

```
IMPLEMENTATION MODULE OrderedList ;
FROM Storage       IMPORT ALLOCATE ;
TYPE
    TREE        = POINTER TO Node ;
    Node        = RECORD
                     Item         : ItemType ;
                     LeftSubTree  ,
                     RightSubTree : TREE
                  END ;
```

```
VAR
    ListInOrder        : TREE ;
    Ordering           : Proc2ItemsBool ;
    OrderingSet        : BOOLEAN ;


PROCEDURE InsertInTree (VAR ThisTree : TREE ;
                             VAR NewItem : ItemType) ;
BEGIN
 IF ThisTree = NIL THEN
    NEW (ThisTree) ;
    WITH ThisTree ∧ DO
         Item       := NewItem ;
         LeftSubTree := NIL;
         RightSubTree := NIL ;
    END (∗ WITH ∗) ;
 ELSIF Ordering (NewItem,ThisTree ∧ .Item) THEN
    InsertInTree (ThisTree ∧ .LeftSubTree,NewItem)
 ELSE
    InsertInTree (ThisTree ∧ .RightSubTree,NewItem)
 END (∗ IF ∗) ;
END InsertInTree ;


              (∗ procedures available to other modules. ∗)


PROCEDURE ProcessEachItem (Process : Proc1Item) ;

  PROCEDURE InOrderTreeWalk (VAR ThisTree : TREE) ;
  BEGIN
   IF ThisTree <> NIL THEN
     InOrderTreeWalk (ThisTree ∧ .LeftSubTree) ;
     Process (ThisTree ∧ .Item) ;
     InOrderTreeWalk (ThisTree ∧ .RightSubTree) ;
   END (∗ IF ∗)
  END InOrderTreeWalk ;

BEGIN      (∗ ProcessEachItem's body ∗)
 InOrderTreeWalk (ListInOrder) ;
END ProcessEachItem ;

PROCEDURE SetOrdering (OrderingProcedure : Proc2ItemsBool) ;
BEGIN
 IF NOT OrderingSet THEN
    Ordering      := OrderingProcedure ;
    OrderingSet := TRUE ;
    Success      : = TRUE ;
 ELSE
    Success := FALSE ;
 END (∗ IF ∗) ;
END SetOrdering ;
```

```
      PROCEDURE Insert (NewItem : ItemType) ;
      BEGIN
       IF OrderingSet THEN
          Success := TRUE ;
          InsertInTree (ListInOrder,NewItem) ;
       ELSE
          Success := FALSE ;
       END (* IF *) ;
       END Insert ;

    BEGIN
     ListInOrder := NIL ;
     OrderingSet := FALSE ;
    END OrderedList .
```

Fig. 13.23.

Figure 13.24 shows a program module which reads a file of product descriptions and produces a list of those records in which the QuantityInStock field is less than or equal to the ReorderLevel field. This list is created in alphabetical order of the Supplier field, and for records with the same supplier in increasing order of the difference between their QuantityInStock field and their ReorderLevel field. Note the simplicity of WriteProductsToReorder and how this organisation allows the procedure which determines the ordering of items to be as complex as necessary.

```
    MODULE ReorderLevelsBySupplier ;
     FROM InOut IMPORT ReadCard,WriteCard;
     FROM OrderedList IMPORT (* TYPE *) ItemType,Proc1Item,Proc2ItemsBool,
                      (* PROCEDURES *) SetOrdering, Insert, ProcessEachItem;
     FROM SimpleFile IMPORT (* TYPE *)   FILE,
                      (* PROCEDURES *) Connect, OpenRead, OpenWrite, Close,
                                        ReadFromFile, WriteToFile,
                                        DisConnect,EOF ;
     VAR
         ProductFile   : FILE ;
         ProductRec   : ItemType ;
     TYPE
         LessOrEqual = (FirstLess,Same,SecondLess) ;

    PROCEDURE Compare (VAR Name1,Name2 : ARRAY OF CHAR) : LessOrEqual ;
    VAR
         Finish,CharPos : CARDINAL;

     PROCEDURE CompareCharacterPair (Ch1,Ch2 : CHAR) : LessOrEqual ;
     BEGIN
```

```
  IF Ch1 = Ch2 THEN
    RETURN Same
  ELSIF Ch1 < Ch2 THEN
    RETURN FirstLess
  ELSE (*TRUE Ch2 < Ch1 *)
    RETURN SecondLess
  END (* IF *)
END CompareCharacterPair ;

BEGIN (* Compare's body *)
 CharPos := 0 ;
 IF HIGH (Name1) < HIGH (Name2) THEN
   Finish := HIGH (Name1) + 1 ;
 ELSE
   Finish := HIGH (Name2) + 1 ;
 END (* IF *) ;
 WHILE (CharPos <> Finish) AND
       (Name1[CharPos] <> 0C) AND (Name2[CharPos] <> 0C) AND
       (Name1[CharPos] = Name2[CharPos]) DO
         INC(CharPos) ;
 END (* WHILE *) ;

 IF (CharPos = Finish) THEN
   IF HIGH(Name1) = HIGH(Name2) THEN
     RETURN Same
   ELSIF (HIGH(Name1) < HIGH(Name2)) AND (Name2[CharPos] <> 0C) THEN
     RETURN FirstLess
   ELSIF (HIGH(Name2) < HIGH(Name1)) AND (Name1[CharPos] <> 0C) THEN
     RETURN SecondLess
   ELSE
     RETURN Same
   END (* IF *)
 ELSE
       RETURN CompareCharacterPair (Name1[CharPos],Name2[CharPos])
 END (* IF *)
END Compare ;

PROCEDURE SupplierThenUnderStock (VAR Item1,
                                      Item2 : ItemType) : BOOLEAN ;
 (* compares Item1 and Item2 on their Supplier field
   RETURNS TRUE   if supplier of Item1 alphabetically ordered
                    prior to supplier if Item2
   RETURNS FALSE if supplier of Item1 alphabetically ordered
                    after to supplier if Item2
   if same supplier then
           RETURNS TRUE if Item1 more out of stock than Item2,
           RETURNS FALSE otherwise. *)
 VAR
    NameOrder : LessOrEqual ;
BEGIN
```

```
NameOrder := Compare (Item1.Supplier,Item2.Supplier) ;
CASE NameOrder OF
    FirstLess      : RETURN TRUE |
    SecondLess   : RETURN FALSE |
    Same         : RETURN (Item1.ReorderLevel – Item1.QuantityInStock) >
                           (Item2.ReorderLevel – Item2.QuantityInStock)
END (* CASE *) ;
END SupplierThenUnderStock ;

PROCEDURE FindProductsToReorder ;
BEGIN
 SetOrdering (SupplierThenUnderStock) ;
 Connect (ProductFile,'Products.Dat',ProductRec) ;
 OpenRead (ProductFile) ;
 ReadFromFile (ProductFile,ProductRec) ;
 WHILE NOT EOF (ProductFile) DO
     IF ProductRec.QuantityInStock <= ProductRec.ReorderLevel THEN
        Insert (ProductRec)
     END (* IF *) ;
     ReadFromFile (ProductFile,ProductRec) ;
 END (* WHILE *) ;
 Close (ProductFile) ;
 DisConnect (ProductFile) ;
END FindProductsToReorder ;

PROCEDURE WriteItem (VAR Item : ItemType) ;
BEGIN
 WriteToFile (ProductFile,Item) ;
END WriteItem ;

PROCEDURE WriteProductsToReorder ;
BEGIN
 Connect (ProductFile,'Reorder.dat',ProductRec) ;
 OpenWrite (ProductFile) ;
 ProcessEachItem (WriteItem) ;
 Close (ProductFile) ;
 DisConnect (ProductFile) ;
END WriteProductsToReorder ;

BEGIN
 FindProductsToReorder ;
 WriteProductsToReorder ;
END ReorderLevelsBySupplier .
```

Fig. 13.24.

The facility for storing procedures in variables and passing them as parameters to other procedures is very useful, however two restrictions must be observed.

a. A procedure which is assigned to a procedure variable or is passed as a parameter to another procedure must not be declared local to any other procedure. This restriction is required to prevent any attempt to extend the scope of a procedure by assigning a local procedure to a global variable.

b. Standard procedures such as CHR, VAL, HIGH, INC etc cannot be stored in procedure variables or passed as procedural parameters. If necessary the programmer can by-pass this restriction by defining his own procedures which merely call standard procedures and these can then be manipulated like other procedures. Procedures declared in standard modules such as InOut and MathLib0 are not standard procedures and so can be manipulated like other procedures.

13.5 SUMMARY

This chapter has introduced the important ideas of recursive data structure and recursive procedure, and useful facilities for manipulating procedures.

a A recursive data structure is a structure which is defined by reference to itself. Such definitions must include a terminating value to prevent infinite recursion. In Modula-2, recursive data structures are implemented using pointers with the value NIL as the terminating value.

b A recursive procedure is a procedure which calls itself. A recursive procedure must include a terminating condition to prevent infinite recursion.

c Linked lists are naturally recursive data structures which can be manipulated by recursive procedures. However, as many of these procedures are tail recursive they can be easily reformulated in terms of repetitive constructs.

d Trees are recursive data structures which involve a special node known as the root node which has no parent node and which permits access to all other nodes. A node of a tree consists of a value held in the node and a series of links to subtrees. A binary tree is a tree in which each node has two links. Trees are manipulated more naturally by recursive procedures than iterative procedures.

e In Modula-2, procedures can be stored in variables like other program objects. The programmer can define procedure types and procedure variables. In addition procedures can be passed as parameters to other procedures thereby permitting general procedures to be written with less general operations supplied as procedural parameters.

TECHNICAL EXERCISES

1   Which of the following diagrams illustrate a valid list and which a valid binary tree?

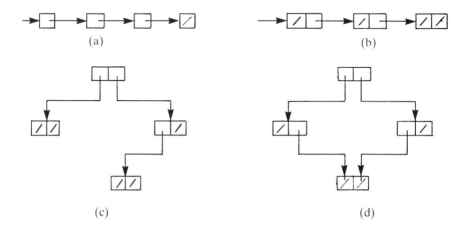

2   Draw the trees resulting from the following procedure calls, assuming that ThisTree is a pointer to a tree which has been initialised to an empty tree each time and that the type of items in the tree are CARDINAL values.

a   InsertInTree (ThisTree,6) ;
InsertInTree (ThisTree,4) ;
InsertInTree (ThisTree,5) ;
InsertInTree (ThisTree,8) ;
InsertInTree (ThisTree,2) ;
InsertInTree (ThisTree,7) ;

b   InsertInTree (ThisTree,1) ;
InsertInTree (ThisTree,2) ;
InsertInTree (ThisTree,3) ;
InsertInTree (ThisTree,6) ;
InsertInTree (ThisTree,7) ;
InsertInTree (ThisTree,8) ;

What happens when the items are already in order?

3   Assume the declarations

```
TYPE
    ListOfChar   = POINTER TO CharNode ;
CharNode         = RECORD
                      Head : CHAR ;
                      Tail : ListOfChar ;
                   END ;
PROCEDURE WriteCharList (VAR CharList : ListOfChar) ;
BEGIN
```

```
IF CharList <> NIL THEN
      Write(CharList∧.Head) ;
      WriteCharList (CharList) ;
   END (∗ IF ∗)
END WriteCharList ;
```

When WriteCharList is called in a program it writes out an indefinite sequence of 5s (555555555...). State what is wrong with the procedure and how it can be corrected to write out the characters in a list of characters.

4   Write a recursive procedure WriteReverseCharList which will write out the characters in a sequence of characters in reverse order.

5   There are two other general tree walking algorithms besides the in-order traversal. These are
a pre-order traversal which processes the items in the node, then recursively calls itself on the left subtree and then recursively calls itself of the right subtree.
b post-order traversal which recursively calls itself on the left and right subtrees and then processes the item in the node.

In what order will the nodes of the following tree be processed during
a a pre-order traversal,
b a post-order traversal?

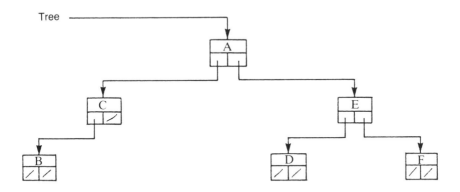

Write two procedure WalkTreePreOrder and WalkTreePostOrder which take a procedural parameter and excute the procedure on each node in the tree. Why would these procedures not be made directly available to other modules?

6   Write a procedure DoItToNumbersBetween whose first parameter is a procedural parameter and the second and third are two CARDINAL values indicating the starting and finishing values. The procedure should execute

the procedure passed to it as its parameter on all numbers between the starting value and the finishing value.

Write procedure calls to write out the

a square,

b cube,

c factorial

of numbers between 1 and 7.

7 a Write a declaration of an array which can hold 3 parameterless procedures.

b Assume that Create, Amend, Delete are three parameterless procedures. Write statements which will put these procedures into the first three elements of the array.

c For each, write a procedure call using the array.

8 Assuming a type

```
TYPE
    ProcREAL1REAL = PROCEDURE (REAL) : REAL ;
```

Write a function procedure IntegralOf which takes a procedure of type ProcREAL1REAL, two REAL values for a lower and upper bound, and a CARDINAL value for the number of intervals as parameters, and returns as its result the integral of the function procedure between the lower and upper bounds using the trapezium rule with the specified number of intervals for calculating the area under a curve.

PROGRAMMING EXERCISES

1 Modify the tree implementation of the OrderedList module to provide the following procedure to other modules,

```
TYPE
    Ordering      = (InOrder,PreOrder,PostOrder) ;
    ProcItem1Bool = PROCEDURE (VAR ItemType) : BOOLEAN ;

PROCEDURE ProcessEachItemSatisfying (Criteria : ProcItem1Bool ;
                                     Process : Proc1Item ;
                                     WhichOrder : Ordering) ;
    (* Starting at the first item of the ordered list execute Process
       on each item which satisfies the Criteria. *)
```

and modifying ProcessEachItem so that it takes an extra parameter to indicate whether this should be done in pre-order, post-order or in-order (see technical exercise 5).

PROCEDURE ProcessEachItem (Process : Proc1Item ;
                          WhichOrder : Ordering) ;
    (* Execute Process on each item of the ordered list in the order
        specified by WhichOrder. *)

2 Redesign the procedure Insert to have InsertInTree as a local procedure, and allow InsertInTree to access Insert's parameter NewItem as a non-local variable (look at ProcessEachItem as a guide). Discuss the respective merits of the method in the text and the redesigned version.

3 Write a program module which uses the OrderedList module to read in the Lilliput student file and order it so that the list is ordered first by course and then by student name. Allow the user to choose then whether the list is to be written to a file or to be shown on the visual display screen.

4 Write a program which reads the Lilliput student file and uses ProcessEachItemSatisfying to generate a list of all students whose names begin with a character specified by the user and who have been deleted.

ANSWERS

1 **a** is a valid list.
 b is a valid binary tree where all the left branch subtrees are empty trees.
 c is a valid binary tree.
 d is not a valid tree as the bottom node has two parent nodes, nor is it a straight forward list.

2

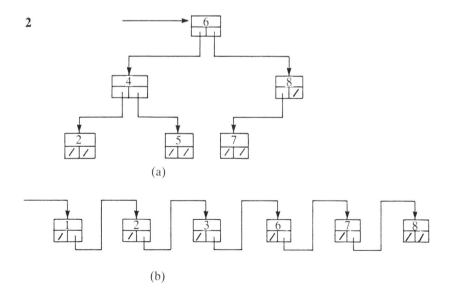

(a)

(b)

In the latter case the left subtrees are not used as all insertions take place at the end of the right subtree links, essentially the tree is an ordered linked list and the efficiency of accessing an item in the lists deteriorates to that of a linked list.

3 The recursive call to WriteCharList makes no progress towards the terminating condition of the recursive procedure as each recursive call passes on unmodified the list it was given and therefore repeatedly writes out the first character in the list. The procedure can be corrected by altering the procedure to call itself on the tail of the list which it is given

    WriteCharList (CharList∧.Tail)

4 A recursive procedure to write out a list of characters in reverse order is

```
PROCEDURE WriteReverseCharList (VAR CharList : ListOfChar) ;
BEGIN
    IF CharList <> NIL THEN
        WriteReverseCharList (CharList∧.Tail) ;
        Write(CharList∧.Head) ;
    END (* IF *)
END WriteReverseCharList ;
```

5 a A C B E D F   **b** B C D F E A

```
PROCEDURE PreOrderTreeWalk (VAR ThisTree : TREE) ;
BEGIN
 IF ThisTree <> NIL THEN
    Process (ThisTree∧.Item) ;
    PreOrderTreeWalk (ThisTree∧.LeftSubTree,Process) ;
    PreOrderTreeWalk (ThisTree∧.RightSubTree,Process) ;
 END (* IF *)
END PreOrderTreeWalk ;
```

```
PROCEDURE PostOrderTreeWalk (VAR ThisTree : TREE) ;
BEGIN
 IF ThisTree <> NIL THEN
    PostOrderTreeWalk (ThisTree∧.LeftSubTree,Process) ;
    PostOrderTreeWalk (ThisTree∧.RightSubTree,Process) ;
    Process (ThisTree∧.Item) ;
 END (* IF *)
END PostOrderTreeWalk ;
```

These procedures could not be made directly available to other modules from the current implementation of OrderedList as it is hiding the tree data structure which the procedures have to be given as a parameter. In addition by declaring them as local procedures to ProcessEachItem they can refer to the formal procedural parameter but cannot then be exported.

6 Assume the declaration

```
TYPE
      ProcCardinal = PROCEDURE (CARDINAL) ;
```

and declarations of procedure WriteSquare, WriteCube and WriteFactorial which
are normal procedures which take one CARDINAL value parameter.

```
PROCEDURE DoItToNumbersBetween (Proc : ProcCardinal ;
                    StartingVal,FinishingVal : CARDINAL) ;
   VAR
      Number : CARDINAL ;
   BEGIN
   FOR Number := StartingVal TO FinishingVal DO
         Proc (Number) ;
   END (* FOR *) ;
   END DoItToNumbersBetween ;
```

a DoItToNumbersBetween (WriteSquare,1,7)

b DoItToNumbersBetween (WriteCube,1,7)

c DoItToNumbersBetween (WriteFactorial,1,7)

Notice how inefficient the processing is. There is often a severe penalty for
generality. This is especially apparent in **c**.

7 a VAR
Procs : ARRAY [1..3] OF PROC ;

b Procs [1] := Create
Procs [2] := Amend
Procs [3] := Delete

c Procs [1]
Procs [2]
Procs [3]

8 A crude solution is

```
PROCEDURE IntegralOf (FuncProc : ProcREAL1REAL ;
                    Lower, Upper : REAL ;
                    NoOfIntervals : CARDINAL) : REAL ;
   VAR
      Interval, TempResult    : REAL ;
      Count                   : CARDINAL ;
   BEGIN
   Interval   := (Upper-Lower) / FLOAT(NoOfIntervals) ;
   TempResult := ((FuncProc(Lower)+FuncProc(Upper))/2.0) ;
   FOR Count := 1 TO NoOfIntervals-1 DO
         INC(TempResult,FuncProc(Lower+FLOAT(Count)*Interval)) ;
   END (* FOR *) ;
   RETURN TempResult * Interval ;
   END IntegralOf ;
```

Chapter 14

Low Level Facilities, Opaque Export and Generic Data Types

This book is primarily concerned with teaching Modula-2 as a high level programming language. However the language has significant advantages over many other high level languages in that it provides facilities for low level programming. Low level programming involves accessing the hardware of the computer directly. The language definition for Modula-2 does not insist that these low level facilities are provided in the language; they are optional. However, in practice, most Modula-2 compilers provide them.

These low level facilities are

1. the ability to convert a value of one type into a value of another type and thereby evade type checking,
2. the ability to declare variables and specify that they are located at particular memory addresses,
3. the ability to determine low level information about variables and types and to write general procedures which can process variables of any type,
4. the ability to substitute an alternative storage allocation module for use by NEW and DISPOSE.

It is not our intention to teach low level programming in this book as this is a complicated discipline in its own right. Rather we give an indication of the kinds of problems which can be tackled and how these can be solved in Modula-2.

Modula-2 provides a high level facility allowing a type to be exported from a module without the need to state how the type is represented. This is known as **opaque export** of a type. In the current definition of Modula-2 there are problems with the security of types which are exported opaquely due to their low level implementation. The insecurities are discussed and recommendations for their secure use are given.

Additionally low level facilities can be used to construct modules which provide generic data types. These are data types whose components' type need not be specified. The illustrative module provides a type Queue where the items in the queue can be of different types.

14.1 TYPE TRANSFER FUNCTION PROCEDURES

Modula-2 is a strongly typed language. The type specified in a variable declaration indicates the permissable range of values which can be stored in a variable and the operations which can be performed on it. This allows the

461

compiler to check that the programmer's understanding of a problem is consistent with the declarations of variables and the operations allowed on them. In general strong type checking is a boon to the programmer. However, there are occasions when the programmer knowingly wishes to override the restrictions and perform operations not normally associated with the type. Rather than provide a facility for overriding the type checking, Modula-2 provides facilities for converting a value of one type into a value of another type thereby permitting the programmer to perform the operations he requires. It is an advantage of the language that this cannot be done unwittingly.

The main memory of a computer consists of a sequence of memory locations which are also termed **words**. On some computers a word consists of 8 bits of data (called a byte); other common word lengths are 16 and 32 bits of data. The distinguishing feature of a word is that each word has a unique **address**. When a program is compiled and linked it is translated into machine instructions which refer to specific words in memory. For many programs it is irrelevant exactly how data is represented in the computer's memory, or where specific pieces of information are placed in memory. Hence, it can be left to the compiler to generate addresses for these data items in a way which mirrors the behaviour intended in the original program. However, there are occasions when it is necessary to convert data of one type into data of another type, and to refer to specific details of the computer. Consequently, it is then necessary to be aware of how data is stored in memory.

We have already seen specialised forms of type conversions. The standard function procedures ORD and CHR convert CHAR values to CARDINAL values and vice versa. These are such useful conversions between types that standard procedures are provided to achieve it.

Modula-2 provides a standard way of converting a value of one type into a value of another type **as long as the internal representations of the values are of the same length**. This restriction requires knowledge of the internal representation of types. Let us assume that the computer we are using has a 16 bit machine word consisting of two bytes of data (8 bits each), and that the types CARDINAL, INTEGER, BOOLEAN, CHAR and BITSET are each represented by one word in memory. Assumptions about other types will be introduced as needed.

For each type Modula-2 provides a **type transfer function** which has the same name as the type, and which when given a value of another type returns the corresponding value of the specified type. Assuming the declarations

```
VAR
        A : CARDINAL ;
        B : BOOLEAN ;
        C : CHAR ;
        D : BITSET ;
```

and the sequence of assignment statements

```
A := 13 ;
B := TRUE ;
C := 'A' ;
D := {1,3,7} ;
```

then the assignment statement

```
A := CARDINAL (D)
```

assigns to A the CARDINAL value corresponding to the bit pattern representing the set of bits {1,3,7}. Likewise the assignment statement

```
C := CHAR (B)
```

assigns to C the character code corresponding to the bit pattern representing the BOOLEAN value TRUE.

Type transfer functions are automatically provided for user defined types, so that values of other types can be converted to and from a user defined type. For example, assume that the compiler represents subranges of CARDINAL and INTEGER in 1 word, and arrays of characters as consecutive bytes two characters to a word, and assume the declarations

```
TYPE
        Cardinal1To52   = CARDINAL [1..52] ;
        Char2           = ARRAY [1..2] OF CHAR ;
VAR
        Initials        : Char2 ;
        WeekNo          : Cardinal1To52 ;
```

then the following assignment statements are permitted

```
WeekNo := Cardinal1To52 (C)
Initials := Char2 (A)
A := CARDINAL (Initials)
C := CHAR (WeekNo)
```

Note though that neither the type CHAR nor the subrange Cardinal1To52 require the full sixteen bits of a word to represent all the valid values of the type. There will be CHAR values which have no correspondence in the type Cardinal1To52 and which cause an execution error if an attempt is made to assign their nonexistent equivalent to WeekNo.

As a further example, suppose that the number of memory locations required to represent arrays and records is simply the sum of the number of words required to represent all components and fields respectively. Then it is permissible to use a type transfer function as shown in Fig. 14.1a because the array and record occupy the same number of memory locations, but not as shown in Fig. 14.1b as these variables are not the same size.

```
TYPE
        ThreeWordArray = ARRAY [1..3] OF CARDINAL ;
        ThreeWordRecord = RECORD
                                A,B : CARDINAL ;
                                C   : BITSET ;
                                END ;
VAR
        X : ThreeWordArray ;
        Y : ThreeWordRecord ;
BEGIN
 X := ThreeWordArray (Y)
END
```

(a) valid use of type transfer function.

```
TYPE
        ThreeWordArray = ARRAY [1..3] OF CARDINAL ;
        FourWordRecord = RECORD
                                A,B,C,D : BITSET ;
                                END ;
VAR
        X : ThreeWordArray ;
        Y : FourWordRecord ;
BEGIN
 X := ThreeWordArray (Y)
END
```

(b) erroneous use of type transfer functions.

Fig. 14.1.

14.2   DECLARATIONS OF VARIABLES AT ABSOLUTE ADDRESSES

When variables are declared, memory locations are automatically allocated by the compiler for these variables. On many computers particular memory locations are reserved for special purposes. Placing particular values in these memory locations causes the computer to perform particular operations such as writing out a character to the screen. If a program requires access to specific memory locations of the computer then it is necessary to override the automatic allocation of memory locations and state explicitly where the variable is to be situated in memory.

The memory address for a variable can be specified in its declaration, for example the declarations

```
VAR
        X [400]      : CARDINAL ;
        Y [0FFH]     : BITSET ;
        Z [255]      : CARDINAL ;
        Fred         : CARDINAL ;
```

specify that variable X is to be located starting at the absolute memory address 400, Y is to be located starting at the absolute address hexadecimal FF, Z is to be located starting at the absolute address 255, and Fred is to be allocated memory automatically by the compiler and its position in memory is irrelevent as far as the program is concerned.

This facility should be used with the utmost care. When a program is running it is not the only thing to be held in the computer's main memory. At the same time parts of the operating system are also in memory and, unless you know exactly where these are, you may inadvertently overwrite part of the operating system and thereby cause the program to behave unpredictably. In addition it is also possible to cause inadvertent structure sharing. In the above set of variable declarations both Y and Z are declared to start at the same memory location so that any alteration of the value of Y will also cause the value of Z to alter and vice versa.

The kinds of problem which need declarations that specify an absolute address are illustrated in the following example, based upon a fictitious computer. It illustrates the kind of information which you will have to determine from the manufacturer's hardware manual. The kinds of operations are realistic but the addresses used and the order of operations will vary from one make of computer to another.

Example. Using a screen map to display information on a visual display screen

Many computers use a so called screen map to represent the information which is displayed on the visual display screen. This screen map is a series of words in main memory which correspond to particular character positions on the visual display screen. If the visual display screen consists of 25 rows of characters with 80 characters on each row then the screen map in main memory may consist of a sequence of 2000 words starting at a particular memory location. Suppose that this sequence of words is arranged so that the first 80 words correspond to the top row of character positions on the screen, the second 80 words to the second row etc, and that the first word of such a subsequence corresponds to the first character on the row, the second word to the second character on the row etc.

Additionally assume that the screen map starts at the memory location hexadecimal 0F800, the computer's word consists of 16 bits and the first byte represents the character on the screen and the second byte indicates the characteristics associated with the character such as the colour of the character and the colour of the background it is on. If a value is placed in the first byte of one of these words it causes the corresponding ASCII character to be displayed at the appropriate character position on the visual display screen with the attributes specified by the second byte.

A program can refer to this screen map in order to perform output to the visual display screen. To do this a suitable declaration of a variable is required which will be mapped onto this sequence of 2000 words. Let us assume that CHAR variables and variables of type BITSET occupy one word of memory, and that arrays are allocated as areas of contiguous memory, but because characters can be represented in one byte, arrays of characters are represented with two characters to a word. This prohibits a declaration of the screenmap as a simple array of characters. A suitable declaration for the screen map would be

```
VAR
    ScreenMap [0F800H] : ARRAY [1..2000] OF BITSET ;
```

A character is written on the screen by specifying a row and column number at which to display it, and from these the appropriate position in the array is calculated in which to store the character.

```
PROCEDURE WriteCh (Ch : CHAR ;
                   Row,Col : CARDINAL) ;
BEGIN
    ScreenMap[(Row−1)*25 + Col] := ScreenMap[(Row−1)*25 + Col] * {8..15} +
                                                    BITSET (Ch) ;
END WriteCh ;
```

This removes the current character at the corresponding screen position by taking the intersection of the appropriate word with the BITSET {8..15} which leaves the attribute as it was. The new character is then displayed by taking the union of the resulting BITSET value with the BITSET which corresponds to the character.

A better declaration for ScreenMap is to specify that it is a two dimensional array thereby reflecting the two dimensionality of the screen in the internal representation

```
CONST
    RowMax  = 25 ;
    ColMax  = 80 ;
```

```
VAR
    ScreenMap [0F800H] : ARRAY [1..RowMax] [1..ColMax] OF BITSET ;
```

so that WriteCh can be written

```
PROCEDURE WriteCh (Ch : CHAR ;
                   Row,Col : CARDINAL) ;
BEGIN
  ScreenMap [Row,Col] := ScreenMap [Row,Col] * {8..15} + BITSET (Ch) ;
END WriteCh ;
```

This facility also allows the programmer to utilise other special memory locations for performing various operations, such as controlling a printer or controlling a communications port to allow data to be transferred to and from other computers.

Registers

Computers have special memory locations known as registers which have special properties. On some computers these can be referred to like any other memory location by an absolute address, however on other computers these are referred to by special names. For the latter cases Modula-2 provides special procedures or variables which permit access to registers. These are provided in a separately compiled module, but because machine architectures vary so widely there is no agreed standard. You will have to consult the documentation for your implementation of Modula-2 for specific details.

14.3 THE MODULE SYSTEM

Modula-2 provides a standard module called SYSTEM which provides several types and procedures for low level processing. This module is required by the compiler itself. It is therefore stored in a different way from other modules and is called a pseudo-module. The facilities which it provides are requested and used in exactly the same way as facilities in other modules.

SYSTEM makes available
1. two types, WORD and ADDRESS,
2. three function procedures, TSIZE, SIZE and ADR.
In addition it provides facilities for coroutines and interrupts to be discussed in the following chapter.

In the previous section declarations of variables at particular memory locations were illustrated. For some programs it is irrelevant exactly where specific pieces of information are placed in memory but it is necessary to find out how the compiler has allocated memory for variables. The module SYS-TEM provides these facilities.

The types ADDRESS and WORD are provided so that low level programs can manipulate a computer's main memory directly. The type ADDRESS is defined as though it is declared

TYPE
     ADDRESS = POINTER TO WORD ;

Variables of type ADDRESS are able to hold values which are addresses of particular memory locations. Such variables can be used with the dereferencing symbol ∧ so that the value held in the variable can be used as an address of a memory location. Variables of type WORD are able to hold any value which can be stored in one word of memory irrespective of its type. Note that the type WORD need not correspond to the smallest addressable unit of memory. On many computers the smallest addressable unit is a byte even though the computer may have a 16 bit or 32 bit word.

The function procedure ADR can take any variable as a parameter and returns as its result the address where the variable is positioned. The procedure heading for ADR is

     PROCEDURE ADR (AnyVariable : AnyType) : ADDRESS ;

Notice that ADR provides the inverse of declaring variables at absolute memory locations. Normally the compiler allocates memory locations for variables and ADR can be used to find out the memory address at which a variable starts.

The procedures SIZE and TSIZE are used to determine the number of the smallest addressable units required to represent variables and types. SIZE takes any variable as an actual parameter and returns as its result the number of units used to represent the variable. TSIZE can be given any type as an actual parameter and returns as its result the number of units required to represent a variable of that type. The results of both procedures are CARDINAL values. The procedure headings for these are

PROCEDURE SIZE (VAR AnyVariable: AnyType): CARDINAL ;

PROCEDURE TSIZE (AnyType): CARDINAL ;

Note that SIZE takes a variable parameter so that this procedure is restricted to use with variables, a literal constant or result from a calculation cannot be passed as an actual parameter to it.

For example, Fig. 14.2 shows a module which gives information about the addresses where the variables X and AWord are located in the computer's memory, the values held within them and the number of units used to represent these variables. Notice that the addresses and the value of AWord are converted to CARDINAL values in order to use WriteCard to write them out.

An important feature of SIZE and TSIZE is that they increase the capability of writing programs which can be transported to different computers using different Modula-2 compilers without alterations, even though the programs may use system specific information. This information can be derived using SIZE and TSIZE rather than using constants.

```
MODULE LowLevel ;
    FROM SYSTEM           IMPORT (* TYPES *) ADDRESS, WORD ,
                                  (* PROCEDURES *) ADR, SIZE, TSIZE ;
    FROM MoreInOut        IMPORT (* PROCEDURE *) WriteStringCard ;

    VAR
        AnAddress    : ADDRESS ;
        AWord        : WORD ;
        X            : CARDINAL ;

    BEGIN
     X := 3 ;
     AWord := WORD (X) ;
     AnAddress := ADR (X) ;
     WriteStringCard('The address of X is ',CARDINAL(AnAddress),10) ;
     WriteStringCard('The size of X is ',SIZE(X),10) ;
     WriteStringCard('The cardinal value of X is ',X,10) ;
     WriteStringCard('The address of AWord is ',CARDINAL(ADR(AWord)),10) ;
     WriteStringCard('The size of AWord is ',TSIZE(WORD),10) ;
     WriteStringCard('The cardinal value in AWord is ',CARDINAL(AWord),10) ;
    END LowLevel .
```

Fig. 14.2.

The types WORD and ADDRESS are special in that they directly reflect the organisation of a computer's memory. To make them even more useful they are defined as being compatible with other types though these are compiler dependent. The rules for compatibility with other types are

1. the type ADDRESS is compatible with all pointer types, and one of the types CARDINAL, LONGCARD or LONGINT,

2. the types with which WORD is compatible are implementation dependent, usually type transfer functions are necessary. The use of the type transfer function WORD, as illustrated in Fig 14.2, increases portability of a program by making the code independent of any one Modula-2 compiler,

3. a formal parameter of type WORD is compatible with all types whose size is one word, any storable value which is represented in one word can be passed as the corresponding actual parameter. A formal parameter whose type is specified as VAR WORD must be passed a variable which is represented in one word,

4. a formal parameter of type ARRAY OF WORD is compatible with an actual parameter of any type, unstructured or structured.

In the present discussion we assume that ADDRESS is compatible with the type CARDINAL.

Figure 14.3 illustrates the use of some of these facilities. CopyMemory accepts as its first formal parameter any variable, usually an array or record, and copies this data into the area of memory starting at the address of OutArea. The FOR loop copies the word referenced by InAddress to the word OutAddress, both of which are incremented to reference the next words on each iteration. This procedure can be used to copy the contents any area of memory to any other area of memory as illustrated by the calls in Fig. 14.3b.

Notice that OutAddress is used in conjunction with the dereferencing operator ∧ in order to use the value in OutAddress as the address at which to store the next word.

```
IMPLEMENTATION MODULE MemoryCopy;
   FROM SYSTEM IMPORT (* TYPES *) ADDRESS, WORD, (*PROCEDURES *) ADR,
                      TSIZE ;

   PROCEDURE CopyMemory (VAR InData : ARRAY OF WORD ;
                         CopyLength : CARDINAL ;
                         VAR OutArea : ARRAY OF WORD) ;
      VAR
         InAddress,OutAddress : ADDRESS ;
         Count : CARDINAL ;
      BEGIN
      InAddress  := ADR(InData);
      OutAddress := ADR (OutArea) ;
      FOR Count := 0 TO CopyLength – 1 DO
         OutAddress∧ := InAddress∧ ;
         INC(InAddress,TSIZE(WORD)) ;
         INC(OutAddress,TSIZE(WORD)) ;
      END (* FOR *) ;
      END CopyMemory ;

END MemoryCopy .
```

(a) an implementation module to copy an area of memory.

```
DesignerOfPascal      := 'Niklaus Wirth' ;
NumberOfWords         := (*... depends on size of components ...*) ;
CopyMemory (DesignerOfPascal,NumberOfWords,DesignerOfModula2) ;

CopyMemory (DesignerOfModula2,3,ScreenMap[3,3]) ;
```

(b) calling CopyMemory.

Fig. 14.3.

Figure 14.4 shows a safer high-level procedure to copy an array to another array which includes checks that the data actually fits in the destination array. However, it cannot be used on arbitary sections of an array in the way that CopyMemory can. Note that any unutilised space at the end of OutArray is not initialised by the procedure. In general, the high-level procedure should be used if the additional flexibility of the low-level version is not required.

```
PROCEDURE CopyArray (VAR InArray : ARRAY OF WORD ;
                     VAR OutArray : ARRAY OF WORD ;
                     VAR Success  : BOOLEAN) ;
VAR
     Count : CARDINAL ;
BEGIN
  IF HIGH (InArray) > HIGH (OutArray) THEN
        Success := FALSE
  ELSE
        Success := TRUE ;
        FOR Count := 0 TO HIGH (InArray) DO
             OutArray[Count] := InArray[Count] ;
        END (* FOR *) ;
  END (* IF *)
END CopyArray ;
```

Fig. 14.4.

It should be noted that the type transfer function ADDRESS and the function ADR have two distinct purposes which should not be confused. Given the declarations

```
VAR
     X [400]   : CARDINAL ;
     Y         : ADDRESS ;
```

and assuming that X has been assigned a value 200 decimal, then

```
Y := ADR (X)
```

assigns the address of X to Y (400), whilst

```
Y := ADDRESS (X)
```

assigns the value held in X to Y. In the former case the assignment statement

```
Y∧ := 3
```

assigns 3 to the memory location 400, but in the latter case it assigns 3 to the memory location 200. ADR returns the address of a variable; ADDRESS allows a value, which may be retrieved from a variable, to be treated as an address.

14.4   THE MODULE Storage

In Chapter 11 it was noted that when NEW and DISPOSE are required for creating and destroying nodes, the procedures ALLOCATE and DEALLOCATE have to be imported from Storage. NEW calls ALLOCATE and DISPOSE calls DEALLOCATE which allocate and deallocate memory for nodes. The correspondence between the procedures is

```
TYPE
      NodePntr = POINTER TO Node ;
      Node = (*... some record type ...*) ;
VAR
      ThisNode : NodePntr ;
NEW (ThisNode)          = ALLOCATE (ThisNode,TSIZE(Node))
DISPOSE (ThisNode)      = DEALLOCATE (ThisNode,TSIZE(Node))
```

More generally NEW, DISPOSE, SIZE and TSIZE can take an indefinite number of parameters. The first parameter is the pointer variable and the rest are values for tag fields governing variants which can occur in the record. Figure 14.5 shows the declaration of a variant record and how calls to TSIZE and NEW are dependent upon any tag field included in the actual parameter lists of the call.

```
TYPE
      Sex                 = (male,female) ;
      MaritalStatus       = (single,married) ;
      Node = RECORD
              FirstName, Surname : ARRAY[0..19] OF CHAR ;
              CASE sex : Sex OF
                 male   : I
                 female : CASE status : MaritalStatus OF
                              single  : I
                              married : MaidenName : ARRAY[0..19] OF CHAR
                          END (* CASE *) ;
              END (* CASE *) ;
              END (*RECORD *) ;

TSIZE (Node,female,married) ;
      returns as its result the size of a node which includes the
      field MaidenName.
NEW (ThisNode,female,single) ;
      does not allocate space in the node for the field MaidenName.
```

Fig. 14.5.

When NEW is called with no tag fields, such as

NEW (ThisNode)

sufficient memory is allocated to cope with the largest variant. By specifying particular values for tag fields in the call to NEW, memory is allocated for the specified variant which can be more efficient than the default allocation of sufficient memory to cope with the largest variant. This should be used with care. If a node is created for a variant the tag field of the node should not be altered to indicate a larger variant. If there is sufficient main memory do not include tag fields in calls to NEW.

Note that a programmer is not allowed to write procedures which have an indefinite number of formal parameters, so it would not be possible for a programmer to write his own version of the procedures NEW and DISPOSE. Instead these are translated into calls to ALLOCATE and DEALLOCATE which have two formal parameters. A programmer can write his own storage allocation module including declarations of his own procedures ALLOCATE and DEALLOCATE and import these into modules. Calls of NEW and DISPOSE will then use the programmer's procedures ALLOCATE and DEALLOCATE. In this way the sophistication of storage allocation for pointers can be as simple or complex as a program requires. Note however that the new definitions of ALLOCATE and DEALLOCATE must be compatible with the type

PROCEDURE (VAR ADDRESS , CARDINAL)

14.5 OPAQUE EXPORT AND ITS INSECURITIES

In previous chapters we have seen that procedures, variables, types and constants can be made available to other modules from an implementation and definition module pair by declaring them in the definition module. It was also pointed out in Chapter 6 that allowing variables to be imported into other modules can undermine the security of the module and it was advised that such variables should be treated as 'read only' by modules which import them. Similar problems arise when the definition module contains declarations of types to be made available to other modules. A module can declare variables of the imported type. However, the definition module provides sufficient information to allow the module to access these variables directly, without using the procedures provided. To overcome this insecurity Chapter 11 illustrated how a module can make available multiple versions of a data structure.

Modula-2 permits a module to make available a type to other modules whilst hiding the detail of the type from the importing module. This is achieved through the **opaque export** of the type. A definition module can contain type declarations which do not specify the full declaration of the type. For example, a definition module can make available a type Queue without having to specify the full declaration (see Fig. 14.6a). QueueModule's implementation module then contains the full declaration of the type and procedures for manipulating objects of that type (see Fig. 14.6b). A module can import the type Queue and procedures for manipulating variables of this type without knowing the details of the type (see Fig. 14.6c).

The benefit of this kind of facility is that modules can make available new types to other modules. These types can then be used in the importing module like basic types without knowing the detail of their implementation. Variables can be declared as and when needed in the importing module though the implementation detail of the type is hidden. You have already seen opaque types. FILE is an opaque type available from SimpleFile, and WORD and ADDRESS are opaque types available from SYSTEM.

Figure 14.7 gives a full implementation module for QueueModule providing the opaque type Queue, and the procedures InitialiseQueue, AddToQueue, RemoveFromQueue, EmptyQueue, FullQueue and LengthOfQueue for manipulating queues. Note that, for the sake of clarity, the module has been simplified from that shown in Chapter 11. In particular, no protection is incorporated against using queues which have not been initialised. The earlier procedure CreateQueue has been renamed to InitialiseQueue to reflect that a variable of type Queue is created in a declaration and must be initialised before it is used. DestroyQueue is omitted as variables of type Queue are discarded when the variable's lifetime ceases as determined by the scope rules. DestroyQueue's procedure heading must not appear in the corresponding definition module.

This version of QueueModule illustrates how opaque types provide new types which can be used by other modules. The following points should be noted.

1. Modula-2 restricts the types which can be exported opaquely from an implementation module. The definition of the language leaves it to specific implementations of the language to determine what these are, however it requires that at least all pointer types can be exported opaquely. The norm, therefore, is for an opaque type to be implemented in the implementation module as a pointer to a header record which forms the basis for the data structure. The data structures representing objects of the type are created and manipulated by procedures in the implementation module.

2. Variables of an opaque type are declared in the importing module, therefore they are not hidden in the way that variables declared within an

DEFINITION MODULE QueueModule ;

```
(* Warning – Do not use assignment between variables of type Queue,
            and do not pass them as value parameters to procedures. *)
TYPE
    Queue ;       (* opaque type *)
    ItemType =    (*... Whatever the user requires inserted here ...*)

    (* headings of procedures which can be imported to manipulate
       variables of type Queue. *)

END QueueModule .
```

    (a) Definition module for opaque export.

IMPLEMENTATION MODULE QueueModule ;

```
(* declarations which form an abstract data type of a
   queue of values determined by the imported type ItemType.
*)
TYPE
    QueueItemPntr     = POINTER TO QueueItem ;
    QueueItem         = RECORD
                           Item : ItemType ;
                           NextItem : QueueItemPntr
                        END ;
                                (* declaration of the opaque type *)
    Queue             = POINTER TO QueueRecord ;
    QueueRecord       = RECORD
                           HeadQueue ,
                           EndQueue   : QueueItemPntr ;
                           SizeQueue  : CARDINAL
                        END ;
    (* declarations of procedures for manipulating variables of type
       Queue. *)
BEGIN
    (* initialisation statements *)
END QueueModule.
```

    (b) Implementation module for opaque export.

```
MODULE ImportQueue ;
    FROM QueueModule IMPORT (* TYPE *)          Queue, ItemType,
                             (* PROCEDURES *)                          ;
    VAR
        TenQueues       : ARRAY [1..10] OF Queue ;
        AnotherQueue : Queue ;

END ImportQueue .
```

    (c) Module importing the opaque type.

Fig. 14.6.

```
IMPLEMENTATION MODULE QueueModule ;
 FROM Storage IMPORT ALLOCATE, DEALLOCATE ;
 (* Data declarations which form an abstract representation of a queue of CARDINAL values. *)
 TYPE
     QueueItemPntr      = POINTER TO QueueItem ;
     QueueItem          = RECORD
                            Item : ItemType ;
                            NextItem : QueueItemPntr
                          END ;

     Queue              = POINTER TO QueueRecord ;
     QueueRecord        = RECORD
                            HeadQueue ,
                            EndQueue   : QueueItemPntr ;
                            SizeQueue : CARDINAL
                          END ;

(* Procedures available for use by other modules *)

 PROCEDURE LengthOfQueue(VAR ThisQueue : Queue) : CARDINAL ;
 BEGIN
  Success := TRUE ;
  RETURN ThisQueue ∧ .SizeQueue
 END LengthOfQueue;

 PROCEDURE InitialiseQueue (VAR NewQueue : Queue) ;
  (* initialises NewQueue to be a new queue ready for use. *)
 BEGIN
  NEW (NewQueue) ;
  WITH NewQueue ∧ DO
     HeadQueue := NIL ;
     EndQueue   := NIL ;
     SizeQueue := 0 ;
  END (* WITH *) ;
  Success := TRUE ;
 END InitialiseQueue ;

 PROCEDURE AddToQueue(VAR ThisQueue : Queue ; Data : ItemType) ;
  VAR
     NewItem : QueueItemPntr ;
 BEGIN
  NEW (NewItem) ;
  WITH NewItem ∧ DO
     Item := Data ;
     NextItem := NIL ;
  END (* WITH *) ;
  WITH ThisQueue ∧ DO
     IF HeadQueue = NIL THEN
         HeadQueue := NewItem
     ELSE
```

```
            EndQueue∧.NextItem := NewItem ;
      END (*IF*) ;
      EndQueue := NewItem ;
      INC (SizeQueue)
  END (* WITH *) ;
  Success := TRUE ;
END AddToQueue ;

PROCEDURE RemoveFromQueue(VAR ThisQueue : Queue ; VAR Data : ItemType);
  VAR
      OldItem : QueueItemPntr ;
BEGIN
  WITH ThisQueue∧ DO
            IF HeadQueue <> NIL THEN
            OldItem     := HeadQueue ;
            Data        := HeadQueue∧.Item ;
            HeadQueue := HeadQueue∧.NextItem ;
            IF HeadQueue = NIL THEN
                EndQueue := NIL ;
            END (* IF *) ;
            DEC (SizeQueue) ;
            DISPOSE (OldItem) ;
            Success    := TRUE ;
        ELSE
            Success    : = FALSE ;
        END (*IF*)
  END (* WITH *)
END RemoveFromQueue;

PROCEDURE FullQueue(VAR ThisQueue : Queue) : BOOLEAN ;
BEGIN
  Success := TRUE ;
  RETURN FALSE ;
END FullQueue;

PROCEDURE EmptyQueue(VAR ThisQueue : Queue) : BOOLEAN ;
BEGIN
  Success := TRUE ;
  RETURN ThisQueue∧.SizeQueue = 0
END EmptyQueue;

END QueueModule .
```

Fig. 14.7.

implementation module are hidden. As a consequence, the body of the implementation module cannot perform initialisation, and it is necessary to have procedures for initialising an object of the type. In QueueModule, InitialiseQueue is provided to initialise a new queue.

3.   The procedures for manipulating a queue require a parameter to indicate on which object of the type an operation is to be performed. In QueueModule each of the procedures takes a parameter of type Queue so that the call of a procedure indicates which queue to use.

This facility for creating new types whose implementation detail is hidden is very powerful. However, there are problems concerning the security of the module.

1.   QueueModule does not guard against any of the operations being performed on a queue before it has actually been initialised. For example a module might import the type and procedures and omit calls to InitialiseQueue as in Fig. 14.8a. This is true of all types. Variables cannot be guaranteed to have been initialised before they are used, and it is the responsibility of the programmer to initialise variables.

2.   As opaque types are typically implemented as pointers, assignment within an importing module does not have the general meaning associated with variables of other types, but has the meaning associated with assignment between pointer variables. This results in structure sharing. For example, in Fig. 14.8b Parasite points at the same structure as Disaster. Any items added to Disaster are consequently added to Parasite, and vice versa, because they point to the same representation.

3.   When a pointer is passed as a value parameter to a procedure a copy of the pointer is taken and structure sharing is introduced. It is not unreasonable to expect a variable of an opaque type which is passed as a value parameter to be copied into the formal parameter, however as they are normally implemented as pointers to data structures this results in unanticipated structure sharing. Any modifications to the structure pointed to by the formal parameter also affect the structure pointed to by the actual parameter (see Fig. 14.8).

4.   When two opaque types are compared for equality, the comparison gives the result TRUE if the variables are structure sharing rather than if they are identical structures.

Note that all of these points are obvious if the data type is considered as a pointer rather than as the opaque type it is meant to be. A program may need to copy variables of an opaque type so a procedure to perform this operation should be added to QueueModule. The procedure must copy the entire structure

```
FROM QueueModule IMPORT Queue, InitialiseQueue, AddToQueue,
                            RemoveFromQueue,EmptyQueue ;
VAR
      Parasite,
      Disaster        : Queue ;
      SomeThing       : ItemType ;
      Count           : CARDINAL ;

BEGIN
  FOR Count := 1 to 5 DO
      ReadThing (SomeThing) ;
      AddToQueue (Disaster,Something) ;
  END (* FOR *) ;
  WHILE NOT EmptyQueue (Disaster) DO
      RemoveFromQueue (Disaster,SomeThing) ;
      Process (SomeThing) ;
  END (* WHILE *) ;
END
```
(a) lack of initialisation.

```
BEGIN
  InitialiseQueue (Disaster) ;
  Parasite := Disaster ;
  AddToQueue (Disaster,SomeThing) ;
  AddToQueue (Parasite,SomeThing) ;
END
```

(b) Assignment causing structure sharing.

```
PROCEDURE BlowIt (ValueParameterQueue : Queue) ;
BEGIN
  AddToQueue (ValueParameterQueue,SomeThing) ;
END BlowIt ;

BlowIt (Disaster) ;
```

(c) Value Parameter causing structure sharing.

```
IF Parasite = Disaster THEN ... END (* IF *)
```

(d) Equality test for structure sharing.

Fig. 14.8. Problem cases for opaque export.

and make a new variable point at the duplicate structure. The procedure heading could be

```
PROCEDURE CopyQueue (VAR ExistingQueue, DuplicateQueue : Queue) ;
```

and, assuming that OldQueue and NewQueue are variables of type Queue and that OldQueue refers to a valid queue, it can be called

CopyQueue (OldQueue,NewQueue)

thus permitting two identical queues which do not structure share. Similarly the normal equality test can only be carried out by providing a procedure to explicitly test that the contents of the variables are identical.

Ideally, we should not be discussing the low level implementation detail of opaque types as they are intended to hide this detail. However, it is necessary to be aware that the underlying mechanism supporting them is based upon pointers and that assignment and value parameters may cause structure sharing. Opaque types are entirely secure if the following rules are adhered to adhered to .

1. variables of opaque types like other types must be suitably initialised,
2. assignment and equality should not be used between variables of opaque types,
3. variables of opaque types should not be passed as value parameters.

Opaque types are a powerful facility if these rules are followed.

The opaque types WORD and ADDRESS provided in SYSTEM are exempt from these limitations. These types can be manipulated like any standard type such as CARDINAL or INTEGER. The reason is that they are both implemented as one word variables rather than as pointers (in fact it is normally the case that pointers are implemented as addresses!).

14.6 GENERIC TYPES — A GENERAL QUEUE

The previous versions of QueueModule have provided queues where the type of each item is determined by the type declaration of ItemType. The user has to alter this in the definition module and then recompile the definition and implementation modules. This restricts the module to providing queues whose items must be of the same type, for example queues of CARDINAL values only. There are occasions when a module requires two or more queues where the items of each queue are of different types (as with FreeQueue and WaitQueue in the Lilliput program), or even situations when it is necessary to include items of different types in the same queue. The standard way of dealing with the former situation is to duplicate the entire module in another module with a different name. The normal way of dealing with the latter case is to use a variant record as the type of the items to be held in the queue, and allow the variant record to permit all possible item types.

The low level facilities of Modula-2, however, allow modules to be written where the items in a queue, stack, tree etc. can be of different types. Essentially the implementation module remains noncommittal about the type of the items and its role is restricted to maintaining the structure of the data structure. All concern for the types of items in the structure is transferred to importing modules. Such types are known as generic types.

The modifications to the earlier version of QueueModule in this chapter are

1.   The Item field of QueueItem records is declared as ADDRESS so that it can be used as a pointer to an object of any type.

2.   Procedures which insert items into the queue and remove items from the queue must accept objects of any type as actual parameters. The module SYSTEM permits this through the formal parameter ARRAY OF WORD.

3.   The data to be included in the queue has to be copied to an area of memory pointed to by a QueueItem record. This area of memory has to be released when an item is removed from the queue. The procedures ALLOCATE and DEALLOCATE provided in Storage permit this if they are supplied with a parameter indicating the size of the area of memory to be allocated.

Figure 14.9 shows a compressed definition module for the general version of QueueModule. The formal parameters for data items are of type ARRAY OF WORD, therfore WORD has to be imported from SYSTEM. As ARRAY OF WORD allows any actual parameter in calls to the procedures, any valid calls of the procedures in the version of QueueModule in Fig. 14.7 are also valid calls to the procedures of the generalised module. No modifications to modules which import from this module are required, only the usual recompilation when a definition module is changed.

Figure 14.10 shows the completed implementation module for this generalised queue module. In the implementation module AddtoQueue uses ALLOCATE to request memory for an item and copies the item into this area, it also notes the size of the item in the Length field of the node which points to the item. RemoveFromQueue uses the Length field when using DEALLOCATE to release the area of memory. Note that the module body initialises the variable TSizeOfWord to the size of the type WORD so that the module is independent of the smallest addressable unit of any particular computer.

It is instructive to look back at QueueModule of Chapter 6 and compare it with Fig. 14.10. The level of complexity of the implementation module is related to how generally useful the module needs to be. If a time efficient program is an important criteria for a problem then it may be necessary to study an existing implementation module in detail and adapt it to be maximally efficient. As indicated in Chapter 12, on occasions it can be useful to implement a simple version of an implementation module and later develop a more sophisticated version. However, it is important that changes to a definition module are minimised if the module is being used in many programs and by other programmers.

```
DEFINITION MODULE QueueModule ;
  FROM SYSTEM IMPORT WORD ;
(* Warning – Do not use assignment between variables of type Queue,
             and do not pass them as value parameters to procedures. *)
  VAR
      Success : BOOLEAN ;
      (* Each operation sets Success to TRUE if it succeeds,
                      otherwise it is set to FALSE. *)
  TYPE
      Queue ; (* Queue exported opaquely *)

  PROCEDURE InitialiseQueue (VAR NewQueue : Queue) ;

  PROCEDURE AddToQueue(VAR ThisQueue : Queue ;
                                  Data : ARRAY OF WORD) ;
  (* adds Date as a new item in ThisQueue. *)

  PROCEDURE RemoveFromQueue(VAR ThisQueue : Queue ;
                                VAR Data : ARRAY OF WORD);
  (* returns the item at the head of ThisQueue in Data and removes
     it from the queue. *)

  PROCEDURE FullQueue(VAR ThisQueue : Queue) : BOOLEAN ;
  PROCEDURE EmptyQueue(VAR ThisQueue : Queue) : BOOLEAN ;
  PROCEDURE LengthOfQueue(VAR ThisQueue : Queue) : CARDINAL ;
END QueueModule.
```

Fig. 14.9.

```
IMPLEMENTATION MODULE QueueModule;
  FROM SYSTEM        IMPORT (* TYPE *) ADDRESS, WORD,
                              (* PROCEDURE *) ADR,TSIZE ;
  FROM Storage       IMPORT (* PROCEDURE *) ALLOCATE, DEALLOCATE ;
  FROM MemoryCopy    IMPORT (* PROCEDURE *) CopyMemory ;

(* The boolean variable Success is declared in the definition module *)
  TYPE
      QueueItemPntr       = POINTER TO QueueItem ;
      QueueItem           = RECORD
                              Item      : ADDRESS ;
                              NextItem : QueueItemPntr ;
                              Length    : CARDINAL ;
                            END ;

      Queue               = POINTER TO QueueRecord ;
      QueueRecord         = RECORD
                              HeadQueue    ,
                              EndQueue     : QueueItemPntr ;
                              SizeQueue    : CARDINAL ;
                            END ;
```

```
VAR
     TSizeWord : CARDINAL ;


(* Procedures available for use by other modules *)

PROCEDURE LengthOfQueue(VAR ThisQueue : Queue) : CARDINAL ;
BEGIN
 Success := TRUE;
 RETURN ThisQueue∧.SizeQueue ;
END LengthOfQueue;

PROCEDURE InitialiseQueue (VAR NewQueue : Queue) ;
(* initialises NewQueue to be a new queue ready for use. *)
BEGIN
 NEW (NewQueue) ;
 WITH NewQueue∧ DO
     HeadQueue        := NIL ;
     EndQueue         := NIL ;
     SizeQueue        := 0 ;
 END (* WITH *) ;
 Success := TRUE ;
END InitialiseQueue ;


PROCEDURE AddToQueue(VAR ThisQueue : Queue ;
                                    Data : ARRAY OF WORD) ;
 VAR
     ItemCell : ADDRESS ;
     NewItem  : QueueItemPntr ;
BEGIN
 ALLOCATE (ItemCell,(HIGH(Data) + 1) * TSizeWord) ;
 CopyMemory (Data,HIGH(Data)+1,ItemCell∧) ;
 NEW (NewItem) ;
 WITH NewItem∧ DO
     Item     := ItemCell ;
     NextItem := NIL ;
     Length   := (HIGH(Data) + 1) * TSizeWord ;
 END (* WITH *) ;
 WITH ThisQueue∧ DO
     IF HeadQueue = NIL THEN
             HeadQueue := NewItem
     ELSE
             EndQueue∧.NextItem := NewItem ;
     END (*IF*) ;
     EndQueue := NewItem ;
     SizeQueue : = SizeQueue + 1
 END (* WITH *) ;
 Success := TRUE
END AddToQueue ;
```

```
PROCEDURE RemoveFromQueue(VAR ThisQueue : Queue ;
                                         VAR Data : ARRAY OF WORD) ;
    VAR
        OldItem : QueueItemPntr ;
    BEGIN
     IF ThisQueue ∧ .HeadQueue = NIL THEN
        Success := FALSE
     ELSE
        WITH ThisQueue ∧ DO
         OldItem    := HeadQueue ;
         CopyMemory (HeadQueue ∧ .Item ∧ ,HeadQueue ∧ .Length DIV TSizeWord,Data) ;
         HeadQueue := HeadQueue ∧ .NextItem ;
         IF HeadQueue = NIL THEN
             EndQueue := NIL
         END (* IF *) ;
         SizeQueue := SizeQueue – 1 ;
         END (* WITH *) ;
         DEALLOCATE (OldItem ∧ .Item,OldItem ∧ .Length) ;
         DISPOSE (OldItem) ;
         Success := TRUE
     END (* IF *)
    END RemoveFromQueue;

    PROCEDURE FullQueue ( VAR ThisQueue : Queue) : BOOLEAN ;
    BEGIN
     Success := TRUE;
     RETURN FALSE ;
    END FullQueue;

    PROCEDURE EmptyQueue (VAR ThisQueue : Queue) : BOOLEAN ;
    BEGIN
     Success := TRUE;
     RETURN ThisQueue ∧ .SizeQueue = 0
    END EmptyQueue;

BEGIN
 Success    := FALSE ;
 TSizeWord := TSIZE (WORD) ;
END QueueModule.
```

Fig. 14.10.

14.7 SUMMARY

In this chapter the low level facilities of Modula-2 have been introduced.
These are

1 procedures for converting values of one type to values of another type. Such conversions involve no calculations, but are used simply to override normal type checking.

2 declaring variables to be located at specific machine memory locations.

3 facilities in the module SYSTEM for determining, as a program runs, where variables are located in memory and their sizes, and for writing general procedures which accept any variable as a parameter through the use of formal parameters of type ARRAY OF WORD.

4 the ability to tailor storage allocation for pointer types by providing alternative versions of ALLOCATE and DEALLOCATE which are called by NEW and DISPOSE.

These facilities should be used with care. They allow a programmer to access low level detail only when it is needed, but they also allow the programmer the freedom to sabotage the program and computer if not used correctly.

The discussion has not been exhaustive as low level programming is a complex topic in its own right and requires detailed knowledge of the hardware of the computer which is being programmed. When low level facilities are being used, access to the details of the hardware should be localised to specific modules. If these are transported to a different computer, modification to such programs are restricted to easily identifiable parts of the program.

This chapter has also illustrated how low level facilities can be used to provide generic types to support data structures which are independent of the types of items in the data structure.

TECHNICAL EXERCISES

1 Write declarations for three variables, one which occupies a memory location at hexadecimal 0A30 of type BITSET, another which occupies a memory location at decimal 500 of type CHAR, and one which occupies 5 memory locations starting at hexadecimal 0A40 with the first two locations holding values of type CARDINAL and the remaining three holding values of type BITSET.

2 Assume the declarations

```
VAR
    A : CARDINAL ;
    B : CHAR ;
```

```
C : (v1,v2,v3) ;
D : RECORD
      a : CARDINAL ;
      b : CHAR ;
      c : CHAR ;
    END ;
E : ARRAY [0..2] OF BITSET ;
```

and that CARDINAL, CHAR, BITSET and enumeration types are represented in a 16 bit word, and that records and arrays occupy the sum of the space required to represent individual fields and components respectively.

Write assignment statements to

a store in A the CARDINAL equivalent of B

b store in A the CARDINAL equivalent of C

c store in A the sum of (the CARDINAL equivalent of B) and A

d store in D the contents of E

e store in B the CHAR equivalent of D.a

f store in E[1] the BITSET equivalent of D.c

What problems may case e. cause?

3   Write a program module which will determine how the BOOLEAN values TRUE and FALSE are represented on your computer.

4   Write a procedure called BitPattern which will accept a value of any type whose values occupy one word of memory and writes out the value as a binary number.

Write a procedure which will accept a variable of any type as a parameter (using ARRAY OF WORD) and uses BitPattern to write out each word of the variable as a binary number.

5   Assume that a computer maintains a twenty-four hour clock which is automatically updated every second. Additionally assume that the particular machine has a 16-bit word and that CARDINAL and BITSET variables occupy one word. The computer uses 2 16-bit memory locations at addresses hexadecimal 200 and 201 and the computer automatically increments the former every second. When the value in location 200H represents 12 o'clock bit 0 of location 201H is either set to 1 if it was previously 0 and set to 0 if it was previously 1 and location 200H is reset to 0. When bit 0 of location 201H is 0 this indicates morning and 1 indicates afternoon.

Write a module which would access these memory locations to provide procedures to

a update their values to represent the number of seconds since midnight when given a time in hours, minutes and seconds (such as 12:03:47),

b return the current time in hours, minutes and seconds when requested to do so,

assuming that the procedures accept and return the time as three CARDINAL values indicating the time on the twenty-four hour clock.

PROGRAMMING EXERCISES

1 Write a program module to test that QueueModule of Fig. 14.10 allows items of differing types to be inserted into a queue.

2 Given the following definition module called SterlingModule which provides an opaque type Sterling, write the corresponding implementation module to implement the operations and a test program to demonstrate that it performs correctly. Use the following types inside the implementation module.

```
Sterling            = POINTER TO PoundsAndPence ;
PoundsAndPence      = RECORD
                         Credit : BOOLEAN ;
                         Pounds : PoundsType ;
                         Pence  : PenceType ;
                      END (* RECORD *) ;
```

```
DEFINITION MODULE SterlingModule ;
  TYPE
      PoundsType       = LONGCARD ;
      PenceType        = [0..99] ;
      Sterling ;                         (* opaque type *)
  (* The next four procedures are of the format Val3: = Val1−Val2 etc*)
  PROCEDURE Add       (VAR Val1,Val2,Val3: Sterling) ;
  PROCEDURE Multiply  (VAR Val1,Val2,Val3: Sterling) ;
  PROCEDURE Subtract  (VAR Val1,Val2,Val3: Sterling) ;
  PROCEDURE Divide    (VAR Val1,Val2,Val3: Sterling) ;
        (* in each case the result of Val1 OP Val2 is stored in Val3 *)
  PROCEDURE Initialise   (VAR Val : Sterling) ;
        (* compulsory initialisation of variables of type Sterling *)
  PROCEDURE Assign (VAR Val : Sterling ;
                        PoundVal : PoundsType ;
                        PenceVal : PenceType ;
                        Sign : BOOLEAN) ;
  PROCEDURE WriteSterling (VAR Val : Sterling) ;
  PROCEDURE ReadSterling  (VAR Val : Sterling) ;
        (* input/output through InOut *)
END SterlingModule .
```

3 Write a stack module which provides a generic data type STACK and appropriate operations. Test the module thoroughly.

ANSWERS

1 VAR
      A [0A30H] : BITSET ;
      B [500]   : CHAR ;
      C [0A40H] : RECORD
             C1,C2   : CARDINAL ;
             C3,C4,C5 : BITSET
             END ;

2 **a** A := CARDINAL (B)

    b A := CARDINAL (C)

    c A := A + CARDINAL (B)

    d D.a := CARDINAL (E[0]) ;
      D.b := CHAR (E[1]) ;   (∗ but D.b: = CHR(E[1]) ; is preferred ∗)
      D.c := CHAR (E[2]) ;   (∗ but D.c: = CHR(E[2]) ; is preferred ∗)

Note that as D's type is declared in full in the variable declaration there is no type identifier associated with D and therefore no type transfer function which can be used even though D and E are the same size. If D was declared

    TYPE
        DsType = RECORD
               a : CARDINAL ;
               b : CHAR ;
               c : CHAR ;
             END ;
    VAR
        D : DsType ;

then

    D := DsType (E)

can be used.

    e B := CHAR (D.a) but B := CHR (D.a) is preferred

    f E[1] := BITSET (D.c)

The assignment statement in e. can be a problem if the value in D.a is greater than the largest character code.

3 MODULE LowLevelBoolean ;
    FROM MoreInOut   IMPORT WriteLnString ;
    FROM InOut   IMPORT WriteCard, WriteLn ;
    VAR

```
      BoolVal : BOOLEAN ;
      CardVal : CARDINAL ;
  BEGIN
   BoolVal := TRUE ;
   CardVal := CARDINAL (BoolVal) ;
   WriteLnString ('True is represented by ') ;
   WriteCard (CardVal,10) ;
   BoolVal := FALSE ;
   CardVal := CARDINAL (BoolVal) ;
   WriteLnString ('False is represented by ') ;
   WriteCard (CardVal,10) ;
   WriteLn ;
  END LowLevelBoolean .
```

4   Assuming a 16 bit machine

```
  PROCEDURE BitPattern (Val : WORD) ;
   CONST
      WordSize = 15 ;
   VAR
      Count : CARDINAL ;
  BEGIN
   FOR Count := 0 TO WordSize DO
      IF Count IN BITSET (Val) THEN
            Write ('1')
      ELSE
            Write ('0')
      END (* IF *)
   END (* FOR *)
  END BitPattern ;


  PROCEDURE BitPatternOfStructure (VAR AnyStructure : ARRAY OF WORD) ;
   VAR
      Count : CARDINAL ;
  BEGIN
   FOR Count := 0 TO HIGH (AnyStructure) DO
      BitPattern (AnyStructure[Count]) ;
      WriteLn ;
   END (* FOR *) ;
  END BitPatternOfStructure ;
```

5

```
  MODULE Timer ;
   VAR
      Time [200H]          : CARDINAL ;
      amORpm [201H]        : BITSET ;

   PROCEDURE GetTime (VAR Hours, Minutes, Seconds : CARDINAL) ;
   BEGIN
    Hours := Time DIV 3600 ;
    IF 0 IN amORpm THEN
```

```
            Hours := Hours + 12 ;
       END (* IF *) ;
       Minutes := (Time DIV 60) MOD 60 ;
       Seconds := Time MOD 60 ;
    END GetTime ;

    PROCEDURE NewTime (Hours,Minutes,Seconds : CARDINAL) ;
    BEGIN
      IF Hours >= 12 THEN
         Hours := Hours – 12 ;
         amORpm := {0} ;
      ELSE
         amORpm := {} ;
      END (* IF *) ;
      Time := Hours * 3600 + Minutes * 60 + Seconds ;
    END NewTime ;

BEGIN
  amORpm := {} ;
  Time := 0 ;
END Timer .
```

Chapter 15

Concurrent Cooperating Processes, Coroutines and Interrupts

This chapter provides a very elementary introducton to the topic of concurrent cooperating processes in order to describe and illustrate facilities provided in Modula-2. The interested reader should consult the books listed in the bibliography under the heading **Cooperating Processes** for further discussion of this interesting area of computer science.

15.1 CONCURRENT COOPERATING PROCESSES

Concurrent processes are a collection of independent processes or programs which are executed in parallel. There are only a few computers at present which have multiple processors of comparable power capable of true parallel processing. Most computers consist of one central processor and a limited number of special purpose processors for operating input and output devices when input and output operations are requested by the central processor. We will refer to such computers as single processor computers, because the central processor has overall control of the execution of programs written for the computer.

On a single processor computer the central processor is unable to execute two programs at the same moment of time. The term concurrent processes is also used to refer to situations where two or more processes have begun execution and have not yet terminated. The computer's central processor then alternates between each by executing part of one process, then suspending this process and executing part of another process. These are said to be concurrent processes though at any one moment the central processor is only executing one process. Many mainframe computers have sophisticated operating systems which swap between different programs so that tens of people may share the same computer with little awareness that other people are also using the computer at the same time. This is known as time sharing. In computers which have more than one processor these processes may be genuinely executed in parallel.

Modula-2 was designed primarily for use on computers with only one processor, however the ideas are pertinent to computers capable of genuine parallel processing. In the following we assume a single processor computer.

Cooperating processes have to be synchronised with each other in such a way that when needed they provide information to other processes, and wait for other processes to provide information. This requires that processes are able to communicate with each other.

The Standard Module Processes

Sequential programs, such as those illustrated so far, can be considered as programs involving only one process consisting of the program module body and the procedures it calls. In Modula-2 concurrent processes are written as independent parameterless procedures which are run concurrently with the main module body. These procedures are not called but are invoked in a special way which initiates them as independent processes.

The standard module Processes provides procedures for starting other procedures as processes, scheduling execution of these procedures and for allowing processes to communicate with each other. Its definition module is shown in Fig. 15.1.

```
DEFINITION MODULE Processes ;

TYPE
    SIGNAL ;                    (* opaque type SIGNAL. Variables of type SIGNAL
                                   are used by processes to synchronise their
                                   joint efforts. The operations which can be
                                   performed on such variables are Init, SEND
                                   and WAIT. *)

PROCEDURE StartProcess (P : PROC ; WorkSpaceSize : CARDINAL) ;
    (* The parameterless procedure P is allocated a work space of size
       WorkSpaceSize words, and execution of this procedure starts. *)

PROCEDURE Init (VAR s : SIGNAL) ;
    (* The signal s is initialised. This procedure must be called on
       variables of type SIGNAL before any calls to SEND and WAIT are
       made on the signal. *)

PROCEDURE WAIT (VAR s : SIGNAL) ;
    (* The process calling WAIT(s) is suspended and added to the
       collection of processes waiting on the signal. *)

PROCEDURE Awaited (s : SIGNAL) : BOOLEAN ;
    (* Returns TRUE if one or more processes are waiting for the
       signal s, otherwise FALSE. *)

PROCEDURE SEND (VAR s : SIGNAL) ;
    (* If none of the other processes are waiting on this signal then
       this has no effect and the process calling SEND(s) continues
       with the statement after the call.
       If there are processes waiting for this signal then the current
       process is suspended and execution of one of the processes
       waiting for the signal is resumed. *)
END Processes .
```

Fig. 15.1.

Figure 15.2 shows a skeleton module involving three processes, the module body, WriteFred and WriteBill. The module body must initialise the procedures as processes and in this sense is special compared with the procedures.

The calls to StartProcess allocate sequences of words as a work space for the processes and initiates execution of each of the processes. The amount of work space required by a process is dependent upon the number and size of variables local to the process and to procedures which it calls. The work space is used as a run time stack and must also cater for actual parameters. In addition, this work space is used to remember the state of a process when it is suspended. The amount of work space can be calculated for a process by referring to the implementation dependent detail of space required for variables and parameters. However, when space is not critical, it is advisable to allow a liberal amount of work space for a process.

```
MODULE ThreeProcesses ;
FROM Processes IMPORT StartProcess ;

PROCEDURE WriteFred ;
BEGIN
     (*......*) ;
END WriteFred ;

PROCEDURE WriteBill ;
BEGIN
     (*......*) ;
END WriteBill ;

BEGIN
  StartProcess (WriteFred,200) ;
  StartProcess (WriteBill,200) ;
  (*......*) ;
END ThreeProcesses .
```

Fig. 15.2.

Once WriteFred and WriteBill have been initiated, these are executed concurrently with the module body. The program terminates when any one of the processes terminates.

Synchronising Process Execution

The module Processes provides a type SIGNAL and two communication primitives, SEND and WAIT, for synchronising the execution of cooperating processes. We will refer to variables of type SIGNAL as signals. These can be thought of as an association of a BOOLEAN condition with a queue of processes waiting for the condition to hold.

A process can be in one of three states
1. it is being executed,
2. it is waiting in the queue associated with a particular signal,
3. it is a runnable process which is not currently being executed. The module Processes maintains a queue of runnable processes for processes which are not currently being executed and which are not waiting on any signal's queue.

The procedure WAIT adds the process calling it to the collection of processes waiting for the condition associated with the specified SIGNAL variable, and holds up the process until a subsequent call of SEND allows it to continue. The process at the front of the runnable processes queue is then selected and execution of it is resumed.

When SEND is called, this indicates that the condition associated with the SIGNAL variable holds and therefore one of the processes waiting for the condition can continue execution. On single processor computers, execution of the current process is suspended and it is put at the end of the runnable processes queue and the process waiting at the front of the queue associated with the SIGNAL variable resumes execution. If a call is made of SEND and no process is waiting for this signal then SEND has no effect and the current process continues execution.

For example, the module in Fig. 15.3 involves two processes, the main program module and the parameterless procedure WriteRestOfMessage. The two processes use the signal StartOfMessage to synchronise their execution. The steps in the execution of this program are
1. the main module begins execution as the first process,
2. the call of StartProcess causes the main module process to be put on the (empty) queue of runnable processes and WriteRestOfMessage to start to execute,
3. WriteRestOfMessage calls WAIT which causes this process to be added to the (empty) queue of processes waiting for the StartOfMessage signal. The process at the front of the queue of runnable processes, the main module process, resumes execution and writes out the start of the message,
4. it then calls SEND on the signal StartOfMessage which causes this process to be added to the (now empty) queue of runnable processes, and the process at the front of StartOfMessage's queue, WriteRestOfMessage, to resume execution. It writes out its message.

Steps 3 and 4 are repeated until the FOR loop terminates, thereby causing the main module process and program to terminate.

The order of initialisation in the main module is important, the SIGNAL variable has to be initialised before the process WriteRestOfMessage is initiated so that it can wait on this signal. When the program terminates WriteRestOfMessage is still waiting for another process to send this signal, this process however dies when the entire program terminates.

This module uses the knowledge that on a single processor computer SEND causes the calling process to be suspended on the queue of runnable processes. See technical exercise 4 on how this can be written so this is not the case.

```
MODULE TwoProcesses ;
  FROM Processes     IMPORT (* TYPE *) SIGNAL,
                            (* PROCEDURES *) Init, SEND, WAIT, StartProcess ;
  FROM MoreInOut     IMPORT (* PROCEDURE *) WriteLnString ;
  FROM InOut         IMPORT (* PROCEDURE *) WriteString ;
  VAR
      StartOfMessage      : SIGNAL ;
      Count               : CARDINAL ;

  PROCEDURE WriteRestOfMessage ;
  BEGIN
    LOOP
        WAIT (StartOfMessage) ;
        (*TRUE first part of message written *)
        WriteString ('.. and Process 2 writes this.') ;
    END (* LOOP *) ;
  END WriteRestOfMessage ;

BEGIN
  Init (StartOfMessage) ;
  StartProcess (WriteRestOfMessage,2000) ;
  FOR Count := 1 TO 10 DO
      WriteLnString ('Process 1 writes this ') ;
      (*TRUE first part of message written *)
      SEND (StartOfMessage) ;
  END (* FOR *) ;
END TwoProcesses .
```

Fig. 15.3.

Communicating Data between Processes — Monitors

The example in Fig. 15.3 does not require that the processes pass information between each other, other than the information communicated through the SIGNAL variable that a particular condition has been achieved. More typically cooperating processes have to pass other information between each other. As processes are only initiated once, this information cannot be by parameter passing, and has to be achieved through allowing each process access to variables which they share. This is achieved by the use of so-called **monitors**, which contain shared variables and guarantee that the procedures which access these variables are not executed in parallel with each other.

In Modula-2, a monitor is written as a module regulating access to hidden variables which are used by two or more processes. The essential characteristic of a monitor is that it guarantees that only one of the procedures in the monitor can be executed at any one time. Any process which uses a procedure from a monitor is temporarily delayed if one of the procedures of the monitor is being executed by another process until that procedure terminates or issues a call of WAIT. A monitor is declared as a module with a priority specified in square brackets in the module heading. Priorities are discussed at greater length later in the chapter.

Monitors typically require that conditions associated with the shared variables result in holding up the current process until another process has performed some operation on the shared variable. This is illustrated by the following problem whose solution uses a monitor to synchronise the efforts of two processes.

Example — Report Generation

Many data processing problems require that reports are generated from data held in files. Such reports have to be formatted so that they are readable and this usually involves laying out the report in a format different to that of the input file. For example page breaks, headings and sub-headings have to be inserted into the report which are not present in the file. Such programs can be written as normal sequential programs and the programming exercises at the end of the chapter include an exercise to write a report generation program as a sequential program to give you an indication of the complexity involved. However, these kinds of programs can be written naturally as cooperating processes.

The problem we shall discuss is to read a file of text and to write out the information in the file to another file, a line printer or the visual display screen. A fixed number of lines per page is required with page numbers at the bottom of each page. This problem can be analysed as a sub-problem of reading the contents of the file one record at a time and converting the information into a textual format, and a sub-problem of formatting the report. Each of the sub-problems can be programmed as a separate process, one producing lines to be included in the report and the other consuming these by including them in the report. The gulf between the two sub-problems is bridged by passing data between the processes, and synchronising their execution. A module containing a hidden circular buffer can be used to allow processes to communicate with each other. Figure 15.4 illustrates the structure of this problem in terms of the abstract ideas of producer and consumer processes and is typical of the structure of many problems involving cooperating processes. The producer deposits data in the buffer and the consumer removes data from the buffer.

Producer   Consumer

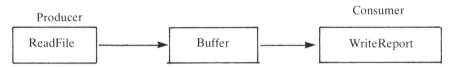

Fig. 15.4.

Both sub-problems can be written as parameterless procedures. Figures 15.5 and 15.6 show initial analyses of each sub-problem. The module body has to initiate each as a separate process. However the detail of this is omitted until consideration has been given to the way that the processes can communicate with each other.

```
PROCEDURE ReadFile ;
BEGIN
  (*... open input file for reading ...*) ;
  WHILE (*... not reached end of the file ...*)
      (*... try to read record from file ...*) ;
      (*... if a valid record read then convert the record into text
              and put it in the buffer
          otherwise send some indication in a line through to the buffer
              that the end of the file has been read ..*) ;
  END (* WHILE *) ;
  (*... close input file ...*) ;
END ReadFile ;
```

Fig. 15.5.

```
PROCEDURE WriteReport ;
BEGIN
  (*... open output channel and perform any initialisation ...*) ;
  (*... get next line from the buffer ...*) ;
  WHILE (*... the producer has not been exhausted ...*) DO
      (*... initialise line count ...*) ;
      (*... start new page ...*) ;
      (*... increment page count ...*) ;
      WHILE (*... the producer has not been exhausted ...*) AND
          (*... not end of current page ...*) DO
```

```
                (*... write out data in line retrieved ...*) ;
                (*... increment line count ...*) ;
                (*... get next line from the buffer ...*) ;
        END (* WHILE *) ;
        IF (*... not at end of current page ...*) THEN
            (*... write out blank lines to end of page ...*) ;
        END (* IF *) ;
        (*... end current page ...*) ;
    END (* WHILE *) ;
    (*... close output channel ...*) ;
    END WriteReport ;
```

Fig. 15.6.

Let us consider the buffer module in detail before developing the sub-problems further. The analyses of the sub-problems indicate that the buffer module must provide an operation to put a line into the buffer, PutLineInBuffer. This takes a line of text from the producer process and places it in the buffer in the next available line. A procedure whose heading is

```
    PROCEDURE PutLineInBuffer (VAR Line : ARRAY OF CHAR) ;
```

is assumed. WriteReport requires an operation to retrieve the next line from the buffer. A Procedure whose heading is

```
    PROCEDURE GetLineFromBuffer (VAR Line : ARRAY OF CHAR) ;
```

is assumed. When the process depositing data in the buffer has exhausted its data it deposits a special line of data which the other process can interpret as indicating that no further data is available from the buffer.

The purpose of the buffer module is to synchronise the processes and allow access to a shared buffer variable. Let us assume that this buffer variable is an array of ten character arrays whose declaration is

```
    CONST
        BufferLength    = 10 ;
    TYPE
        Lines           = ARRAY [0..79] OF CHAR ;
        BufferType      = ARRAY [0..BufferLength−1] OF Lines ;
    VAR
        Buffer          : BufferType ;
        NoOfLines       : [0..Bufferlength] ;
```

and that the module variable NoOfLines keeps track of the number of lines in the buffer currently in use.

PutLineInBuffer

If the buffer is full PutLineInBuffer must wait until there is an available line into which it can deposit data. A module variable LineInNo keeps track of the line of the buffer where data is to be deposited next. The data is then deposited into the next available line and the procedure signals to the other process that the buffer contains data to be processed. This requires two SIGNAL variables NotFull and NotEmpty. The condition associated with the former is that there is at least one vacant line in the buffer into which data can be deposited. The condition associated with the latter is that the is at least one line in the buffer containing data which can be removed. Figure 15.7 shows a possible formulation of PutLineInBuffer.

```
PROCEDURE PutLineInBuffer (VAR Line : ARRAY OF CHAR) ;
BEGIN
  IF NoOfLines = BufferLength THEN
      WAIT (NotFull) ;
  END (* IF *) ;
  (*TRUE NoOfLines < BufferLength *)
  Copy (Buffer[LineInNo],Line) ;
  LineInNo: = (LineInNo + 1) MOD BufferLength ;
  INC (NoOfLines) ;
  SEND (NotEmpty) ;
END PutLineInBuffer ;
```

Fig. 15.7.

GetLineFromBuffer

A line can only be retrieved from the buffer if one or more have been made available by the producer process. If there are no lines available in the buffer then GetLineFromBuffer must hold up the consumer process until a line is available. When the producer process signals that there are lines available in the buffer, GetLineFromBuffer can resume and remove a line. This procedure has to know which line to retrieve from the buffer so a module variable LineOutNo can hold the index of the next line to be removed from the buffer. GetLineFromBuffer can be formulated as shown in Fig. 15.8.

```
PROCEDURE GetLineFromBuffer (VAR Line : ARRAY OF CHAR) ;
BEGIN
  IF NoOfLines = 0 THEN
      WAIT (NotEmpty) ;
  END (* IF *) ;
  (*TRUE NoOfLines > 0 *)
  Copy (Line,Buffer[LineOutNo]) ;
  LineOutNo := (LineOutNo+1) MOD BufferLength ;
  DEC (NoOfLines) ;
  SEND (NotFull) ;
END GetLineFromBuffer ;
```

Fig. 15.8.

Two points are worthy of note which have consequences for other procedures provided in the buffer module.

1.   The body of the module must suitably initialise the variables of the module. This requires initialising the SIGNAL variables, and LineInNo, LineOutNo and NoOfLines. LineInNo and LineOutNo must be initialised to the same value and NoOfLines initially must indicate that the buffer is empty by being set to 0. This will cause GetLineFromBuffer to wait and suspend the consumer process when it starts execution.

2.   The main module process must be held up on another SIGNAL variable so that the program is not completed prematurely by executing it from the runnable processes queue. The module body must wait until both the producer and consumer have completed their tasks. To this end CloseProducer and CloseConsumer must guarantee that the main module body cannot continue until both the consumer and producer have finished.

3.   On a single processor computer, where processes are implemented as coroutines (see section 15.2), termination of any one of the processes causes the the entire program to terminate. In order that the program only terminates when the main module's body has run to completion a fourth SIGNAL variable, Indefinitely, is introduced to hold up the consumer and producer processes indefinitely once they have completed their tasks.

4.   The heading of BufferModule indicates that it is a monitor by specifying a priority for the module. On a single processor computer only one of the procedures in BufferModule can be executed at any one time, however the inclusion of the priority prohibits parallel execution of the procedures in the module even on computers capable of true parallel processing.

Figure 15.9 shows BufferModule as a local module and the completed procedures ReadFile and WriteReport. BufferModule can be written as an implementation module with an accompanying definition module to make it available to many report generating programs.

```
MODULE ReportGenerator ;
   FROM SimpleFile      IMPORT (* PROCEDURES *) Connect,OpenRead,ReadFromFile,
                                  EOF,Close,DisConnect,
                                  (* TYPE *) FILE ;
   FROM MoreInOut       IMPORT (* PROCEDURES *) WriteLnString ;
   FROM InOut           IMPORT (* PROCEDURES *) ReadString,WriteString,
                                  WriteCard,WriteLn,OpenOutput,CloseOutput ;
   IMPORT Processes ; (* for BufferModule *)


   (* the monitor *)
   MODULE BufferModule [3] ;
```

```
FROM Processes IMPORT (* PROCEDURES *) Init,WAIT,SEND,StartProcess,
                      (* TYPE *)        SIGNAL ;
EXPORT StartProcesses, PutLineInBuffer, GetLineFromBuffer,
       CloseProducer, CloseConsumer ;


VAR
      MainModuleContinue      ,           (* both producer and consumer
                                             have run to completion *)
      Indefinitely            ,           (* condition never achieved *)
      NotFull                 ,           (* the buffer is not full. *)
      NotEmpty                :           SIGNAL ; (* the buffer is not empty *)
      ProducerFinished        ,
      ConsumerFinished        :           BOOLEAN ;

PROCEDURE StartProcesses (ProducerProcess,ConsumerProcess : PROC) ;
BEGIN
  StartProcess (ConsumerProcess,4000) ;
  StartProcess (ProducerProcess,4000) ;
  WAIT (MainModuleContinue) ;
END StartProcesses ;

PROCEDURE CheckFinished ;
BEGIN
  IF ProducerFinished AND ConsumerFinished THEN
          SEND (MainModuleContinue) ;
  END (* IF *)
END CheckFinished ;

PROCEDURE CloseProducer ;
BEGIN
  ProducerFinished := TRUE ;
  CheckFinished ;
  WAIT (Indefinitely) ;
END CloseProducer ;

PROCEDURE CloseConsumer ;
BEGIN
  ConsumerFinished := TRUE ;
  CheckFinished ;
  WAIT (Indefinitely) ;
END CloseConsumer ;

PROCEDURE CopyInTo (VAR To,From : ARRAY OF CHAR) ;
  VAR
     LengthOfTo, LengthOfFrom, CharPos : CARDINAL ;
BEGIN
  LengthOfTo     := HIGH(To) + 1 ;
  LengthOfFrom   := HIGH (From) + 1 ;
  CharPos        := 0 ;
  WHILE (CharPos <> LengthOfTo) AND (CharPos <> LengthOfFrom) DO
```

```
            To[CharPos] := From[CharPos] ;
            INC (CharPos) ;
      END (* WHILE *) ;
      FOR CharPos := LengthOfFrom+1 TO LengthOfTo DO
            To[CharPos] := ' ' ;
      END (* FOR *) ;
   END CopyInTo ;


   CONST
      BufferLength              = 10 ;
   TYPE
      Lines                     = ARRAY [1..80] OF CHAR ;
   VAR
      Buffer                    : ARRAY [0..BufferLength-1] OF Lines ;
      NoOfLines                 : [0..BufferLength] ;
      LineInNo, LineOutNo       : [0..BufferLength-1] ;

   PROCEDURE GetLineFromBuffer (VAR Line : ARRAY OF CHAR) ;
   BEGIN
    IF NoOfLines = 0 THEN
       WAIT (NotEmpty) ;
    END (* IF *) ;
    (*TRUE NoOfLines > 0 *)
    CopyInTo (Line,Buffer[LineOutNo]) ;
    LineOutNo := (LineOutNo+1) MOD BufferLength ;
    DEC (NoOfLines) ;
    SEND (NotFull) ;
   END GetLineFromBuffer ;


   PROCEDURE PutLineInBuffer (VAR Line : ARRAY OF CHAR) ;
   BEGIN
    IF NoOfLines = BufferLength THEN
       WAIT (NotFull) ;
    END (* IF *) ;
    (*TRUE NoOfLines < BufferLength *)
    CopyInTo    (Buffer[LineInNo],Line) ;
    LineInNo := (LineInNo + 1) MOD BufferLength ;
    INC (NoOfLines) ;
    SEND (NotEmpty) ;
   END PutLineInBuffer ;


 BEGIN (* Body of BufferModule – initialisation *)
  NoOfLines := 0 ;
  LineInNo  := 0 ;
  LineOutNo := 0 ;
  ProducerFinished := FALSE ;
  ConsumerFinished := FALSE ;
  Init (MainModuleContinue) ;
  Init (NotFull) ;
  Init (NotEmpty) ;
```

```
  Init (Indefinitely) ;
END BufferModule ;


CONST
    DoneFlag    = 0C ;
VAR
    InFileName : ARRAY [1..20] OF CHAR ;

PROCEDURE ReadFile ;
  VAR
    InFile        : FILE ;
    Rec           : RECORD
                       Line : ARRAY [1..80] OF CHAR ;
                    END (* RECORD *) ;
BEGIN
  Connect (InFile,InFileName,Rec) ;
  OpenRead (InFile) ;
  REPEAT
      ReadFromFile (InFile,Rec.Line) ;
      PutLineInBuffer (Rec.Line) ;
  UNTIL EOF (InFile) ;
  Rec.Line [1] := DoneFlag ;
  PutLineInBuffer (Rec.Line) ;
  Close (InFile) ;
  DisConnect (InFile) ;
  CloseProducer ;
END ReadFile ;

PROCEDURE WriteReport ;
  CONST
    PageLength        = 55 ;
    PaperLength       = 66 ;
    TopMargin         = (PaperLength–PageLength) DIV 2 ;
    BottomMargin      = (PaperLength–PageLength+1) DIV 2 ;
  VAR
    Line                      : ARRAY [0..79] OF CHAR ;
    LineCount, PageCount      : CARDINAL ;

  PROCEDURE WriteHeading ;
   VAR
     BlankLines : CARDINAL ;
  BEGIN
   FOR BlankLines := 1 TO TopMargin DO
     WriteLn ;
    END (* FOR *) ;
  END WriteHeading ;

  PROCEDURE WriteFooting ;
   VAR
```

```
        BlankLines : CARDINAL ;
    BEGIN
      FOR BlankLines := 1 TO BottomMargin DO
         WriteLn ;
      END (* FOR *) ;
      WriteCard (PageCount,44) ;
      WriteLn ;
    END WriteFooting ;

  BEGIN
    PageCount := 0 ;
    OpenOutput ('') ;
    GetLineFromBuffer (Line) ;
    WHILE (Line[0] <> DoneFlag) DO
        LineCount := 0 ;
        WriteHeading ;
        INC (PageCount) ;
        WHILE (Line[0] <> DoneFlag) AND (LineCount <> PageLength) DO
             WriteLnString (Line) ;
             INC(LineCount) ;
             GetLineFromBuffer (Line) ;
        END (* IF *) ;
        FOR LineCount := LineCount TO PageLength–1 DO
             WriteLn ;
        END (* FOR *) ;
        WriteFooting ;
    END (* WHILE *) ;
    CloseOutput ;
    CloseConsumer ;
  END WriteReport ;

BEGIN
  WriteLnString ('Type filename of input file – ') ;
  ReadString (InFileName) ;
  StartProcesses (ReadFile,WriteReport) ;
  WriteLnString ('Program Terminating.') ;
END ReportGenerator .
```

Fig. 15.9.

If this program is executed by a computer capable of true parallel processing then each of the processes would be written as a separate program module to be run on one of the processors and the BufferModule would be provided as an implementation and definition module pair. Each process would use the procedures it requires from BufferModule and as it is a monitor (indicated by the priority [3] in the module heading) it prevents both processes using it simultaneously.

On a single processor computer control is switched from one process to the other each time a process sends a signal to the other. This has the net effect of ReadFile reading a record and placing a line in the buffer and then switching control immediately to WriteReport which then removes the line from the buffer, processes it and then waits because the buffer is empty. Despite BufferModule providing a buffer of ten lines, only one line of the buffer at most contains data at any one time. If the processes are started in the opposite order then ReadFile initially fills the entire buffer and then the processes alternate with WriteReport taking a line of data out of the buffer and ReadFile placing the data from the next record into the line of the buffer that has become available.

This phenomenon arises simply because on a single processor computer a call of SEND implicitly puts the calling process on the queue of runnable processes, if there is a process waiting for that signal. Figure 15.10 shows alternative formulations of GetLineFromBuffer and PutLineInBuffer which make use of one SIGNAL variable and the fact that when PutLineInBuffer signals that the consumer process can run, this causes the producer process to wait in the queue of runnable processes. If these procedures are used in BufferModule, the producer process only signals to the consumer process once the buffer is full.

```
PROCEDURE GetLineFromBuffer (VAR Line : ARRAY OF CHAR) ;
BEGIN
 IF NoOfLines = 0 THEN
      WAIT (Full) ;
 END (* IF *) ;
 (*TRUE NoOfLines > 0 *)
 CopyInTo (Line,Buffer[LineOutNo]) ;
 LineOutNo := (LineOutNo+1) MOD BufferLength ;
 DEC (NoOfLines) ;
END GetLineFromBuffer ;

PROCEDURE PutLineInBuffer (VAR Line : ARRAY OF CHAR) ;
BEGIN
 IF NoOfLines = BufferLength THEN
      SEND (Full) ;
 END (* IF *) ;
 (*TRUE NoOfLines < BufferLength *)
 CopyInTo (Buffer[LineInNo],Line) ;
 LineInNo := (LineInNo + 1) MOD BufferLength ;
 INC (NoOfLines) ;
END PutLineInBuffer ;
```

Fig. 15.10.

Using the queue of runnable processes has several implications for the rest of the module.

1.   In the version of the procedures in Fig. 15.10, it is critical that the consumer process is waiting before the producer process signals that there is data available in the buffer. If this is not the case a situation can arise where the producer has filled the buffer and is waiting for the consumer to indicate that the buffer is not full and the consumer is waiting for the producer to indicate that the buffer is not empty having missed its earlier signals. (Recall that SEND has no effects if there are no processes waiting on that SIGNAL variable.) StartProcesses already achieves this, but the processes could not be started in the other order.

2.   The producer may terminate when the buffer is only partially full. This can be prevented by allowing CloseProducer to include a call of SEND on Full to allow the consumer to remove any remaining lines in the buffer.

Deadlock

When writing cooperating processes it is essential that a situation is not reached where a process is waiting for another process which is itself waiting for the former process. This situation is referred to as **deadlock** or **deadly embrace** as each process is waiting for the other and neither can continue. It is always the case that if no process is currently running, the runnable processes queue is empty and there are processes waiting in signal queues then the program terminates without the waiting processes being executed to completion.

15.2   COROUTINES

On a single processor computer processes are implemented as coroutines which are the same as processes except that

1.   it is known that only one coroutine is executed at any one time. This is not the case with processes.

2.   control is passed from one coroutine to another by explicit tranfers of control from the current coroutine to another coroutine. Execution of the current coroutine is suspended until control is explicitly passed back to it from another coroutine. In contrast, processes are scheduled from within the Processes module.

Modula-2 provides procedures called NEWPROCESS and TRANSFER in the module SYSTEM for creating coroutines and passing control between them. Their procedure headings are

```
PROCEDURE NEWPROCESS (ParameterlessProcedure : PROC ;
                      WorkSpaceAddress : ADDRESS ;
                      WorkSpaceSize : CARDINAL ;
                      VAR Coroutine : ADDRESS (* PROCESS *)) ;
PROCEDURE TRANSFER (VAR Source,Destination : ADDRESS (* PROCESS *)) ;
```

The early definition of SYSTEM included a type PROCESS for coroutines which has since been removed and ADDRESS is used in its place. Check your implementation for the precise detail for creating and transfering between coroutines. In the following discussion ADDRESS is used but PROCESS is indicated in comments where it would have been used. Try not to confuse coroutines with processes though the names NEWPROCESS and PROCESS make this difficult.

NEWPROCESS initialises the parameterless procedure as a coroutine with a particular workspace specified by a starting address and a size. The variable parameter Coroutine is initialised to a memory address identifying the coroutine and this variable is used in calls of TRANSFER. TRANSFER transfers control from the source coroutine to the destination coroutine. The current state of the source coroutine is stored in its workspace and execution of the destination coroutine is resumed using the identifying address held in the parameter Destination.

The example program in Fig. 15.11 illustrates how these procedures are used to create coroutines and pass control between them. The program simply writes 'Hello Peter Hello Ian' a hundred times on separate lines. Note that the module body constitutes a coroutine which does not need to be created. When the call to TRANSFER in the module body is executed the current state of this coroutine is remembered in the main program's work space and the variable MainProgram is initialised so that subsequent transfers to it resume the module body.

Coroutines cannot be an obligatory part of the language definition, as computers capable of true parallel processing use different techniques to provide concurrent processes. However, implementations of Modula-2 for single processor computers are expected to provide them. On single processor computers these procedures are used inside the module Processes to implement concurrent processes. On such computers coroutines can be used to provide alternative ways of controlling the interaction between them to that provided in Processes.

```
MODULE IllustrateCoroutines ;
FROM SYSTEM       IMPORT (* TYPE *) ADDRESS, WORD, (* PROCESS, *)
                         (* PROCEDURES *) NEWPROCESS, TRANSFER, ADR, SIZE ;
FROM MoreInOut    IMPORT WriteLnString ;
FROM InOut        IMPORT WriteString ;
VAR
      Coroutine1, Coroutine2, MainProgram : ADDRESS (* PROCESS *) ;
      WorkSpace1, WorkSpace2 : ARRAY [1..200] OF WORD ;
PROCEDURE Ian ;
BEGIN
 LOOP
    WriteLnString ('Hello Peter.') ;
    TRANSFER (Coroutine1,Coroutine2) ;
  END (* LOOP *) ;
END Ian ;

PROCEDURE Peter ;
 VAR      Count : CARDINAL ;
BEGIN
 Count := 0 ;
 LOOP
    WriteString (' Hello Ian.') ;
    IF Count = 100 THEN
          TRANSFER (Coroutine2,MainProgram) ;
    ELSE
          INC (Count) ;
          TRANSFER (Coroutine2,Coroutine1) ;
    END (* IF *) ;
  END (* LOOP *) ;
END Peter ;
BEGIN
 NEWPROCESS (Ian,ADR(WorkSpace1),SIZE(WorkSpace1),Coroutine1) ;
 NEWPROCESS (Peter,ADR(WorkSpace2),SIZE(WorkSpace2),Coroutine2) ;
 TRANSFER (MainProgram,Coroutine1) ;
END IllustrateCoroutines .
```
Fig. 15.11.

15.3   INTERRUPTS

In the above examples of communicating processes and coroutines each of the processes or coroutines has known when to communicate with another process or coroutine. The programmer knows as he writes the program where calls to SEND and WAIT or TRANSFER have to appear in the program. In some situations, however, it is not known when communication between processes will take place.

Though few present day computers involve multiple processors of equal power, most modern computers use processors inside peripheral devices such as keyboards and printers. These processors are less powerful than the central processor and are designed to provide particular operations, however they do execute in parallel with the central processor. It is wasteful of the central processor if it always has to wait for these processors to complete their operations before continuing execution of a program. It is therefore usual for peripheral processors to be allowed to interrupt the central processor so that it can transfer control to a section of code designed to service the interrupting device. As computers can be connected to several peripheral devices, it is normal for a peripheral device to be assigned an **interrupt vector address**. The peripheral processor signals to the central processor via its interrupt vector address that it needs attention which identifies the peripheral device so that control can be transferred to the appropriate device handler.

In Modula-2, this facility is usually provided through coroutines and a procedure called IOTRANSFER available in SYSTEM. Its procedure heading is

```
PROCEDURE IOTRANSFER (VAR Source,Destination : ADDRESS ;
                      VectorAddress : CARDINAL) ;
```

The source coroutine is a device handler designed to cope with interrupts generated by the peripheral device which uses the specified interrupt vector address. A call to IOTRANSFER suspends the source coroutine (device handler) and transfers control to the destination coroutine. However, when an interrupt is generated through the specified interrupt vector address, this coroutine is suspended and control is passed to the original source coroutine (device handler). This can be thought of as splicing into the destination coroutine a call to TRANSFER at the point where execution had reached when the interrupt occurred.

This mechanism is implementation dependent and details of its use, such as the appropriate vector addresses and the absolute addresses used by devices, are machine specific. Here we outline the principles involved but for precise details you will have to refer to your implementation of Modula-2 and the hardware manual of your computer. It should be noted that the use of interrupts is usually the province of an operating system (or some other control program) and that their use may adversely affect the operating system.

In addition peripheral devices usually have access to specific memory locations which they use to communicate data to the device handler. These memory locations are typically used to indicate

1. the status of the device — for example whether the peripheral processor is executing or waiting,
2. the data to be given to or received from the peripheral device.

Figure 15.12 shows a program to list the contents of a file of text, with 80 characters per line, to the visual display screen. If a key is typed at the keyboard then the listing of the file is suspended until another key is pressed. The module InterruptListing alternates execution between two coroutines, depending on whether the character 'C' or a different character is typed at the keyboard. The character 'A' causes the program body coroutine to resume and allows the entire program to be aborted. InterruptListing embodies a fourth coroutine, ControlListing, which handles the interrupts generated from the keyboard and determines which of the other three coroutines to transfer control to. The procedure StartListing is exported from InterruptListing to allow the program module to specify the parameterless procedures which are to be executed as coroutines.

The program module declares two parameterless procedures, ReadFile and InfiniteLoop, which are passed to StartListing as the two coroutines to be executed. ReadFile is the main coroutine, and InfiniteLoop is executed when Readfile is interrupted. InfiniteLoop does nothing, but serves to hold up ReadFile when a character other than 'C' or 'A' is typed at the keyboard.

The procedure CheckCharacter determines the character which was typed to cause the interrupt. The way this character is found depends upon how the computer handles interrupts. One possibility is that the character is found by inspecting a particular memory location using an absolute address or a further possibilty is that the normal input routine from the keyboard can be used to read the character. Additional complications can arise if the keyboard generates multiple interrupts when a key is held down. CheckCharacter might also have to cope with these by repeatedly using IOTRANSFER to transfer control to the background coroutine until no further interrupts arrive, before returning its result.

Most computers are capable of having several different types of peripheral device connected to them and therefore a program may contain modules for handling more than one device. Some of these devices need to be handled more urgently than others. Computers often employ a **priority interrupt** mechanism to cope with this. In Modula-2 the priority of the device handling module is determined by the priority specified in the module's heading. The module InterruptListing has a priority 3. A module can only be interrupted by an IOTRANSFER in another module if the latter has a higher priority than the former. Note that a priority cannot be specified in a definition module and that the numbering of priorities is implementation dependent.

When assigning priorities to modules, great care is required. In particular, a procedure cannot be called from within a module which has a lower priority than the module containing its declaration. This restriction does not apply to modules which have no priority in their declaration. This is one way of achieving mutual exclusion for monitors on multi-processor computers.

Notice that the structure of ReadFile is in part determined by the example application. It is usual to include the opening and closing of the file as part of this procedure. Recall from Chapter 12 that OpenInput requests the user to input at the keyboard the name of the file as the source of the input for subsequent calls to procedures in InOut. If StartListing is called before the name of the file is input then problems arise with the user's reply to the request for the input filename. When he types the filename at the keyboard this generates interrupts which are then being handled by the module InterruptListing. This problem can be overcome by using the procedures provided in SimpleFile in Chapter 10, though the filename cannot be passed as a parameter to ReadFile which has to be a parameterless procedure in order to be a coroutine.

```
MODULE ListFile ;
  IMPORT SYSTEM                (* For InterruptListing *) ;
  IMPORT Terminal              (* For InterruptListing *) ;
  FROM InOut        IMPORT  (* VARIABLE *) Done, (* CONSTANT *) EOL,
                            (* PROCEDURE *) Read, OpenInput, CloseInput ;
  FROM MoreInOut    IMPORT  (* PROCEDURE *) WriteLnString ;

  MODULE InterruptListing [3] ;
    FROM SYSTEM       IMPORT  (* TYPE *) ADDRESS, (* PROCESS, *) WORD,
                      (* PROCEDURES *) TRANSFER, ADR, SIZE, IOTRANSFER,
                                        NEWPROCESS ;
    FROM Terminal IMPORT BusyRead ;
    EXPORT (* PROCEDURES *) StartListing, EndListing ;
    VAR
        Control, Listing, Background, MainProg        : ADDRESS (* PROCESS *) ;
        WrkSpace1, WrkSpace2, WrkSpace3               : ARRAY [1..500] OF WORD ;

    PROCEDURE ControlListing ;
      TYPE
              ContinueHaltAbort = (Continue,Halt,Abort) ;
      VAR
              Command          : ContinueHaltAbort ;

      PROCEDURE CheckCharacter () : ContinueHaltAbort ;
          (* gets the character typed which caused the interrupt,
                  if character is 'a' or 'A' RETURNS Abort
                                   'c' or 'C' RETURNS Continue
                  otherwise              RETURNS Halt
              This procedure might use BusyRead, or absolute memory
              addresses to get the character input. *)
      END CheckCharacter ;
```

```
BEGIN
 Command := Continue ;
 LOOP
    CASE Command OF
         Halt     : IOTRANSFER (Control,Background,60B) |
         Continue : IOTRANSFER (Control,Listing,60B) |
         Abort     : TRANSFER (Control,MainProg) |
    END (* CASE *) ;
    Command := CheckCharacter () ;
 END ;
END ControlListing ;

PROCEDURE StartListing (ListingProc,BackgroundProc : PROC) ;
BEGIN
 NEWPROCESS (BackgroundProc,ADR(WrkSpace1),SIZE(WrkSpace1),Background) ;
 NEWPROCESS (ControlListing,ADR(WrkSpace2),SIZE(WrkSpace2),Control) ;
 NEWPROCESS (ListingProc,ADR(WrkSpace3),SIZE(WrkSpace3),Listing) ;
 TRANSFER (MainProg,Control) ;
END StartListing ;

PROCEDURE EndListing ;
BEGIN
 TRANSFER (Listing,MainProg) ;
END EndListing ;

END InterruptListing ;

PROCEDURE InfiniteLoop ;
BEGIN    LOOP END
END InfiniteLoop ;

PROCEDURE ReadFile ;
 VAR
    Line : ARRAY [0..80] OF CHAR ;

 PROCEDURE ReadLine (VAR Line: ARRAY OF CHAR) ;
  VAR
      Ch        : CHAR ;
      Count     : CARDINAL ;
 BEGIN
  Count := 0 ;
  Read (Ch) ;
  WHILE Done AND (Ch <> EOL) AND (Count <> HIGH(Line)) DO
         Line[Count] := Ch ;
         INC (Count) ;
         Read (Ch) ;
  END (* WHILE *) ;
  Line[Count] := 0C ;
  EndListing ;
 END ReadLine ;
```

```
BEGIN
  ReadLine (Line) ;
  WHILE Done DO
        WriteLnString (Line) ;
        ReadLine (Line) ;
  END (* WHILE *) ;
  END ReadFile ;

BEGIN
  OpenInput ('') ;
  IF Done THEN
        StartListing (ReadFile,InfiniteLoop) ;
        CloseInput ;
  ELSE
        WriteLnString ('File not opened correctly.') ;
  END (* IF *) ;
  WriteLnString ('Program terminated.') ;
  END ListFile .
```

Fig. 15.12.

15.4 SUMMARY

1 Modula-2 provides a high level facility for writing programs which involve communicating processes. This is provided in a standard module called Processes. It provides the type SIGNAL for declaring variables used in controlling communication between processes, and the communication primitives WAIT and SEND. WAIT holds a process up on a signal until a certain condition holds and SEND allows a process to communicate generally to other processes that a condition now holds. In addition, the module provides procedures for creating processes and initialising SIGNAL variables. Processes themselves are written as parameterless procedures.

2 Modula-2 optionally allows lower level facilities for providing coroutines on single processor computers. The procedures NEWPROCESS and TRANSFER are provided in the module SYSTEM if they are available. These permit explicit transfer of control from one particular coroutine to another.

3 Modula-2 optionally provides a procedure IOTRANSFER for allowing peripheral processors to interrupt the central processor and to cause control to be transferred to a module for handling the device.

TECHNICAL EXERCISES

1   Describe in English what the following procedure does.

```
PROCEDURE WhatDoIDo (VAR A : CARDINAL) ;
BEGIN
  WAIT (Fred) ;
  SEND (Bill) ;
  A := 100 ;
END WhatDoIDo ;
```

What is wrong with the following call of StartProcess?

```
StartProcess (WhatDoIDo,1000)
```

2   What is wrong in the following pair of procedures if they are provided in BufferModule?

```
PROCEDURE GetLineFromBuffer (VAR Line : ARRAY OF CHAR) ;
BEGIN
  IF NoOfLines <> BufferLength THEN
    WAIT (Full) ;
  END (* IF *) ;
  (*TRUE NoOfLines > 0 *)
  Copy (Line,Buffer[LineOutNo]) ;
  LineOutNo := (LineOutNo+1) MOD BufferLength ;
  DEC (NoOfLines) ;
  IF NoOfLines = 0 THEN
    SEND (Empty) ;
  END (* IF *) ;
END GetLineFromBuffer ;

PROCEDURE PutLineInBuffer (VAR Line : ARRAY OF CHAR) ;
BEGIN
  IF NoOfLines <> 0 THEN
    WAIT (Empty) ;
  END (* IF *) ;
  (*TRUE NoOfLines < BufferLength *)
  Copy (Buffer[LineInNo],Line) ;
  LineInNo := (LineInNo + 1) MOD BufferLength ;
  INC (NoOfLines) ;
  IF NoOfLines = BufferLength THEN
    SEND (Full) ;
  END (* IF *) ;
END PutLineInBuffer ;
```

3   Write a module involving three processes, Jim, Jane and Joan, sharing access to a CARDINAL variable X which always holds a value between 1 and 3 inclusive. Joan must wait if X <> 1, Jane must wait if X <> 2 and Jim must wait if X <> 3. When Joan runs it sets X to 2, Jane sets X to 3 and Jim sets X

to 1. Each process should write out the value of X before it alters its value. The processes communicate via a SIGNAL variable CanRun on which they are queued when they have to wait, and on which they call SEND to signal that another process can run after they have altered the value of X. Initialise the variable X and start the processes so that the program writes 123 and then terminates.

4 Rewrite the program in Fig. 15.3 as coroutines rather than communicating processes.

PROGRAMMING EXERCISES

1 Put BufferModule into a separate implementation and definition module, and **alter the module** ReportGenerator to use this definition and implementation module pair.

If your computer is a single-processor computer, make the alterations to BufferModule suggested by Fig. 15.10 and the accompanying commentary and test the resulting module.

2 Modify ReportGenerator to
a use BufferModule in the separately compiled modules of exercise 1,
b accept the product description file of Chapter 13 ordered on the Supplier field of the records as input,
c and to produce a report such that a new page is started for each supplier and the name of the supplier appears only at the top of each page.

3 Write ReportGenerator as a sequential program.

4 Find out if your implementation of Modula-2 and computer support interrupts. If they do consult the hardware manual for the computer to determine how to control a printer and the keyboard. Write a program which permits a user to print a file to the printer and to input data at the keyboard to another file by implementing these as separate coroutines which use device handling modules to handle interrupts generated by the keyboard and the printer to transfer control between the coroutines. (Allow yourself several months to achieve a correct program!)

ANSWERS

1 WhatDoIDo waits in the queue associated with the SIGNAL variable Fred until it is at the front of the queue and another process SENDs on this SIGNAL variable. When this happens it signals to any process waiting on the SIGNAL

variable Bill that it can continue, and then returns the value 100 through its variable parameter A.

The procedure call

```
StartProcess (WhatDoIDo,1000)
```

is invalid as WhatDoIDo is not a parameterless procedure.

2 As there are N lines in the buffer, both the conditions

```
NoOfLines <> BufferLength
NoOfLines <> 0
```

are true when NoOfLines has a value between 2 and N-1 inclusive. This causes both the processes calling GetLineFormBuffer and PutLineInBuffer to wait on the signals Full and Empty respectively. Each process is waiting for the other to communicate that it can continue and neither can run. This is known as deadlock or deadly embrace.

3
```
        MODULE JimJoanAndJane ;
        FROM Processes IMPORT (* TYPE *) SIGNAL,
                         (* PROCEDURES *) SEND, WAIT, Init, StartProcess ;
        FROM InOut      IMPORT WriteCard, WriteLn ;
        VAR
            X          : CARDINAL ;
            CanRun   : SIGNAL ;

        PROCEDURE Joan ;
        BEGIN
            IF X <> 1 THEN
                 WAIT (CanRun) ;
            END (* IF *) ;
            WriteCard (X,1) ;
            X := 2 ;
            SEND (CanRun) ;
        END Joan ;

        PROCEDURE Jane ;
        BEGIN
            IF X <> 2 THEN
                 WAIT (CanRun) ;
            END (* IF *) ;
            WriteCard (X,1) ;
            X := 3 ;
            SEND (CanRun) ;
        END Jane ;

        PROCEDURE Jim ;
        BEGIN
```

```
            IF X <> 3 THEN
                WAIT (CanRun) ;
            END (* IF *) ;
            WriteCard (X,1) ;
            X := 1 ;
            SEND (CanRun) ;
        END Jim ;

    BEGIN
      Init (CanRun) ;
      X := 1 ;
      WriteLn ;
      StartProcess (Jim,2000) ;
      StartProcess (Jane,2000) ;
      StartProcess (Joan,2000) ;
      END JimJoanAndJane .
```

4 MODULE TwoCoroutines ;
```
    FROM SYSTEM      IMPORT (* TYPE *) ADDRESS, (* PROCESS *), WORD,
                            (* PROCEDURES *) NEWPROCESS, TRANSFER, ADR,
                            SIZE ;
    FROM MoreInOut   IMPORT (* PROCEDURE *) WriteLnString ;
    FROM InOut       IMPORT (* PROCEDURE *) WriteString ;
    VAR
        Count                   : CARDINAL ;
        WrkSpace                : ARRAY [1..500] OF WORD ;
        Coroutine1,Coroutine2   : ADDRESS (* PROCESS *) ;

    PROCEDURE WriteRestOfMessage ;
    BEGIN
      LOOP
          WriteString ('.. and Process 2 writes this.') ;
          TRANSFER (Coroutine2,Coroutine1) ;
      END (* LOOP *) ;
    END WriteRestOfMessage ;

    BEGIN
      NEWPROCESS (WriteRestOfMessage,ADR(WrkSpace),SIZE(WrkSpace),Coroutine2) ;
      FOR Count := 1 TO 10 DO
          WriteLnString ('Process 1 writes this ') ;
          TRANSFER (Coroutine1,Coroutine2) ;
      END (* FOR *) ;
    END TwoCoroutines .
```

Bibliography

Elementary Computing

Bartee, T. *Digital Computer Fundamentals* (McGraw-Hill 1985).
Emery, G. *Elements of Computer Science* (Pitman 1979).
Thewlis, P.J. & Foxon, B.N.T *From Logic to Computers* (Blackwell 1983).

Logic and Computers

Gries, D. *The Science of Programming* (Springer-Verlag 1982).
Reynolds, J.C. *The Craft of Programming* (Prentice-Hall 1981).

Program Development

Grogono, P.B. & Nelson, S.H. *Problem Solving and Computer Progamming* (Addison Wesley 1982).
Van Tassel, D. *Program Style, Design, Efficiency, Debugging and Testing* (Prentice-Hall 1978).
Pressman, R.S. *Software Engineering: A Practitioner's Approach* (McGraw-Hill 1982).

Data Structures

Wirth, N. *Algorithms and Data Structures* (Prentice-Hall 1986).
Welsh, J., Elder, J & Bustard, D. *Sequential Program Structures* (Prentice-Hall 1984).
Pfaltz, J.L. *Computer Data Structures* (McGraw-Hill 1977).

Cooperating Processes

Glass, P.L. *Real-Time Software* (Prentice-Hall 1984).
Hoare, C.A.R. *Communicating Sequential Processes* (Prentice-Hall 1985).

Modula-2

Wirth, N. *Programming in Modula-2* (Springer-Verlag 1986).

518

Appendix 1

Syntax Diagrams

Index for Syntax Diagrams

Modules˙

1. Compilation Unit :

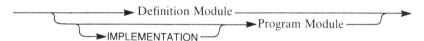

2. Program Module :

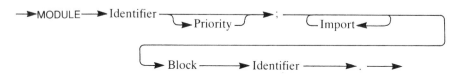

3. Module Declaration :

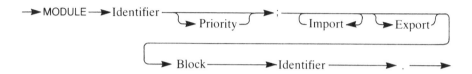

4. Definition Module :

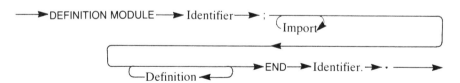

5. Priority :

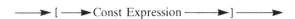

6. Import :

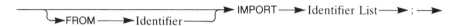

7. Export :

8. Definition :

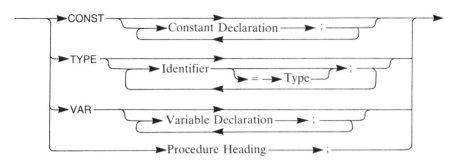

9. Block :

10. Declaration :

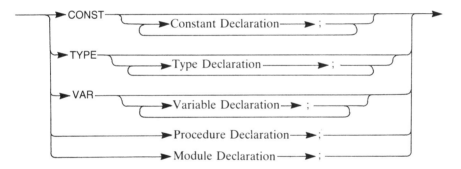

Procedures

11. Procedure Declaration :

12. Procedure Heading :

13. Formal Parameters :

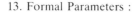

14. FP Section :

15. Formal Type :

Statements

16. Statement Sequence :

17. Statement :

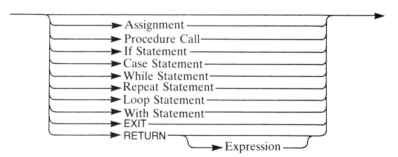

18. Assignment :

19. Procedure Call :

20. Actual Parameters :

21. If Statement :

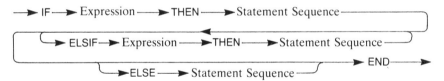

22. Case Statement :

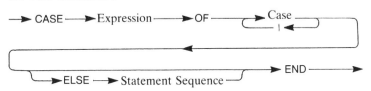

23. Case :

24. Case Label List :

25. Case Labels :

26. While Statement :

27. Repeat Statement :

28. For Statement :

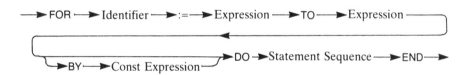

29. Loop Statement :

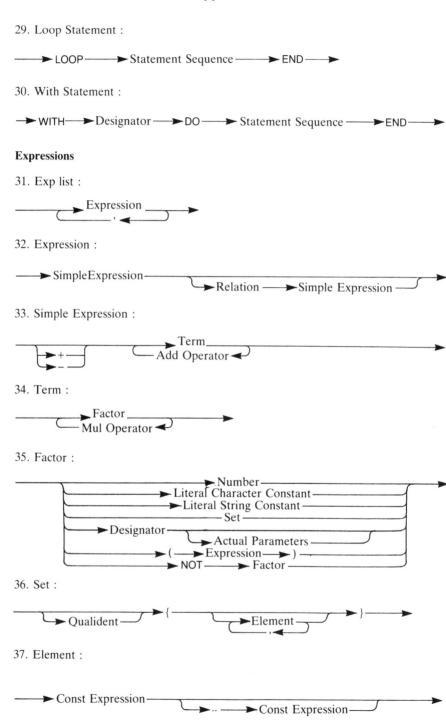

30. With Statement :

Expressions

31. Exp list :

32. Expression :

33. Simple Expression :

34. Term :

35. Factor :

36. Set :

37. Element :

Declarations

38. Constant Declaration :

39. Const Expression :

40. Simple Const Expression :

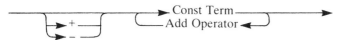

41. Const Term :

42. Const Factor :

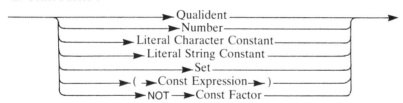

43. Type Declaration :

44. Type :

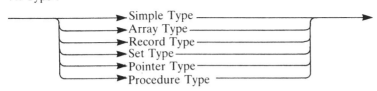

45. Simple Type :

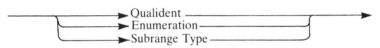

46. Enumeration :

→ (─→ Identifier List ─────→) ─────→

47. Subrange Type :

48. Array Type :

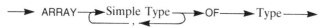

49. Record Type :

───→RECORD───→Field List Sequence─────→ END───→

50. Field List Sequence :

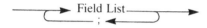

51. Field List :

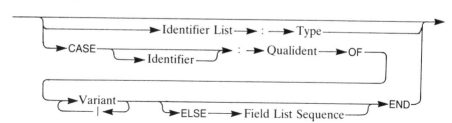

52. Variant :

53. Set Type :

────→ SET OF─────→Simple Type─→

54. Pointer Type :

──────→POINTER TO─→Type───→

55. Procedure Type :

56. Formal Type List :

57. Variable Declaration :

Operators

58. Mul Operator :

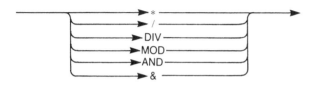

59. Add Operator :

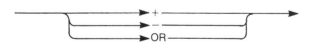

60. Relation :

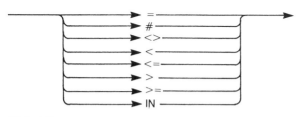

Object Names

61. Designator :

62. Qualident :

63. Identifier List :

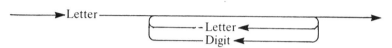

64. Identifier :

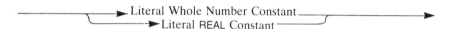

65. Number :

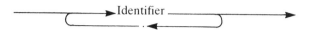

66. Literal Whole Number Constant :

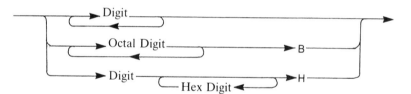

67. Hex Digit :

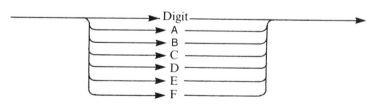

68. Literal REAL Constant:

69. Scale Factor :

70. Digit :

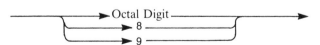

71. Octal Digit :

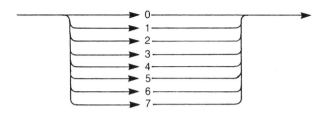

72. Literal String Constant :

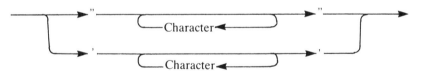

73. Literal Character Constant :

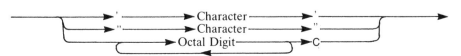

74. Character :

the printable characters of the character set of the computer, usually ASCII.

75. Letter :

upper and lower case alphabetic characters.

Appendix 2

Reserved Words and Symbols

Reserved Words

AND	ELSIF	LOOP	REPEAT
ARRAY	END	MOD	RETURN
BEGIN	EXIT	MODULE	SET
BY	EXPORT	NOT	THEN
CASE	FOR	OF	TO
CONST	FROM	OR	TYPE
DEFINITION	IF	POINTER	UNTIL
DIV	IMPLEMENTATION	PROCEDURE	VAR
DO	IMPORT	QUALIFIED	WHILE
ELSE	IN	RECORD	WITH

None of the reserved words can be used as identifier names in any context.

Delimiters

.	,	..	;	:	(	)
[	]	{	}	^	|	

Operators

~

*	/	&				
+	−					
<	>	<=	>=	<>	=	#
:=						

The relational operators are not applicable to arrays and records.

Appendix 3

Standard Identifiers

The standard identifiers are automatically imported into every module. Consequently these names cannot be declared as identifier names in module blocks, however they can be redeclared in procedure declarations thereby creating a hole in the scope of the standard use of the name. In general, avoid using these names for other objects.

Standard Types

BITSET	BOOLEAN	CARDINAL	CHAR
INTEGER	PROC	REAL	
LONGCARD	LONGINT	LONGREAL	

Standard Values

TRUE   FALSE   NIL

Standard Procedures (F denotes function procedure)

Note that many of the standard procedures cannot be written by a Modula-2 programmer as they take an indefinite number of actual parameters or take parameters of widely differing types.

ABS	(F)	ABS(AnyValue)	= result is the absolute value of AnyValue, result type is the same as the type of the parameter.
CAP	(F)	CAP (Ch)	= if Ch is a lower case character then the result is the equivalent upper case character, if Ch is an upper case character result is the same character.
CHR	(F)	CHR (v)	= result is the character whose ordinal number is v.
DEC		DEC (v)	= v := v−1 – can be used with subrange
		DEC (v,n)	= v := v−n and enumeration types. –
DISPOSE		DISPOSE (Pntr)	= DEALLOCATE (Pntr,TSIZE(TypeOfPntr))
EXCL		EXCL (s,e)	= excludes the element e from the set s
FLOAT	(F)	FLOAT (Card)	= result is the REAL value representation of the CARDINAL value Card.
HALT		HALT	= terminate program.
HIGH	(F)	HIGH (Array)	= result is the index of the upper bound of Array
INC		INC (v)	= v := v+1 – can be used with subrange
		INC (v,n)	= v := v+n and enumeration types. –
INCL		INCL (s,e)	= includes the element e in the set s
MAX	(F)	MAX (T)	= result is the maximum/minimum value
MIN	(F)	MIN (T)	of the type T. T can be any basic type, enumerated type or subrange type.
NEW		NEW (Pntr)	= ALLOCATE (Pntr,TSIZE(TypeOfPntr))
ODD	(F)	ODD (x)	= result is the result of the BOOLEAN expression x MOD 2 <> 0
ORD	(F)	ORD (Val)	= result is the CARDINAL value which is the ordinal number of Val. Val's type can be any enumeration type, CHAR, INTEGER or CARDINAL.
TRUNC	(F)	TRUNC (RealVal)	= result is the CARDINAL value which corresponds to RealVal truncated to exclude its fractional part.
VAL	(F)	VAL (AType,v)	= result is the value of type AType whose ordinal value is v. AType can be any enumeration type, CHAR, INTEGER or CARDINAL.

Appendix 4

Standard Modules

InOut

```
DEFINITION MODULE InOut ;
CONST
        EOL = 36C ;
VAR
        Done : BOOLEAN ; (* set to TRUE if procedure successful. *)
        termCH : CHAR ; (* see specific procedures. *)

PROCEDURE OpenInput (DefaultFileExtension : ARRAY OF CHAR) ;
    (* Prompts at the screen for a file name accepted from the keyboard
        which is opened for input. Subsequent input procedures in InOut
        then take input from the file. Done is set to FALSE if the file
        was not successfully opened.
        If the file name accepted at the keyboard ends with a . then the
        default file extension is appended to the file name. *)

PROCEDURE OpenOutput (DefaultFileExtension : ARRAY OF CHAR) ;
    (* Prompts at the screen for a file name accepted from the keyboard
        which is opened for output. Subsequent output procedures in InOut
        then send output to the file. Done is set to FALSE if the file
        was not successfully opened.
        If the file name accepted at the keyboard ends with a . then the
        default file extension is appended to the file name. *)

PROCEDURE CloseInput ;
    (* Closes the input file, subsequent input is then taken from the
        keyboard. *)

PROCEDURE CloseOutput ;
    (* Closes the output file, subsequent output is then sent to the
        screen. *)

PROCEDURE Read (VAR Ch : CHAR) ;
    (* Reads a character from the current input channel.
        If the character read is the end of file character Done is set
        to FALSE. *)

PROCEDURE ReadString (VAR s : ARRAY OF CHAR) ;
    (* Reads a sequence of characters not containing space or control
        characters. Leading spaces are ignored and the character sequence
        is terminated by any character whose character code is <= space.
        The character which was input to terminate the character sequence
        is held in termCH. The character del backspaces when input is
        from the keyboard. *)
```

PROCEDURE ReadCard (VAR x : CARDINAL) ;
(* Reads a nonnegative whole number into x from the current
input channel. If a CARDINAL value was not read Done is set to
FALSE. *)

PROCEDURE ReadInt (VAR x : INTEGER) ;
(* Reads a positive or negative whole number or 0 into x from
the current input channel. If an INTEGER value was not read Done
is set to FALSE. *)

PROCEDURE Write (Ch : CHAR) ;
(* Writes the character Ch to the current output channel. *)

PROCEDURE WriteString (s : ARRAY OF CHAR) ;
(* Writes the sequence of characters in s to the current
output channel. *)

PROCEDURE WriteCard (x,n : CARDINAL) ;
(* Writes the value x in a fieldwidth n characters wide to the
current output channel. If the field width is wider than
necessary leading spaces are written to fill the field. *)

PROCEDURE WriteInt (x : INTEGER ; n : CARDINAL) ;
(* Writes the value x in a fieldwidth n characters wide to the
current output channel. If the field width is wider than
necessary leading spaces are written to fill the field. *)

PROCEDURE WriteLn ;
(* Terminates the current line and starts a new line on the
current output channel. *)

PROCEDURE WriteOct (x,n : CARDINAL) ;
(* Writes the value x in octal in a field width n characters wide. *)

PROCEDURE WriteHex (x,n : CARDINAL) ;
(* Writes the value x in hexadecimal in a field width n characters
wide. *)

END InOut .

RealInOut.
DEFINITION MODULE RealInOut ;
VAR
Done : BOOLEAN ;

PROCEDURE ReadReal (VAR RealVariable : REAL) ;
(* Reads a real number from the current input channel according to the
syntax

where Scale Factor is as defined in Appendix 1.
The variable Done is set to TRUE if a valid number was read.
7 digits at most are significant excluding leading zeros and
the maximum exponent is 38 characters.
The number is terminated by any character whose character code is
$<=$ space.
The character del backspaces when input is from the keyboard. *)

PROCEDURE WriteReal (RealValue : REAL ;
                      FieldWidth : CARDINAL) ;
  (* Writes the real value to the current output channel in the
     specified field width. If fewer character positions are required
     leading spaces are written to fill the field. *)

PROCEDURE WriteRealOct (RealValue : REAL) ;
  (* Writes the real value in octal with exponent and mantissa. *)

END RealInOut .

Terminal.

DEFINITION MODULE Terminal ;

PROCEDURE Read (VAR Ch : CHAR) ;
  (* Reads a character from the keyboard. *)

PROCEDURE BusyRead (VAR Ch : CHAR) ;
  (* Reads a character from the keyboard if one has been typed,
     if no character has been typed the procedure returns immediately
     with Ch having the value 0C. *)

PROCEDURE ReadAgain ;
  (* Causes the last character read to to be returned again on the
     next call of Read. *)

PROCEDURE Write (Ch : CHAR) ;
  (* Writes the character value Ch to the screen. *)

PROCEDURE WriteLn ;
  (* Terminates last line and starts a new line for input and output. *)

PROCEDURE WriteString (CharacterSequence : ARRAY OF CHAR) ;
  (* Writes the character sequence to the screen. *)

END Terminal .

MathLib0,

DEFINITION MODULE MathLib0 ;

PROCEDURE sqrt	(Val : REAL) : REAL ;
PROCEDURE exp	(Val : REAL) : REAL ;
PROCEDURE ln	(Val : REAL) : REAL ;
PROCEDURE sin	(Val : REAL) : REAL ;
PROCEDURE cos	(Val : REAL) : REAL ;
PROCEDURE arctan	(Val : REAL) : REAL ;
PROCEDURE real	(Val : INTEGER) : REAL ;
PROCEDURE entier	(Val : REAL) : INTEGER ;

END MathLib0 .

SYSTEM (pseudo-module).

DEFINITION MODULE SYSTEM ;
TYPE
     WORD ;   ADDRESS ;   (* PROCESS ; *)

PROCEDURE ADR (AnyVariable : AnyType) : ADDRESS ;
(* Returns the address of AnyVariable. *)

PROCEDURE SIZE (VAR AnyVariable : AnyType) : CARDINAL ;
(* Returns the size of AnyVariable in the units of the smallest
addressable memory units. *)

PROCEDURE TSIZE (AnyType) : CARDINAL ;
(* Returns the number of smallest addressable units required to
represent variables of the specified type. TSIZE can be called with additional parameters of
tag fields of a record to determine the
space required to represent a particular variant of a variant
record. *)

PROCEDURE NEWPROCESS (ParameterlessProcedure : PROC ;
WorkSpaceAddress : ADDRESS ;
WorkSpaceSize : CARDINAL ;
VAR Coroutine : ADDRESS (* PROCESS*)) ;
(* Initialises the parameterless procedure as a coroutine with
a work space of a particular size. *)

PROCEDURE TRANSFER (VAR Source, Destination : ADDRESS (* PROCESS *)) ;
(* Transfers control from the source coroutine to the destination
coroutine. *)

(* this module may contain other system dependent facilities e.g. *)

PROCEDURE IOTRANSFER (VAR Source, Destination : ADDRESS (* PROCESS *) ;
VectorAddress : CARDINAL) ;
(* Transfers from the source to the destination coroutine, but when
an interrupt occurs through the specified vector address control
is transfered from the destination to the source coroutine. *)

END SYSTEM .

Storage.

DEFINITION MODULE Storage ;

PROCEDURE ALLOCATE (VAR StartingAddress : ADDRESS ;
Size : CARDINAL) ;
(* Allocates the requested number of smallest addressable units
as an area of memory and initialises StartingAddress to be the
address of the start of this are of memory. *)

PROCEDURE DEALLOCATE (VAR StartingAddress : ADDRESS ;
Size : CARDINAL) ;
(* Deallocates the specified number of smallest addressable units
which start at the specified starting address. *)

PROCEDURE Available (Size : CARDINAL) : BOOLEAN ;
(* Returns TRUE if the requested amount of storage is available,
otherwise FALSE. *)

END Storage .

Processes.

See Fig. 15.1.

Appendix 5

The ASCII Character Set

		0	1	2	3	4	5	6	7
	0	null	soh	stx	etx	eot	enq	ack	bel
	1	bs	ht	lf	vt	ff	cr	so	si
	2	dle	dc1	dc2	dc3	dc4	nak	syn	etb
	3	can	em	sub	esc	fs	gs	rs	us
	4	sp	!	''	#	$	%	&	'
H	5	(	)	*	+	,	−	.	/
I	6	0	1	2	3	4	5	6	7
G	7	8	9	:	;	<	=	>	?
H	8	@	A	B	C	D	E	F	G
	9	H	I	J	K	L	M	N	O
	10	P	Q	R	S	T	U	V	W
	11	X	Y	Z	[	/	]	^	←
	12	`	a	b	c	d	e	f	g
	13	h	i	j	k	l	m	n	o
	14	p	q	r	s	t	u	v	w
	15	x	y	z	{	|	}	~	del

Character Code = (HIGH $*$ 8 + LOW)

Index